Foundation ActionScript for Macromedia Flash MX

Sham Bhangal
Ben Renow-Clarke

Foundation ActionScript
for Macromedia Flash MX

© 2002 friends of ED

First Printed June 2002

Trademark Acknowledgements

friends of ED has endeavored to provide trademark information about all the companies and products mentioned in this book by the appropriate use of capitals. However, friends of ED cannot guarantee the accuracy of this information.

Published by friends of ED

30-32 Lincoln Road, Olton, Birmingham.
B27 6PA. UK.
Printed in USA

ISBN 1-903450-073X

Credits

Authors
Sham Bhangal
Ben Renow-Clarke

Additional Material
Daniel Squier
Andrew Tracey

Commissioning Editor
Matthew Knight

Technical Editors
Daniel Squier
Andrew Tracey
Dan Britton
Julie Closs

Author Agent
Gaynor Riopedre

Project Manager
Vic Idiens

Reviewers
Sally Cruikshank
Leon Cych
Todd Darling
Brian K. James
Steve Kirby
Steve McCormick
Mike Pearce
Jake Smith
Steve Webster
Stephen Williams

Managing Editors
Ben Huczek
Mel Orgee

Graphic Editors
Matt Clark
Ty Bhogal

Indexer
Simon Collins

Cover Design
Matt Clark
Katy Freer

Proof Reader
Jason Cuthbert

Sham Bhangal

Sham Bhangal originally started his career as an engineer specializing in industrial computer-based display and control systems. In his spare time he took up freelance web design, a hobby that grew slowly until it became his main career. He now writes extensively for friends of ED and is engaged in all aspects of web design. Sham lives in rural Somerset with his partner Karen.

Ben Renow - Clarke

www.keeki.com

Benjamin Ewen James Renow-Clarke is a very long name. As far as Ben is concerned, home is the small village of North Cerney, England, from which he is currently temporarily exiled. Ben has just bought a fancy new computer and web domain, both of which he promises to fill with "junk" soon.

I promised to dedicate a book to some friends I met while putting up fences in Countisbury for the National Trust in 1995. So, even though there's no way any of them will be reading it, this is for you Cara, Helen, Richard, Nadine, Andy, Paula, and the others that I've forgotten.

4.   More power, less script   101

5.   Movies that remember how to do things   139

6.   Objects   165

7.   Objects on the stage   199

8. Making Plans   223

9. Modular ActionScript   281

10. Sound   315

11. Sprites   357

12.   Drawing API   391

13.   Coding the stun:design site   419

Introduction

Welcome

With the release of Flash MX, scripting in Flash has moved from being a desirable asset to an essential skill in the world of web design. ActionScript is, quite simply, the center of power in Flash, and it's no surprise that most of the advances in Flash MX are script-centric.

ActionScript is that scary code stuff that programmers do, right? Wrong. What ActionScript does is to add power and potential to your design work. It's not going to turn you into someone who speaks in ones and zeros, only comes out after dark, and whose idea of design is a different HTML color. It's going to turn you into someone who finally has the power to achieve what they want with their web design, rather than being hemmed in by frustrating limitations.

This book will take you from knowing little or nothing about ActionScript to a position where you have a real Foundation of knowledge that you and your design work can build some awe-inspiring structures on.

What you need to know

You've picked up this book, so we guess that you've got the Flash basics under your belt. You will probably have built some basic timeline-based movies with tweens and so on, and may have read an introductory book to Flash such as friends of ED's acclaimed *Foundation Macromedia Flash MX*.

If you haven't, we do recommend looking at Foundation Macromedia Flash MX, or even at the more visually-orientated Macromedia Flash MX Express, first.
All these books, and much more, can be examined in more detail at www.flashmxlibrary.com.

You may even be aware of this book's Flash 5-based predecessor *Foundation ActionScript*. This book shares a few surface similarities, but you'll quickly see that this book has been totally rewritten around the quite different demands of Flash MX (just take a look at the table of contents if you don't believe us!).

If you did read *Foundation ActionScript*, then there is much valuable information within these pages for you. There will inevitably be a little crossover, though, and you might want to take a look at friends of ED's *Flash MX Upgrade Essentials*. This will get you up to speed with all the new features in Flash MX as quickly as possible, without any unnecessary repetition.

If you didn't read *Foundation ActionScript*, but dabbled with ActionScript with Flash 5, be prepared to meet some new ways of working. There are plenty of people out there coding in Flash 5 style in Flash MX, and this is easy to do. This risks missing out on taking advantage of the advances made with MX, and we're not going to do that. Everything will be fully explained, so don't worry – you'll be miles ahead of everyone else on the web by the end.

Support: fast, free, and friendly

Got a problem? Can't get one of our exercises to work? Can't find a bit of code that we've promised you? friends of ED offer free technical support for all of our books to make sure that you experience an unhindered path through the pages of this book. So, if you've got a problem, don't hesitate to get in touch.

You can reach us at support@friendsofED.com, quoting the last four digits of the ISBN in the subject of the e-mail (that's 073x), and even if our dedicated support team are unable to solve your problem immediately, your queries will be passed onto the people who put the book together - the editors and authors - to solve.

We'd love to hear from you, even if it's just to request future books, ask about friends of ED, or tell us how much you loved *Foundation Macromedia Flash MX ActionScript!*

> *To tell us a bit about yourself and make comments about the book, why not fill out the reply card at the back and send it to us!*

If your enquiry concerns an issue not directly concerned with book content, then the best place for these types of questions is our message board lists at http://friendsofed.infopop.net/2/OpenTopic. Here, you'll find a variety of designers talking about what they do, who should be able to provide some ideas and solutions.

For news, more books, sample chapters, downloads, author interviews and more, send your browser to www.friendsofED.com. To take a look at the brand new friends of ED Flash MX bookshelf from which this book comes, take a look at flashmxlibrary.com.

FLAs for download

There's a wealth of code and support files available for this book, organized by chapter at the Foundation ActionScript for Macromedia Flash MX page at www.friendsofED.com.

If you haven't got a copy of Macromedia Flash MX yet, then you can download a fully-functional 30-day trial from those nice people at www.macromedia.com.

You can also access the fully functioning website that you'll be building throughout the latter parts of this book as a case study from the friends of ED site. Talking of which:

The case study: stun design

During this book we will be creating a website from scratch, called *stun:design*. This website uses some features that are not included with the default installation of Flash MX. You do not have to install the following items to make the website work, but if you do, you will be using exactly the same environment that we did. The three items are:

Microsoft TrueType Fonts for the Web:

Some time ago, Microsoft released a core set of fonts to be used for the web. The theory was that if all users had these fonts installed, HTML web designers could assume that if they used these fonts only, then their web pages would look exactly the same for every user.

This has not taken off, but this is not a problem for the typical Flash designer, *because we can embed the fonts we want to into the SWF itself, and the user doesn't have to have them installed to see the same site.*

The TrueType fonts for the web are cool, because, as their name implies, they are specifically designed for the web. The stun:design site uses the **Trebuchet MS** font, and you can download it free from

www.microsoft.com/typography/fontpack/default.htm

This allows you to install the Trebuchet font for either PC or Mac. If you don't download this font, the FLA files will default to _sans, which is not a problem, but the site was designed with Trebuchet in mind.

Macromedia Extensions Manager

The Macromedia Extensions manager allows you to install **Extensions**, specially created additions to the Flash authoring environment. It is *not* installed by default, although you can find the installer for it in the **goodies/Macromedia/Extensions Manager** subdirectory of the Flash MX install CDROM. You need to install it to install the extension we used in creating our final HTML files for the stun:design site, as noted below.

Extension MX_139598; Center in browser

The Flash SWFs we will be creating for the stun:design site use the following HTML sizing information (File > Publish Settings… > HTML);

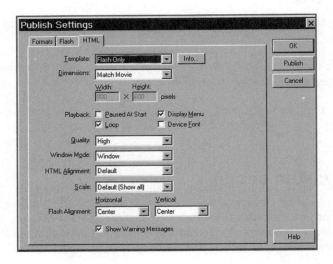

This will give you the following output if you publish the SWF (SHIFT+F12)

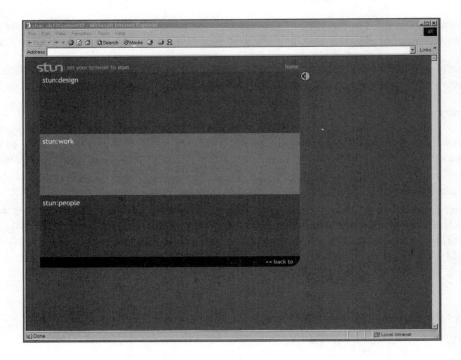

That's fine, but the web page looks odd because it is not centered. Most, if not all professional Flash pages look like this:

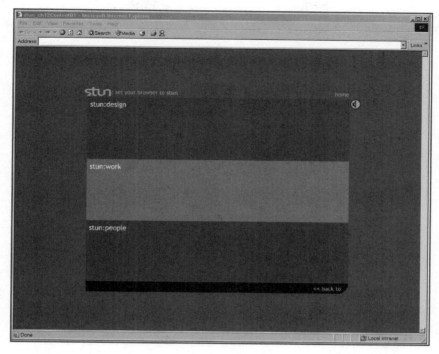

The ability to center in this way is a common question asked by beginners. The rather clever Jason Walker has produced a simple but highly effective Macromedia Extension that does this for you. You can load the extension from the Macromedia site (search on 'MX139598'). Although this extension was designed for Flash 5, it's simply a HTML template, and is therefore version independent. Simply download the file and install it using the Extensions manager (if you also have Flash 5 installed, be sure to select Flash MX in the dropdown at the top of the Extension Manager screen).

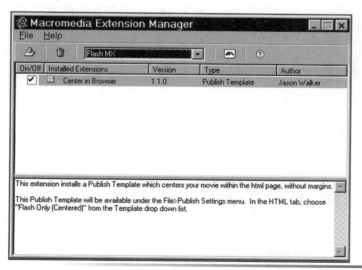

If you now select Flash Only (Centered) from the File > Publish Settings… > HTML tab, Template: dropdown, you will see a properly centered, non scaling SWF if you use the settings shown below:

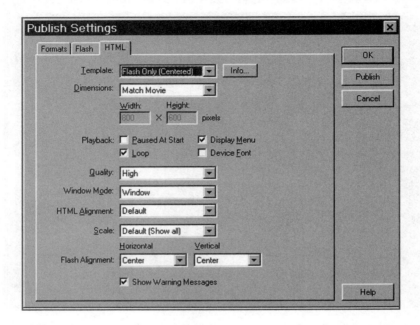

Layout conventions used in this book

We've tried to keep this book as clear and easy to follow as possible, so we've used the following text conventions throughout:

When you first come across an important word it will be in **bold** type, then in normal type thereafter.

We've used a fixed-width font for `code`, `file names`, and `any other text you need to type in for yourself`. Sections of code that need to be added to an existing script are additionally highlighted in bold type.

You'll see menu commands written in the form Menu > Sub-menu > Sub-menu.

When there's some information we think is really important, we'll highlight it like this:

This is very important stuff – don't skip it!

Worked exercises are laid out like this:

1. Open up Flash.

2. Create a new movie file, and add a circle in the middle of the stage.

Etc...

When we ask you to enter code that spills onto two lines **without** using a cariage-return, we'll use a code continuation character, like this. ➥

PCs and Macs

To make sure this book is as useful to you as possible, we've tried to avoid making too many assumptions about whether you're running Flash on a PC or a Mac. However, when it comes to mouse clicks and modifier buttons, we can't generalize – there's no two ways about it, they're different!

When we say 'click', we mean *left*-click on the PC or simply *click* on the Mac. On the other hand, a right-click on the PC corresponds to holding down the Ctrl button and clicking on the Mac. We abbreviate this to Ctrl-click.

Another important key combination on the PC is when you hold down Ctrl while you press another key (or click on something). We abbreviate this sort of thing as Ctrl-click. The Mac equivalent is to hold down the Command key (also known as the *Apple* or *Flower* key) instead, so you'll normally see this written out in the form Ctrl/Cmd-click.

Here's a quick rundown of the most common commands:

PC	Mac
Right-click	Ctrl-click
Ctrl-click	Apple-click
Ctrl-Z (to undo)	Apple-Z
Ctrl-Enter	Apple-Enter

Okay; now that we've taken care of the preliminaries, let's go to work!

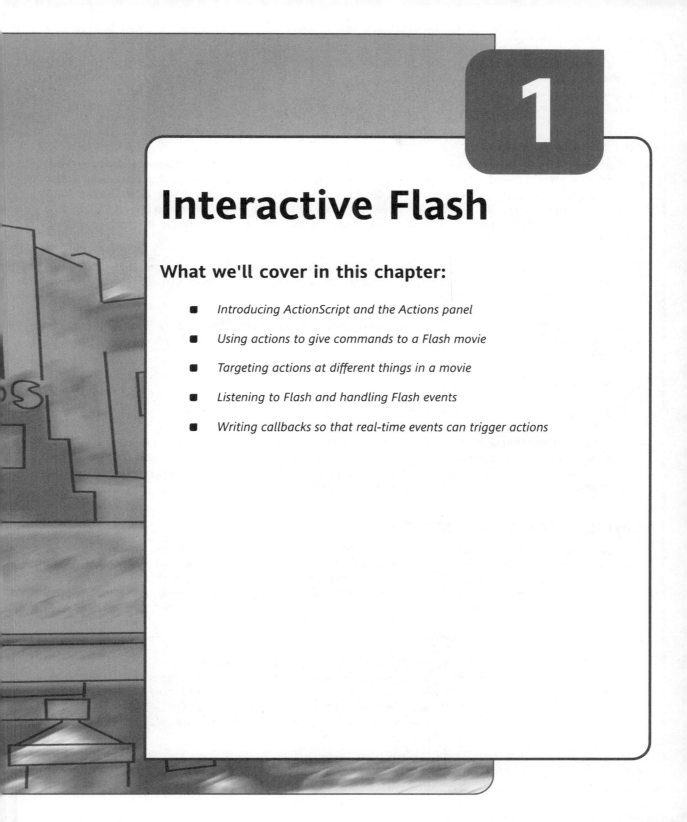

Interactive Flash

What we'll cover in this chapter:

- *Introducing ActionScript and the Actions panel*
- *Using actions to give commands to a Flash movie*
- *Targeting actions at different things in a movie*
- *Listening to Flash and handling Flash events*
- *Writing callbacks so that real-time events can trigger actions*

So, what's this ActionScript business all about? You may well have done loads of great stuff with Flash already, but you still keep hearing people say you've barely scratched the surface, because you haven't learned to **program** your movies... On the other hand, programming's supposed to be a strange and highly complex business, practiced by myopic young men with pale skin and peculiar taste in clothes.

If you're anything like me, that's a path in life you'd probably rather avoid.

Fortunately, there's some good news. Programming's a bit like mountaineering: there are dedicated full-timers who might spend every waking minute preparing to tackle the north face of the Eiger, even if that means their day-to-day lives come to resemble some kind of hideous training regime. However, there are plenty more folks who'll just take a few weeks out from 'normal life' to join a trek up Mount Kilimanjaro, and get back home tanned, fit, and with a whole new perspective on things – not to mention a great big wad of stunning photos!

I'm not going to suggest that learning ActionScript is somehow going to get you fit and tanned. But it can help you to race ahead with making rich, powerful, truly fantastic Flash movies that will leave most non-ActionScripting Flash-meisters standing.

So, to get back to the point. What's this ActionScript business all about? Well, as far too many irritating game show hosts have reminded us over the years: "the clue is in the question". There are two words to consider:

- Action

- Script

We all know what these mean: an action is something you do, and a script is something actors read so that they know what to say and do when they go on stage or in front of a camera. Well, that's really all there is to it. ActionScript is like a script that we give to a Flash movie, so that we can tell it what to do, and when to do it – that is, we give it **actions** to perform.

Giving your movies instructions

Actions are the basic building blocks of ActionScript. It's sometimes helpful to think of them as instructions we give to the movie, or even better, as **commands**. We tell the movie to stop. We tell it to start again. We tell it to go to such and such a frame, and start playing from there. You probably get the idea. Whenever we want to tell our movie to do something that it wouldn't normally do anyway, we can do so by giving it an action.

Since this book is about ActionScript, I'll stick with using the word 'actions'. If you mention actions to programmers who don't use Flash though, they may look at you blankly for a moment, before saying "ah, you mean commands!". In my opinion, it's well worth keeping the idea that 'actions are the same thing as commands' at the back of your mind!

As you'll know if you've sneaked a look at the ActionScript Dictionary (Help > ActionScript Dictionary), there are stacks of different actions available in Flash MX, which makes it (a) possible to do all sorts of weird and wonderful things to your movies, and (b) pretty hard to know where to start. Don't worry though – I've a cunning plan! We'll start off by looking at some simple actions that let us start and stop a movie's main timeline, and then go on to look at jumping about from one frame to another. Nothing too tricky to begin with.

Before we start writing actions though, I need to make an important introduction. The **Actions panel** will be your partner in crime throughout this chapter, the rest of the book, and your future career as an ActionScript hero! Let's check it out.

Working with the Actions panel

The Actions panel is where we'll be writing all our ActionScript, so it'll pay for you to know your way around it before we make a proper start.

First, you need to open it up – as with any panel, there are several ways to do this, but the simplest is to click on the panel's title bar, which you should spot near the bottom of the screen.

> ▶ **Actions - Frame**

If you don't see it here, you can always select Window > Actions (or use the keyboard shortcut F9) to call it up. Another option is to click on the little arrow icon (🗷) (which Flash uses to represent all things ActionScript) at the far right of the Property inspector.

This is how it should look when you open it up for the first time:

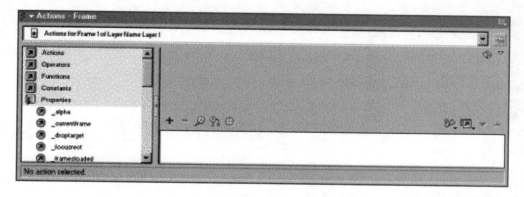

Let's take a look at what we've got here. Up at the top, there's a bar saying:

> Actions for Frame 1 of Layer Name Layer 1

This tells us that any actions we add are going to be **attached to** the first frame of the layer called Layer 1. Actions are always attached to something: usually a keyframe on the timeline or an instance on the stage. This tells you what and where that something is.

We'll see what that means for us shortly, but it's worth noting here and now that this text will change automatically when we start selecting other things in our movie.

If the selection changes, the script that's displayed will also change. So, if you've written some script and it suddenly seems to vanish, it's probably because you've clicked outside the window and selected something else by mistake. Don't panic though – you can get your work back by reselecting the original frame.

> *One very common mistake (and one that even the pros aren't immune to) is to type a load of ActionScript into the Actions Panel, watch the movie totally fail to do what you expect, and scratch your head for hours, not realizing that your script is attached to the wrong thing! It's always worth checking that this box says what you expect it to.*

On the left side, there's a list of little 'book' icons 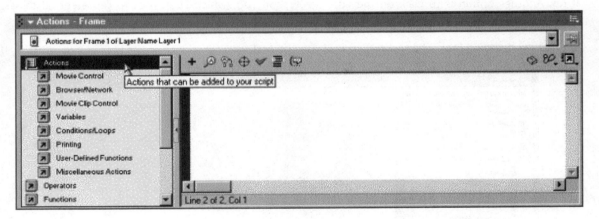, the first of which contains its own great long list of actions. The other books contain operators, functions, constants, and other bits and pieces we can use to tie lots of actions together in the way we want. If you hover the mouse pointer over one of them, a tooltip should appear, giving you a brief definition of its contents and where it's used.

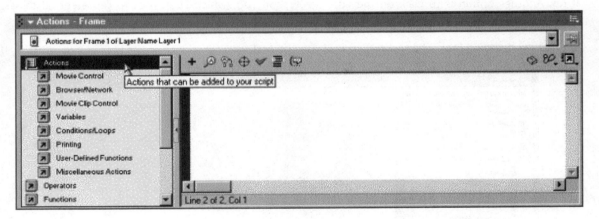

Don't worry about the details of all these for now though; you'll learn about them soon enough. This is the **Actions toolbox**, and it gives us a neat little way to write code in a no-brain 'building blocks' fashion.

If you open up the Actions book (just click on the icon), and then open the Movie Control book inside, you'll see the following list of actions:

Double-click on stop, and you'll add a `stop()` action to your 'Actions for Frame 1 of Layer Name Layer 1' script:

We've now got an action called **stop**, which is attached to the first frame on the layer called Layer 1. Say you now added a whole bunch of cool tweens to later frames on the main movie timeline... There wouldn't be much point: when you ran it, it would get as far as frame 1, read the script, and stop dead. The `stop()` action does precisely what it says, just as the `play()` action makes the movie start playing, and so on.

> Don't worry about the brackets and the semi-colon for now – they are programming conventions and their purpose will become clear later on.

Picking your scriptwriting mode

Well, we've made a start. All the actions we're ever going to need are stashed away inside those book icons, so we could carry on using this technique to write all the code we're ever likely to need. What's more, Flash won't let you make any changes to the script that could break it (such as mistyping the `stop()` action as `slop()`), so you literally *can't* put a foot wrong along the way.

Back in Flash 5 this safe, controlled **Normal mode** was undeniably the best way to start out writing ActionScript. However, there's another option to consider: **Expert mode** lets us bypass the books, allowing us to type the code in directly.

If you have a nervous disposition, this may seem like a worrying step. "It's only the first chapter, but already you're expecting me to be an expert?" you cry... But honestly, it's not like that at all! Macromedia added so many enhancements to the Actions panel for Flash MX that there's really no need at all to use Normal mode any more. Expert mode contains all the helpful features you might need, but saves you the trouble of searching through all those books for the particular action you want – now you can just type it in.

Okay, so maybe you don't believe a word of what I'm saying here. Let's switch to Expert mode, and I'll prove it to you!

Find the Options button 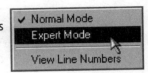, in the bottom right-hand corner of the Actions panel, click on it, and select Expert Mode from the little menu that pops up:

Your Actions panel should now look like this:

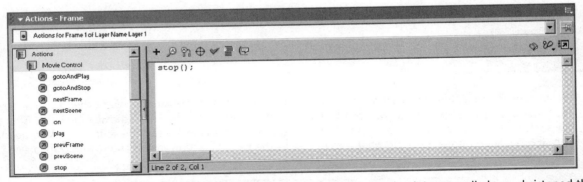

As you can see, we've now got a lot more white space for writing script (Macromedia have christened this the **Script pane**), and even a flashing cursor to help us with typing it in! This is just like any other simple text editor you might have come across: you can add and delete text as you'd expect, cut and paste, even highlight lines and drag them wherever you want.

It all works here – so what more could we ask for? Well, a few things actually.

First of all, we want something that'll tell us if we've made a mistake. Try changing `stop();` to `slop();` and you'll see (if you look carefully) that the first four letters have changed from blue to black. The Script pane will normally show all action names (or **keywords**) in blue, though you may want to use the Preferences dialog (CTRL/CMD+U) to change this color to something a little more visible.

Secondly, we could do with fixing that 'disappearing script' problem I mentioned a couple of pages back. Just select frame 10 and add a keyframe (F6) to see what I mean – look, no more script! Of course, that's not quite true. Your script is still attached to frame 1, but you're looking at the script attached to frame 10. Check the text at the top of the panel if you want proof:

So what if you want to work on frame 10 while you're looking at the script in frame 1?

Easy! Just click on frame 1 again, and then press the drawing pin button  that's just to the right of the text box:

Now that you've pinned the current selection (frame 1) to the Actions panel, you can do whatever you like with frame 10 without affecting what's shown in the Script pane. Have a go and see for yourself. Select frame 10, and you'll still be able to see your stop() action from frame 1.

This is a very useful feature to know about, but only so long as you remember to turn it off when you start trying to add actions elsewhere! Press the pin button again to unpin the script, and click back on the first frame. Now we're ready to carry on.

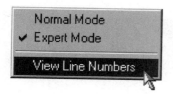

One more thing you can do to make the Script pane a little friendlier is to turn on line numbering. Just press the Options button  again, and select View Line Numbers from the menu:

Now you'll see that each line of your script has a number shown against it in the left-hand margin:

```
1 stop();
2
```

This can be very handy for tracking down problems in your scripts. If Flash has problems when you run the movie, it can use the line numbers to tell you which bits of script are causing the problem.

One more thing that's well worth knowing is that the Flash scripting pane is a bit strange about case-sensitivity. ActionScript itself isn't case-sensitive, but the **syntax highlighting** (which makes all your actions turn blue) is case-sensitive for actions. For example, if you wrote a script containing the action STOP(), it would work just fine when you played the movie. However, it wouldn't be highlighted in the scripting pane, since that expects the action to read stop().

> *There are several more helpful features built into the Actions panel – you've probably already noticed all the buttons running along the top of the Script pane. We won't examine them right away though; it'll be easier to demonstrate what they do once we've a little more script under our belts.*

The Actions panel will lie at the center of all the ActionScript that you'll ever write. We'll explore a few more of its mysteries as we work through the book, but you now have enough to make a start and create your first ActionScript-enabled movie.

Using actions to control the root timeline

We're going to start with a simple example that shows how easily we can bypass the usual flow of a movie with just a tiny bit of ActionScript.

1. Create a new movie and add a new layer to the root timeline. Rename the original layer as graphics, and the new layer as actions.

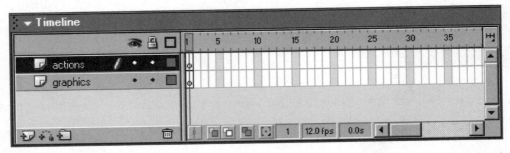

This is a good way to start all your ActionScripted movies. The script doesn't care what layer it's on, so you can put it on a layer of its own. This will help keep the timeline uncluttered, letting us add and remove graphics to and from the other layers without any risk of damaging our lovingly crafted script. Let's add those graphics now.

We don't really need any terribly fancy graphics to demonstrate what's going on with the timeline. For simplicity's sake, let's just create a simple motion tween between two points.

2. Select frame 1 on the graphics layer, and use the Oval tool to draw a circle on the left-hand side of the stage. Now select frame 20 and press F5 to insert a frame.

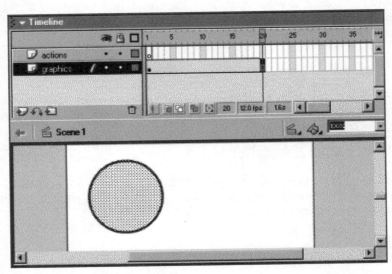

3. Right-click (or CTRL-click if you're on a Mac) on the new frame, and select Create Motion Tween from the menu that appears. Now hold down the SHIFT key and drag the circle over to the right-hand side of the stage.

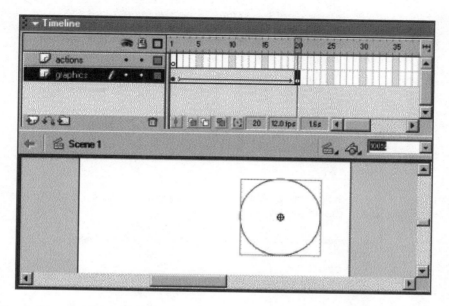

If the Actions panel is still showing, (providing you haven't played with the tween and the circle is still selected!) you'll notice that it now contains the following helpful words:

Current selection cannot have actions applied to it.

That's because the tweening process has made our circle into a graphic symbol, and graphics are one thing that we can't attach ActionScript to. Ah well, at least the panel told us.

That doesn't stop us controlling the circle, though. If you now test the movie (press CTRL/CMD+ENTER) you should find yourself with a circle that moves steadily across the screen from left to right. The circle's movement depends on the timeline, and we know that ActionScript can be used to control that. Let's prove it.

4. Select frame 1 on the actions layer and take a look at the Actions panel. Make sure the Script pane is active (by clicking in it with the mouse so that the margin turns blue – it's gray when inactive) and you should see the cursor blinking away right next to it. You're about to begin your hand-coding journey, so flex your fingers, crack those knuckles, and type exactly what we saw before:

```
1  stop();
2  |
```

> *You may have noticed that just after you entered the first bracket, a little tooltip popped up showing you the full command, but that it swiftly disappeared again when you entered the second bracket. This is another of the Actions panel's helping hands that I mentioned earlier, called a* **code hint**. *This is Flash's way of telling you that it's recognized what you're typing, and that all you need to enter now is a closing bracket and a semi-colon to finish off the job.*
>
> *It may not look like much now, but when we start looking at more complicated actions later on you'll begin to find it invaluable. If you ever want to see the code hint again, you can click between the brackets at the end of the action and press the* **Show Code Hint** *button*  *at the top of the panel.*

5. Place the cursor at the beginning of line 1, hit ENTER to shift the action down to line 2, and fill the now-blank first line as shown below:

```
1  // stops the movie
2  stop();
```

Don't worry about the fact that this new line appears in gray. This is how Flash shows **comments**, lines of script that serve no purpose except to help you keep track of what's going on. They don't actually contain any instructions, they just provide space within your ActionScript for you to keep notes and reminders.

When the movie runs, Flash will completely ignore all the gray text (everything following the double slash) so you can add as many comments as you like – in fact, I strongly recommend that you do just that!

A well-commented script is far easier to understand than one with non-stop pages and pages of actions. It's therefore much easier to debug six months later when you've forgotten what was going through your mind when you wrote it. Ideally, don't just state what a bit of script *is*, but describe how it fits in with the rest of your movie. Also, note that comments traditionally come just before the lines of script they're describing. Of course it's really up to you where you put them; but if you're going to be showing off your code to admiring colleagues (or asking them to help you fix it) it's better to stick with convention and put them first.

6. If you take a look at the timeline, you'll see that there's now a little 'a' showing in the first frame:

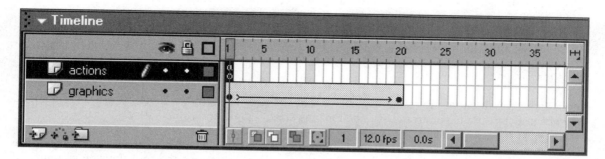

This reminds us that there are actions attached to this frame. Run the movie again and you'll see what a difference our single action has already made: as expected, the circle doesn't move.

That's all well and good, but on its own, this isn't really that exciting, let alone useful. Ten pages in, and all we've done with ActionScript is stop our movie doing anything at all... Okay, it's time we introduced a couple more actions before *you* decide it's time to stop.

7. Head back to the Actions panel and delete all the script we've written so far. Replace it with the following lines:

```
// jump to frame 20 and then stop
gotoAndStop(20);
```

Run the movie again, and you'll see once again that the circle's dead still. This time though, it's dead still on the right-hand side of the stage, because we've stopped it at frame 20.

8. Now select frame 20 on the actions layer, press F6 to insert a keyframe, and attach these lines of script:

```
// jump to frame 10 and then play
gotoAndPlay(10);
```

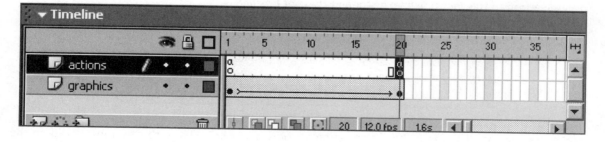

Now we should have a little more action to see on the stage. When the movie starts up, it will see the gotoAndStop() action we've attached to frame 1. This tells it to jump ahead to frame 20 and stop, so it will do just that.

However, attached to frame 20 is an action telling our movie to jump back to frame 10 and start playing again. Even though the movie will have stopped playing at this stage (that is, it won't be moving automatically from one frame to the next), it still has to follow instructions.

So, we see the circle jump back to the middle of the stage and start to move smoothly across to the right... Of course, once we reach frame 20 again, we're sent back to play from frame 10, and so on, and so on, for as long as you care to watch it.

Hmm. That's a little more interesting to look at, but still doesn't seem like much to write home about. Why not just start the tween from the middle of the stage – same end result surely?

Maybe, but the important thing we've seen here is that we can use a couple of simple actions to **override what would normally happen** in the movie. In this case, we've stopped the root timeline and jumped about from frame to frame.

This is just the tip of the iceberg – there's plenty more in a movie that we can turn to our bidding...

Who are you talking to?

One of the most important things to understand about actions is that they always have a **target**. If we think of them as commands again, it's fairly obvious that each command is directed at someone or something. Thinking back to when my parents would tell me (for the fifteenth time) to go clean my bedroom, they might just say:

> Get up there and clean that darned bedroom *now*!

Now that was fine when I was the only person in the room, but when my sister was there too, they'd need to say:

> *Ben*, get up there and clean that darned bedroom now!

So what's all this got to do with ActionScript? Well, we already know that actions are basically just commands to the Flash movie, telling it to do something. We know that they're always attached to something, and so far that's always been a keyframe on the root timeline. When we attached a simple `stop()` action to the root timeline, it stopped *the root timeline*.

> *Flash will always assume (unless it's told otherwise) that an action is targeted at the thing it's attached to.*

That being the case, how do we target an action at something else? What if there's a movie clip on the stage? They have their own timelines, quite separate from the main one; say we want to mess about with the movie clip's timeline.

The first solution that might spring to mind is to open up the movie clip's timeline, and attach the action to that. That's certainly the obvious way to do it, and back in Flash 5 that's precisely how you *would* do it every time. Unfortunately though, that approach has a few problems:

- As soon as you start writing more complex movies, you'll end up with lots of little bits of script dotted around all over the place. Before you can fix your bugs, you'll have to find them!

- Once you add script to a movie clip, you're stuck with it. If you want lots of identical instances that all do the same thing, then that's fine. But if you want to make one that's even slightly different, you'll need to create a completely new movie clip.

Flash MX won't actually *stop* you building script into your movie clips (there are still some times when it's useful to be able to do that), but it's much more useful in the long run if you can learn to keep all your code in the main timeline and use ActionScript-only techniques to pick your targets.

Controlling movie clips on the stage

It's all very well *saying* that, but how do we *do* it? Well, the answer comes in two parts.

First we need to give the movie clip a name. "But it already has a name!" I hear you cry... When you create a movie clip (or any kind of symbol), it appears in the Library panel with a name against it – normally 'Symbol 1' or something like that, unless you change it to something else.

In fact, this name doesn't mean anything at all to ActionScript; it's just a label that Flash gives it to make life easier for you when you're making movies. What's more, the items you see in the Library aren't actually part of the movie – it's only when you drag an **instance** of the symbol onto the stage that it becomes a thing that we can control with ActionScript.

Once you've done that, the Property inspector gives us a neat little way to christen that instance with its very own name. Say you have a movie clip in the library called Symbol1, and you've just dragged it onto the stage. This is what the Property inspector might look like:

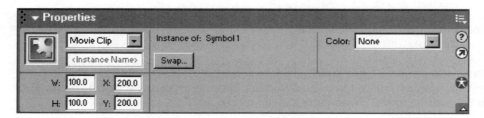

There's a text box just below where it says Movie Clip, which holds the following text in gray:

<Instance Name>

No prizes for guessing, but this is where you give your movie clip instance a name! Let's assume for now that you call it myClip_mc:

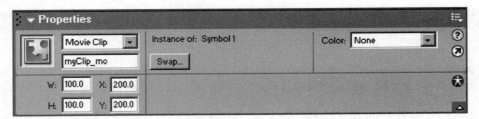

You may be wondering what the _mc suffix is all about. Why not just call it myClip? It's simply to make it clear that it's the name of a movie clip instance. You'll soon come to appreciate how useful it is to have a simple reminder like this, so that when we see it in code, we know immediately that it's referring to a movie clip. What's more, the Actions panel also recognizes _mc instance names as movie clips, so it can prompt us with options that are specifically relevant to movie clips.

You'll see the use of suffixes come into play in more detail later in the book, but here's a quick list of all of the suffixes that Flash recognizes, and what they mean:

_mc	movie clip
_btn	button
_sound	sound
_video	video
_str	string
_array	array
_txt	text field
_fmt	text format
_date	date
_color	color
_xml	XML
_xmlsocket	XMLsocket

The first two are the ones you'll use most often, but it's worth knowing what the others are so that you'll recognize them when you see them.

Now that our instance has a name, we can use ActionScript to talk to it. This is where the second part comes in: **dot notation**.

The **dot** (a.k.a. **period** or **full stop**) might be the smallest text character going, but when it comes to ActionScript, it's also one of the most important. This is how we use it to tell Flash that we want to stop the timeline of the movie clip instance called myClip_mc:

```
myClip_mc.stop();
```

In terms of our earlier room-tidying analogy, this is just like saying:

```
Ben.go tidy your room!
```

The bit before the dot tells Flash who (or rather, what) the bit afterwards (the action) is directed towards. In these examples, we stop the timeline of the instance whose name is myClip_mc, and tell Ben to go tidy his room.

Let's bolt together all that we've learnt so far.

Talking to different timelines

In this exercise, we're going to use ActionScript to control a couple of cars. The graphic symbols I've used can be found in the download for this chapter (in the file car.fla), though there's nothing to stop you from creating your own!

1. Create a new Flash document, and select File > Open As Library to pull the redCar graphic from car.fla into the library. Drag an instance onto the left-hand side of the stage, and press F8 to convert it to a movie clip called carRunning.

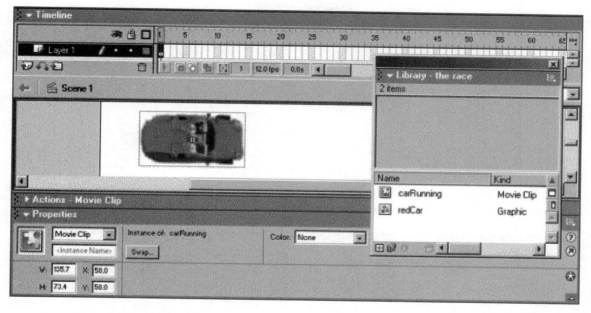

2. Double-click on the unnamed instance to edit the movie clip in place. Select frame 2 of the timeline and press F6 to insert a keyframe. Select the graphic again, and use the Property inspector to move it vertically (that is, change its y-coordinate) by one pixel. If you run the movie now, you'll see the car judder slightly up and down, which tells us that its engine is running.

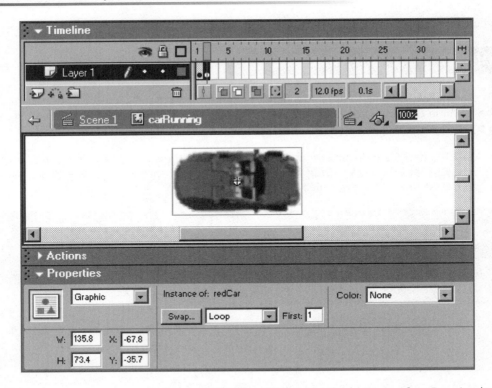

3. Click on Scene 1 to return to the main timeline. Make sure the instance of carRunning is selected and use the Property inspector to set its instance name to myCar_mc.

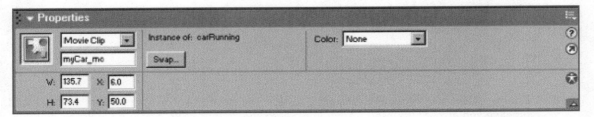

4. Select frame 50 and press F5 to insert a frame. Use Insert > Create Motion Tween and hold down SHIFT while you drag the car across to the right-hand side of the stage. Run the movie again, and you'll see the car judder its way across the stage. So far, so good!

5. Now it's time to add some ActionScript, so create a new layer called actions and select frame 1 in the timeline.

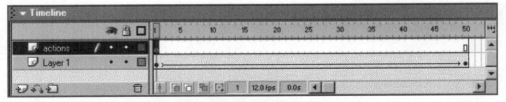

6. Open up the Actions panel and enter the following script:

```
// stop the car traveling
stop ();
```

Since we've attached our script to the root timeline, Flash assumes that the `stop()` action is directed at the root timeline. That's where our car's motion is controlled, so the car should stop traveling.

Test the movie and you'll see this is true. More importantly though, while the car may not actually be going anywhere, its engine still appears to be running. That's because the juddering motion is part of the movie clip, so it's controlled by a separate timeline.

7. One way we could stop the car's timeline would be to open up the movie clip and attach a `stop()` action to its timeline. That'd do the trick, but would quickly get fiddly if we wanted to do more complex things and found ourselves having to switch back and forth between the timelines.

There's no point anyway, since we have a perfectly good way to do the same thing directly from the root timeline. Change your script so that it looks like this:

```
// stop the car's engine
myCar_mc.stop();
```

and try the movie again. You'll now see that the car is moving across the screen, but no longer shaking. Either someone's fixed the dodgy engine, or they've left it out of gear and forgotten to put on the handbrake!

In terms of our movie, we've now stopped the `myCar_mc` timeline, but left the root timeline alone. If we stopped both of them, the car wouldn't move at all:

```
// stop the car moving at all
stop();
myCar_mc.stop();
```

The other big advantage of using dot notation and scripting everything from the main timeline is that we can now do different things to different instances.

8. Create a new layer, and add a new instance of `carRunning` called `myCar2_mc`. You may want to rename these layers as `car1` and `car2`. Make sure your new car is well below the original and recreate the motion tween I described earlier on.

Run the movie, and you'll see that the first car is still dead as a duck, but the second car is still running (even if it's not going anywhere right now...)

9. Finally, let's prove that it's not just down to chance that one's running while the other isn't. Change the last line of your script to read:

```
// stop the car moving at all
stop();
myCar2_mc.stop();
```

Run the movie one last time, and sure enough, the engine in the first car (myCar_mc) now runs, while the second (myCar2_mc) is motionless.

Arguments

Of course, my parents had an easy time of it with the bedroom-cleaning instructions. Living in a fairly small house, with just one room each for my sister and me, they didn't have to tell me which room they meant. If I'd been one of the Getty children, my parents might have had to say:

John-Paul, get up to bedroom number seven this instant or it's no rum truffles for you!

My parents didn't need to add extra details about *which* room they meant, because it was obviously *my* room. John-Paul's parents had to add an extra bit of information: *which one* of his bedrooms he had to clean!

This extra piece of information that qualifies the initial command is called an **argument**. No, this doesn't mean that John-Paul refused to clean his room and started a family row. It's just a name we give to values that help to determine what an action does for us.

The stop() action doesn't take any arguments, since Flash knows exactly what to do without any help. It just means **stop the timeline**.

On the other hand, gotoAndPlay() tells Flash to skip to a particular frame and start playing from there. Obviously, we need to tell Flash exactly *which* frame to go to, so we always need to give it an argument:

```
gotoAndPlay(10);
```

The action tells Flash that it should start playing from a new frame, while the argument tells it which frame that is.

Listening to what your movies are telling you

So far, all the ActionScript we've looked at has been fairly predictable and not terribly exciting. That's because we've figured everything out in advance – before we've even run the movie, we know exactly what actions we want to give our movie, and exactly when we want them to kick in.

When you think of Flash, you probably think of **interactivity**: whoever ends up watching your movie should be able to react to what they see and hear, and make things happen in the movie spontaneously. That's probably why you're here in the first place, learning how to add some more of that interactive power to your designs.

Interactivity is a two-way process, though. As well as giving out commands, we need some way to respond to what's going on when the movie runs. We need some way to **trigger** actions whenever some event happens while the movie's running – when the movie finishes loading, when the user presses a button, when the hero of our adventure game catches all the magic artichokes before the villain's bomb goes off... I think you probably get the idea.

When I was a child, I was given a cuckoo clock as a present. Well, actually, a cuckoo clock only in the loosest sense of the word, given that it was in the shape of a cartoon lion with a swinging tail as a pendulum. Every time the clock struck the hour, the lion would wake up, open its mouth and growl. He could act as an alarm clock too, giving an almighty roar as the alarm went off.

As I've said, there were two things that set my lion into action:

- When the clock reached the beginning of the hour, it was time to growl.
- When the alarm time arrived, it was time to roar.

So, in this case there were two **events** that the lion was waiting for. As soon as either occurred, the lion would perform the appropriate **action** (a roar or a growl).

In fact, the magic word here is **event**. We need a way to write ActionScript that can react to events that happen during the course of the movie – that is, what we really want to say is:

Whenever *this event* happens, perform *these actions*...

Or, to be more succinct, "if *this* happens, do *that*".

> *ActionScript is called an **event-driven language**, which sounds like complicated programming-speak until you realize that, just like the lion, it's set up to wait for something to happen and then react to it – nothing more complicated than that.*

Events in Flash

So what sort of event happens in a Flash movie? Well, it could be something obvious that happens externally, say the user pressing a button on your web site or typing on the keyboard. An event can also be something less obvious that happens internally within Flash, like loading a movie clip or moving to the next frame on the timeline.

Whether we're dealing with an internal event or an external event, we can write a sequence of actions (called an **event handler**) that will run whenever that event occurs.

In the real world, you can see all sorts of event/event handler pairs around you. For example, your electric kettle waits for the water to start boiling (the event) and has a special circuit that switches the power off (the event handler) when this occurs. Another example would be your central heating: when your apartment falls to a certain temperature (the event, where this temperature is decided by how you've set the thermostat) your heating kicks in (the event handler) to make things warm and toasty again.

External events

Back in the Flash world, let's consider the simplest event/event handler partnership – a button press:

- The button `push_btn` sits there waiting for some user interaction.

- The user presses `push_btn`, and this shows up as a Flash event called `onPress`.

- Flash looks for an event handler that's been assigned to that particular event on that particular button: `push_btn.onPress`.

- If it finds one it runs the ActionScript inside it, otherwise it does nothing.

Press me for something to happen!!   Roar!!

The most important thing to notice about events is that they're very specific to the thing that generated them. Say we had another button called `red_btn`. If we pressed that, it would also generate an `onPress` event, but it wouldn't trigger anything unless we'd specifically defined an event handler for `red_btn.onPress`.

Yes, the dot notation gets everywhere! Don't panic though, the rules are similar to before: the bit before the dot tells Flash where the bit afterwards is *coming from*. It's really just as it was with actions, except that it's telling us *where an event came from* rather than *where an action's going*.

Internal events

This event/event handler relationship is fairly easy to spot when we're talking about external events like a button press. However, internal events aren't always so obvious, since movies generate them automatically.

Probably the easiest one to get your head around is the `onEnterFrame` event, which is generated every time a timeline's playhead enters a new frame. Yeah, but what does this mean in practical terms? Well, it means that it's dead easy to write a bit of script that Flash will then run for *every* frame.

Say we want to make the timeline run at double speed: `_currentframe` refers to the number of the frame we're currently on, so we could write an `onEnterFrame` event handler that contains the action `gotoAndStop(_currentframe+2)`.

- The movie starts, generating an `onEnterFrame` event.
- This triggers `gotoAndStop(1+2)`, sending us to frame 3.
- This generates another `onEnterFrame` event.
- This triggers `gotoAndStop(3+2)`, sending us on to frame 5.
- And so on...

Basically, we skip every other frame, so the movie appears to run at twice normal speed. If we did the same thing using `gotoAndStop(_currentframe-1)`, we could even make the movie run backwards, as every time the playhead enters a frame, it would be told to go to the frame before the one it is currently in, where it would find the same command again.

Okay, this may not seem like particularly useful stuff just at the moment; but that's just because we're still fooling around with the timeline. Once we've tackled a few more actions, you'll start to realize just how powerful this `onEnterFrame` business really is.

Before doing that though, we need to get down to business and look at how we actually write these fabled event handlers.

Introducing callbacks

Earlier on, I described event-driven programming in these terms:

> Whenever *this event* happens, perform *these actions*.

We now know that *this event* might be something like `push_btn.onPress`, and that *these actions* are what we call the event handler. We can express that in ActionScript like this:

```
push_btn.onPress = function() {
    // actions here make up the event handler
};
```

Hmm. It's not nearly as intuitive as `stop()` and `play()` were – I confess, there's a bit more to this one than we've talked about so far. But before you shrug your shoulders and start checking the index for what = and `function` are all about (because I know you want to know!) just stop for a moment; we'll get onto all that soon enough. All that matters here is this:

> *Whatever actions we write between the curly brackets { and } will be run whenever someone presses the button called* push_btn.

The technical name for this wee beastie is a **callback**, and while it may look a bit intimidating at first, you'll forget all about that once you've used it a couple of times.

Between you and me, there are plenty of Flash 5 ActionScripters who would rather walk over hot coals than start using callbacks! That's not because they're actually hard to use – on the contrary, they're an absolute cinch once you get the brackets in the right place – but because they use more letters than the old Flash 5 technique, which uses a nice short little action called `on()` to do pretty much the same thing.

Before you ask, yes, we can use `on()` in Flash MX; but it's really quite a lame duck compared to a callback, since it only lets you define event handlers for the timeline it's directly attached to.

Nesting spiders – argh!

I hate anything that has lots of brackets and commas and dots and stuff. Rather like some people hate spiders because they have too many legs, I just hate lines with too many brackets.

I managed to get my head around this with ActionScript when I realized that these aren't the sorts of brackets that require you to reach for a calculator and start thinking: they're just there to help arrange things into groups, like this:

> All small dogs (including dachshunds and terriers) should go to the tree on the left, but all other dogs (including beagles and Alsatians) should go to the tree on the right.

I'd say that this looks a *lot* less frightening than:

$$s = ?(u+v)t +5(a^2+20c) -1$$

Ugh! Spiders! I know a lot of the stuff below will look like that awful equation, but it's not as bad as all that. Most of the time, it's just a shorthand way of writing the 'dogs and trees' sentence. When any sort of math gets involved, it's usually of the $2 = 1 + 1$ variety.

Let's get over any apprehension about callbacks as quickly as possible, and put them through their paces.

Making actions run when you press a button on the stage

We're going to base this example on the earlier FLA we made with the racing cars going across the screen, so either open up your own copy, or grab the file called `therace.fla` from this chapter's download folder.

1. We're going to begin by adding some buttons to the stage, so you may like to close up the Actions panel for the time being. First, create a new layer called controls, and place it above the car layers.

2. Now, rather than creating buttons from scratch, let's pull some good-looking ones from out of the Macromedia buttons library (Windows > Common Libraries > Buttons). Open the Circle Buttons folder, and drag one 'next' and one 'previous' onto the stage.

3. Drop the buttons at either side of the stage, and add a horizontal line between them:

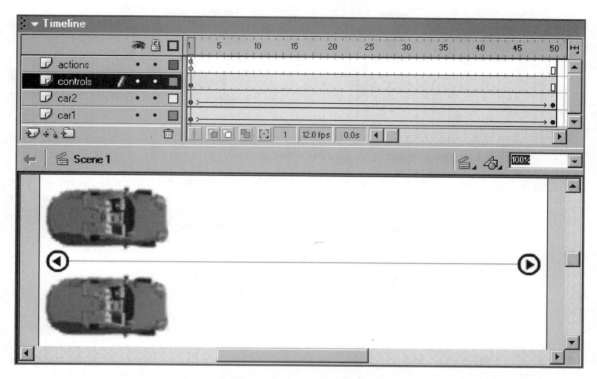

4. Select the left-hand button, and pop down to the Property inspector to give it the instance name `back_btn`. Do the same for the right-hand button, calling it `forward_btn`. Any guesses for what they're going to do?

5. Okay, it's time to open up the Actions panel again. Make sure that frame 1 of the actions layer is selected (so that the bar at the top of the panel reads 'Actions for Frame 1 of Layer Name actions'), delete the existing script, and enter the following:

```
// stop the cars traveling
stop();

// callback for onPress event on 'back' button
back_btn.onPress = function() {
    // jump to the previous frame and stop
    gotoAndStop(_currentframe-1);
};

// callback for onPress event on 'forward' button
forward_btn.onPress = function() {
    // jump to the next frame and stop
    gotoAndStop(_currentframe+1);
};
```

That looks a bit intimidating, but actually, there's less script there than it might seem, mainly because of all the comments I've put in. Let's consider it one piece at a time.

We begin by telling the root timeline to stop in its tracks. Otherwise, the cars would zoom straight across the stage and there would be nothing for us to do.

Next, there's a callback, which listens out for an onPress event coming from our 'back' button. If it picks one up (as it will if someone presses the button), then we use the gotoAndStop() action to jump to the previous frame.

The next callback's pretty much the same, only it listens out for an onPress event coming from the 'forward' button and jumps to the next frame on picking one up.

Each time you write a callback, you'll notice that after you type the first { bracket, Flash will start to indent your script. Likewise, just as soon as you type the closing bracket } it will automatically 'outdent' back to where it started. This incredibly useful feature is called Auto-formatting, and it can be a real lifesaver, especially later on when we start putting braces inside braces.

> *If the formatting of your code ever goes a bit awry for some reason, you can easily bring it back into line by clicking the* **Auto Format** *button* ▦ *in the Actions panel.*

6. Now run the movie, and you should see a couple of motionless cars. Been there, done that. So what? Try clicking on the 'forward' button, and you'll see both cars inch forward. Likewise, a click on the 'back' button and both cars will move back again.

    Yes, with just a couple of really-not-so-scary callbacks, we've wired up a couple of buttons that give us complete control over the movie's main timeline! Not bad, eh?

    Now you may have felt the need to point out that with both cars covering exactly the same ground, it's really not much of a race... Yes, the foolish and short-sighted approach I used for animating the cars (two motion tweens on the same timeline – d'oh!) doesn't really do the movie any favors.

    What if there was a quick and simple way to separate them? Preferably involving ActionScript and not too many long words...

Animating movie clips with ActionScript

Okay, this isn't strictly part of the chapter's storyline, but I'm not going to leave you wondering for the sake of a lesson plan... after all, this is supposed to be fun!

So far, we've done all our animation using tweens, and all our actions have been aimed at one timeline or another: stopping, starting, jumping about the place, and so on. That's a pretty good place to start if you're already quite familiar with Flash, since we're mainly tackling things you're already aware of.

Now that you've begun to get a bit of a grasp on ActionScript stuff like targeting actions at movie clips and wiring up event handlers, I can start to reveal the truth...

We don't need the timeline to animate a movie clip.

Rather than explaining that statement, I'm going to show you the alternative.

1. Back at the races, click on frame 50 in the actions layer and drag down to frame 2 in the car1 layer, so that frames 2 to 50 are selected on every one of the four layers:

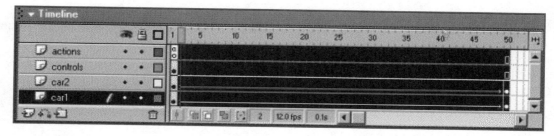

2. Now right-click (or CTRL-click) on the selection to call up a menu, and select Remove Frames to get rid of everything following frame 1. Yes, that's right. We want to lose *everything* except the contents of frame 1 in each layer.

3. Select frame 1 in the actions layer and open up the Actions panel. You'll need to make the following highlighted changes to get the first set of buttons working:

```
// stop the cars traveling
stop();

// callback for onPress event on 'back' button
back_btn.onPress = function() {
    //move myCar_mc horizontally -10 pixels
    myCar_mc._x -= 10;
    };

// callback for onPress event on 'forward' button
forward_btn.onPress = function() {
//move myCar_mc horizontally +10 pixels
    myCar_mc._x += 10;
};
```

Test the movie now, and you'll find that the top set of buttons controls the top car, while the bottom car sits still. Let's fix that.

4. Now add the following script to the end of what's already there:

```
// callback for onEnterFrame event
onEnterFrame = function() {
    // move the myCar2_mc across to mouse position
    myCar2_mc._x = _xmouse;
};
```

This lets us controls the second car using the mouse. Just as _currentframe refers to the current frame number, _xmouse refers to the mouse's current x-position, and we've used this to update the car's position. Because it's inside the onEnterFrame callback, it's updated twelve times every second, which keeps the position up to date.

Run the movie again. Now you can use the two sets of controls to maneuver each car separately.

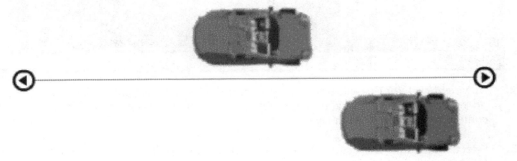

This animated effect is way more advanced than anything we've done before: it's truly interactive. Our original car race movie just moved the cars from left to right, and that's all it will ever do. This time, we can control the cars using buttons and the mouse.

Even simple interactivity like this opens up fantastic possibilities that we didn't have before. With a little imagination, you could replace each of the cars with a bat, and bounce little squares back and forth across the screen, just like one of those old TV video game consoles...

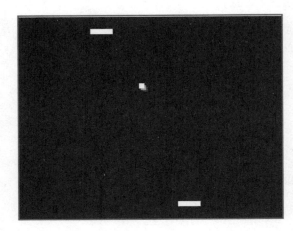

Tennis anyone? Take a look at `pong.fla` in the download to see how easy it is to create an interactive bat.

As another option (perhaps just a *little* more exciting): you could change one of the cars into a spaceship, so it could be The Lone Crusader © on his mission to save the world from the evil alien hordes...

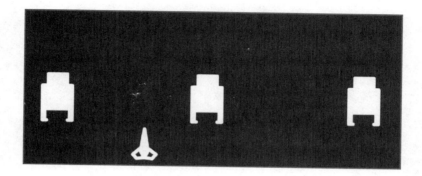

This time, your Starfleet SpaceCruiser™ has to dodge the alien plasma bolts... *save those cities young pilot!* Have a look at `spaceinvaders.fla` from the download if you want to see this screen moving.

I'm afraid we're not yet *quite* advanced enough to start adding alien hordes or the associated bloolly bloolly bloolly Blooop sound effects just yet... But hey, we've only been learning this stuff for twenty minutes!

Remember that all this movement comes from just a few lines of ActionScript! Even better, they're the same lines of ActionScript every time, and the whole thing is only one frame long! We're already up to the maximum interactivity offered by home computer entertainment systems when I was a kid – just think what we could achieve with another few frames and forty more lines of ActionScript...

This is why it pays to know ActionScript. It's so much more versatile and dynamic than plain Flash that it quickly leaves traditional Flash animation standing in the corner feeling sorry for itself!

Summary

In this chapter, you've gone quickly through the basic concepts behind event-driven programming. We started off by looking at how to attach script to the root timeline, and then saw how to write **actions** that control the timeline. Along the way, you learnt about **targets** and **instance names**.

After that, we introduced the idea of **events** and **event handlers**. Instead of writing plain actions that Flash will run regardless, we can enable a movie to trigger off scripts while it's running. By writing **callbacks** that wire up event handlers to button events, we can even give users a way to control what's going on in real time while the movie runs.

Don't worry if you didn't understand every single detail of what we've covered here; we've covered a lot of ground in quite a short space of time. Also, at this stage, a lot of it may seem a little abstract and theoretical, because we don't have all the tools in place to try out all the possibilities this stuff opens up.

As long as you've got all the exercises up and running though, you should be able to cope just fine with what we've got coming up. From here onwards, we'll be moving through the surrounding concepts in greater depth – but at a much more leisurely pace.

2

Movies that remember

What we'll cover in this chapter:

- *How to use variables as containers for storing information*

- *Different types of variables – numeric, string and Boolean*

- *The use of expressions to generate values to be stored in variables*

- *Taking user interactivity beyond button pressing using input and output text*

- *How to use arrays to deal with more complex, related information*

So far, all our ActionScript has dealt with what's going on in the present – for example, what the *current* frame is, or where the mouse pointer is *at this moment*. Of course, technology hasn't progressed far enough to let us peer into the future – not even with Flash MX! But looking at what's happened in the *past* isn't a problem. The only reason that all our movies so far have been stuck in the present is that they have no **memory**.

It might not be obvious right away what advantages there are to having a memory. After all, there's plenty you can do in Flash already, and we've already seen how a little bit of ActionScript manages to raise the bar on that. What do we need memory for?

Once again, the answer has everything to do with interactivity. If you want to make a movie that really makes a user feel they're involved with what's happening on the screen, you need to ensure there's a bit of continuity to the experience. For example, take the Starfleet SpaceCruiser™ game we just looked at in Chapter 1 – think how much less fun it would be to play if we couldn't give it any kind of scoring system...

> *In short, there's nothing wrong with movies that have no memory – just as there's nothing wrong with movies that don't use ActionScript at all. It's just that there's a whole lot more you can do with than you can without.*

Having a memory means having a place to store **information**, or **data**. Once Flash has stored a piece of data, it can keep it there for as long as it likes, and call it up whenever required. It can still respond instantly to whatever's going on (as we saw in the last chapter), but once it has a memory, it can choose *not to*, and respond whenever it chooses!

Even more importantly, once Flash has somewhere to *store* data, the user can send it much more interesting messages (like text and numbers) than they'd ever manage by clicking on a button!

Virtually all your ActionScript-enabled movies are going to use some kind of data, and it's fairly normal to find that you'll want to change it from one moment to the next. For precisely that reason, the ActionScript 'containers' we use for holding data are designed so that it's extremely easy to vary their contents – that's why they're called **variables**.

Here's an official-sounding definition:

> *A variable is a named memory location for holding data that's prone to frequent change.*

In the first part of this chapter, we'll take a look at what this definition really means, and see how Flash uses variables to keep track of what's going on, to make decisions and predictions, and to perform calculations.

Does it sound like we're in for some heavy math? No, and don't let the idea put you off! Variables don't need to be used to contain things like the speed of light squared – they can just as easily be used to specify how high you want your cartoon Flash character to jump. It's not math; it's just a powerful way to get Flash to do the fun things you want it to.

So, without further ado...

Introducing variables

A **variable** is a named 'container' that we can use to store data that we need to use several times (and possibly change) during the course of the movie. Whenever you need to use the data, you give Flash the variable name, and it will look in the right place and retrieve it for you. If you've never wrangled with code before, this concept may be confusing, so let's consider it in non-programming terms.

Your wallet is designed specifically to hold money – hopefully you have some to put in it! At any given time, there will be a particular amount of money in the wallet, which will go up and down as you visit ATM machines and stores full of cool and tempting goodies. The wallet probably isn't worth much itself – it's the money inside that defines its value. Whatever you paid for it, your local superstore isn't going to accept an empty wallet as payment for produce!

To put it another way, the wallet is a container that you recognize as holding your money. When you hear the word 'wallet', you know that what you'll find inside is money – never socks or frozen pizza. You also know that the amount of money in there will never stay the same for long.

Of course, you might use other containers to store money too. You might have a tin in the kitchen to pay for coffee, tea, and chocolate biscuits. You might have a piggy bank or a bottle into which you throw all your small change throughout the year. (If you're like me, you might spend that big bottle of money on a small bottle of something else at Christmas.) You have different containers because you need separate places to store money that's set aside for different purposes.

So, I have three different storage places, each holding separate quantities of money that fluctuate constantly:

- my **wallet**, containing my day-to-day money
- my **tin**, with money for tea and biscuits
- my **bottle**, containing my Christmas money

You can think of these storage places as being my 'variables': each contains a different value that may change at any time. My first variable is my `wallet`, and the value it contains is the amount of money that I have to spend on everyday items. I also have a `tin` variable that holds tea money, and a `bottle` variable that holds beer money.

An important aspect of my high-level financial management is that I keep money for the right purpose in the right variable. Imagine the tragedy of confusing my `tin` variable with my `bottle` variable, so that at the end of the year I have enough cash to buy tea for the whole of China, but only $2.50 for a glass of beer on Christmas Eve!

Hopefully, I'm not very likely to confuse physical items like a tin, a bottle, and a wallet, but we don't have that luxury when we're programming. To ward off potential tragedy, I'll have to stick labels on the front of my containers, or name my variables, so that I can be sure to know what each one holds.

Even then, we can still get lost; we can have containers that have the same name, but in different places! For example I might have a bottle in the kitchen labeled 'Christmas', for buying a Christmas drink or two, and a piggy bank in the living room labeled 'Christmas', containing savings for my Christmas gifts for my friends and family.

*In the same way that we can have containers for Christmas money in two rooms, we can have variables on different timelines. Obviously, you therefore have to know **where** each of your containers are as well as the name of the container. If not, my friends might be a bit annoyed when they see me at Christmas and I'm very drunk, having spent all the money meant for their gifts on beer!*

Values and types

In the real world, we're surrounded by different kinds of storage spaces, designed to hold different things:

- Your wallet is designed to store money
- Your fridge is designed to store food
- Your closet is designed to store clothes

In ActionScript too, there are different kinds of values that we might want to stow away for later use. In fact, there are three such **value types**:

- Strings, which are sequences of letters and numbers (plus a few other characters) such as 'Sham', or 'Hello', or 'a1b2c3'. String values can be any length, from a single letter to a whole sentence, and they're especially useful for storing input from visitors to your site.

- Numbers, such as 27, or -15, or 3.142. As we'll discuss later, putting numbers in variables can be useful for keeping track of the positions of things in your movies, and for controlling how your ActionScript programs behave.

- Booleans, which are 'true' or 'false' values that can be useful for making decisions.

Some programming languages can be very fussy when it comes to storing different types of data, forcing you to work with variables that can only store one kind of value. If this were true in the real world, you'd discover it was physically impossible to hide chocolate at the back of the bedroom closet or put your jeans in the refrigerator. And what a cruel world that would be!

ActionScript isn't like that. It's an **untyped language**, which means that you don't have to specify what sort of values a variable will hold when you create it. What's more, ActionScript variables can hold different kinds of data at different times. In most cases, Flash can work out for itself what the type is – it's not infallible though, so this flexibility sometimes means we need to exercise a little strictness ourselves. Sometimes it's important to be strict with Flash, and tell it what sort of data to accept – like telling your kids not to leave their shoes in the fridge – and we'll look at some examples of this later on in the chapter.

> *Always try to work with the value type that's **most appropriate to the particular problem you're solving**. For example, we'd all like to be able to converse with machines in a language like the one we use to talk to each other. Strings are useful here, because they represent a friendly way for Flash to communicate with the user. On the other hand, they're no good for defining a complex calculation, for which you'd want to use numbers.*

Literals and Expressions

Shortly, we'll look at some examples that will start to demonstrate just how useful variables can be. When we get there, we'll find that Flash gives us quite a lot of help in doing so, but it's often nice to know what kind of thing to expect.

The easiest way to store a value in a variable is to use an equals sign = like this:

```
Variable = Value;
```

Whatever value (whether it's a string, a number, or a Boolean) you specify on the right gets stored in the variable you've named on the left.

The easiest way to specify what you want to store is to use a **literal value**, So let's see what that means.

Literal Values

Imagine we have an ActionScript variable called myname. If I wanted to store my own name in this variable, I might do it like this:

```
myname = "Sham";
```

Here, "Sham" is a **string literal**: the string value that you want to store in myname is **literally** what appears between those two quotation marks.

To show you how simply computers think you have to do some serious dumbing down yourself. Stop thinking on your normal highbrow level, and think on a purely semantic one. The literal word 'Sham' is always exactly that word and it can never change. You might think that you can add 'rock' to it to create 'Shamrock', but you can't – that's a completely different word. The word 'Sham' is still the word 'Sham', and always will be.

If we want to change something, then we have to make it a variable; as we've just learnt, a variable isn't actually a value itself, it's only a container for a value.

It's important to include the quotation marks in a string literal. Without the quotes, Flash will think that we are referring to another variable. Say we had:

```
myname = Sham;
```

Instead of setting the value of `myname` to the word "Sham", Flash would go looking for a *variable* called `Sham`. If such a variable existed, it might contain any number of different things: probably not what we wanted though! Even if it didn't exist, Flash would still get it wrong. We always need to use the right syntax to tell Flash what we want it to do, and for literal string values, that means using quotes.

> *In case you're wondering, if you do tell Flash by mistake to set a variable to be another variable that doesn't exist, it will set that variable to a special value called* **undefined**. *This isn't the same as holding the string literal* "undefined", *but tells Flash that there's no data whatsoever in there. If you try using an undefined value in your script, Flash will spot that there's something wrong and give you an error.*

In a similar way, we could have another variable called `myage`. To store a value in this variable, we might use a **numeric literal**, like so:

```
myage = 33;
```

After these two lines, the variables `myname` and `myage` can be used in your code as direct replacements for the values they contain. That might not sound like much now, but you'll soon see just how much versatility this can provide.

> *Remember that variables live up to their name: storing a value is no bar to storing a different value (or even a different* **type** *of value) in the same variable later on. Variable* x *may start out holding the numeric value* 10, *but tomorrow I could make it hold a string value just by writing* x = "Sham";.

Expressions

The next way of generating values to be stored in variables is through the use of **expressions**. As we'll see in the exercises, this is where programming does start to look a bit like math, because expressions are often sequences of literals and variables, linked together by mathematical symbols. For example, you might have something like this:

```
result = myage - 10;
```

If `myage` were still storing 33, then Flash would calculate the mathematical expression 33 - 10 to reach the answer 23, and store this new value in `result`.

It's when we start to use expressions like this that we have to think carefully about the types of data being stored by our variables. The price we pay for the ease of using our untyped variables is that it's **our responsibility** to keep track of what they're holding. If we get it wrong, we run the risk of using a value in the wrong place, and producing incorrect results.

Think back to your high school algebra. You can plan an equation like *a* + *b* = *c*, and be sure that it will work even before you know what the exact values of *a* and *b* are. Whatever happens, they're both numbers, and you know that two numbers added together will give you another number. Easy. Programming is only slightly more complex: variables don't always hold numbers – as we know, they can contain other things such as letters and words. We have to be aware of the types of data, and make sure that we don't try to mix two different types together.

If variable a = 2 and variable b = 3, we could add a and b to get a value for c that makes sense, because 2 + 3 = 5.

We get the same with strings, because if variable a = "mad" and variable b = "house", we could add a and b to get a value for c that makes sense: "mad" + "house" = "madhouse".

When we mix variables up though, we can get some unexpected results, so if variable a = "mad" and variable b = 3 and we add them together, the value for c is unlikely to make sense, because "mad" + 3 = "mad3".

To make variables work for us, we have to manipulate types separately and not mix them together. As a rule, if you input all numbers, then you can expect the result to be a number as well. If you input a string, then you can expect the result to be a string. If you mix a number and a string then the result will be a string too. If this doesn't happen, it's important that you know why, because this can be one of the most subtle and difficult errors to find if you are not expecting it. One simple error is assuming that because a string only consists of a number, then Flash will treat it as a number, but this is not the case. For example if you had the following expression:

```
myage = 33 + "3";
```

You might expect the answer to be 36 (33+3), but Flash sees that you defined the second value as a string, and as we just saw, a string plus a number gives a string as the result, so Flash would set myage to be a string value of "333". Now imagine that the second value was a variable that we'd set to a string somewhere else in the movie, possibly by mistake, and you can see how easy it is to quickly get confused.

Determining the type of a variable

Wouldn't it would be handy if we could just ask Flash what type a variable was? Well, luckily there is. We'll use the example we just looked at as our starting point.

1. Open up a new Flash document and type the following line into the Actions panel for the first frame:

    ```
    myage = 33 + 3;
    ```

    This will create the variable myage, and set it to our value.

2. Press CTRL/CMD+ENTER to test-run the movie. As you'd expect, there'll be nothing on the screen, but Flash has stored our variable away in its memory. To see this, go to the Debug menu and choose List Variables. You should see a box like the one on the next page appear:

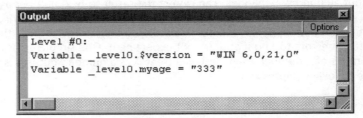

As you can see, the final entry contains our variable (don't worry about the first two, we'll come to them later on). We can clearly see that our variable is set to be the number 36.

3. Now go back to the Actions panel and change the line so that it reads this:

```
myage = 33 + "3";
```

Now when you test your movie and look at the variables, you should see this:

You can see from this that our variable is now a string (notice the double quotes) and that it's set to the value of "333".

Well, that's one way of checking. Once you start building more complicated movies though, it'll become much harder to find the variable you're looking for in this list. That doesn't make it useless though – in fact, should you ever need to do this, you'll find a handy Find command hidden away in the Output window's Options menu, which allows you to search the entire contents of the output window for whatever it is you're looking for. To test this, go to Options > Find and type in myage. Click Find Next, and the variable will be highlighted for you.

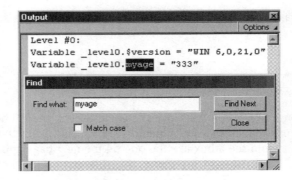

4. Close the SWF window and go back to the Actions panel. Add the following line just after the first:

```
myage = 33 + "3";
trace(myage);
```

The `trace` command is one of the most useful commands in Flash to help you debug your ActionScript. If you run the movie now, you'll see that the Output window appears with just the contents of our variable in it:

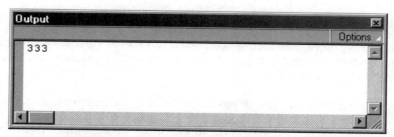

This is helpful enough as it is, but it's not all we can do. To the casual observer that still looks like just a number. Let's see if we can be a bit more explicit.

5. Go back to the Actions panel, and alter your second line so it reads:

```
trace(typeof(myage));
```

Be careful with the brackets here – if you put in too many (or too few) Flash will throw up an error.

The `typeof` command tells Flash that we want it to give us the type of the variable that we've supplied as an argument. The whole of this expression is still taking place within the `trace` command, so it will still output whatever the result is.

If you test the movie now, you should get the following:

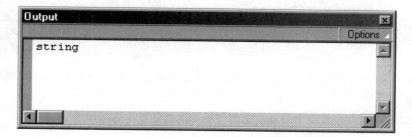

Now we can definitely see what type the variable is!

6. Try changing the variable back to how it was originally:

```
myage = 33 + 3;
```

Then test your movie and see if the Output window contains the expected results.

So, we can now find out what the type of a variable is when things go wrong, but wouldn't it be better if there were a way we could prevent things from going wrong in the first place? Well, later on in the chapter, we'll look at a few ways to do just that.

First, we'll investigate some more ways in which we can use our newfound variable friends, more specifically by using them to increase user interaction.

Input and output

So far, we've really only talked loosely about what variables are and the kinds of values they can store. It's about time we had a proper example of using them, so that you can start to see what they can do for your movies and web sites.

We'll start by using them to store strings, since the practical benefits here are most obvious.

The act of storing strings is closely associated with **input to** and **output from** Flash, simply because users generally prefer to interact with a computer using text rather than raw numbers. Most complex interactions with computers are done using text of some kind, from filling in a form to order something online, to entering keywords into a search engine. Both are much more involved than, say, entering numbers into a calculator, and this is where string variables shine.

Creating an input field

If we're going to use a variable to **store** a string that the user has entered, we need to enable the user to input a string.

1.   Open a new movie and select the Text tool. Now turn your gaze to the Property inspector, and make sure that Input Text is selected in the dropdown menu on the far left-hand side:

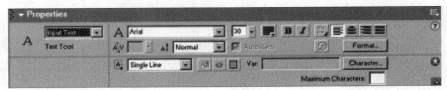

2.   Now click on the stage to create a text field. If you've only worked with static text before, then you'll notice that two things are different:

Firstly, a static textbox has a circle at the top right-hand corner, whereas our input text field has a square at the bottom right.

Secondly, a static textbox will always start its life one character long, and grow as you add more text to it. An input text field, on the other hand, immediately comes up with room enough to enter several characters. There won't be any text placed into it until after you've published the movie, so until then Flash needs to make a rough guess at how much text you might need to enter.

The default size is Flash's best guess; you can make the field longer (or even make room for more than one line of text) by dragging the little square on the bottom right of the text field.

3. Look at the Property inspector again. Now that we've assigned this box as an input field, Flash knows that we'll probably want to store that input in a variable for later use. To make this easy for us, it's provided a textbox (labelled Var:) where we can give it a name for that variable. Since this is our first input box, let's call it `input1`:

4. Now click the Show Border button ☐ so that Flash will draw a box around the text area's limits.

    Since this area will be used for inputting text, a user will want to click on it and make sure it's selected before they type anything in. The border will show the user where to click.

5. Make sure that the text color isn't set to white. This may sound like a really obvious thing to do, but it's easy enough to forget, and annoying if you run the movie and can't think why you don't see any text appearing in the text box...

6. Test the movie. You should see an empty rectangle on the stage. Click inside it, and a text entry cursor will appear. Type in whatever you want. If you type in more than the box can fit, it will scroll to accommodate your input as you type. You can use BACKSPACE, normal copy and paste keys, and most of the other keys you'd expect, though you can't use ENTER to finish your input:

hello Flash!!|

It may appear that Flash isn't doing anything when you type, but it's actually storing whatever goes in your text field inside your `input1` variable. At this point, we could look up `input1` in the variables list, and find (sure enough) that `input1` contains the string literal "hello Flash!!"

If you do this, you may be rather surprised at just how many new variables have appeared. Don't worry about all this extra stuff for now.

Creating an output field

Let's start putting our variables to use: we'll send Flash to retrieve what's been stored in variable `input1` and display it in an **output field**.

1. If the input field is still selected, then click on a blank part of the stage to deselect it. Bring up the Property inspector and change the top dropdown menu to Dynamic Text. This time, make sure the Show Border and Selectable buttons are **not** selected:

We deselect these buttons because the field that we're about to create is for use by Flash, and not by the user. It's being used as a display area, so the user won't need to see it drawn or be able to select it.

2. With the Text tool, add a new text field directly below the existing one, and set it to our variable name: `input1`. Whereas for the input field, the variable name told Flash to take whatever was in the text field and put it into our variable, the dynamic text field is completely the opposite – it will take whatever's in the variable and put it into the text field.

3. Now test the movie. You'll see the same empty rectangle, until you start entering some text. When you do that, the dynamic text field will begin to 'echo' what you've entered.

hello Flash!!

hello Flash!!

You'll also see, though, that it's of fixed length, and it won't scroll in the same way as the input box to display everything that you type in:

see some more>>>

hello Flash!! let's see s

The update speed of both text fields is determined by the frame rate specified for the movie. At the default frame rate of 12fps, the speed of text entry and its echo should look immediate. If you go and change the frame rate via Modify > Document to 1fps, you will see a marked change in the update rate when you test the movie again. When you're done experimenting, return the frame rate to 12fps.

At the moment, Flash is displaying a copy of what we type into the input box in real time, as soon as we type it in. If we make a mistake, Flash displays it for the world to see. We need a way to make Flash wait until we've finished entering our text and are happy with it before considering it the finished article. The easiest way to give us this extra feature and expand on what we've got is to create an enter button.

4.   Select the lower text field (the output box), and change its variable to `output1`:

5.   Next, add a button next to the input text field, and use the Property inspector to give it the instance name `enter_btn`. You should know how to create your own buttons by now, so I'll leave the details down to you. However you do it, make sure that when you specify the enter text for your button, the text is set as static (in other words, it's not still set to Dynamic in the Property inspector):

We now need to wire up the button with a little ActionScript. We'll do this by defining a callback for the button, just like we did in the last chapter.

6.   Select the first frame in the timeline and bring up the Actions panel. We'll start off by putting in the framework for an `onRelease` callback on the `enter_btn` button:

```
enter_btn.onRelease = function() {
};
```

7.   The next step is to write some event handling code, so that something actually happens when the user releases the button and triggers the `onRelease` event. Add the following line:

```
enter_btn.onRelease = function() {
  output1 = input1;
};
```

8.   Now test the movie. This time, when you enter any text, the bottom field doesn't echo our input...

...until we press the Enter button:

anybody home?

Make sure you hang on to this FLA, because we'll be using it several times later on as a simple Flash user interface. I've saved it with the filename `input-output.fla`.

Using String Expressions

Let's recap. To start pulling together the first building blocks for inputting and outputting text within Flash, we've created simple text fields for obtaining and displaying the values of basic variables. Now that you know how to do this, your available lines of communication with the user (and levels of interactivity) have just gone up from basic mouse-clicks to phrases and sentences.

Working with strings

Having got our text input and output working, we're going to look now at how we can use string expressions to give Flash a more human face and communicate with the user on a more personal level. We'll create a string expression that combines the value of the variable `input1` with some extra text to display more than the user might expect.

1.   Open up the FLA that we've just been working on (or use my file `input-output.fla` from the downloads folder).

2.   Select the Enter button yet again, and open the Actions Panel. Then, select the line `output1 = input1;` and alter it so that it matches this:

```
output1 = "Hello" + input1 + "!";
```

Make sure that you include the space after Hello, otherwise Flash will just sandwich all of the words together.

When ActionScript encounters this, it takes the string literal `"Hello"`, adds the contents of the variable `input1`, appends the second string literal `"!"`, and stores the result in the variable out-

`put1`. This may all sound very confusing, but rest assured it'll all make sense when you see it in action!

3. Test the movie and enter your name. Flash should greet you like a long lost friend:

| Sham | **Enter** |

Hello Sham!

While I don't want to undersell what we've done here, I have to point out that there's a slight problem: we haven't been able to empower Flash with the grammatical knowledge to check whether what it's saying to you makes sense. Whatever you type in, Flash will give it back to you as part of the same answer:

| hi there! | **Enter** |

Hello hi there!!

I can't say that I have the solution to this for you here. I've shown you how to use string expressions to build in a degree of personalization, but be aware how quickly the illusion of intelligence falls apart. If you try this within a web site project, be careful. Still, it's reassuring to know that computers still can't be more intelligent than we are!

Naming Variables

Now that you've had just a flavor of how it might be possible to improve the web sites you build by using variables, and before we move on to look at storing numeric values, the time is ripe for us to look a little more deeply into the names we give to our variables. As you'll see, there are two very good reasons why this is an important thing to get right.

In Flash, we can name a variable however we like, *so long as Flash isn't likely to confuse it with something else*. Built into Flash are numerous names and symbols that are important to its correct operation, so we can't use them for our own purposes. These are called **reserved names**, and they include:

- **Actions** and other parts of ActionScript that might be mistaken as *part of an action*, including `{}`, `;`, and `()`. The reserved names that can be used within actions are things like: `break`, `call`, `case`, `continue`, `default`, `delete`, `do`, `else`, `for`, `function`, `if`, `in`, `new`, `on`, `return`, `set`, `switch`, `this`, `typeof`, `var`, `void`, `while`, and `with`.

  Of course, actions themselves cannot be variables; basically if it shows up in dark blue when you type it, then it's a reserved word, and you can't use it. Obviously, don't start your variable name with `//`, because then it just becomes a comment.

- **Spaces** in a variable name will confuse Flash into thinking the name has finished before it actually has. For example, the command `ben renow-clarke = "author"` will look to Flash like a variable called `ben` that's followed by a string of random gibberish. It's usually clearest to use underscores `_` instead.

- Variable names that **begin with numbers** (such as `6y`) won't work either. Use `y6` instead.

- **Operators**, such as +, -, *, and / should also be avoided. Otherwise, Flash may try to treat your variable as a sum to occur between two variables.

  The period character . is actually another operator (though you may not have realized it) so you should steer clear of using it in your variable names as well. However, as you'll see very shortly, it plays a very important role in how we **locate** variables...

With these provisions in mind, valid variable names would be:

- `cow`
- `menu6`
- `label7c`
- `off`

Invalid names would be:

- `on`   – because Flash will expect it to part of an `onEvent` action.
- `label 7c` – because of the space in the middle, Flash will see the `7c` as garbage.
- `6menu`   – because it starts with a number.
- `my-toys`   – because it contains a minus operator, so Flash will assume we actually want the difference between the two variables `my` and `toys`.

Once you've obeyed these rules to keep Flash happy, the important thing is that your variable names keep you happy too. You don't want to spend time figuring out what types they contain or what values they're meant to hold, so be as efficient as you can. Make sure that the names say something about what the variables hold.

For example, if I had three variables holding my three amounts of money, I could name them `dayMoney`, `teaMoney` and `beerMoney`. This will really make debugging a lot easier. As you become more experienced, you may find times when you need to use variables of the same name in different places. As long as you're clear on the reasons why you need to do that, that's fine.

> Note that Flash **isn't** *case-sensitive about variable names, so* `big` *and* `BIG` *will be treated as the same variable.*

Virtually all the variable examples we've looked at so far have dealt with storing strings. Of course that's not the only type of data we can put into an ActionScript variable, so let's take a closer look at the other two types: **number** and **Boolean**.

Working with numbers

In everyday use, numbers can represent more than just raw values. Numbered seats in a cinema don't represent a chair's *value*, but its *position*. The ISBN for this book doesn't represent its value or its position, but is a **reference** or **index** to the book.

To a much greater extent than strings, numbers lend themselves to being operated upon: they can be added to, subtracted from, added together, multiplied, divided, and so on. If you store numbers in variables, all kinds of possibilities are opened up.

Returning to those cinema seats, if we arrange to store the number booked so far in a variable called `seatstaken`, then the number of the next seat available for booking is *always* going to be `seatstaken+1`, regardless of the actual value stored in the variable. Look at this:

```
seatstaken = seatstaken +1;
```

It says: "add one to the current value of `seatstaken`, and store the result back in `seatstaken`". Each time ActionScript encounters it, the number stored in the variable increases by one. Remember: variables are all about giving ActionScript a memory.

Let's try some of this out, using our interface FLA again – you can use `greetings.fla` from the download file if you forgot to save it. In this exercise, we're going to get the user to input some numbers, and then perform some calculations on them.

Simple calculations

In the previous exercise, the values we saw going into `input1` were actually string values, which is to say that they could include more than the numbers 0 to 9 and the decimal point that we would normally expect in numeric values. Before we start using `input1` in numeric expressions, we need to take steps to prevent the user from entering characters that could spoil our work.

1. Select the input text box, and turn your attention back to the Property inspector. Click the Character… button next to the variable field to bring up the Character Options panel:

    As you can see, there are numerous settings here, but we want to allow Only Numerals. We also want a decimal point, so enter one in the And these characters box. Click Done to confirm your options.

2. Now test the movie. You'll find that you are no longer able to enter anything other than decimal numbers, which is a step in the right direction.

```
123.4567890          Enter
```

Hello 123.4567890!

3. Close the SWF and select frame 1 on the timeline. Call up the Actions panel. Now that we know it's safe to treat `input1` as a numeric value, we can perform a bit of simple arithmetic on it, and assign the result to `output1`. We'll try:

```
output1 = input1 * 2;
```

Computer programming languages use the asterisk * to represent multiplication in place of the traditional x. The idea is to remove the chance of confusion with the letter 'x'.

4. Change the second line in the ActionScript to this new command, and test your movie. Our output is now a calculated value based on our input – that is, it's the result of a numeric expression:

```
45                    Enter
```

90

If you like, you can try changing the expression (or even adding buttons with new callbacks of their own) to give the following information:

- `output1 = input1^2;`   for the square of the amount entered
- `output1 = 1/input1;`   for the reciprocal of the amount entered

Here's a shot from one you can find in the downloads folder, saved as `calculator.fla`:

```
5          input*2
           input²
25         1/input
```

Other uses for numeric expressions

Numeric expressions have a lot more to offer than making Flash do sums for us. For example, we could use the results of numeric expressions to control the position or orientation of an instance, allowing us to create some very complex movements. We could have an expression to tell our alien spaceship, Blarg, where to move to after he had made his bombing run on the player!

We can also use numeric expressions to jump to frames within a movie based on **dynamic** values, and not just to the fixed number values we have used so far. This allows us to control timeline flow to a much greater degree; for example, we could jump to an explosion if hit by an alien.

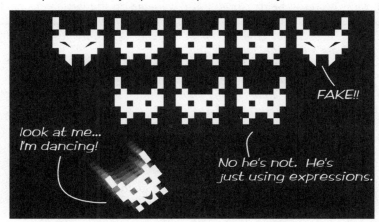

Some of the stuff we've been looking at may have seemed a little removed from space invaders flitting about the screen, and cool, ActionScript-heavy dynamic sites, but we are learning about the cogs that make these things turn. We'll continue to do that in the next section.

Working with Boolean values

If I buy a packet of cookies, I do so because they look tasty and I am not on a diet. This is a very clear-cut decision: if two criteria are met, then I buy the cookies. In general, however, we don't tend to make such straightforward decisions; instead we base them at least partly on a comparison, our mood, or a predisposition. We might even base some decisions on inputs that have nothing to do with the choice at all: "I don't want to talk to him because I don't like the color of his shirt.". Our decisions can have many more outcomes than simply 'I will' or 'I will not'.

Computers, though, stick to decisions of the more clear-cut variety, which is a relief because a computer probably tracks my bank balance and transactions. I wouldn't like my balance to halve suddenly because the computer was having a bad day and I turned up at the bank wearing a lilac shirt. Computers base their decisions on statements of the yes/no or true/false variety. Their decisions have only two possible outcomes at a time, although they can apply lots of yes/no decisions in a row to tackle more complex outcomes.

Suppose, for example, that we wanted to find out whether a number was higher or lower than 100. It could be the price of a share on the stock market: if it is lower, we want to think about buying, and if it is higher, we will think about selling. Depending on which side of 100 the price is, we will perform one of two different sets of actions. Alternatively, it could be that we're writing a space invaders game, where the invaders move down the screen in their attempt to land on your planet. Once the distance of any invader from the top edge of the stage is greater than 100, we know they are at the bottom of the screen, and the player has lost.

Take the first case, and assume that the share price we're interested in is stored in a variable called price. Now have a look at this line of ActionScript on the next page:

```
buy = price < 100;
```

When we've seen code like this in the past, the expression on the right-hand side of the equals sign has been evaluated, with the result being stored in the variable on the left-hand side. But what *is* the value of the right-hand side? Given the title of this section, you won't be surprised to discover that it's a **Boolean value**, which means that buy will be set to true if price is less than 100, or false if price has any other value. Flash's thinking goes like this:

```
If the price is less than 100, then set buy to equal true.
If the price isn't less than 100 (that is, it's greater than or equal to
100), then set buy to equal false.
```

true and false are the *only* Boolean values, and they are the only possible values of the right-hand side.

> Note that true *and* false *here are neither strings nor variables.*
> *They are simply the two possible Boolean values.*

Testing whether statements are true

Until we start to look at conditional operators in the next chapter – which will indeed allow us to perform different actions depending on Boolean values – there's a limit to what we can do with them. However, we can at least check that what I've been saying is true, and use them in some slightly more complex expressions.

1. Let's modify our movie again. Load up input-output.fla (the file we saved earlier), making sure it's free of all the little tweaks we subsequently made to it. Alternatively you can open up greetings.fla again. Select the input text, and change the Character Options again, so that we're only accepting numbers and a decimal point.

2. Now select the first frame in the actions layer and call up the Actions panel. Change the code it contains as follows:

```
enter_btn.onRelease = function() {
    output1 = (input1 < 100);
};
```

3. Run the movie, and you'll see that Flash now looks at any number you enter and compares it with 100. If it's lower, input1 < 100 is a true statement, so you get true:

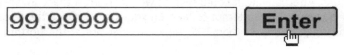

If it's greater than or equal to 100, `input1 < 100` is not true, so you get `false`:

false

Logic operators

Think back to high school when you had lessons on electrical circuits. You may remember that there were logic gates that would open only if their conditions were met. These gates had crazy names like AND, OR, NOT, and NAND, and these **logic operators** also exist in ActionScript. Here is a list of the ones that it recognizes:

```
&&    -   AND
||    -   OR
!     -   NOT
```

If you need to, you can use these logic operators to make your test more selective. That's what we're about to do.

Take our earlier example about share prices. If you were prepared to buy if the price was below 100, then you might want to stop buying if the price went below 80, because such a sharp drop would indicate unfavorable market conditions. In plain text, you would need something like this:

> *If the price is less than 100 AND greater than 80...*

Bringing this closer to our expression in this example, we need:

```
(input1 < 100) AND (input1 > 80)
```

Flash uses the `&&` symbol to signify AND, so the ActionScript we actually want is:

```
(input1 < 100) && (input1 > 80)
```

Testing for more than one thing at a time

Let's change our script to test for the double expression that we looked at above.

1. Alter your frame 1 script to read:

```
enter_btn.onRelease = function() {
    output1 = (input1 < 100) && (input > 80);
};
```

2. Now run the movie. You'll see that you get a `true` result only if the price is between 80 and 100.

42		**Enter**

false

Using similar techniques, you can build up very complex conditions that involve a number of other operators and terms, and we will start using them for real in the next chapter.

Before we do that though, I'm going to show you how you can get more out of your variables by using arrays.

Arrays

The easiest way to think of an **array** is as a container for a collection of variables, which you access using a single name. From the outside, it looks just like a single entity, but it can hold lots of different values at any one time.

In many ways, an array is not dissimilar to a filing cabinet: the cabinet itself has a name, but may contain several drawers, each of which can contain its own information. Each drawer is like a variable in its own right, but it's stored in a cabinet along with the others, because they all hold data that's related in some way:

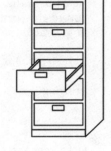

When you're looking at a variable array, you need to specify two things:

- the **name** of the array
- the **index** (or offset number) of the **element** (or 'drawer') you want to use

Say you had an array called `mycolor` containing five pieces of information – that is, five elements. To refer to the first one (that's the bottom drawer in the cabinet), you'd just use:

```
mycolor[0]
```

Note that the index (or offset) is surrounded by square brackets, and yes, the first array location is 0, not 1 as you might have expected. If the fact that there is a 0th drawer confuses you, think of it this way: whenever you see an index value of n, you're referring to the drawer that's offset by 'n' from the bottom. In theory, there's nothing to stop you leaving it empty, but this isn't recommended, for practical reasons you'll learn about later on. It may seem a little odd to begin with, but you'll soon get used to it!

So, an index of 0 gives you the base element. The second element (the first drawer up from the base) would be:

```
mycolor[1]
```

The third (offset by two from the base) is:

```
mycolor[2]
```

and so on. Likewise, say you want to get hold of some information that you know is stored in the third drawer from the bottom of a filing cabinet called "contracts". In ActionScript terms, that filing cabinet is an array called `contracts`, and the third drawer can be accessed as the variable `contracts[2]`.

Reasons for using arrays

There are several reasons why it can be useful to store variables in arrays:

Arrays let you store related information together. Say we're working with a list of birds, and we want to keep together information on all birds that live around water. We might put them into an array called `wadingBirds` – element number one might contain the string "flamingo". We could have other arrays such as `tropicalBirds` (containing "parrot", "hummingbird", and so on...) and another called `tundraBirds` (containing "ptarmigan" and "arctic owl").

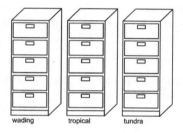

wading   tropical   tundra

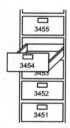

Arrays let you hold information in a specific order. Perhaps we want an array containing the names of pupils at a school, held in the order of their exam rankings (best first, of course!). The variable `pupils[3454]` might well contain the name "Sham B"...

Arrays let you index information. For example, if we had an array to hold theater bookings, we could use the variable `seatingPlan[45]` to hold the name of the person who had booked seat 45. In these circumstances, the numbering scheme is the most important thing, so you'd probably just ignore `seatingPlan[0]` – that is, unless it was a theater whose seat numbering began at zero (run by programmers, no doubt!)

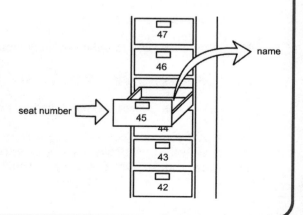

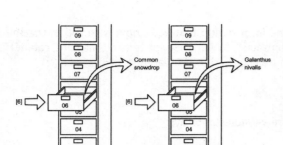

Arrays help you to link information together. Say we have a list of common plant names and another giving their Latin counterparts, and store them in a pair of arrays called `commonName` and `latinName`. Assuming the lists had been arranged properly in the first place, we could cross-reference between the two. For example, say we looked in `CommonName[6]` and found "Common Snowdrop", we could then look at the equivalent variable `latinName[6]` in the other array to find the Latin name "Galanthus nivalis".

Creating a new array

Before we can do anything useful with arrays, we need to learn how to create them and pipe in information. Well, the first bit's simple enough – say we want to create an array called `myarray`:

```
myarray = new Array();
```

No problem! We now have an array, but it doesn't have any elements – it's like a filing cabinet without any drawers. It's easy enough to add them in though:

```
myarray[0] = "Bill";
myarray[1] = "Pat";
myarray[2] = "Jon";
myarray[3] = "Tom";
```

Yes, we can assign values to the elements just as if they were plain old variables. Flash simply expands the array as you add new entries to it. We don't even need to use the same variable type for the different elements. Going on from the example above, we could easily say:

```
myarray[4] = 1981;
myarray[5] = 1984;
myarray[6] = 1987;
```

This isn't the only way to define an array though. We could say:

```
myScores = new Array(1, 45, 34504, 31415);
```

or

```
myPets = new Array("cat", "dog", "pelican");
```

Note that if you set `myarray[19]`, you're creating a **single** element. Flash *won't* create array entries [0] to [18] as well, so you have 'missing drawers' that show up as **undefined**. This could be dangerous if subsequent code expects to see them filled with a sensible value (such as zero or "").

It's much safer if you define each element straight after you define the array. You would give each entry a default value. For example, the default value might be "" if you wanted an array of strings, or 0 for an array of numbers.

There are various other ways to create arrays, but I'd recommend sticking to these ones for now – they should easily meet your demands.

Using variable values as offsets

One particularly useful feature of arrays is that you can specify offsets in terms of other variables. So, you can use an existing variable (defined completely separately from the array) to specify which drawer you want to look in.

Let's take a look at a quick example:

```
offset=0;
mycolor[offset] = "blue";
```

Here, offset is a variable that we've set to zero, and we use it to specify which element in the array mycolor should be given the value 'blue'. In this case, we've effectively said:

```
mycolor[0] = "blue";
```

This approach can be *very* powerful – by simply changing the value of your variable you can use one bit of code to work on as many different drawers as your array has to offer. This means that you can write generalized code for manipulating array elements, and specify the offset quite separately.

Using a number variable to select text string from array

Let's use our faithful interface input-output.fla to take a quick look at arrays in action.

1. Open up the FLA and select the top (input) text field. Open the Property inspector, press the Characters button, and make sure the text field is configured to Only accept Numerals:

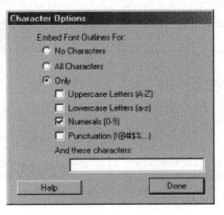

2. Now select frame 1 on the timeline, and make the following changes to the code:

```
bondMovies = new Array();
bondMovies[0] = "Doctor No";
bondMovies[1] = "From Russia With Love";
bondMovies[2] = "Goldfinger";

enter_btn.onRelease = function() {
    output1 = bondMovies[input1];
};
```

Now, when we enter a number in the first field and click on the Enter button, it's used as the offset for our `bondMovies` array. As long as the number entered is between 0 and 2, we'll be rewarded with the name of the relevant film:

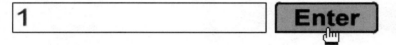

From Russia With Love

...well, if you happen to count them from zero that is.

Let's face it; most people would think your system was broken if they fed in the number 1 and got 'From Russia With Love'... Everyone knows that was the second movie!

3. Well, let's fix this 'broken' movie. Either we can change the array itself, leaving element 0 empty (or maybe hide 'Casino Royale' away in there where nobody's likely to spot it); or we can tweak the off-set. Between you and me, I have a soft spot for anything featuring Peter Sellers, so let's do the sec-ond:

```
enter_btn.onRelease = function() {
    output1 = bondMovies[input1-1];
};
```

4. Now we can run the movie, type a number, press Enter, and see the title we expected:

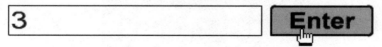

Goldfinger

Hey presto! Enter a number and get back a film title.

Of course, we're barely touching on the power of arrays here, but hopefully you've seen enough to get a feel for what they are and what they do. Trust me, we'll be seeing a lot more of them!

In the next couple of chapters, we're going to look at decision-making and looping, both topics that really make the most of what you can do with both variables and arrays. We'll look at the decision-making functionality that we can build using Boolean values, use ActionScript loops to act on whole arrays in one fell swoop, and even build a fully functioning hangman game to draw all these threads together.

Summary

In this chapter we've looked at how ActionScript uses variables as containers for information we want to use in our movies. We've also gone over the different types of values that a variable can store:

- Strings
- Numbers
- Booleans

We explored the differences between literal values and expressions, and saw how to communicate with a user via string values and text fields. I then talked about rules for naming your variables, so that they're (a) acceptable to Flash, and (b) useful to you. We went on to look at working with numeric values (for performing calculations) and Boolean values (for storing the result of a true/false expression).

Rounding off the chapter, we looked at how arrays make it easy for us to store lots of related data together in a neatly structured way, which, apart from anything else, helps us find it more easily.

You now have a good grounding in variables and values. Although you haven't built that many cool FLAs in this chapter, you have a solid foundation with which to move forward into Chapters 3 and 4, where every new thing you learn will allow you to do something cool and immediately useful. That's what you've built up to by slogging through this one!

As you work through the rest of this book you'll see how variables lie at the heart of virtually all of the most exciting Flash effects you can create. Have a little break, and get ready for Chapter 3.

Movies that decide for themselves

What we'll cover in this chapter:

- *Getting Flash to look at a situation and decide what to do based on what it sees*

- *Sausage notation (or 'How I learned to stop worrying and love brackets')*

- *Giving Flash the intelligence to check passwords*

So far, we've looked at a few simple ways to control Flash movies using actions, event handlers, and variables. The actions are like commands, telling Flash what to do. The event handlers are just sets of actions that get triggered off by events from the movie, so that it can respond in real time to things like button presses and 'entering a new frame'. Variables give Flash a memory, so that we can store information away for when we need it later on.

Already, that gives us quite a lot to play with; but it's not without problems. Think about the last couple of examples from Chapter 2: when we made our 'times by two' movie, we had to set up the input text field so that it would only accept numbers and dots. Otherwise, it might end up trying to double the value of "Platypus", which wouldn't make any sense at all!

That's cool though; we dealt with it. But what about the array of movie titles: it works okay if you put in 1, 2, or 3, but doesn't give us a bean if we try 4, 5, or 6… Who cares? Well whoever's using your movie will care if they're expecting to see something and they see nothing – at least you could put up a sign saying "Sorry, but this array doesn't list movies made after 1963".

This might not seem like much, but it's not something we can do with the tools we've got so far. What we need is a way to **test** whether the input's good or not, and then *act on the result*. To put it in plain English, Flash needs to *make a decision* about what to do.

Decision-making

Real-life decisions are rarely as simple as:

> I'll go to the open-air rock concert if it's not raining.

You're probably far more likely to think:

> If I have enough money, and it's not raining on the day, I'll go to the open-air rock concert. But if I'm late with my job I won't be able to afford the time.

Your decision now is not only based on whether you'll get wet if you go to the concert, but also on whether you have enough money and can spare the time.

These sorts of issues are just as important when you're making decisions in ActionScript – you need to consider exactly what your conditions are, what should happen if they're met, and what should happen if they're not met.

Okay, you may already know what you want to say; but that doesn't mean you know how to state your conditions in a way that Flash is going to understand. Say we write our concert dilemma out like this:

```
if (it's not raining) {go to the concert}
```

Er… what's with all those brackety things? Well the plain brackets (and) are like the ones we use to pass arguments to actions: `gotoAndStop(10)` for example. They're information we give to an action to help it do its job. The curly brackets { and } should look familiar too: when we learnt to write callbacks back in Chapter 1, they're what we used to put round all the event handler actions. They just mean 'do everything in here'.

> *I don't know about you, but I need silly ways to remember things. The way I think of this rather complicated syntax is as a string of sausages, with the contents of each set of brackets being a sausage.*

As we saw though, the real problem is a little more complex than that:

```
if (if I have enough money and it's not raining on the day and I can afford
the time)
   {go to the concert}
```

If you were programming this decision, you'd go through exactly this process. Writing a decision down on paper in the same way that I've done here will help you to make sure you've considered all the conditions that need to be met.

Making decisions in ActionScript – the if action

So what about making this work for real? It's all very well having this sausage notation for working things out, but it's not much help if we can't use it in a movie.

Well, we're actually not so far off using it in a movie. The **condition** (that is, the bit we've placed between the (and) brackets) can only ever be true or false. If it's true, we go to the concert. If it's false, we don't. Simple as that.

Now, if you can manage to stretch your mental faculties back to the previous chapter, you may recall we looked briefly at Boolean variables. These can only ever hold two values: `true` and `false`. What's more, we looked at a couple of ways to generate true and false values, using > and < (to test whether one number is bigger or smaller than another).

So, once we've worked out an expression that gives us a true or false result, we can (a) store it in a Boolean variable, and (b) use that Boolean (or even just the expression itself) as a **condition**. If the condition is met (value is `true`) then Flash has to do something. If it's not (value is `false`) then Flash doesn't have to do that something.

Let's add that information into our sausage notation. Assume we've already defined some Boolean variables like this:

```
haveEnoughMoney = true;
notRaining = true;
affordTheTime = true;
```

We know that `&&` is something we can use to check whether one Boolean AND another are both true. Handily, we can even string several together to check whether one AND another AND another are all true, so this is what we could end up with:

```
if (haveEnoughMoney && notRaining && affordTheTime)
   {go to the concert}
```

If any of the Booleans are set to false, we'll be staying in!

What about telling Flash to go to the concert? How does that shape up ActionScript-wise? That's going to depend on what your movie actually does. Maybe you're going to send a little stick man running up to a big stage where he joins the screaming masses... Or maybe you're just going to make a little message appear, saying "go to the concert". Well, the first one would look more impressive, but the second one would be quicker!

```
if (haveEnoughMoney && notRaining && affordTheTime)
    {trace("go to the concert");}
```

If you want to make your own movie that shows a man running up to join the crowd, then you can write actions to make it do that. The important thing to remember is that you can put *any actions you like* in here, and Flash will perform them for you – but *only if the condition is true.*

So how do we make this into proper ActionScript that a movie's going to understand? We don't have to change a lot. In fact, if you type it in exactly as it stands, it should work just fine. However, in order to keep the syntax checker happy, you need to rearrange it ever so slightly:

```
if (haveEnoughMoney && notRaining && affordTheTime) {
    trace("go to the concert");
};
```

Just put the opening { bracket on the first line, indent the action (to remind you that it's **nested** inside the if statement), put the closing bracket } on a line of its own, and add a semicolon ; on the end. Hey presto!

So, in general, an if statement looks like this:

```
if (condition is true) {
    do this;
    do this;
    do this;
    ...
};
```

The only structural difference between this and my sausage notation is that ActionScript prefers us to split the sausage itself over several lines.

> *The sausage notation will help you to write all your programming decision branches in terms that you can use to set things clearly in your mind before you start programming. You even have the bonus that it's written in correct ActionScript syntax, so you can convert it seamlessly into working code. Don't be put off by the silly 'sausage' name – it really does help!*

Now that we've got the basic idea, let's apply this 'decision-making' system to the kind of situation you might encounter when you're thinking out a Flash movie.

Defining a decision

I'll start by expressing my decision as simply and precisely as possible, in order to get a clear idea of what I want the code to do. Here's the decision I want to make:

I'm writing a game of space invaders in which the player controls a ship that can fire bullets up at the attacking alien hordes. In particular, I'm considering the situation when the bullet has been fired (signified by `bullet_fired = true`), and is moving up the screen (at a speed controlled by the numeric value of `bullet_speed`). If it hasn't already reached the top of the screen (where the y-position is 0), I want to move it further up. If it's *at* the top, I want to stop moving the bullet, remove it from the screen, and set `bullet_fired` to `false`, indicating that the player is allowed to fire again. The value of variable `bullet_y` denotes the bullet's height at any point in time.

When you're faced with such a longwinded problem, there's only one way to simplify it: lose some of the words. The easiest way to do this is to draw a picture – automatically dropping your word count to zero:

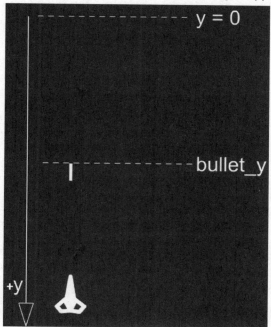

We've got the player's ship at the bottom of the screen, and the bullet at some point above it, moving upwards. The bullet will always move up in a vertical line, so only its y-coordinate will change, decreasing as it moves up the screen until it reaches the top and has a y-coordinate of zero.

We're now concerned with building up a framework of decisions that will result in this behavior. We need to consider two questions:

1. How does the bullet behave when it's on the screen?

2.   How does the bullet behave when it first goes off the top of the screen?

bullet_speed is a variable that we'll use to hold a number, which will tell Flash how many pixels to move the bullet up the screen. Each time the script runs, this value will be subtracted from the bullet's y-coordinate position, moving it to a new position. Making it a high number will make the bullet move quickly; making it smaller will make the bullet move more slowly.

The y-coordinate of the bullet, bullet_y, starts off as a positive value, and reaches zero when it gets to the top of the screen. In other words, bullet_y will be positive before it hits the top and negative once it's gone off the screen. So:

- If bullet_y is positive, the bullet's on the screen and we should keep subtracting bullet_speed so that the bullet moves upwards.
- As soon as bullet_y is less than zero, we no longer need to animate the bullet, although we need it to disappear. We could make it disappear in a number of ways, but the easiest would be to place it off screen, say at bullet_y = -100. Also, once the bullet is off the screen, the player should be allowed to fire again, so we need to tell Flash this by making bullet_fired = false.

So, our decision-making breaks down into two branches. This is how they look in sausage notation:

```
if (the bullet is being fired and its y-position is greater than 0)
  {move the bullet}
```

and:

```
if (the bullet is being fired and its y-position is less than 0)
  {hide bullet and let user fire another}
```

So what happens if the bullet isn't being fired? Well, neither of these branches will be relevant, and neither one will do anything. In fact, that's just what we want: if bullet_fired = false, the bullet should be safely hidden away above the top of the screen, and that's just where we want it to stay!

Let's put some variables into our sausage notation. This gives us:

```
if (bullet_fired is true and bullet_y is greater than 0)
  {set bullet_y equal to bullet_y minus bullet_speed}
```

and:

```
if (bullet_fired is true and bullet_y is less than 0)
  {set bullet_fired equal to false, set bullet_y to -100}
```

Now we just need to convert this into proper ActionScript syntax. This is easy enough to do:

```
if (bullet_fired && bullet_y > 0) {
  bullet_y = bullet_y - bullet_speed;
};
```

and:

```
if (bullet_fired && bullet_y < 0) {
  bullet_fired = false;
  bullet_y = -100;
};
```

There are several things to note about how I've written out the conditions here:

- Each **condition** is *completely contained within the ( ) brackets.*

This shouldn't come as a particular surprise, since that's how we did it before – but be warned! When you start using more complex conditions (with their own sub-terms in parentheses) it's all too easy to forget that *the condition as a whole* needs to be contained.

- I've replaced the sub-condition `bullet_fired is true` with `bullet_fired`.

You may want to think about this for a moment. Just as we can use < and > to test whether one value's bigger or smaller, we can use == to test whether two values are the same. So why don't we do the obvious thing and replace `bullet_fired is true` with `bullet_fired == true`.

Well, `bullet_fired == true` would only ever be true if `bullet_fired` itself was true. Likewise, it would only ever be false if `bullet_fired` itself were false. What we've just proved is that `bullet_fired` will *always* have the same value as `bullet_fired == true`, so one's just as good as the other. It should be fairly obvious which one looks neatest!

One more thing to consider is that the y-coordinate of -100 (which we used to put the bullet well clear of the visible screen) is a fairly arbitrary value. It's obvious what it does now, but six months later you might find yourself asking "What's that -100 doing in there?"

The obvious way to make things clearer is to add a comment by this line. Another way to clarify is by using a descriptively named variable, such as hide. At the beginning of the game you could set hide to -100; then in the main code, you could make statements like `bullet_y = hide`, making it more explicit what this value represents.

Password protection pt.1 – setting up the stage

Let's walk through a simple example, and put all this theory into practice. I've built a techno-gothic screen, whose sole purpose in life is to extract a password from the user. If they fail at this point, they won't be allowed to enter the rest of my site.

> It's important to note here that this is not a secure system. It's a good example of conditions, but don't think this will lock hackers out of your site for more than ten seconds!

1. First of all, open up `password_start.fla` from this chapter's download bundle. It consists of some basic graphics, a text field and a button, and uses the font OCR–Extended. What this movie *doesn't* have is the ActionScript required to make it run – that's where you'll come in!

If you want to use this font in your own movies, you should have no trouble picking it up from most free font sites. If you can't find it elsewhere, try the newsgroup alt.binaries.fonts. I've always found them to be a pretty decent and helpful bunch and someone there has always pointed me to exactly what I wanted whenever I've been looking for some fairly specific fonts.

> *In fact, for the download files, I've applied* Modify > Break Apart *a couple of times (breaking all my type into shapes) and then grouped them together (for ease of use). You should therefore be able to see the screens just as I designed them, whether or not you have this specific font installed on your machine.*

2.   Select frame 1 in the timeline, and you'll find the following screen (which is defined on the graphics layer):

There are two active items on this screen: the hollow rectangle is an Input Text field, where a user can enter their password; the text that reads '_execute' is actually a button, which the user will press after entering their password. Right now, neither one is configured, so that's the first thing we need to change.

3. Select the input text field and use the Property inspector to configure it like the one that's shown below. In particular, set the instance name to `password_txt`, the Line Type  to 'Password' (so that Flash displays only asterisks in the text field when you type into it), and Var to `myPass` (so we can read the password from ActionScript):

4. Now select the button, and set its instance name to `execute_btn`:

The stage is all set up now, so we just need to wire it up to some ActionScript so that our active items can actually do something. Let's pause for a moment and consider what we're trying to achieve.

Password protection pt.2 – working out the ActionScript

Once the user has entered a valid password, we want to take them to the next stage of the movie, which will start at frame 21. I've used the Property inspector to label this frame as accepted. This is the point where your site proper would begin, and this is what they'll see:

accepted::
welcome>

Before I let the user get this far though, I want to check whether they've used the correct password. This needs to be checked just as soon as they press the _execute button in frame 1, so that's where we need to attach the ActionScript that will make the system work. We'll work out that ActionScript now.

We need to make Flash look at what input the user gives us via `password_str`, and compare it with a predefined password. If they're the same, it will let the user into the site.

In recognition of one of my favorite films, I've decided that the password will be "I am The One". Also, to make life easier for the user, I'll make the password case-insensitive, so they can enter 'I am the One', or 'I am the one' or any combination of upper and lower case letters.

Expressed in my shorthand, the decision we need to make here is:

```
if (the lower case version of the text in myPass is "i am the one")
   {go to the 'accepted' frame}
```

Note that I'm not considering what will happen if the password provided isn't a good match. In that event (for now at least) I don't want to do anything. In ActionScript, we need to say:

```
lowerCasePass = myPass.toLowerCase();
if (lowerCasePass == "i am the one") {
  gotoAndStop("accepted");
};
```

The first line sets a variable called `lowerCasePass` to a lower case version of `myPass`, which we get by sticking `.toLowerCase()` onto the end of it. At this stage, you don't really need to worry about *how* this works; just remember *what* it does – that it now doesn't matter what case letters the user enters for their password.

The next three lines of code make up our decision-making system – that is, we have the structure we wanted:

```
if (something) {
  do this;
}
```

Note that our `something` expression uses the double equals sign `==` that I mentioned earlier. This is the **equality operator**, which tests whether the terms on either side have the same value. It will only return `true` if `lowerCasePass` has exactly the same value as the string "i am the one". If that *is* the case, the 'do this' section will be executed, so the movie will jump to the frame we've labeled as `accepted`.

> *This is a slightly different use of the* `gotoAndStop()` *action from what we've seen in the past, but the end result is the same: Flash jumps to the specified frame and stops there.*

We don't want this script to be executed as soon as the movie starts – after all, we need to give our user a chance to enter their password first! Since we want it to run just after the `execute_btn` button has been pressed, it makes sense to put it into a function to be triggered by that button's `onRelease` event. Basically, we're going to turn our code into an event handler, and attach it to a callback for the `execute_btn.onRelease` event:

```
execute_btn.onRelease = function() {
  lowerCasePass = myPass.toLowerCase();
```

```
    if (lowerCasePass == "i am the one") {
      gotoAndStop("accepted");
    };
  }
  stop();
```

Note that we've also had to tell the movie to stop – otherwise it would run straight on to the next page, whether or not our user entered a password, valid or not!

Password protection pt.3 – wiring up the code

Now we're ready to plug our code into the movie and give it a test run.

1. Use the Timeline panel to select the first frame in the actions layer.

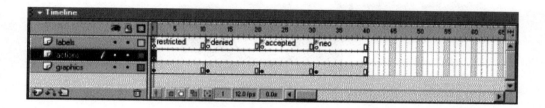

2. Now open up the Actions panel, type in the code, and press the check syntax button 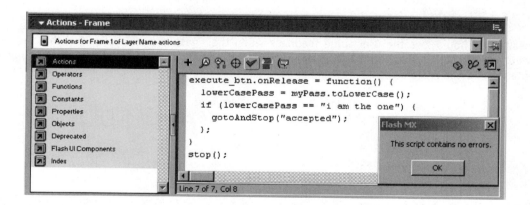 to confirm that it's good to go.

3. You're now ready to test the movie – use Control > Test Movie or press CTRL/CMD+ENTER. Type the password into the input text field (you'll see each character represented by an asterisk, so that no-one can see what you've typed).

4.   Now hit the _execute button. Assuming you typed in the password correctly, you will now see the accepted message shown below:

Alternative actions

So what happens if you enter the wrong password? The answer: nothing at all. In fact, until you key in a valid password, it will look to all intents and purposes as though the 'execute' button is broken! If you've ever come across this kind of behavior, you'll know how frustrating it can be: you've typed in your password, but the movie/web site/application still won't run properly, and doesn't even hint at what's wrong.

Ideally, we should give the user some feedback when their password is invalid, and that means taking another look at our decision-making code. Here's the important bit as it stands, first in my sausage notation, then in ActionScript:

```
if (the text in lowerCasePass is "i am the one")
  {go to the 'accepted' frame}

if (lowerCasePass == "i am the one") {
  gotoAndStop("accepted");
}
```

Probably the most obvious way to deal with an invalid password would be to add another if structure on the end, like this:

```
if (the text in lowerCasePass is "i am the one")
  {go to the 'accepted' frame}
if (the text in lowerCasePass is not "i am the one")
```

```
{go to the 'denied' frame}

if (lowerCasePass == "i am the one") {
  gotoAndStop("accepted");
}
if (lowerCasePass != "i am the one") {
  gotoAndStop("denied");
}
```

That's another new symbol for us: just as == means 'is equal to', != means 'is not equal to'. So, in the second if statement, the condition is only true if the text is *not* equal to our password. This works okay, but it's a bit of a waste of time: we're basically spelling out the same condition twice. It would be much easier just to say:

```
if (the text in lowerCasePass is "i am the one")
  {go to the 'accepted' frame}
otherwise
  {go to the 'denied' frame}
```

Don't go looking for the otherwise action though, because it doesn't exist – Flash uses else to do this:

```
if (lowerCasePass == "i am the one") {
  gotoAndStop("accepted");
} else {
  gotoAndStop("denied");
}
```

Acting on alternatives – the else action

Basically, the else action tells Flash to execute the attached commands whenever the last if condition turns out to be false. The code we've just seen is a good example of the commonest sort of choice you'll find in programming: we have a condition with two possible outcomes (in this case the password is either valid or it isn't) and define an appropriate course of action for each one.

Access denied – using the else action

Let's add this useful little nugget into our password movie.

1. Use the Timeline panel to select the first frame in the actions layer again.

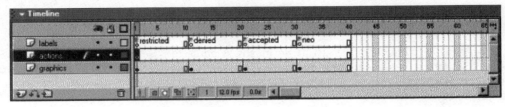

2. Add the new lines of code into the Actions panel, and press ![check] to check the syntax:

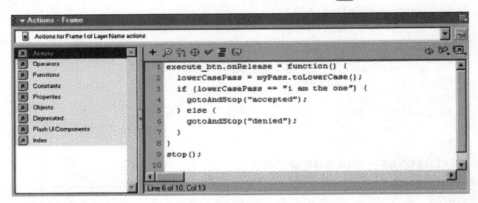

```
execute_btn.onRelease = function() {
    lowerCasePass = myPass.toLowerCase();
    if (lowerCasePass == "i am the one") {
        gotoAndStop("accepted");
    } else {
        gotoAndStop("denied");
    }
}
stop();
```

3. You can now hit CTRL/CMD+ENTER to test run the movie again.

4. Try pressing the execute button when there's no text in the password box. You should now see the denied message shown on the next page:

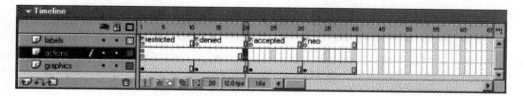

Great! That's just what we wanted – the only problem now is that we can't get back to the original screen to try again. Let's fix that right away.

5. First, select frame 20 on the actions layer. This is the last frame containing our 'access denied' message. Press F6 to create a keyframe here.

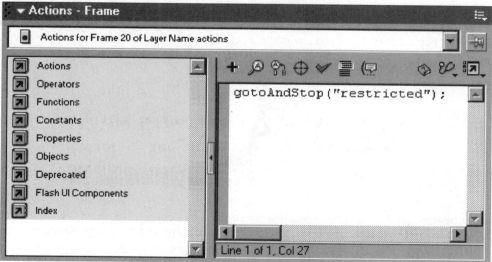

6. Now open the Actions panel and enter the following code:

```
gotoAndStop("restricted");
```

As soon as the playhead reaches frame 20, Flash will send us back to the original screen.

7. This is no good though unless frame 20 actually gets played, so we need to make a slight change to our original code: specifically, gotoAndStop("denied") becomes gotoAndPlay("denied"). Select frame 1 in the actions layer, and make this change so that your Actions panel looks like this:

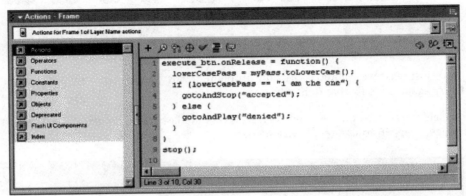

8. Hit CTRL/CMD+ENTER again, and test the movie with no password again. This time, you should find that the denied message is shown for less than a second before it returns you to the password entry screen. Problem solved!

More than one alternative – the else if action

Let's think about how we might improve this system even further. What if we wanted to create a special section of the site for executive users, to whom we've given a different password? If you take a look at frames 31-40, you'll see that I've already made a screen (labeled 'neo') to welcome these VIPs:

We'll also need to pick a separate, executive password – I've chosen the word "Neo" – and some more ActionScript to check whether it's been entered. Let's use some more sausage notation to confirm what we're doing:

```
if (lowerCasePass is "i am the one")
    {go to 'accepted' frame}
otherwise, if (lowerCasePass is "neo")
    {go to 'neo' frame}
otherwise
    {go to 'denied' frame}
```

You might have guessed from this that the ActionScript we need to make this happen looks like this:

```
if (lowerCasePass == "i am the one") {
    gotoAndStop("accepted");
} else if (lowerCasePass == "neo")
    gotoAndStop("neo");
} else {
    gotoAndPlay("denied");
}
```

We've effectively combined the else and if actions, so that we can test for another condition if the first one isn't met. Of course, if neither one is met we'll end up running the else command just like before. All it really means 'if the last condition tested was false, check whether this one's true'.

In fact, ActionScript treats else if as an action in its own right, and there are things you can do with an else if that you can't do with a plain else. For example, you can put as many else if actions as you want after an initial if action, making Flash check whether any number of conditions have been met (are true):

```
if (a) {
    do this;
} else if (b) {
    do this;
} else if (c) {
    do this;
} else if (d) {
    do this;
}
```

Breaking this down a little:

```
if (a) {
    do this;
} else if (b) {
```

Flash will start by looking at the first condition: a. If it's true, Flash will carry out the associated {do this;} action (or series of actions) and then skip past the rest of the if ...else if ... else block. If a is false, Flash moves straight on to the next else if, which tells it to check whether b is true.

Then, if b is true, Flash runs the associated {do this;} action and skips to the end of the block. It won't check c or d , and it won't run their {do this;} actions, *even if* c or d are true.

> This is an important fact to take on board, because it shows the importance of the order in which you enter your else if actions – if several conditions are satisfied, only the first one in the list will ever be acted on.

If, on the other hand, b is false, Flash moves on to c, and so on, and so on. You need to always remember that *only one* of your if/else if/else commands will run, and that it will be the first one in the list whose condition is true.

So, why not just use a string of separate if structures? Well, it's largely a matter of efficiency: once a condition within an else if command has been found to be true, Flash won't bother checking any of the subsequent else if conditions – it just follows the appropriate instruction. If we used separate if actions, we'd force Flash to check every single one, even after it had found a condition that had been met. If you only want one result, this is going to put a completely unnecessary strain on Flash, and possibly slow your movie down.

Essentially, as you go down the ladder of else if actions, you're finding out what *isn't* true, and then homing in on what is true by asking more and more precise questions based on what you know it *might be*.

Imagine that you were writing a piece of code that controlled how a diving space invader attacked the player on its way down the screen, and you wanted to make your space invader do different things as it got closer to the player's ship. You'd write your decision like this:

```
if (distance is greater than 50)
   {make alien stay in formation}
else if (distance is greater than 25)
   {make alien start to fire on the ship and dive in a random direction}
else if (distance is greater than 10)
   {execute kamikaze tactics}
```

If the first condition in the if action is found to be false, you can deduce that on the first else if statement the distance is less than 50, because if it wasn't you wouldn't have got this far down the statement. If the condition in the first else if statement is found to be true, you know that the distance must be greater than 25 but less than 50.

> Note that the ordering of the if...else if *decisions affects the order in which they're checked. If you put the 'greater than 25' decision* **after** *the 'greater than 10' decision, the 'greater than 25' bit would never run!*

So, to make your decision, you're using what you know the distance *isn't*, as well as what it *is*.

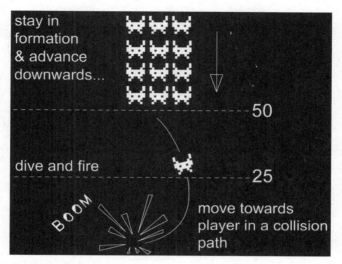

As the demarcation lines used to decide the kamikaze behavior move up the screen, the aliens' scope for attacking will increase, as they acquire more room in which to perform their kamikaze maneuver. So, if you gradually moved the lines upward as the game progressed, your aliens would appear to have grown more aggressive over time. It's amazing how much an object's behavior can be modified by changing a single number.

As you can see from this explanation, else if has many more versatile uses than we're exploiting in our simple password exercise.

Speaking of that, let's get back to it now. We'll plug in our else if action so that Flash can distinguish between the two passwords and direct users to the appropriate part of the site.

Executive access – using 'else if'

Go back to your FLA. Our script should still be in the Actions window

1. Select the first frame in the actions layer and add the new lines of code (highlighted below) to what's already shown in the Actions panel. Remember that the second line converts all passwords to lower case; this is why Neo has become neo. Press [✓] to check the syntax.

```
execute_btn.onRelease = function() {
  lowerCasePass = myPass.toLowerCase()
  if (lowerCasePass == "i am the one") {
    gotoAndStop("accepted");
  } else if (lowerCasePass == "neo") {
    gotoAndStop("neo");
  } else {
    gotoAndPlay("denied");
  }
```

```
    }
    stop();
```

2. Hit CTRL/CMD+ENTER to test run the movie again, and try the new password:

3. Press the execute button and you should see the neo message shown below:

You can find this complete version saved as `password_finished.fla` in the chapter download.

We've now looked at every stage of the `if...else if...else` cycle, considering the decisions that Flash takes at each point along the way. Hopefully, you're now starting to get an idea for just how much flexibility these decision-making structures can give your Flash movies. Now they don't just act and react, but can take a different course of action for each circumstance you plan for.

There's one more way to make decisions using ActionScript. While it doesn't actually do anything new, it can be a lot tidier (not to mention shorter and more readable) than the `if...else if...else` cycle we've used so far.

Handling lots of alternatives – the switch action

When we last saw our password script, the meat of it looked like this:

```
if (lowerCasePass == "i am the one") {
    gotoAndStop("accepted");
} else if (lowerCasePass == "neo") {
    gotoAndStop("neo");
} else {
    gotoAndPlay("denied");
}
```

It doesn't exactly take a degree in rocket science to guess what this does. Take out all the brackets, swap 'is equal to' for the `==` symbols, 'otherwise' for `else`, and stick it all on one line: bingo! You've got something that's pretty close to plain English:

- If `lowerCasePass` is equal to "i am the one", go to accepted and stop there.
- Otherwise, if `lowerCasePass` is equal to "neo", go to neo and stop there.
- Otherwise, go to denied and play from there.

That's perfect for this situation: it's simple, concise, and easy to understand. Believe it or not, rule number one of good programming says that *all* code should aim to be all of these things – maybe someone should tell the programmers that!

In real life though, we might want to add more users to the system, each with their own password, and each with their own set of actions to perform once they've entered it. In that case, we could end up with a great long string of `else if (lowerCasePass == "something")` terms. That's not so bad in itself, but it does mean that we're testing the value of `lowerCasePass` over and over and over....

When that happens, it's worth considering using the `switch` action instead. Let's take a look at our `if...else if...else` password testing script when it's written out using `switch`:

```
switch (lowerCasePass) {
    case "i am the one":
                gotoAndStop("accepted");
                break;
    case "neo":
                gotoAndStop("neo");
                break;
    default:
                gotoAndPlay("denied");
}
```

Hmm. It's a bit further away from plain English than our `if`s and `else`s. So what does it mean?

Let's take it one line at a time:

```
switch (lowerCasePass) {
```

The `switch()` action is very similar to `if()`, in that it uses a sausage-like arrangement of plain brackets and curly brackets. The big difference here is that we don't put a condition (something that will give us a true or false value) inside the plain brackets. Instead, we put in a plain old variable.

So how does it know whether or not to run the actions inside the curly brackets? The answer is that it doesn't need to: *it runs the actions in the curly brackets anyway*.

Okay, you're shaking your head now. Supper's ready, and this is all getting a bit strange. Just bear with me a moment longer, because this is the clever bit that'll one day make your ActionScripting chores seem a hundred times easier!

Take a look at what's inside the brackets, and you'll see it doesn't look like anything we've seen before. There's a couple of new terms – `case` and `break` – plus colons `:` dotted around all over the place. What does it all mean?

Well the first thing Flash sees when it starts running the actions is this line:

```
case "i am the one":
```

This line basically says 'check whether the string "i am the one" is the same as what's being stored in the `switch` variable'. In this case, the `switch` variable is `lowerCasePass`. If it is, then it runs the actions following the colon.

> This `case` thing isn't actually an action, but a special keyword that helps the `switch` action to do its job. This might not seem like much of a distinction, but it's important to remember. If you try using `case` outside the curly brackets of a `switch` statement, Flash won't understand what you mean.

Let's look at what Flash sees when it starts going through those actions. First up:

```
gotoAndStop("accepted");
```

That's safe enough. We know what that does already. What about the next line though?

```
break;
```

This action simply tells Flash to ignore all the rest of the actions inside the curly brackets. If the switch variable `lowerCasePass` *did* contain the string "i am the one", then we're all done now.

What if it didn't then? Well, we carry on through the contents of the curly brackets.

No prizes for guessing what happens if the switch variable contains the string "neo"! The next line primes Flash for precisely that situation:

```
case "neo":
```

And then follows up with actions to run in that case:

```
gotoAndStop("neo");
break;
```

Finally, we set up a `default` case:

```
default:
gotoAndPlay("denied");
```

Note that we don't need to use the `case` keyword here. You can think of `default` as being a bit like `case`'s poverty-stricken cousin: they're both keywords that only mean something when they're used inside a `switch` statement; but while `case` is very fussy about the value of the `switch` variable, `default` sits at the bottom of the pile and grabs anything and everything that `case` lets through to it.

It's quite tempting to describe this default section as 'what happens if none of the other cases work out'. That's certainly what happens in this particular example: if either of the `cases` were good, we'd have hit a `break` by now, and wouldn't even be considering the `default` case.

But what if we took the `breaks` out?

```
switch (lowerCasePass) {
    case "i am the one":
            gotoAndStop("accepted");
    case "neo":
            gotoAndStop("neo");
    default:
            gotoAndPlay("denied");
}
```

Zoinks! Even shorter than before, but is it actually what we want?

Say we've got the value "i am the one" stored in `lowerCasePass`. We hit the first `case` statement, it sees a good match, and gives us the thumbs up to run the subsequent actions. The playhead gets told to jump ahead to the `accepted` frame and stop there, but the ActionScript carries on running.

When we hit the next `case` statement, Flash doesn't bother checking! We're already past security – and it really can't be bothered to throw us out now – so the fact that we're not "neo" doesn't stop us seeing the playhead ordered to the `neo` frame.

That's pretty bad news – but there's worse to come! Not content with letting us into the executive area of the site on the strength of a bog-standard password, we now hit the `default` case, which throws us out of the site regardless!

Okay, I think we've established that's *not* what we want. But that's not to say we should never consider taking out the `breaks` – it's just that in this case we really do need them.

Before we finish off the chapter, let's look at another example of decision-making in a Flash movie, where it *does* make sense for us to use a `switch` statement that doesn't have any breaks.

Switching without breaks

Just for a few pages, let's go back to school. Say we're writing a movie that's going to let members of a college faculty access records. We can assume there are several different types of member to allow for: for simplicity's sake, we'll just consider students, professors, and the head of the faculty.

- Students will want a link to timetables, lab allocations and so on.
- Professors want a link to all those things, plus hall bookings, staff allocations, and so on.
- The faculty head wants all of the above, plus a detailed rundown of the faculty's financial status (and maybe links to stock prices for all the companies he's poured faculty money into over all the years...).

The important thing about this situation is that the information we give to each group isn't always *exclusive* to that group. In our password-handling movie, we always wanted to send the user to one frame *or* another, *or* another, but never to more than one.

In this example, we're dealing with basic faculty information about stuff like lecture timetables, and want to make that available to *everyone*. Then there's staff administration stuff that everyone *except* the students need to know about. Finally there's key financial information that the head of faculty wants to keep to him- or herself.

If you tried scripting this with an if...else if...else structure, it would look a bit of a mess:

```
if (user is a student)
  { show student info }
else if (user is a professor)
  { show staff info, show student info }
else if (user is the faculty head)
  { show accounts, show staff info, show student info }
else
  { tell user that this site is not for them }
```

It'll work, but there's lots of pointless repetition in there. Just for a start, we've three lots of *show student info*, each one of which might consist of *loads* of separate actions...

The answer is to use a switch structure, just like the one we used before, but without any breaks:

```
switch (type of user) {
    case "head of faculty": show accounts
    case "professor": show staff info
    case "student": show student info
    default: tell user that this site is not for them
}
```

We start by finding out what type of user we're dealing with. For the sake of keeping our example simple and flexible, we'll assume that this is something the user just types in.

> *Of course in practice, that's the last thing you'd want to do, since any old John Doe typing in "head of faculty" could then sneak a peek at privileged information! While security's an important issue to be aware of, it's a bit of a red herring while we're still on the learning slopes... That is, unless you're planning to try to base a real 'secure' site on these very simple examples – which I wouldn't recommend for a millisecond!*

If our user claims to be the head of faculty, the first case statement shows them a link to the faculty accounts page. If not, they don't see the accounts.

Either way, we then move on to the second case statement. If we're dealing with a professor (or someone who's already been successfully cased, such as the head of faculty), Flash then shows a link to the staff info page.

Next, we move on to the third case statement, and if we're dealing with a student (or someone who's already been successfully cased, such as the head of faculty or one of the professors), then they get to see a link to the student info page.

Finally, the default action generates a message telling them to go away. Anyone viewing the movie should see this.

Huh? Surely we don't want to tell our bona fide members to go away! This highlights the difference between actions in an `else` clause within an `if...else` structure, and actions in a `default` clause within a `switch` statement:

- An `else` action will *only* run if all the previous `if` tests fail.
- A `default` action will *always* run unless you `break` out before reaching it.

We don't want faculty members to see the default message, so we need to make sure there's a `break` somewhere before hitting the `default` keyword. No problem:

```
switch (type of user) {
    case "head of faculty": show accounts
    case "professor": show staff info
    case "student": show student info, break
    default: tell user that this site is not for them
}
```

Since all faculty members get to see the student info, they all get to `break` out before Flash has a chance to tell them to get lost!

The faculty links page

Now that we have a good idea of how our decision-making script should look, let's put it to work.

1. Open up a new movie, and click on the stage to select it. Now use the Property inspector to set the background color to a pinkish purple color (I've used #CC66FF). Obviously, this isn't essential, but it does help us make things look a little less drab!

2. Now rename Layer 1 as background, and add a white box like the one shown on the next page. Select frame 30 and press F5 to insert a frame there:

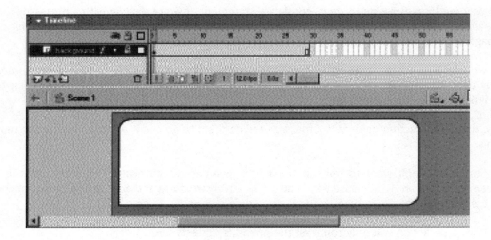

3.   Now add a new layer called text – this will hold all our instructions for the user. On frame 1, we need to see the following:

At the top of the white box, I've created a couple of static text fields. Underneath, there's an input text field, which I've set up like this:

Note that I've checked the Show Border box, named the instance input_txt and set Var to userInput. There's also a Submit button (which I've subtly recycled from last chapter's calculator movie) whose instance name is – predictably enough – submit_btn.

4.   Still on level text, select frame 10 and press F6 to add a keyframe. You can delete the input field and the button from this frame, and change the text in the lower static field so that it looks like this:

Faculty records

Select the page you would like to view:

5. Add another keyframe at frame 20, and change the lower text again, so that it looks like this:

Faculty records

You're not permitted to view our records.

No prizes for guessing what this screen is for!

6. Now it's time to add some frame labels, so that the `gotoAndStop()` actions we're going to use for navigation don't get too abstract. Create a new layer called labels, and use the Property inspector to label keyframes as shown in the timeline below:

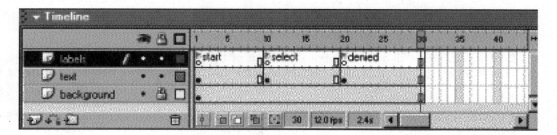

7. Now for another layer, called links. This is where the actual link buttons are going to sit. There are four of them, each based on its own button symbol in the library. Again, I've based them on the calculator buttons from Chapter 2:

7.   Once you've positioned them on the stage, give them the following instance names: `student_btn`, `staff_btn`, `finance_btn`, and `back_btn`. I'll leave you to work out which one's which!

If you run the movie at this point, you'll see some very strange behavior – not at all what we'd hope for. Apart from the fact that it's cycling through the entire timeline, the link buttons are visible and active all the way through, and they're covering up the input text field! What on earth have we done?

Don't panic. This is all quite intentional and part of the plan. We're going to make use of a nifty little trick, which involves making buttons invisible. Now you see them, now you.... where'd they go?

Create another new layer called actions; don't worry, I promise this will be the last new layer! Select frame 1, call up the Actions panel, and click on the pin button, just to make sure we don't accidentally attach any script to the wrong place... Now add the script shown in the screenshot on the next page:

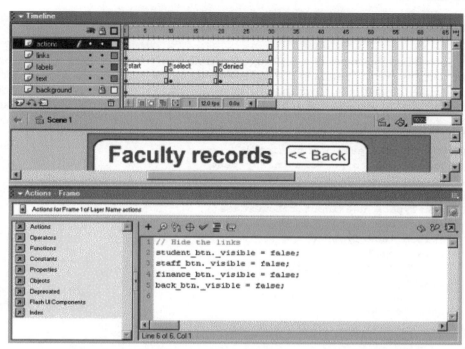

Just as we can use _x to control the x-position of an instance on the stage (as we saw in the last chapter), we can use _visible to control its visibility. By setting _visible to false, we can make an instance invisible.

8. Test run the movie again, and you'll see immediately what a difference this makes! It's still looping though, so let's add a stop() action to the end of the script before we go on:

```
// Hide the links
student_btn._visible = false;
staff_btn._visible = false;
finance_btn._visible = false;
back_btn._visible = false;
// This is where your callbacks should go...
// Stop the movie
stop();
```

Apart from the actual links, our movie offers three ways for a user to interact: via the input text field (where they state their position), the Submit button (which they click to submit that information), and the Back button (which they click to return to the original screen and try again). The input text is automatically stored in the userInput variable, so that's taken care of; we've still got a couple of callbacks to write, though.

9. The Back button's easiest, since all it ever needs to do is send us back to the frame labeled start and stop there.

```
// Callback for 'back' button release
back_btn.onRelease = function() {
```

```
            gotoAndStop("start");
    };
```

9.   The Submit button is more of a challenge. This is what we'll use to trigger our decision-making
      code (like the execute button in our earlier examples). The action we want to take for each case is
      to *show* the relevant button (which will presumably link to some other part of the movie – I'll
      leave that part to you!) We can achieve this by resetting its visibility to true. Hold your breath…

```
// Callback for 'submit' button release
submit_btn.onRelease = function() {
    // Actions to perform in any case
    gotoAndStop("select");
    back_btn._visible = true;
    userType = userInput.toLowerCase();
    // Actions to perform depending on user type
    switch (userType) {
    case "head" :
        finance_btn._visible = true;
    case "professor" :
        staff_btn._visible = true;
    case "student" :
        student_btn._visible = true;
        break;
    default :
        gotoAndStop("denied");
    }
};
```

      …okay, you can breathe out now.

Let's go through this carefully – it's not nearly as hard as it looks!

When someone presses and then releases the Submit button, they trigger off the script above, which starts
off by shuttling them on to the select frame. At this point, all the link buttons are still invisible, so the
stage looks like this:

Faculty records
Select the page you would like to view:

Next, we make the Back button visible and store the lower case version of the variable `userInput` in another variable called `userType`. The stage now looks like this:

Now it's time to look at the real engine behind our movie. We've got a `switch` action that tests for various different values of `userType`:

```
// Actions to perform depending on user type
switch (userType) {
case "head" :
    finance_btn._visible = true;
case "professor" :
    staff_btn._visible = true;
case "student" :
    student_btn._visible = true;
    break;
default :
    gotoAndStop("denied");
}
```

- If the value is head, then it shows the Finance button, and cascades through all the other cases (showing the Staff button and the Student button) before hitting a break.

- Similarly, if the value is professor, it shows the Staff button, falls through to show the Student button too, and stops when it hits break.

- If the value is student, it only shows the Student button before breaking out.

- If the value of userType is none of the above, the default clause sends users hurtling on to the denied frame, where they're politely informed that they don't have permission to view faculty records. None of the link buttons are visible, apart from the Back button, which absent-minded professors can use to return to the first screen and try remembering their job titles again.

Here's the full script listing for `faculty.fla`, which you can also find included in the download for this chapter:

```
// Hide the links
student_btn._visible = false;
staff_btn._visible = false;
finance_btn._visible = false;
back_btn._visible = false;
```

```
// Callback for 'submit' button release
submit_btn.onRelease = function() {
    // Actions to perform in any case
    gotoAndStop("select");
    back_btn._visible = true;
    userType = userInput.toLowerCase();
    // Actions to perform depending on user type
    switch (userType) {
    case "head" :
        finance_btn._visible = true;
    case "professor" :
        staff_btn._visible = true;
    case "student" :
        student_btn._visible = true;
        break;
    default :
        gotoAndStop("denied");
    }
};
// Callback for 'back' button release
back_btn.onRelease = function() {
    gotoAndStop("start");
};
// Stop the movie
stop();
```

Try the movie out one last time, and you'll find that each different type of user is presented with a different selection of link buttons to choose from:

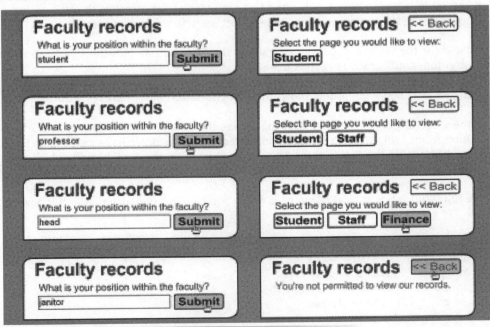

Summary

In this chapter, we've covered a number of ways to make your Flash movies more intelligent by giving them the power to make decisions based on specific circumstances and user input:

- Using `if` and `else` actions, **Booleans** and **conditions** to enable Flash to make decisions and act on them.

- Adding `else if` actions to enable Flash to act on a variety of outcomes.

- Using `switch` actions with `breaks` to allow one of a number of options to happen.

- Using `switch` actions without `breaks` to allow several of a number of options to happen.

We've designed some simple password systems to show this, although I would like to stress, just one last time, that these methods are not very secure, so don't go using them commercially!

Once you've got your head round these basic ActionScript building blocks, you'll be able to go on and create increasingly intelligent Flash movies, with the power to implement intricate decision-making code.

In the next chapter we'll be looking at how to write your code so that it works harder for you.

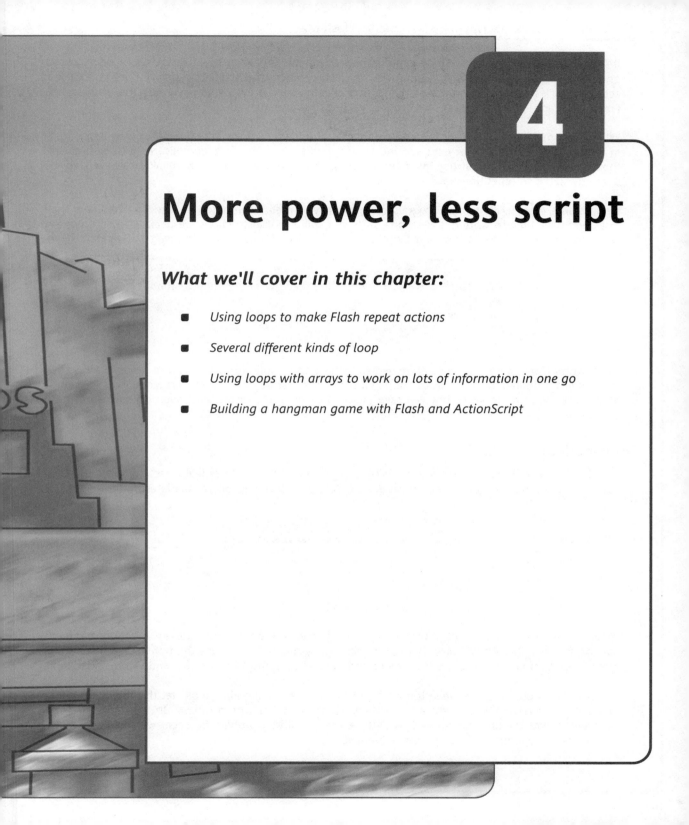

More power, less script

What we'll cover in this chapter:

- Using loops to make Flash repeat actions

- Several different kinds of loop

- Using loops with arrays to work on lots of information in one go

- Building a hangman game with Flash and ActionScript

It's not exactly headline news, but computers are pretty dumb. Whatever far-fetched dreams we may have once had, the 21st Century isn't buzzing with the conversation of HAL-9000s– well, not yet at least! It's actually chock full of silicon number crunchers, and (sorry to say) even your shiny new top-of-the-range PowerMac can't hold a candle to the raw intelligence of the simplest human being.

When it's a matter of crunching through commands and figures though, the computer wins easily, both in terms of speed and accuracy. It's specifically designed to work on large, complicated jobs by breaking them down into gazillions of tiny instructions, and getting them all done in the blink of an eye – so it's perfectly suited to repetitious jobs.

By and large though, it's human programmers who have to tell a computer what to do when, and they just don't have time to write out *every one* of those gazillions of instructions – especially when there are reruns of Star Trek to be watched on TV! And thus it was that **loops** came into being.

> In Flash, a loop is a command (or collection of commands) that makes your movie do something (or collection of somethings) more than once over...

Don't worry if this statement doesn't immediately make the whole world seem like a better place to live in – it's just a definition of the word 'loop'. I'll spend the rest of the chapter persuading you that loops aren't just useful to Trekkies, but can save *you* lots of time and effort, and open up some very cool possibilities...

Timeline loops

The simplest way to make a loop in Flash is by using gotoAndPlay() to repeat a section of the timeline. Say we label frame 1 as 'loop', and attach gotoAndPlay("loop") to one of the later frames:

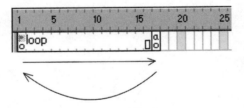

When this timeline plays, it'll play normally as far as frame 17, see the gotoAndPlay() action, and jump back to frame 1. Then it will play through frames 1-17 again, before it runs the frame 17 actions again, jumps back to frame 1, and plays from there until it reaches frame 17 and so on, and so on, and so on...

So, this will set up a loop between frames 1 and 17, and Flash will quite happily let this repetition go on indefinitely. Of course, you might well be thinking, "why bother with a gotoAndPlay() action? Flash normally repeats the timeline anyway." Well there are lots of very subtle differences we could talk about, but one real biggie that makes the rest redundant:

- An automatic timeline loop is simple and dumb. It plays the whole timeline. It plays the whole timeline again. It plays the whole timeline again. And so on. What's more, any old user can tweak the player settings to turn it off – no good if your movie depends on it...!

- A `gotoAndPlay()` timeline loop puts you, the author of the movie, in control of the looping. You can specify where the loop starts and where it stops, so it doesn't need to loop the entire timeline; you can even have several loops on the same timeline! You can use it within movie clips too. Even better, none of those pesky loop-stopping users can break it!

Timeline looping can be a very useful technique for getting the most out of what's already there on the stage, but it doesn't really give us much of the value-added interactive power that ActionScript promises.

The real subject of this chapter involves another, quite different approach to looping. Instead of repeating a sequence of frames on the timeline, let's see how we can repeat a set of actions.

ActionScript loops

Loops really come into their own when we start using them to repeat scripts that we've already written. Maybe you have a great long list of variables that all need to be tweaked in just the same way, or lots of movie clip instances on the stage that all need to be shifted one pixel to the left. It's easy to write an action to change one of them, and not so hard to write a couple more. By the time you've written four hundred and twenty-eight though, you might be starting to flag a little...

If, on the other hand, you write out your action once and stick it inside an ActionScript loop, you can tell the loop to repeat that action as many times as you like. Yes, it's time to capitalize on the fact that your computer will never get bored doing simple repetitive jobs!

An ActionScript loop is a totally different beast from a timeline loop. A timeline loop involves playing through a sequence of frames, whereas an ActionScript loop exists entirely within a single frame. The ActionScript loop is defined in the lines of script you've attached to that frame, so Flash will stay on the same frame for as long as those lines are looping.

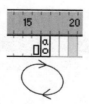

ActionScript has several looping actions, specifically designed to help us out with this sort of thing. They all use the sausage-like notation we saw in the last chapter, so they hopefully won't look too alien to you!

while loops

A **while loop** is probably the simplest of all ActionScript loops to understand, since it's really not much different from a simple `if` statement:

```
while (condition) {
   do these actions;
}
```

In fact, the only thing that *is* different from an `if` statement is the name of the action. Well, that and the end result of course! We give it a condition (something that will *always* turn up either true or false) and some actions to perform **while** the condition's true. Unlike in an `if` statement, Flash won't stop and move on once it's run the actions – it'll perform them over and over and over for as long as the condition's true. It'll only move on to the next line of script (or the next frame) when the condition turns out to be false.

That means that something like this...

```
while (false) {
   // actions
};
```

...won't do a thing. The condition is always false, so any actions we put in the body will never run. On the other hand, something like this...

```
while (true) {
   // actions
};
```

...will kill your movie stone dead. The condition is always true, so the loop goes on forever!

You can try making this happen if you like, but be warned: your computer may lock up for a while when Flash tries to compile the SWF. When Flash spots your mistake, it will show you the following message:

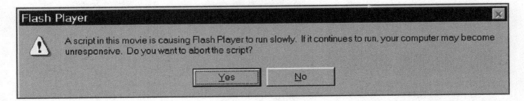

If you do ever see this dialog, I strongly suggest hitting Yes. Although Flash can detect these 'forever' loops, they can still *crash your computer* if you press No and let them run – I've seen the evidence for myself.

> *Any ActionScript loop that repeats indefinitely can be described as a* **forever loop**. *These will normally only ever happen if something's gone wrong.*

Useful things to do with while loops

So how can we do something useful with a `while` loop? Simple: base the condition on a variable, and put actions in the body of the loop that can change that variable. Here's a simple example:

```
myCounter = 0;
while (myCounter < 10) {
  myCounter++;
};
```

We set up a variable called `myCounter`, giving it a value of 0. When we start the `while` loop, the condition we give it basically says: 'the value of variable `myCounter` is less than 10'. Well, at this stage, that's most certainly true, so we run the actions inside the body of the loop.

There's only one action in the loop body, and while it may look a little odd, it's really nothing special: `myCounter++` is just a shorthand way of saying 'add one to the number stored in `myCounter`'. So that's just what Flash does, just before it reaches the end of the loop.

Since we're still working through a while action, we loop back to the start. `myCounter` now has a value of 1, so `myCounter < 10` is still true. We therefore run `myCounter++` and loop back to the start again. And again. And again. And this keeps happening until the value of `myCounter` reaches 9. At that point, we add 1 to the value, loop back to the start, test whether the new value is less than 10 – it's not! Now the condition is false, so Flash can stop looping and move on.

Of course, this just gives us the bare bones of a useful loop: it's not terribly exciting if it just adds lots of 'one' to a boring old number variable... Let's flesh things out, so that our simple `while` loop actually does something practical in a movie.

Making actions run several times in a row

This quick example is going to demonstrate a few of the things it's possible to do with a simple `while` loop.

1. Create a new Flash document and select frame 1 on the main timeline. Open up the Actions panel, and click on the pin button to pin it to the current frame. Now add the following script:

```
myCounter = 0;
while (myCounter < 10) {
  // actions to loop go here
  myCounter++;
};
```

This is our basic loop, which will run a complete ten cycles.

2.   The simplest thing we can do with this is to trace out the value of myCounter for each loop:

```
myCounter = 0;
while (myCounter < 10) {
  // actions to loop go here
  trace(myCounter);
  myCounter++;
};
```

Run the movie, and sure enough, this is what we get:

This reminds us that myCounter takes values of 0, 1, 2, and so on up to 9, before the loop stops (when it hits 10). It's important to remember that we never actually *see* the value of myCounter traced as 10 because the loop stops as soon as it gets that value.

3.   This business of counting from 0 to 9 instead of counting from 1 to 10 should remind you of something we saw back in Chapter 2: arrays.

As you may recall, a single array can hold lots of different variables – the **elements** of that array. We can tell Flash which element we want to work with by specifying a particular offset number (or **index**). If we use a variable to specify the offset, then the element we deal with depends on the variable's value. Then we can pick and choose from the array's elements by changing the value of that offset variable... You still with me?

Anyway, the upshot of this is that we can write generalized code for manipulating array element number i, and specify the value of i quite separately. If we happen to be looping through all possible values of i, this approach can be *very* powerful!

So let's try using myCounter as the offset value, used to specify one particular element in an array.

```
bondMovies = new Array("Doctor No", "From Russia With Love",
                      ➥"Goldfinger", "Thunderball");
myCounter = 0;
while (myCounter < 10) {
  // actions to loop go here
  trace( bondMovies[myCounter] );
  myCounter++;
};
```

Now we get something more like this:

Instead of just showing the counter value, we're using it to show the first ten values from our bondMovie array. The only problem is that there are only four entries.

4. There's no point in looping ten times if there are only four entries in the array In fact, we only need our loop to loop for as long as the array element we're looking at has a well-defined value. In other words, we should be looping 'while bondMovies[myCounter] is not undefined'. Sounds like we need to change our loop condition:

```
bondMovies = new Array("Doctor No", "From Russia With Love",
                      ➥"Goldfinger", "Thunderball");
myCounter = 0;
while ( bondMovies[myCounter] != undefined) {
  // actions to loop go here
  trace( bondMovies[myCounter] );
  myCounter++;
};
```

Run the movie once again, and you'll see that this has done the trick

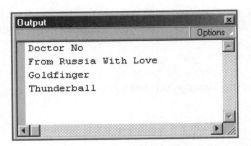

As soon as `myCounter` reaches 4, the while loop spots that `bondMovies[myCounter]` isn't defined, so the loop cuts out before it gets a chance to trace the word 'undefined'.

Okay, this may seem like pretty cool stuff if you happen to enjoy making lists of movie titles. But what about doing some real Flash stuff?

Using loops to control what's on the stage

This time, we're going to use a similar loop to put a whole set of movie clips on the stage. Along the way, I'll introduce a couple of useful tricks for controlling movie clips that we haven't seen before.

1. Create another new Flash document, make sure the stage is active and use the Property inspector to give it a black background. In the Timeline panel, rename Layer 1 as particles, and create a new layer above it called actions:

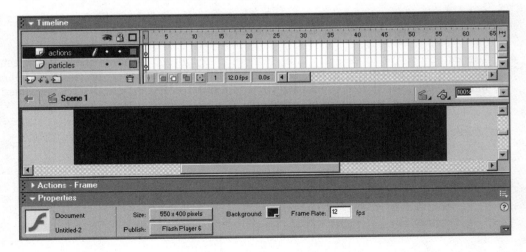

2. Select the particles layer and use Insert > New Symbol (or press CTRL/CMD+F8) to create a new movie clip called particle. Now use the Color Mixer panel to set up a radial fill style that fades from opaque white at the center to transparent white at the perimeter:

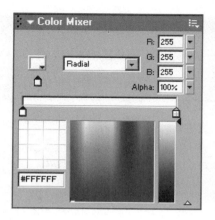 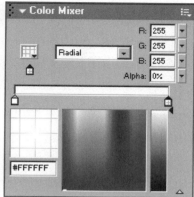

3.   Add a circle with no stroke to the particle movie clip. Use the Property inspector to give it a diameter of 80 pixels (W:80.0, H:80.0) and place it bang in the center of the stage (X:-40.0, Y:-40.0):

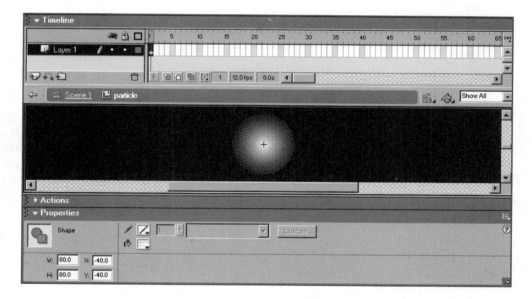

Now click on the Scene 1 link to head back to the main timeline.

4.   Press CTRL/CMD+L to call up the Library panel, and drag the particle item onto the stage to create an instance of the movie clip. Select the instance and use the Property inspector to place it at X:290, Y:190. While you're at it, don't forget to give it an instance name: particle_mc.

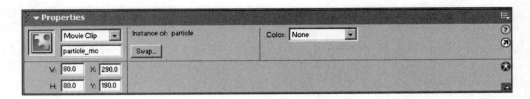

> Remember, we always put _mc at the end of a movie clip instance name to remind us what sort of instance we're dealing with.

5. Now select frame 1 of the actions layer, open up the Actions panel, and click on the pin button to pin it to the current frame. Now add the following script:

```
i = 0;
while (i < 10) {
  // actions to loop go here
  i++;
}
```

This is just the same loop as we used before, except that we're using a variable called i as our counter instead of myCounter.

So what about all that stuff I said in Chapter 2 about naming your variables sensibly? Okay, this is a bit of an exception: when we're writing actions inside loops, we often end up using the counter variable rather a lot, for array offsets and other such things. If you call it something like myCounter, these actions can get very long and complex looking. It's therefore quite common to use a variable called i, j, or k instead. I won't bore you with an explanation of *why* these particular names are used; suffice to say they hark back to the days of mainframe computers that had just 16K of memory! I promise it won't take you long to get used to this little quirk.

6. Now we're going to add an action into our loop that will duplicate the particle movie clip for us:

```
i = 0;
while (i < 10) {
  // actions to loop go here
  duplicateMovieClip(particle_mc, "particle"+i+"_mc", i);
  i++;
}
```

This is something totally new – and very useful! It shouldn't take a genius to work out *what* an action called **duplicateMovieClip** does, but *how it works* is another matter...

This action takes a grand total of three arguments. The first is the instance name of the movie clip we want to duplicate – in this case it's particle_mc – which doesn't need any quotes around it. The second argument is where we specify what the duplicate should be called. Each instance should have a unique name, so we build this up from two string literals and the counter variable. We're naming each duplicate instance as:

```
"particle"+i+"_mc"
```

So when i has a value of 0, this works out as `particle0_mc`. Likewise, when i has a value of 1, it works out as `particle1_mc`. And so on. The third argument tells Flash which **depth level** to place the duplicate on. The only thing you really need to know about this (for now at least) is that you can only have one movie clip on each depth level; put two at the same depth and the second will replace the first. We therefore need to change this argument for each new duplicate, so we use the counter variable i again.

The end result is that we wind up with ten duplicates of the `particle_mc` movie clip instance, called `particle0_mc`, `particle1_mc`, `particle2_mc`, and so on. All this from one action inside a loop! Let's do something with them...

7. Now that we have a grand total of eleven movie clip instances on the stage, we can start dragging them around the place in a variety of weird and wonderful ways. Say we recycle the mouse following callback we brewed up at the end of Chapter 1:

```
onEnterFrame = function() {
    // move particle to mouse position
    particle_mc._x = _xmouse;
    particle_mc._y = _ymouse;
};
```

Just pop this on the end of your script, run the movie, wiggle your mouse around, and watch that particle go!

8. Ahem. Well, we now have *one* particle following the mouse around; what about the other ten? Of course, we don't want to write separate actions to control every single one. That would be rather silly now that we have the power of loops to fall back on.

```
onEnterFrame = function() {
  j = 0;
  while (j < 10) {
    // move particle to mouse position
    particle_mc._x = _xmouse;
    particle_mc._y = _ymouse;
    j++;
  };
};
```

The only problem with this is that we're now updating the position of particle_mc ten times over, when we actually want to reposition a *different* instance each time.

9.   Ideally, we want to build another string like "particle"+j+"_mc", and use *that* to specify which instance to reposition. Unfortunately, we can't just put.

```
"particle"+j+"_mc"._x = _xmouse;
```

because Flash will think that you're trying to assign the value of _xmouse to something that isn't a variable or a property. It's not smart enough to spot that you're actually talking about the _x property of an instance called particle0_mc or whatever

We need to give it a helping hand, and this leads us straight on to our second crafty trick for the day: instead of writing...

```
"particle"+j+"_mc"._x = _xmouse;
```

we can put...

```
_root["particle"+j+"_mc"]._x = _xmouse;
```

The _root bit on the beginning tells Flash to look in the main (or 'root') timeline, and the stuff inside the square brackets [] tells it the name of the thing to look for. It's as if _root is an array whose elements hold things like movie clips, and use names instead of numbers. Once we've pulled out the element we want, we can use it as normal:

```
onEnterFrame = function() {
  j = 0;
  while (j < 10) {
    // move particle to mouse position
    _root["particle"+j+"_mc"]._x = _xmouse;
    _root["particle"+j+"_mc"]._y = _ymouse;
    j++;
  };
};
```

Now you'll find that all the duplicates follow your mouse pointer around, while the original sits still in the middle of the stage. Progress to be sure – but we're not done yet!

10. To finish things off, let's stagger the duplicate particles so that they form a blobby line between the original and the current mouse position. The original particle is centered on X:290, Y:190, so we start by working out the x and y differences between this point and the position of the mouse:

```
onEnterFrame = function() {
  // work out distances from center to mouse
  xDist = _xmouse - 290;
  yDist = _ymouse - 190;
```

Now, we're ready to move on to our loop, where we'll move each particle to X:290, Y:190 plus j tenths of the distance to the mouse:

```
  j = 0;
  while (j < 10) {
    // move particle to center plus j tenths of the distance
    _root["particle"+j+"_mc"]._x = 290 + (xDist * j/10);
    _root["particle"+j+"_mc"]._y = 190 + (yDist * j/10);
    j++;
  };
};
```

This means that particle0_mc will be in the same place as the original instance, while particle1_mc will be one tenth of the way to the mouse pointer. particle2_mc will then be two tenths of the way there, and so on, until we reach particle9_mc at nine tenths of the way to the pointer.

Test the movie again, and you'll see some fairly impressive results, even if we did need to do a little math to get them...

It's still not *quite* what we set out to achieve though! There's a big fat blob at one end (where particle0_mc sits on top of the original) and a conspicuous gap at the pointer itself, where we have no particle at all. This all boils down to that old 'counting from zero' business I mentioned before. This is one time where it would be much more useful if we could start counting from 1 (placing the first duplicate at one tenth of the distance) and finish at 10 (placing the last duplicate at ten tenths of the distance – smack bang on top of the pointer!)

11.   In fact, it turns out that nothing could be simpler. Both of our loops currently use `i++` (or `j++`) to bump up the loop counter at the end of each cycle. So what about changing the counter at the *start* of each loop instead? You'll need to change both loops, so here's the full script:

```
// set up particles
i = 0;
while (i < 10) {
  i++;
  // duplicate the particle_mc instance
  duplicateMovieClip(particle_mc, "particle"+i+"_mc", i);
};
onEnterFrame = function() {
  // work out distances from center to mouse
  xDist = _xmouse - 290;
  yDist = _ymouse - 190;

  j = 0;
  while (j < 10) {
    j++;
    // move particle to center plus j tenths of the distance
    _root["particle"+j+"_mc"]._x = 290 + (xDist * j/10);
    _root["particle"+j+"_mc"]._y = 190 + (yDist * j/10);
  };
};
```

Now we start each loop with a counter value of 0. The first thing we do is bump it up to 1, use that value to do stuff with `particle1_mc`, and then loop back. The counter's less than ten, so we run the loop actions again: bump the counter up to 2, use it to do stuff with `particle2_mc`, and then loop back again.

We keep doing that until the counter's 9. That's still less than 10, so we run the loop actions, which bump it up to 10, use it to do stuff with `particle10_mc`, and loop back again. Only now does the `while()` action wise up to the fact that its `counter<10` condition *isn't actually true any more*...!

Run the movie one last time, and you'll see a beautiful, homogenous line of particles stretching out from the middle of the stage to wherever your mouse pointer happens to be. Hey presto!

Now that we've seen a little of what you can do with a `while` loop or two, let's take a quick look at the other sorts of loop available in ActionScript. "Other sorts of loop?" I hear you cry... "Surely there can't be any *more* ways to send scripts running round in circles?" Well, no.... and yes.

Most of the loops we've looked at so far use a pretty standard system: set up a counter variable, add one to its value every cycle, and test each time whether it's gone above a certain value. This approach is *so* ubiquitous that there's a special action devoted to it...

for loops

Whenever you build a loop that uses some kind of counter variable to count how many cycles you've gone through, it's worth considering the humble `for` loop as an option. It doesn't actually add anything new to the possibilities offered by `while()`, but it lets you set things out in a way that brings all the counter-specific actions together on one line, neatens things up, and should help you to keep things nice and clear.

Let's consider a loop that we've already looked at:

```
myCounter = 0;
while (myCounter < 10) {
  trace(myCounter);
  myCounter++;
};
```

There are four important parts to this loop, one on each of the first four lines:

- initialize the counter variable `myCounter`

- specify the loop condition `myCounter<10`

- perform the main loop action `trace(myCounter)`

- bump up the value of the counter with `myCounter++`

If we rewrite this loop as a `for` loop, we can cut this down to two lines:

```
for (myCounter = 0; myCounter < 10; myCounter++) {
  trace(myCounter);
};
```

We've now defined the whole range of the loop within the first line, so there's no need to set up a counter before the loop, and no need to change its value as one of the looped actions. ActionScript takes care of all that for us.

Okay, you're probably not convinced yet. These `for` loops certainly don't lend themselves to useful explanations like 'while the counter's less than 10, perform the following actions', and they *will* take a bit of getting used to.

*The crucial thing to register is the fact that every factor that could possibly influence how many cycles this loop goes through is **specified in the** `for()` **action itself.** Since these factors are all in one place, you'll find it a lot easier to keep track of what the loop's doing when you come across it buried in a mountain of other stuff. Since you can see how many loops it needs to cycle through, it's less likely to give you a nasty surprise when you test your code. Also, you can easily modify a `for` loop so that it only cycles once – this can be tremendously useful while developing your code, since if you can see it working for a single loop, you can be confident that it will run for many cycles.*

Of course, we can still use the counter for all sorts of things other than simply counting how many times we've looped: as the index for an array or variable, or for deriving a sequence of numbers (such as a math times table; 5, 10, 15, 20, 25, and so on.)

Let's take a closer look at each of the three arguments we stick in the `for()` action.

init

The first argument is where you set up the counter variable. It's normal to set this to zero, though you're free to use any value you like. You can also name the counter as you wish. The total number of loops must always turn out to be a numeric variable, so valid start counter values are:

```
counter = 0         the counter starts at zero
i = startValue      the counter i starts at the value of numeric variable startValue
```

condition

This is just like the condition in an `if` statement or a `while` loop: as long as the expression evaluates to true, the loop will continue cycling. Inside a `for` loop though, the condition should always refer explicitly to the counter; normally in a form like 'counter is less than the stop value'. Valid examples are:

- `i < 10`   loop as long as i is less than ten.
- `counter >= 200`   loop as long as counter is greater than or equal to 200.
- `x < xMax`   loop as long as x is less than xMax.

In the last case though, it's important that you *don't let your loop actions change the value of* xMax – well, not unless you really know what you're doing (in which case you'll probably be using another kind of loop anyway!) Flash won't stop you doing this, but it will make your code very unpredictable, and may even result in a forever loop.

One condition that beginners often get stuck with is:

- `counter == 10`

Although this is okay as a condition, it's probably not what you want for a `for` loop – unless `counter` equals 10 on the first loop, it will stop the loop immediately, and not do anything at all.

next

This is where you specify what should happen to the counter after every loop. Possible things you can add here are:

- `i++`   add 1 to `i`.
- `counter--`   subtract 1 from `counter`.
- `i = i+2`   add 2 to `i`.

We've already encountered the `++` trick for adding one to the value of a variable; here's its partner in crime: `--` which takes one *off* the value. Anything else you want to do to the counter needs to be written out in full.

Some useful examples of for loops

If you want to see the following `for` loops in action, simply use the Actions panel to attach them to frame 1 of a new movie, and hit CTRL/CMD+ENTER to give the movie a test run. The Output window will then show you the `counter` value for each cycle (or iteration) of the loop.

Simple loop

This loop will count upwards from 0 to 12:

```
for (counter=0; counter <= 12; counter++) {
  trace (counter);
}
```

Reverse loop

This one will count down from 12 to 0:

```
for (counter=12; counter >=0 ; counter--) {
  trace (counter);
}
```

Two at a time

This will count upwards from 0 to 12 in steps of 2, and show the value of counter once the loop has terminated:

```
for (counter= 0; counter <= 12; counter = counter+2) {
  trace (counter);
}
trace (counter);
```

This demonstrates that the value of the counter just after the loop completes is *the first value that doesn't satisfy our condition. In this case, that's 2 more than the maximum value of 12: namely, 14.*

Looping through elements in an array

As we've now established, loops are pretty darned useful for making a lot of actions run in a very short space of time. In particular, `for` loops give us a very tidy way to cycle through lots of values with just a couple of lines of code. One particularly useful thing we can do with loops is using them to work with arrays.

Say you've written a set of actions that all act on element `i` of an array. By looping through all available values of `i`, you can quickly apply them to every element in the array. So, a small piece of code can be made to work on large amounts of data.

We already saw a simple example of how you can use a `while` loop to look at all the elements in an array – we even persuaded it to stop when the array ran out of defined elements! In fact, the combination of loops and arrays is *so* important that we're going to return to it now, and look at a few more of the things they let us do.

Applying an operation to all the elements in an array

Consider an array of two hundred values between 1 and 20, which we've stored in an array called `rawdata`. I'd like to create a corresponding list of percentage values in a second array called `percent`. The non-loopy way to do this (or should it be 'the *totally* loopy way'?) would be to write out two hundred lines of script like this:

```
percent[0]  = rawData[0]*5;
percent[1]  = rawData[1]*5;
percent[2]  = rawData[2]*5;
percent[3]  = rawData[3]*5;
...
percent[198] = rawData[198]*5;
percent[199] = rawData[199]*5;
```

The sensible way to do it would be to use a loop – and since we know how many elements there are, it makes sense to use a `for` loop. First, we need to work out a generalized action for our 'convert to percent' process.

That's not too hard: percent just means 'out of one hundred', and 1 in 20 is just the same as 5 in 100. So we just need to multiply all our numbers by five. Assuming we're using a counter variable called `i`, we can just say...

```
percent[i]  = rawData[i]*5;
```

Now we loop through all values of `i` from 0 to 199, applying it each time until you've converted the whole array:

```
for (i=0; i<200; i++) {
  percent[i] = rawData[i]*5;
}
```

What if we don't know how many elements there are in the array? We've already seen one way to deal with it using a `while` loop, which we *could* translate into `for`-style notation:

```
for (i=0; rawData[i]!=undefined; i++) {
  percent[i] = rawData[i]*5;
}
```

Hmm. Well Flash won't actually *stop* us doing this, but it still goes against everything we've just learnt about for loops. Sure, the loop condition still depends on i, but only very loosely; it depends a lot more on the contents of the rawData array, and it's not at all obvious how many times we expect to loop... This is one situation where things are best left to while loops!

On the other hand, if we had some way to ask the array directly how many elements it had, then we could still get away with a condition like i<lengthOfArray. Of course, there's just such a way: all arrays have a property called length, which tells you how many elements it contains. So it looks like our best bet is to use i<rawData.length like this:

```
for (i=0; i<rawData.length; i++) {
  percent[i] = rawData[i]*5;
}
```

> *The length property is common to all arrays, and tells us the number of elements they contain. This technique gives us a very simple way to put limits on all our array loops.*

Searching an array for a specific value

Another thing we can do using a combination of loops and arrays is to search through the elements in an array until we find a particular value. Say we have an array of book titles called myLibrary, and use a variable called searchString to hold the name of a book we're looking for. There are two ways we could approach this.

We could say:

```
searchString = "The Wasp Factory";
i = 0
while (library[i] != searchString && i < library.length) {
    i++
}
if (library[i]==searchString) {
    trace("Match found: item number " + i);
} else {
    result = "No matches found.";
}
```

We don't know in advance how many loops we're going to need before we find a match, so we set up a while loop. We then keep adding one to the value of i until library[i] matches our search string or we run out of array elements. We then use an if...else to check whether the loop ended because a match had been found (in which case we trace out the relevant element number) or because it got to the end of the array without finding any matches at all (in which case we say just that).

On the other hand, we might want to do it like this:

```
searchString = "The Wasp Factory";
matchesFound = 0;
for (i = 0; i < library.length; i++) {
    if (library[i] == searchString) {
        trace("Match found: item number " + i);
        matchesFound++
    }
}
trace("Number of matches found: " + matchesFound);
```

This time, we assume that we're going to search the whole library, on the basis that there may be more than one copy of the book we're looking for. We therefore use a for loop which cycles as many times as there are elements in the array (thanks, once again, to the length property). Every time around, the if statement will check whether there's a match with the search string. If there is, we trace out details of the match, and bump up the number of matchesFound. Once the whole array has been searched, we trace out the total matchesFound value.

Cross-indexing a pair of arrays

Once we've figured out how to search an array, we're only one step away from cross-indexing with another array. Let's consider two arrays, each containing a list of plant names: each element in the first contains the common name of a plant, while the corresponding element in the other holds the Latin name of the same plant. They might look like this:

```
commonNames = new Array("foxglove", "palm tree", "rose",
                   ➡ "Californian poppy", "witch hazel")
latinNames = new Array("digitalis", "trachycarpus", "rosa",
                   ➡ "Escholzia californica", "hammamelis mollis")
```

What if we know the common name of a particular plant, but want to find out what its Latin name is. We might ask the question, 'what is the Latin name for the Californian poppy?' We just need a loop that will cycle through elements in the commonNames array until it finds one that contains the string "Californian poppy". It could then use the successful index value (in this case 3) to call up the corresponding element from the latinNames array and find the answer: "Escholzia californica".

Here's how you might do it:

```
offset = 0;
search = "Californian poppy";
while (commonNames[offset] != search && offset < commonNames.length) {
    offset++;
}
if (commonNames[offset] == search) {
    trace("Match found: " + latinNames[offset]);
} else {
    result = "No matches found.";
}
```

In this case, we don't necessarily want to search on every element – we'll stop just as soon as we've found a match. Since we can't know in advance how many elements we'll need to search on, a `for` loop isn't suitable, so we use a `while` structure. As before, it loops around incrementing our `offset` variable for as long as (a) the element `commonNames[offset]` doesn't match our search term, and (b) `offset` is less than the array length.

So, when the `while` loop finishes, it could be for one of two reasons: either we've found a match or we've reached the end of the array and found none. This method – finding an index and applying it to another related array – is known as **cross-indexing**.

Now that you've seen a few theoretical examples of combining loops with arrays, it's time to put your newfound skills to work. We're going to use Flash and ActionScript to create a game of 'Hangman', using arrays and loops together with more than a little string variable manipulation.

As ever, a nice practical example should help lift the whole thing right off the page!

Hangman

It's an old game that's been around for centuries. Pick a word at random, write it out using blanks in place of each letter, and challenge a friend to guess what it is by picking letters from the alphabet. If they choose a letter that's in the word, you show them where it is in the word by filling in a blank. If they pick one that isn't, you add pieces to a drawing of a scaffold. After five or six wrong guesses, the scaffold is complete, and you start adding a figure hanging from the gibbet. After about ten wrong guesses, the figure is complete – HANGMAN! The only way for your friend to win is by guessing all the letters in the word before they're hanged.

Hangman is a brutal game when you think about it, and there's no hiding the fact that it's a game about someone getting hanged. All the fluffy bunnies in the world aren't going to soften the blow, but I've decided all the same to get my own version looking like it was all drawn and painted by a child.

Let's start with a quick walkthrough, to give us an idea of how the gaming experience should pan out for our players:

1.   When we start the movie, we'll see the following scene:

An empty field on a sunny day, with a title, a solitary flower and play game button, which we can press to start the game.

2. Once we press the button and the game starts, we're presented with a simple interface: a box for typing in our guesses, an enter button to submit them, and a list of question marks indicating how many letters there are in the word we have to guess:

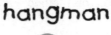

???? ?

guess a letter: [   ] enter

3. The next step is to type in a letter and hit the enter button. Let's say our mystery word is 'flash' and I've just tried the letter 'a'. This is what I should see:

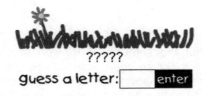

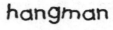

??a??

guess a letter: [   ] *enter*

There's one 'a' in the word 'flash', so Flash replaces the relevant question mark with the letter itself.

4. Say we now try a few more letters, such as 'u', 'x', 'q', and 'z'. Okay, let's just say we're being deliberately dumb here... None of these letters occur in the word 'flash', so they're all bad guesses – so we have to pay the price:

Four wrong letters, so four sections of the gallows appear... If we don't start making some decent guesses soon, we'll be hung out to dry! As you can see from the screenshot, I'm just about to guess the letter 'g'. I haven't pressed enter yet, so all is not lost...

5. Let's assume I now replace the 'g' with an 'f', hit enter, and suddenly realize what the word is. Follow it up with 'l', 's', and 'h', and the word is complete. This is what I should now see:

The gallows vanish, and our would-be victim is now free to wander through the sunlit fields with a big red flower in his hand. How sweet.

6. However, there's an alternate reality in which I didn't recant my faith in the letter 'g'. I left a 'g' in the input box and hit enter! With no clue to what the word could be, I floundered around with such desperate guesses as 'm', 'n', 'o', 'p', and 'q'... Yes, I was so desperate (and forgetful) that I tried 'q' again! By that time though, there was no hope:

Our hero meets a grisly end, and the only solace to be found is in the little button that reappears behind the gallows, hinting that we can actually have another go.

Well, that's the game – and I did warn you things might get a little unpleasant! Now that we've got a good idea of how the game 'hangs' together, let's start looking at how we can build it in Flash.

> *If you're in a rush and don't want to create all these graphics from scratch, you can find them all in this chapter's download, in the library of a file called* hangman_start.fla. *In case you're wondering, the font I've used throughout is called "kids".*

We'll start by breaking it down into symbols that we need in the library. I've used four graphics (called flower, grass, sun, and title – no prizes for guessing what they all are...), plus two buttons (enter and play) and put all the 'hanging' material and interface stuff into a couple of movie clips (called hanging man and interface).

There's nothing terribly special about the buttons (one's a black box behind a bit of static text that says 'enter', the other's just a bit of text that says 'play game' – select and press F8 to convert them to symbols and you're done), and the graphics should be self-explanatory (the sun's an orangey circle, the title says 'hangman', and so on – select and hit F8 again... I'm sure you get the idea) so I'll skip straight on to how we build the two movie clips!

The 'hanging man' movie clip

This is where we pull together our scenery, and animate the awful process of a hanging...

1. First, we need to create a total of four layers, which you should call labels, flower, hangman, and background:

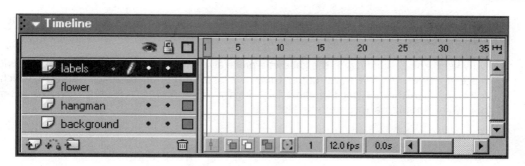

2. Select the background layer, and pull some sun and grass onto it from the library:

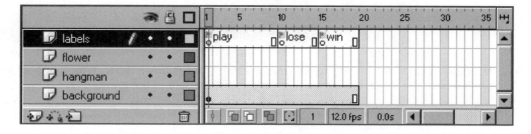

    Select frame 19 and press F5 to insert a frame. We want this scenery on display throughout the clip.

3. Now select frame 1 on the labels layer, and press F6 to insert a keyframe. Press F5 to insert a frame at 19, and F6 to add keyframes at 10 and 15. Use the Property inspector to label your three keyframes as play, lose, and win respectively. Your timeline should now look like this:

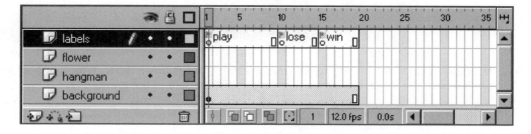

4. Now for the creative part... we're going to add the frame-by-frame animation of the gallows and hanging man. Select frame 1 of the hangman layer and use F6 to insert a keyframe. Select frame 19, and press F5 to insert a normal frame. It should now look like an albino version of the background timeline.

    Select frame 2, hit F6 to add a keyframe, and draw a horizontal brown line along the top of the grass. Select frame 3, hit F6 to add a keyframe, and add a vertical brown line at the right-hand end.

Select frame 4, hit F6 to add a keyframe, and add a diagonal brown line connecting the two lines you just drew.

Now keep going, building up the gallows a piece at a time, and then adding our hapless victim (one piece at a time – no, I've never understood that bit either) until you reach frame 10, which is where folks go when they've lost the game Each keyframe represents one step closer to doom! By this point, you should have something like this:

I've also added in some text here, just to emphasize the fact that our tale is over...

5.   Of course, if our player has won the game, we need to reward their efforts and give them a nice uplifting image. Select frame 15, and hit F6 to add a keyframe. You can delete the gallows from this frame, and replace them with something happier:

6.   Now for a nice little finishing touch. Select frame 1 of the flower layer, drag a copy of the flower symbol onto the stage, and nestle it down somewhere safe in the grass:

Now add a keyframe at frame 15, and drag the flower across so that it looks as if it's being held in our hero's hand:

Select frame 19 and press F5 to insert a frame.

Phew! After all that hard work, your 'hanging man' timeline should be looking like this:

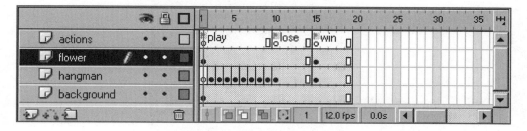

Aren't you glad I didn't show you that before we started? Now that we've dealt with the aesthetics of our game, let's take a look at the user interface.

The 'interface' movie clip

You'll be glad to hear that this movie clip's a great deal simpler than the last one! There's one layer, one keyframe, and no fancy graphics to labor over. In fact, the following image sums it up quite well:

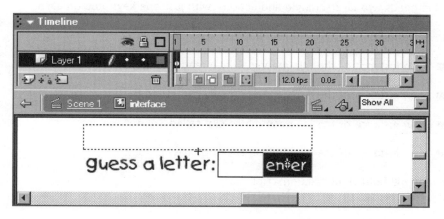

There are just four things on the stage:

- A dynamic text field called `display_txt` at the top (for which Var is set to `display`)

- A static text field on the left, reading 'guess a letter'

- An input text field called `input_txt` (for which Var is set to `input`)

- An instance of the enter button, which I've called `enter_btn`

We only want the player to enter lower case characters, so select the input text field and hit the Character button on the Property inspector. In the Character Options dialog, check the boxes for Only and Lowercase Letters (a-z), and press Done to confirm.

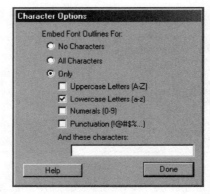

Once you've created each of these and set them up on the stage as described, you're all done. Now we're ready to take a look at the main timeline, arrange our movie clips, and wire them all up with a little ActionScript...

The main movie timeline

This timeline needs two layers, movie and actions, with just one keyframe on each:

- movie contains...

    - an instance of the title graphic, which reads 'hangman'

    - an instance of the hanging man movie clip called `hangman_mc`

    - an instance of the interface movie clip called `interface_mc`

    - an instance of the play button called `playGame_btn`

- actions will hold all our ActionScript

Here's how the stage should look once everything's in place:

Well, we've got all the pictures in place – how about a little code? Now the code for this game might look a little hairy at times, but don't panic! Nothing we do here will be hideously complicated; if it all starts to look like a mess of brackets and semicolons swimming about in front of your eyes (yes, that sometimes happens to me too) just take it one line at a time. Look for the structures you understand and think how they're being used to form the game we described earlier on.

Adding in the ActionScript

Select frame 1 on the actions layer, open up the Actions panel, click down that pin button, and get ready to wire everything together. Although there are lots of actions for us to put in over the next couple of pages, they all need to be attached to the same frame. What's more, they break down into three neat pieces:

- Movie setup – actions to run when the movie starts

- Game setup – actions to run when we click play game to start the game

- Game play – actions to run when we click on enter to submit a guessed letter

Let's get stuck in!

1. The first chunk of code we need to add will set our movie up when it starts running. We begin by creating three arrays:

```
// initialize array of words
wordList = new Array("computer", "apple", "coffee", "flash",
                ➥ "animal", "america", "panel", "window",
                ➥ "import", "number", "string", "cake",
                ➥ "object", "movie", "aardvark", "kettle");
// initialize arrays for letters
```

```
lettersNeeded = new Array(10);
lettersGuessed = new Array(10);
```

The first of these lists all the words we're going to choose from. If you want to, you can add more by simply sticking them on the end of the list. Words must be in lower case letters (since that's all we'll allow the user to enter) and can have up to ten letters, but no more.

This is simply because the two other arrays we define here are only big enough to hold ten characters. Remember that zero is counted as the first element, so asking for ten elements will give you elements numbered from 0 to 9.

We're going to be using the elements of `lettersNeeded` to store letters from our mystery word, while `lettersGuessed` array elements will hold a mixture of question marks and letters that the player has guessed correctly – these are the letters we'll show them while they're playing the game.

2. We then have to stop the main timeline, stop the `hangman_mc` timeline, and hide the game interface:

```
stop();
hangman_mc.stop();
interface_mc._visible = false;
```

Now that we've set up the movie with arrays and stopped timelines, it's time we laid down some actions that will get us ready for a game.

3. When the player presses the play game button, there are several commands we need to give Flash before we can let them start guessing letters. We can put these into an event handler for the `onRelease` event of the `playGame_btn` instance. It'll start out like this:

```
playGame_btn.onRelease = function() {
    hangman_mc.gotoAndStop("play");
    playGame_btn._visible = false;
    interface_mc._visible = true;
```

First, we initialize the hangman movie clip, sending its play head to the first frame. In fact, at this point in the game, it's probably there already – but we'll want to run these actions again when we set things up for a rematch, so this is an important thing to do.

We then make the play game button invisible (since we don't need it now) and make the game interface visible; we're certainly going to need that!

4. Next up in the event handler, we select a word at random from the `wordList` array:

```
randomNumber = Math.round(Math.random()*(wordList.length-1));
selectedWord = wordList[randomNumber];
```

At first glance, you may think the first line looks pretty terrifying. All it actually does is pick a random whole number between 0 and `wordList.length-1`, and store it in a variable called `randomNumber`.

We then use that number to specify one of the elements in the `wordList` array, and pull out the word it contains, and store this randomly selected word in `selectedWord`.

5. The next step is to set up a variable that's going to help us keep track of how many more letters the player still has to guess. At this stage, they've guessed none, so this is just the number of letters in the word:

```
lettersLeftToGo = selectedWord.length;
```

6. Now it's time to break our word down into a list of letters. As I mentioned before, the `lettersNeeded` array is going to store all the letters our player has to guess. We set this up using a `for` loop, and cycle through each letter in the word, putting it into the corresponding element in the array:

```
for (i=0; i<selectedWord.length; i++) {
    lettersNeeded[i] = selectedWord.charAt(i);
}
```

The `charAt(i)` bit at the end of the second line is new, but all it actually means is 'get the character at position i' of the `selectedWord` variable it's stuck on the end of.

7. We do a similar thing for the `lettersGuessed` array, but fill every slot with a question mark — only fair, since the player hasn't guessed any letters yet!

```
for (i=0; i<selectedWord.length; i++) {
    lettersGuessed[i] = "?";
}
// initialize display of lettersGuessed by player
interface_mc.display = lettersGuessed.join("");
};
```

The last line here, just before we finish off the event handler, uses another new trick to join together all the element values in `lettersGuessed`. We send the result (which will be a long string of question marks) to `interface_mc.display`; that is, the variable called `display` from the `interface_mc` movie clip, whose value gets shown in the dynamic text field.

Phew! Let's stop for a moment and take a quick breather. That's a lot of script, and a fair few new tricks along the way. Try running the movie now, and press the play game button. Sure enough, the button vanishes, the interface appears, and a string of question marks appears just below the grass:

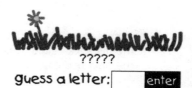

Now select Debug > Show Variables, and you can check out the contents of all our arrays:

```
Output                                                              [x]
                                                          Options
     12:"object",
     13:"movie",
     14:"aardvark",
     15:"kettle"
  ]
Variable _level0.lettersNeeded = [object #2, class 'Array'] [
     0:"a",
     1:"p",
     2:"p",
     3:"l",
     4:"e"
  ]
Variable _level0.lettersGuessed = [object #3, class 'Array'] [
     0:"?",
     1:"?",
     2:"?",
     3:"?",
     4:"?"
  ]
Variable _level0.selectedWord = "apple"
Variable _level0.lettersLeftToGo = 5
Variable _level0.i = 5
Movie Clip: Target="_level0.hangman_mc"
Movie Clip: Target="_level0.interface_mc"
```

> *As well as helping to reassure you that things are going to plan, this should also serve as a reminder that the information you store inside a Flash movie isn't that hard to pull out again. Sure, once you've compiled a SWF and set it loose in the outside world, it won't be quite this easy to peer inside for a quick peek at what's going on; but it's certainly not impossible. Anyone with a bit of tech-savvy and enough perseverance can figure out exactly what words you've got stored in* wordList *and cheat you out of a victory... You have been warned!*

That aside, we've got a game to finish off, and an enter button to wire up. Let's get to it!

8. The enter button (instance name enter_btn) is actually *inside* the movie clip instance called interface_mc, so we need to set up our callback like this:

```
interface_mc.enter_btn.onRelease = function() {
```

Suffice to say, interface_mc.enter_btn just means 'the instance called enter_btn that's *inside* the instance called interface_mc'. We'll learn a lot more about these dot-based shenanigans in the next few chapters; so don't let this oddity put you off just yet.

9. The first thing Flash has to do once the player hits enter is to assume that they've guessed wrong:

    ```
    wrong = true;
    ```

    Now we just loop through all the letters in the word (as stored in the lettersNeeded array) and change this value as soon as we find a match with the input text field in interface_mc:

    ```
    for (i=0; i<selectedWord.length; i++) {
        foundLetter = lettersNeeded[i] == interface_mc.input;
        if (foundLetter) {
            // guess matches a letter in the word
            wrong = false;
            lettersLeftToGo--;
            lettersGuessed[i] = interface_mc.input;
        }
        interface_mc.display = lettersGuessed.join("");
    }
    ```

    The variable foundletter gets its value from the expression lettersNeeded[i] == interface_mc.input, which will always be Boolean. It will only be true if the letter our player just entered is the same as the letter in element i of the lettersNeeded array.

    We also bump down the number of letters left to guess, change the appropriate question mark in the lettersGuessed array so that it shows the correct letter, and use join() again to update the display.

    Hang on a minute though! What if we picked the same letter more than once? If it matched the first time, it would match again, and again; lettersLeftToGo would hit zero before very long, suggesting that we'd won the game. It looks like we need to be a little more picky with the condition in our if statement.

10. Make the following highlighted additions to the for loop we just wrote:

    ```
    for (i=0; i<selectedWord.length; i++) {
        foundLetter = lettersNeeded[i] == interface_mc.input;
        notGuessed = lettersGuessed[i] != interface_mc.input;
        if (foundLetter && notGuessed) {
            // guess matches a letter we haven't already found
            wrong = false;
            lettersLeftToGo--;
            lettersGuessed[i] = interface_mc.input;
        }
        interface_mc.display = lettersGuessed.join("");
    }
    ```

    Now we check that our player's input is *not* the same as element number i in the array lettersGuessed. Now, if foundLetter and notGuessed are *both* true, we know we've got a brand new correct guess!

133

11. Next, we empty out the input box, so that it's all ready for our player to have another go:

```
interface_mc.input = "";          // reset input text box
```

12. If the player's guess was no good (or they were foolish enough to guess at a letter they'd already got) the variable wrong will still have a Boolean value of true, in which case the next few lines kick in:

```
if (wrong) {
    hangman_mc.nextFrame();
    if (hangman_mc._currentFrame == 10) {
        // GAME OVER!!
        interface_mc._visible = false;
        playGame_btn._visible = true;
    }
}
```

First, we use nextFrame() to bump the hangman_mc play head onto the next frame. We then check whether that happens to be frame 10, also known as HANGMAN!

If it is, we run the 'Game Lost' actions: these just hide the interface and show the play game button (so the player can play the game again if they feel the need). If it's not frame 10, we don't need to show anything here.

13. Last bit now! We just need to test whether all the letters have been guessed correctly. If they have, the value of lettersLeftToGo should be down to 0. We use this fact to control whether or not the 'Game Won' actions should be run:

```
if (lettersLeftToGo == 0) {
    // GAME WON!!
    hangman_mc.gotoAndStop("win");
    interface_mc._visible = false;
    playGame_btn._visible = true;
}
};
```

These simply send hangman_mc to the win frame (where we get to see our hero holding a flower and smiling in gratitude), hide the interface, and show the play game button.

Now we're all done, you can sit back and relax – and maybe have a quick game! Of course, the tension won't be quite so high now that you've seen the full list of words our movie gets to choose from. All the same though, it's nice to see that all this script will actually *do* something.

Summary

In the course of this chapter, we've looked at three different ways to make something loop in Flash:

- Timeline loops using the `gotoAndPlay()` action

- ActionScript loops using the `while()` action

- ActionScript loops using the `for()` action

That's not to say there are no other looping actions: there's **do...while**, which is almost exactly the same as `while`, except that it tests its condition *after* running the loop actions each time; there's also **for...in**, which we can use to loop through all the elements in an array, or all the instances in a timeline. When all's said and done though, they don't really offer much beyond what we've already achieved. As we've seen, even `for` loops are really just a specialized version of your basic `while` loop; just a particularly useful one! I haven't set out to try and be comprehensive here, since the three we've covered should do for most of your needs. The only question is when you should use which one.

Here are some simple rules of thumb for deciding when (and when not) to use an ActionScript loop or a timeline loop:

- If you want Flash to perform an action (or set of actions) many times over in the shortest possible period of time, you should use an ActionScript loop. Every cycle of the loop is attached to one frame, so (unless you run over 200,000 cycles, when Flash starts getting a little nervous) they'll always complete before you move on to the next frame.

- If you want to make something move gradually across the stage, you're best off using a timeline loop to nudge it by a few pixels for each frame. An ActionScript loop will work its magic much, much faster, so all you're likely to see would be the start and end points.

If you've settled on an ActionScript loop, picking between `while` and `for` loops is fairly simple:

- If the values you use to define the looping behavior are all known in advance, then it's best to use a `for` loop. Otherwise, a `while` loop will almost always do the trick.

This chapter has had the biggest variety of examples so far, because the full range of your ActionScript skills you've been learning is really starting to come together. You've learned some important new techniques, and even more important, you've seen large sections of ActionScript working together in a finished application.

Don't worry if you've only skimmed though this. The important thing is that a standard has been set in your mind, and you've probably picked up a lot of useful little snippets without even realizing it. That's what coding is all about. You're probably looking at all the long pieces of code and saying 'Why has he done that? Why didn't he do it this way?' The proof is when you start doing your own programs and recognize things you're trying to do in terms of the programs I've listed here.

Each of the last three chapters has been an important step forward; building up the range of things you can do once you start throwing information around behind the scenes of your movies. Now that you've seen how to work with variables, arrays, decision-making, and looping, you should be getting a very good idea of just how much a few lines of ActionScript can add to your Flash movies.

You're not even halfway through the book yet, and you're already moving away from the level of 'novice' ActionScripter. In the next few chapters, we're going to look at some more ways of bundling together actions and information, and start thinking about how our scripts are structured. You may already feel confident enough to wire the odd snippet of ActionScript into your own projects; if so, that's great! Soon enough though, you'll be all set to start taking on some full-sized challenges.

Movies that remember how to do things

What we'll cover in this chapter:

- *Introducing functions as containers for storing actions*

- *Breaking tasks down into subtasks and using functions to structure your code*

- *Using callbacks to set up functions*

- *Using functions to recycle blocks of script*

- *Using arguments and returning results*

As we've seen, the ability to handle information in your movies opens up a lot of possibilities. A few chapters back, we introduced variables as containers for data, whether that data's in the form of a string, a number, or a 'true or false' Boolean value. We also looked at arrays, which let us store lots of variables under a single name.

Variables and arrays help us to store and organize our data – but data's only half the deal when it comes to writing scripts: what about actions? Literally anything we do with ActionScript is going to involve at least one action (or command), giving Flash an explicit instruction to **do** something or other. That's the whole point of ActionScript – of course, that's why it's called *Action*Script in the first place!

This is where functions come in. Say you have a sequence of actions you need to use at several different points in a movie: rather than writing it out in full each time, you can just write a function declaration that contains these actions, and call out for that function whenever you want them to run. You just need to give Flash the name of the function; it will track down the function definition for you and make sure it runs everything inside.

> *In many ways, a function does for actions what a variable does for data: it acts as a container for things we want to re-use later in the movie.*

This turns out to be very useful for organizing your scripts too. Functions let you wrap whole blocks of script into an easy-to-handle lump, and if you pick those script blocks wisely, you'll ensure that each one focuses on one specific **subtask**.

Breaking down the task

Think about the whole business of writing a script in everyday terms: whatever you happen to be working on, you're essentially trying to break one complex task down into several simpler ones.

When you go shopping, there are lots of actions you'll perform as part of the overall task: walk to the store, find the items you want to buy, take them to the checkout, find out how much they cost, hand over a sum of money, receive change (hopefully!), leave the store, and walk home again.

This is all so obvious that you barely need to think about it: if someone asks you to fetch something from the store, you already know what that's likely to entail. Of course, they'll need to tell you what they want, and possibly which store they want it from, but the basics of 'go shopping' are already there.

Most of the examples we've looked at so far have involved taking an overall task and breaking it straight down to the level of individual actions. This works well for the small programs we've been dealing with so far, but once they start to grow in size, things can quickly turn nasty! As I'm about to demonstrate, functions give us an opportunity to break down our overall movie mission into tasks and subtasks just as quickly or slowly as we want to.

So, there are two very good reasons for using functions to wrap up your code into blocks:

- **re-usability** – you can use each block over and over again with the minimum of fuss

- **structure** – you can break up huge reams of code into easily identifiable sections

Now you know why functions are a good thing, let's look at how we can actually use them.

Bundling together actions and running them afterwards

Working with functions really isn't hard at all, especially in light of what we've already done since the beginning of this book. There are really only two steps involved:

1. **declare** the function, giving it a name and telling it what actions to perform
2. **call** the function, telling Flash to summon it up and run those actions

Say we were writing a monster attack game, and wanted a function called 'hideAllMonsters' that would make all the monsters invisible in one fell swoop. It will probably contain a loop that cycles through all relevant values of counter variable i, making monster number i invisible each time around. Here's what the function definition might look like:

```
hideAllMonsters = function() {
    for(i=0 ; i<numberOfMonsters ; i++) {
        _root["monster"+i+"_mc"]._visible = false;
    }
};
```

> When it comes to picking a good name for a function, the issues are similar to those we looked at for naming variables: make it something relevant and recognizable, and take care not to use one of Flash's reserved words.

Of course, this should look very familiar: we're defining our function by writing a **callback**, just as we've done in the past for all our event handlers. In fact, this isn't the only way to define a function, but this is easily the most flexible approach, and what's more, it's one you've already seen! Let's take a quick look at the other way though, just so you can see how they differ:

```
function hideAllMonsters() {
    // actions here
};
```

This is the way that Flash 5 ActionScripters will most often write a function: it's just using an action called function, followed by the name of the function being declared and the usual sausage-like arrangement of brackets, where we write out the actions that make up the function body.

We're doing largely the same thing when we write a callback. The big difference is that we don't tell the function action what name to use – for that reason, we call it an **anonymous function**. Instead, we use = to store this nameless function in a container called hideAllMonsters. This container can be *anywhere* in the movie (and not just in the current timeline, which is where the old-style function will always be stuck). This is why callbacks are perfect for defining event handlers like this:

```
monster1_mc.onEnterFrame = function() {
    // actions for attacking Tokyo
};
```

So what about *using* these function-thingies then? Simple. Use them just as if they were actions. Here's how we might call our monster-hiding function from elsewhere in the script:

```
if (mutantInvisibilityRayIsActive) {
    hideAllMonsters();
};
```

You can think of a function as being like your own custom action, one that's totally exclusive to your movie!

Using functions to hide away evil math

Let's start with a very simple example. Say you're writing a Flash movie that has to perform an evil bit of math on a variable called myVariable. It's not nice, but it's sometimes necessary to get the jaw-dropping effects you're after. Okay, we'll hold back on the *really* evil math for now, and just do something like 'add 5 and double'. That seems simple enough; you're probably already thinking of something along the lines of:

```
myVariable = 4;          //input number
myVariable += 5;         //add five
myVariable *= 2;         //double it
trace(myVariable);       //show the result on the screen
```

Well that's easy enough; but what if you need to do exactly the same thing another twenty times in various places throughout your movie? Of course you could just type out the same code over and over again, but this will quickly get to be a real drag – especially if your calculation runs to more than a couple of simple expressions and you wind up having to type out seven or eight lines every time!

This is the perfect time to use a function, so let's fix one up. First, we need to write a declaration:

```
notSoEvilMath = function() {
    myVariable += 5;
    myVariable *= 2;
};
```

There we are; we've now created a simple function to take myVariable, add five, and double it. Now we can use a notSoEvilMath() function call in place of our original math:

```
myVariable = 4;          //input number
notSoEvilMath();         //add five and double its value
trace(myVariable);       //show the result on the screen
```

Create a new Flash movie and attach these two little chunks of script to the first frame. Make sure they're in the same order as I've shown them.

> *It's very important to always write a function declaration **before** you call it; otherwise Flash won't understand the function call and will just ignore it. This is why it's a good idea to declare all your functions near the beginning of the first frame, before you write any script that needs to call them.*

Run it, and you should see the Output window pop up with the answer:

There you are, a simple function declaration and function call.

Okay, you may be thinking it looked easier to do it the old way; don't forget though, your functions will often be much more complicated than one simple expression!

There's another benefit to using functions here: say you suddenly find you need to alter the code so that it triples the input instead of doubling it. If you'd done it ten times the long-handed way, you would need to change ten different lines of script. With the function, you only need to change one character on one line:

```
notSoEvilMath = function() {
    myVariable += 5;
    myVariable *= 3;
};
```

Every time it's called now, `notSoEvilMath()` will add five and *triple* the value of `myVariable`, just as if that was what it had always done:

Functions are one of those things that once you've used them a few times, you can't imagine how you ever managed without them! Of course, their usefulness becomes more obvious when you're using them for something practical, and when you're using them several times in one movie. Let's look at another situation where functions can help us out...

Using functions to take care of repetitive jobs

Think back to the Hangman game we put together at the end of the last chapter, and the faculty records movie we made in the one before that. In both cases, we used _visible to make buttons appear and disappear when we wanted. This is a very powerful way to control what's seen on the stage in Flash MX, and you'll often find it being used to substitute one button (or movie clip) for another.

For example, the Hangman movie had a 'play game' button and an 'interface' movie clip. We only ever wanted one of them on the screen at any particular time: we needed the interface while we were playing the game, and we needed the button while we weren't. That meant saying...

```
playGame_btn._visible = false;
interface_mc._visible = true;
```

...at one point in the script, and...

```
playGame_btn._visible = true;
interface_mc._visible = false;
```

...a little later on. If you're very keen-eyed, you'll have already spotted that these two bits of script are almost identical. The only difference boils down to which instance gets shown, and which one gets hidden. In fact, even this isn't much of a difference: in both cases, the visible one gets hidden, while the invisible one gets unhidden... We can write this out in script as follows:

```
playGame_btn._visible = !playGame_btn._visible;
interface_mc._visible = !interface_mc._visible;
```

The ! sign is called a NOT operator, and shows us the opposite Boolean value of whatever comes straight after it. If playGame_btn._visible is false, !playGame_btn._visible must be true, and vice versa. In effect, both lines of code now say:

```
if it's hidden, show it - if it's showing, hide it
```

...with one doing that for each instance. We now have a script that can be reused whenever we need to swap these two instances over, so let's make it into a function:

```
swap = function() {
    playGame_btn._visible = !playGame_btn._visible;
    interface_mc._visible = !interface_mc._visible;
};
```

Once you've added this declaration to your hangman script, you can replace each of the false/true pairs with a quick and simple call to the new swap() function:

```
// define callback for release of 'play game' button
playGame_btn.onRelease = function() {
    hangman_mc.gotoAndStop("play");   // initialize hangman movie clip
    swap();             // hide 'play game' button and show game interface
```

```
        ...
    };
    interface_mc.enter_btn.onRelease = function() {
        wrong = true;
        ...
        if (wrong) {
            hangman_mc.nextFrame();
            if (hangman_mc._currentFrame == 10) {
                // GAME OVER!!
                swap();
            }
        }
        if (lettersLeftToGo == 0) {
            // GAME WON!!
            hangman_mc.gotoAndStop("win");
            swap();
        }
    };
```

We've only used it three times, but it's already making the script shorter and easier to follow. Think how much more of a difference it would make if we had ten or twenty swaps to do...!

Note that in this case, you can get away with declaring the swap() function at the end of your script. This is because the only sections of script that ever call it are tucked away inside event handlers, so they won't be run until the user presses one of the buttons on the stage. By that time, all the script on frame 1 should have run, so Flash will know all about your function and what to do about lines that just say swap().

Choosing which actions to bundle together where

Say we want a script that tells our movie to go shopping ten times in a row. In the past, we'd write a loop (probably a for loop, since we know it needs to cycle ten times) containing all the actions involved in 'going shopping'. If there are only two of three of these actions, that's probably fine as it is; but what if there are two or three *hundred*? Don't laugh! It's quite possible...

Sure, we can still pop them all inside the for loop, but it'll make our script a real pain to follow. Another option is to define a function called 'goShopping', which contains all the same actions. The loop that calls it ten times over will then look like this:

```
for(i=0; i<10; i++) {
    goShopping();
};
```

That simplifies things here, but what about in the function declaration? Oh no.... now *that's* going to go on for six or seven pages, and we've got the same problem of readability we had before!

Actually, we've already worked out a way round this particular problem. A 'go shopping' task is too big and complex, so we break it down into subtasks. What about this?

```
for(i=0; i<10; i++) {
    walkToStore();
    findItems();
    walkToCheckout();
    findCost();
    payForGoods();
    checkChange();
    walkHome();
};
```

Of course, we'd have to work out how all these other functions work and declare them as well, but each one will be *much* smaller than the goShopping() declaration would have been.

Making multi-talented functions

Another thing we can spot here is **redundancy**: that is, three of these functions are doing almost exactly the same thing! The only difference between walkToStore(), walkToCheckout(), and walkHome() is the destination they send our imaginary customer walking off to. So, is there anything we can do about this? Of course there is!

We've already seen that some actions (gotoAndPlay() for example) will let us feed in arguments between the brackets that influence how they're carried out by Flash. Well, we can do exactly the same thing with functions.

Say we set up a general function called walk(), which let us feed in a string argument that told it where we want to walk to. In a very simple movie (no, don't worry; I'm not planning to drag you through the 300-line version!), we might declare it like this:

```
walk = function(destination) {
    var destination;
    gotoAndStop(destination);
};
```

The main difference between this and the other functions we've declared is the fact that we've stuck a variable called destination between the brackets following function – this variable is called a **function parameter**. We use it to store the value of the argument with which the function was called. We've also used the keyword var to tell Flash that destination should be treated as a **local variable**.

Confused yet? Let's take a step or two back and think about what happens when we call the walk() function.

Say we write a line of script like this, which calls the walk() function using the argument "home":

```
walk("home");
```

Flash sees this, and since it doesn't recognize walk() as an ActionScript action, it hunts around for a function called 'walk'. It finds the declaration we wrote and spots that there's one parameter in there, which is a variable called destination. Currently, destination has no value, but that doesn't last long:

Flash now takes the argument value "home" and stores it in `destination`, ready for the following actions to make use of it.

The keyword `var` lets Flash know that we only want to use the `destination` variable while we're inside this function. Outside the function called 'walk', it simply won't exist. This is actually a very sensible thing to do: say we add another function called `run()`, and want to use `destination` as the name of the parameter in *that* function as well. As long as we use `var` there as well, the two variables can quite happily take the same name without conflicting with one another.

> *Since arguments and parameters always go together, it's easy to get one confused with the other. It's worth remembering that they're quite separate: an argument is part of a specific function call and exists outside the function. The corresponding parameter is part of the function itself and (assuming it's defined there as a local variable, which it almost always should be) doesn't exist anywhere else.*

Parameters really open up the possibilities of what a function can do, and can help to turn a simple bundle of actions into a truly powerful mechanism in your script.

Now we can write our script like this:

```
for(i=0; i<10; i++) {
    walk("store");
    findItems();
    walk("checkout");
    findCost();
    payForGoods();
    checkChange();
    walk("home");
};
```

Later on, if I wanted to make the 'walking' part of this movie any more complex, I'd just need to change the declaration. I wouldn't need to do anything to the three calls inside `goShopping()`, since they just tell Flash to 'use this string to do whatever actions are in the `walk()` function'.

Returning values from a function

Earlier on, we created a `notSoEvilMath()` function, which quite happily changed the value of `myVariable`, but was pretty useless when it came to any other variables. Say we wanted to do the same math on variables like `alienHeight` or `bulletSpeed`...

Well, what about using an argument to tell the function which variable it needs to work its magic on? We could redefine the function like this:

```
notSoEvilMath = function(localVariable) {
    var localVariable;
    localVariable += 5;
    localVariable *= 2;
};
```

...and call it from our script like this:

```
notSoEvilMath(alienHeight);
```

There's just one problem with this. We're not actually passing the `alienHeight` variable into the function – *only its value*. Inside the function, we can do whatever we like to the **value**, but it won't have any effect on what's stored in `alienHeight`.

> *You can think of our function as having a **copy** of* `alienHeight` *to play with: we can do what we like with the duplicate, but the original will always be unaffected.*

We've now localized the code within the function, making it separate from the rest of the script, so we need a way to tell the movie what the result of our function was. So what about doing something with `localVariable`? That's where we're storing the value while it's inside the function, so there's no problem with tweaking that. But because it's a local variable, it doesn't actually exist outside the function declaration. How can we send the tweaked value back to `alienHeight`?

Easy! We can add a handy little action called `return` to our declaration, like this:

```
notSoEvilMath = function(localVariable) {
    var localVariable;
    localVariable += 5;
    localVariable *= 2;
    return localVariable;
};
```

We perform our calculation in exactly the same way as we did before, but on the final line of the function, we use the `return` action to tell Flash that it should pass the value of `localVariable` back to the script that called the function in the first place.

Once we've done that, the function call itself takes on this `return`ed value, so we can trace it out like this:

```
trace( notSoEvilMath(alienHeight) );
```

Even better, we can use it to update the value of `alienHeight`, which is what we wanted to do in the first place:

```
alienHeight = notSoEvilMath(alienHeight);
```

Okay, hang on a minute. We're passing in `alienHeight`, but the function doesn't mention that at all, and we're returning `localVariable`, but then using `alienHeight` to store the answer... Aargh! What's going on?

Well, first off, don't worry – you're not being dumb. This is a common stumbling block that most folks hit when they encounter functions for the first time. Let's walk through what Flash is actually doing.

When Flash sees this:

```
alienHeight = notSoEvilMath(alienHeight);
```

it knows that it has to do two things:

- **Run the function called `notSoEvilMath()` using the value of `alienHeight` as part of its calculations.** Let's assume that `alienHeight` starts out with a value of 4. Flash goes to the function declaration, sees that the parameter `localVariable` has been set up to catch an argument, and stores a value of 4 inside it. Next, it adds 5 (giving 9) and doubles the variable value (giving 18). The final line tells it to return the variable value as the overall result of the function.

- **Change the value of `alienHeight` to whatever value gets returned by the function.** We know the function returns a value of 18, so this is the new value of `alienHeight`.

The great thing about this is that the arguments *outside the function* are completely separate from the parameters *inside the function* – so, we can now pass **any value** to the function, and do what we like to the result. For example:

```
notSoEvilMath = function(localVariable) {
    var localVariable;
    localVariable += 5;
    localVariable *= 2;
    return localVariable;
};
x = 4;
y = 5;
x = notSoEvilMath(x);
trace("Value of x is: " + x);
y = notSoEvilMath(y);
trace("Value of y is: " + y);
y = notSoEvilMath(x);
trace("Value of y is: " + y);
```

This would give us the following output:

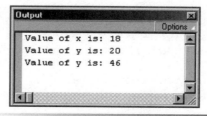

The variable x starts out with a value of 4, so it ends up as 18. Variable y starts out as 5, so the function pops that value into localVariable, adds five (giving 10), doubles it (20) and throws that last figure back as the new value of y. Finally, we apply the function to x (which now has a value of 18 of course); plus 5 gives 23, and twice that is 46. Now that we're starting to use functions like the pros, we can store that result anywhere we like, so we pop it into y!

Give this a try for yourself, using different values and variables, and different combinations. You can even play around with the actions inside the function itself, and see what you can come up with!

Calling functions with multiple arguments

We can expand our functions further by giving them more than one parameter. For example, if you wanted a function to multiply two values together, you could do something like this:

```
function multiply(a, b) {
    var a, b;
    return a*b;
};
x = 5;
y = 10;
z = multiply(x, y);
trace(z);
```

This would output the value 50. You'll notice here that we've done something slightly different in that we've put the expression in the return command. This is a handy shortcut to use when you're returning simple expressions.

Hopefully, you're now starting to appreciate exactly why functions are worth using in your scripts. On the other hand, you may be wondering how all this stupid math stuff could possibly be any use in your quest to build a stunning bit of Flash to impress the world with. Okay then, before I throw any more scary words and concepts at you, let's spend a little time building up a practical example, so that you can actually *see* these little critters in action...

Running in circles

Say I wanted to give you a real scare. Well, I could put a sheet over my head and jump out at you shouting BOO! On the other hand, I could stay where I am and whisper the word *trigonometry* at you. Similar effect, I should imagine... That's certainly been my reaction in the past!

Well don't panic. I'm not about to try and give you a boring lesson in pure math. I'm just going to show you two very cool little functions that you and your movies might find rather useful...

```
circleX = function(distance, angle) {
    var distance, angle;
    return distance * Math.sin(Math.PI * angle/6);
};
circleY = function(distance, angle) {
    var distance, angle;
```

```
        return -distance * Math.cos(Math.PI * angle/6);
};
```

Now, if you can look at these without breaking out in a cold sweat, that's great. If not, it doesn't matter, because I'm not going to talk about *how* these functions work, and you don't need to understand any of what's going on inside them. All that's really important is *what* they do.

So far in this book, all the ActionScript animation we've looked at has dealt with things moving about the stage in straight lines. Even the moving blobs we created in Chapter 4 were basically just an animated straight line connecting the pointer to a fixed point on the stage.

That's pretty cool, as far as it goes... but what about making circles instead? Sounds hard, but with these two functions, it's not actually a problem. We can use them to turn circle-based values like 'distance from center' and 'angle' (that is, how far round the circle we are) into x and y coordinates that we can use to position things on the stage.

Let's start off by drawing a clock face – well, the numbers on a clock face anyway.

1. Create a new Flash document, and create a dynamic text field on the stage. Make sure it's big enough to hold the text '12' in whichever type you decide to use. Name it `number_text` in the instance name field of the Property inspector.

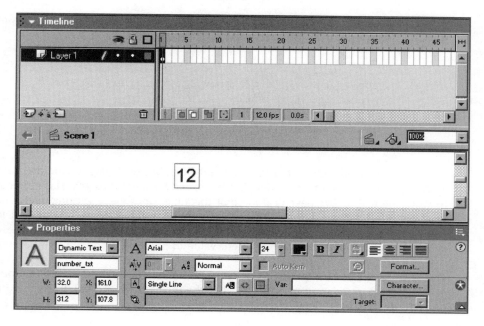

2. Use the Property inspector to place it at X:200, Y:200, replace '12' with a capital letter 'O', and press the button to center justify the text. Name the instance `number_txt`.

3. Now add a new layer called actions, open up the Actions panel, and click on the pin button to make sure we don't lose focus by accident. Let's start by putting in the two functions I showed you just a few moments ago – just key them in exactly as shown:

```
circleX = function(distance, angle) {
    var distance, angle;
    return distance * Math.sin(Math.PI * angle/6);
};
circleY = function(distance, angle) {
    var distance, angle;
    return -distance * Math.cos(Math.PI * angle/6);
};
```

4. Now for our main script. It's actually going to be very simple: we'll just loop through values 1 to 12, and make a duplicate of the number_txt text field each time:

```
for (i=1; i<13; i++) {
    duplicateMovieClip(number_txt, "number"+i+"_txt", i);
    //position text field
    //change text in text field
};
```

As you can see, I've added a couple of comments to mark where we need to add a couple more things in. We'll start with the second of these, since it's the simpler of the two:

```
for (i=1; i<13; i++) {
    duplicateMovieClip(number_txt, "number"+i+"_txt", i);
    //position text field
    //change text in text field
    _root["number"+i+"_txt"].text = i;
};
```

This is a new way of setting the text in a text field, but hopefully it shouldn't faze you too much. In the past, we've used the Var field in the Property inspector to give Flash the name of a variable to store the text in. We haven't done that this time: since we're making twelve copies of the text field, they'd all end up using the *same* variable! Instead, we've hacked straight into the dynamic text field's text property – just as we've done in the past with other properties like _x, _y, and visible – and changed it to the current value of i.

This gives us twelve new text fields, showing numbers 1 through 12 – note that our for loop starts at i=1, and stops as soon as i hits 13. Run the movie now, and you'll see them all sitting on top of each other:

Ugh... let's move them, quick!

Okay, the plan is to put our twelve new text fields in a circle around the original one, which still has its top left-hand corner sitting at X:200, Y:200. This is where our functions come in – we give them two arguments: a distance from the center, and the number of a position round the edge of the circle. Here's the script you need to add:

```
for (i=1; i<13; i++) {
    duplicateMovieClip(number_txt, "number"+i+"_txt", i);
    //position text field
    _root["number"+i+"_txt"]._x = 200+circleX(100, i);
    _root["number"+i+"_txt"]._y = 200+circleY(100, i);
    //change text in text field
    _root["number"+i+"_txt"].text = i;
};
```

For each text field, we set the x-position to 200 plus the return value of `circleX()`, and set the y-position to 200 plus the return value of `circleY()`. We'll look at how we've called these functions in a moment. First though, reassure yourself that this does actually work by testing the movie now. This is what you should see:

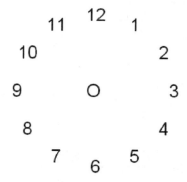

Cool! We've made a circle without having to resort to any evil mathematical equations... Well, actually we did have to, but they're hidden away inside the functions, so we don't need to worry about them. All that really matters to us is this pair of lines:

```
_root["number"+i+"_txt"]._x = 200+circleX(100, i);
_root["number"+i+"_txt"]._y = 200+circleY(100, i);
```

...and the fact that `circleX()` gives us the x-position for each number, while `circleY()` gives us the y-position for each number. What about all those numbers we've used on the right-hand side though? They do look a bit confusing, so let's figure out what they all do.

Changing how the circle appears

All the values in the first line determine x-positions for the text fields, while all those in the second control their y-positions. There are three different things for us to look at in each line, and each controls a different aspect of how the overall circle appears.

1. First up, we have the 200s that go on the beginning of each line's right-hand side. These just tell Flash what point on the stage to draw the circle around. Try changing them to see how they affect things:

    ```
    _root["number"+i+"_txt"]._x = 250+circleX(100, i);
    _root["number"+i+"_txt"]._y = 250+circleY(100, i);
    ```

    Now you should see something like this:

    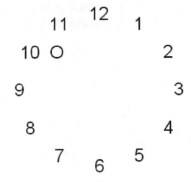

    The central 'O' is still where it was, but all the numbers have moved down and across to the right because we've added 50 to the center coordinates.

2. Okay, so the first pair of values controls the position of the circle. What about the first of the arguments in each of our functions? At the moment, they're both set to 100, so let's try changing them and see what happens. Don't forget to put the 200s back first:

    ```
    _root["number"+i+"_txt"]._x = 200+circleX(200, i);
    _root["number"+i+"_txt"]._y = 200+circleY(50, i);
    ```

    We've doubled the top value, and halved the bottom one, so you should now get something like this:

Yes, we can use the first argument in circleX() to control how wide our 'circle' is, and the first argument in circleY() to control how tall it is. In fact, the values we give tell Flash the horizontal and vertical distances from center to edge, so this 'circle' is all of 400 pixels wide and 100 high.

Now for the second of the arguments. Right now this is simply i for both of them, and you can probably guess that this is what controls the angle (or rotation) of each position – that is, whereabouts on the circle each number will appear. If the second argument has a value of 6, we'll get a position at the bottom of the circle. Likewise, a value of 9 gives a position on the far left of the circle. To see this in effect, let's play with the values again:

```
_root["number"+i+"_txt"]._x = 200+circleX(200, i+2);
_root["number"+i+"_txt"]._y = 200+circleY(50, i+2);
```

This will give you the following:

```
            9      10      11
      8                          12
   7                O                1
      6                          2
         5       4       3
```

All the numbers have shifted round the clock face by two places. Even better, we don't even need to stick to using whole numbers: for example, a value of 1.5 will give us a position halfway between the 1 and 2 positions. So what about halving the value of i?

```
_root["number"+i+"_txt"]._x = 200+circleX(200, i/2);
_root["number"+i+"_txt"]._y = 200+circleY(50, i/2);
```

Now the numbers will run from clock positions 0.5 to 6, so they're all on the right-hand side of the circle, and none remain on the left:

```
           1    2   3   4  5
                            6
      O                    7
                         8
      12   11   10   9
```

As you can see, with these two circle functions, we can do some pretty impressive stuff. What's more, we don't need to know anything about what goes on inside them; we can just plug in a few numbers and draw circles, ovals, and arcs to our hearts' content!

Before we get too carried away with this, there's another important lesson to learn about functions and what we can do with them.

Nesting functions

It may seem like an obvious point to make, but there's no reason why you can't call one function from inside another. Say we have a simple function called `double()`, declared like this:

```
function double(x) {
    var x;
    x = x * 2;
    return x;
}
```

Now, if we wanted to create a new function `quadruple()` that multiplies a specified value by four, we can set it up so that it calls our `double()` function twice over:

```
function quadruple(y) {
    var y;
    y = double(y);
    y = double(y);
    return y;
}
```

In fact, we could make this even shorter by actually passing the first `double()` function call as an argument in the second:

```
function quadruple(y) {
    var y;
    y = double(double(y));
    return y;
}
```

Here, Flash first calculates the result of the second function call, and then uses this value as the argument for the first function call. Now, if you followed it up with something like this:

```
x = 4;
x = quadruple(x);
trace(x);
```

...you'd get the value 16 in the Output window: first it doubles 4 to get 8, and then it doubles 8 to get 16. Easy.

But what does this mean for our scriptwriting in general?

It means that we can have as many layers of functions as we want between our overall problem and the separate actions that make up a scripted solution. Not only can we break the task down into various subtasks, but we can break each of them down into their own 'sub-subtasks', and so on, and so on, for as long as we find it useful.

Using nested functions

The most obvious benefit of nesting functions is that we can call our own functions from inside an event handler. For instance, if we put our clock face script inside the onEnterFrame event handler for the root timeline, we could update it in real time.

1. Let's have some fun with this right away, and make the number circle follow our mouse pointer around the stage. We just need to put the main script in an onEnterFrame event handler (so it updates all the text field positions once every frame) and change the 200s to _xmouse and _ymouse respectively:

```
onEnterFrame = function() {
    for (i=1; i<13; i++) {
        duplicateMovieClip(number_txt, "number"+i+"_txt", i);
        //position text field
        _root["number"+i+"_txt"]._x = _xmouse+circleX(100, i);
        _root["number"+i+"_txt"]._y = _ymouse+circleY(100, i);
        //change text in text field
        _root["number"+i+"_txt"].text = i;
    }
};
```

Run the movie again, and sure enough, the circle of numbers goes where the mouse pointer leads it. Wherever the pointer is, it's always in the middle of the circle.

2. Now let's see what happens if we use the mouse pointer to control our circle's width and height. Don't forget to put the positioning 200s back in, or you'll see some very strange things going on...

```
_root["number"+i+"_txt"]._x = 200+circleX(_xmouse-200, i);
_root["number"+i+"_txt"]._y = 200+circleY(_ymouse-200, i);
```

Now, as you move the mouse pointer across the stage, the width of the circle changes accordingly. Likewise, the circle height changes as you move the mouse pointer up and down the stage:

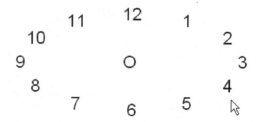

I've used _xmouse-200 and _ymouse-200 here, so that the circle collapses down on itself when the pointer's directly over the center (that is, when both have values of 200).

3. No, it isn't looking much like a circle any more, is it? Let's use the same value to control both the width and the height. We'll get it from the x-coordinate of the mouse pointer, and store it in a variable called size:

```
size = _xmouse-200;
_root["number"+i+"_txt"]._x = 200+circleX(size, i);
_root["number"+i+"_txt"]._y = 200+circleY(size, i);
```

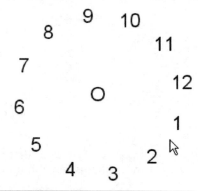

4. We've figured out how to tweak the position of the circle, and we've just been fiddling with the width and height. What else is there? Well, there's still another function argument to play with.

Let's use _ymouse to control the rotation of our number circle. Since _ymouse can take values up to five hundred or so, we'll divide it by 100 first, giving us lots of fine control but with a rotation range of about 5 – that's almost halfway round the clock, which should be enough for us to see that it's working okay:

```
size = _xmouse-200;
rotation = i + _ymouse/100;
_root["number"+i+"_txt"]._x = 200+circleX(size, rotation);
_root["number"+i+"_txt"]._y = 200+circleY(size, rotation);
```

Of course, we still need to add i to the _ymouse-based value; otherwise all the text fields would end up in the same place. Now the circle turns round as you move the mouse up and down:

5. Let's quickly recap on our full script listing:

```
circleX = function(distance, angle) {
    var distance, angle;
    return distance * Math.sin(Math.PI * angle/6);
};
circleY = function(distance, angle) {
    var distance, angle;
    return -distance * Math.cos(Math.PI * angle/6);
};
onEnterFrame = function() {
  for (i=1; i<13; i++) {
    duplicateMovieClip(number_txt, "number"+i+"_txt", i);
    //position text field
    size = _xmouse-200;
    rotation = i + _ymouse/100;
    _root["number"+i+"_txt"]._x = 200+circleX(size, rotation);
    _root["number"+i+"_txt"]._y = 200+circleY(size, rotation);
    //change text in text field
    _root["number"+i+"_txt"].text = i;
  }
};
```

Not bad, considering what we've achieved!

Using more function nesting to tidy up our script

Before we wrap this chapter up, let's see if we can't tighten up our script a little. Not everything in the onEnterFrame event handler actually needs to be there, and it makes sense to put the lines of code that actually position the text fields into their own function (so we can turn variables like size and rotation into function parameters, and make it easier to customize in future...)

Let's leave the opening pair of functions alone (unless you're feeling very adventurous!) and brew up a couple of brand new ones just underneath.

1. The first of these new functions is called createTextFields(), and creates all the text fields for us when the movie starts:

```
createTextFields = function () {
    for (i=1; i<13; i++) {
        duplicateMovieClip(number_txt, "number"+i+"_txt", i);
        // change text in text field
        _root["number"+i+"_txt"].text = i;
    }
};
```

I'm assuming that the actual text we put into each of the fields isn't going to change while the movie's running, so I've set that up here as well.

2. I'm putting all the other stuff into a function called positionTextFields().

    ```
    positionTextFields = function (centerX, centerY, size, rotation){
      var centerX, centerY, size, rotation;
      for (i=1; i<13; i++) {
        field = "number"+i+"_txt";
        _root[field]._x = centerX + circleX(size, i+rotation);
        _root[field]._y = centerY + circleY(size, i+rotation);
      }
    };
    ```

    This has four parameters, which control exactly where the circle appears, how large it is, and how far round the numbers start counting.

3. Now that all our positioning script is tidily wrapped inside a function, the onEnterFrame event handler gets a lot simpler:

    ```
    onEnterFrame = function () {
        positionTextFields(200, 200, _xmouse-200, _ymouse/100);
    };
    ```

4. Finally, we need to run the createTextFields() action, so that the fields actually get set up:

    ```
    createTextFields();
    ```

    We can leave everything else to the onEnterFrame handler function.

5. Here's the finished script:

    ```
    // DECLARE FUNCTIONS FIRST
    circleX = function (distance, angle) {
        var distance, angle;
        return distance*Math.sin(Math.PI*angle/6);
    };
    circleY = function (distance, angle) {
        var distance, angle;
        return -distance*Math.cos(Math.PI*angle/6);
    };
    createTextFields = function () {
        for (i=1; i<13; i++) {
            duplicateMovieClip(number_txt, "number"+i+"_txt", i);
            // change text in text field
            _root["number"+i+"_txt"].text = i;
        }
    };
    positionTextFields = function (centerX, centerY, size, rotation){
    ```

```
        var centerX, centerY, size, rotation;
        for (i=1; i<13; i++) {
            _root["number"+i+"_txt"]._x =
                        centerX + circleX(size, i+rotation);
            _root["number"+i+"_txt"]._y =
                        centerY + circleY(size, i+rotation);
        }
    };
    // DECLARE onEnterFrame EVENT HANDLER
    onEnterFrame = function () {
        positionTextFields(200, 200, _xmouse-200, _ymouse/100);
    };
    // ACTIONS TO RUN WHEN MOVIE STARTS
    createTextFields();
```

Hmm. It's actually a bit *longer* than it was before. So why is it worth making all those changes? Well, apart from the slight improvement in speed (now that we're not making a whole set of duplicate text fields every frame), we've pulled out the main circle variables as parameters in the positionTextFields() function. This makes it loads easier to change how we control the appearance of the circle. Of course, we've hardwired certain features into the function – for example, the width and height will always be the same, the numbers will always be evenly spaced round the whole circle, and so on. There's nothing to stop you changing that, though...

Now that you've seen how easy it is to use functions like circleX() and circleY() to make a funky little circle of text fields, you might like to start experimenting with them for yourself. What we've done here is only the tip of the iceberg, and there are plenty of other possibilities left for you to explore! What about changing the value of rotation steadily from one frame to the next? Or using different values of size for the different text fields, so they spiral into the center? Or even changing the text fields for something completely different like an animated movie clip...? Now you have the basics down, the sky's the limit!

Summary

Functions give us a way to bundle up useful sets of actions so that we can define them once and reuse them as many times as we like. Not only can this help to cut down on repetition and keep our scripts shorter, but it can also help us make them more structured.

By breaking each task in your movie down into several well-defined subtasks, you can keep your blocks of script relatively short and focused on specific goals. This makes it much easier to build up your movie script in nice, easy-to-digest chunks. What's more, by nesting functions inside other functions, you can put as many levels of functions as you need between the overall goal of the movie and the individual actions that actually get the job done.

Let's recap the benefits of using functions:

- **conciseness** – define the function once, and you can call it as many times as you like

- **maintainability** – change the function definition once, and you update its functionality throughout the movie

- **versatility** – use arguments to apply the same function to different things

Now that we've started to look at how we can structure the actions behind our scripts, we're ready to go a step further and bring data back into the frame. In the next chapter, we'll see how we can bundle together functions *and* variables, helping us make scripts that are even more self-contained and reusable.

The practical benefits of this may not seem particularly obvious at this stage, since even the largest scripts we've written so far have been pretty small (by professional standards anyway). All the same, I'm taking it as read that you'll want to move on to larger projects, so stick at it and you'll soon be in a position to reap the rewards. Buckle up now – Base Camp 1 is well behind us, and the slopes are starting to kick in. Take a break and prepare to unlock the ancient secrets of Mount ActionScript...

6

Objects

What we'll cover in this chapter:

- *Using objects to describe things with state and behavior*

- *Storing related collections of variables and functions*

- *Creating custom object classes*

- *Working with ActionScript's core built-in objects*

We spent a lot of the last chapter discussing how functions can help to give your scripts a nice, clear structure – especially when you choose them wisely and name them sensibly! One of the techniques we looked at dealt with nesting functions inside one another. That way, we can break down any complex task into a few slightly simpler subtasks, break each of those down into even simpler sub-subtasks, and so on, until each one reaches a level where it just needs a few simple actions to do its job. We end up with lots of short, tightly focused functions, each playing its own special part in the overall movie script.

On their own, functions can be fairly useful, but they also have one or two drawbacks:

- A function can't remember anything for itself. Any variables you use set up inside the declaration will be created when the function starts to run and destroyed as soon as it's done. If you call a function three times in a row, it will do exactly the same thing every time, because the third call doesn't know anything about the first two...

- If a function does make a lasting change to the movie, it's because it contains script that acts on things that are defined somewhere else in the movie. For example, the swap() function we considered for the Hangman game refers specifically to a named button instance *and* a named movie clip. Neither of these things is part of the function; but it's no use to anyone unless both of them exist in the movie.

Okay, but so what? We've used functions, and they worked fine. What's the problem?

The problem is this: as your movies get bigger and bigger, it gets harder to keep track of what's where. This makes it much harder to get away with writing functions like swap(), because they rely on things that may or may not exist somewhere out there in the murky depths of your Flash Magnum Opus...

In order to help avoid this sort of thing, we need to learn how to work with **objects**.

Introducing objects

Okay. What on *earth* have objects got to do with ActionScript? Objects are things like chairs, TVs, coffee pots, and bicycles. By and large, we know how to use them already, and they live in the real world. So why are we talking about them here?

In fact, it's precisely *because* objects are familiar things from the real world that they're useful to us.

Say you have a car – it could *be* a red Ferrari with a 2400cc engine. Lovely. Common sense tells you there are certain things it can *do*: start, stop, change gear, reverse, and so on. It's nice to imagine actually doing those things, but there's no great mental strain involved...

On the other hand, say you have a brick – it could *be* one kilo in weight, brown, made of clay, and part of the top of a wall. But it can't *do* much; it just sort of... sits there.

These two examples highlight the important characteristics of real objects: they're things that have **state** (all the things they *are* – where they are, what they look like, what they're made of, and so on) and **behavior** (all the things they can possibly do to change that state in some way). Because they're examples of objects that we've all encountered in the real world, we already have a good idea of what these things can and can't be. Common sense tells us that we can't change gear on a brick (unless, perhaps it's one of those lovely new Lego bricks), so we're not likely to try!

Based on this idea, ActionScript objects give us another sort of descriptive container (like variables are for data, and functions are for actions) that can *be* and *do* lots of different things: just like the objects we see around us in the real world. The 'being' is taken care of by variables (for values that can vary, such as position) and constants (for values that can't, such as engine capacity), while the 'doing' is all defined in terms of functions.

> *In the simplest possible terms, we can think of an object as a bunch of related variables, constants, and functions, wrapped together in a bundle to making a neatly self-contained building block that we can use in our movie script.*
>
> *When we're dealing with objects, there are special technical names we give to these variables and functions: the variables in an object are known as its properties, while the functions are referred to as its methods.*

Once you start digging around behind the scenes, you'll find that objects are pretty fundamental to everything that goes on in Flash and ActionScript. We don't need to create them all from scratch, as we've done in the past with variables and functions, because Flash already has plenty of built-in objects for us to play with – and not all of them new to us...

Seeing arrays in a new light

Back in Chapter 2, we started playing about with arrays. As we've seen since then, they can be terribly useful for storing lots of variables in one place, and with the power of loops added in, they're clearly a force to be reckoned with.

Well, you ain't seen nothing yet!

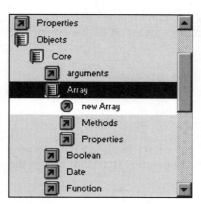

The humble array happens to be one marvelous example of an ActionScript object. We already know it as a container that holds lots of variables; it also has a few tricks up its sleeve (as you may have guessed after seeing that `join()` business I used during the Hangman game). You can see what's on offer by taking a look in the Actions toolbox (on the left side of the Actions panel), where you'll find Array listed under Objects > Core, with three entries beneath it in the hierarchy:

The array constructor method

The first of these is new Array, and this is a special sort of action known as a **constructor**. Why? Because it's what we use to *construct* the Array object in the first place. We've seen this used quite a few times already – for example:

```
letters = new Array("f","l","a","s","h");
```

This tells Flash to construct a new object of type Array, giving it five string elements (with values as shown) and storing it in the container `letters`. Of course, that's pretty much as you understood it before – or at least, I hope it is!

Other array methods

Now take a look in the Methods book, and you'll see a list of all those tricks I mentioned before:

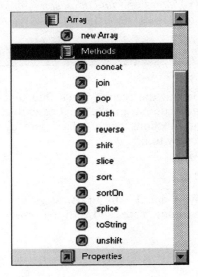

You should recognize at least one of these – we used `join()` in chapter 4 to join together all the elements in a long string. It took one argument, which specified a string for it to place between each element and the next:

```
letters.join();          // returns "f,l,a,s,h" (default)
letters.join("");         // returns "flash"
letters.join(" ");        // returns "f l a s h"
letters.join("+");        // returns "f+l+a+s+h"
```

Just like the functions we saw toward the end of the previous chapter, the `join()` method simply returns a value – a string in this case – and has no effect on the array on which it operates. That's not always the case though:

```
letters.reverse();         // reverses the order of elements
letters.join("")           // now returns "hsalf"
lettersGuessed.sort();     // sorts elements alphabetical
```

```
lettersGuessed.join("");    // now returns "afhls"
letters.push("MX");         // adds new final element "MX"
letters.join("")            // now returns "hsalfMX"
```

I won't go through the rest of the array methods, or we'll be here all day! Besides, the ActionScript Dictionary (under the Help menu) does a pretty good job of describing what they do if you feel the need to find out more.

The important thing is that you know how to use them: simply write the name of the array you want to work on, add a dot, and write the name of the method you want to apply followed by a pair of brackets. Sometimes you'll want to add an argument or two between the brackets, but more often than not, you'll just leave them empty.

> *Keen-eyed readers will notice that we've now used exactly the same dot notation to run actions, functions, and now methods. Hmm.... very spooky!*

Array properties

Look in the Properties book, and you'll find a single entry called `length`. Of course, this is just the property we used in chapter 4 to tell us how many array elements to loop through:

```
elementsInLettersArray = letters.length
```

No brackets here, because it's a property, and not a method. Okay, been there, done that. But is that *it* for the array properties – what about all the elements? Surely they're array properties too?

Yes, they are. But think about it for a moment, and you'll see why they aren't amongst the built-in properties listed in the Actions toolbox – it's because they're *not* built-in! All the elements we add to an array are **custom properties**. In other words, they don't need to exist until our script specifically defines them, so they aren't part of ActionScript's general definition of what an array is.

General definitions vs. specific objects

It's important to know about the differences between these general definitions and the specific objects that we use in our scripts. It's terribly easy to get the two confused, particularly when we're using the same word 'object' (or, in this particular case 'array') to refer to both. For that reason, we have names for each: the general definition is known as a **class**, while the corresponding object your script gets to muck about with is called an **instance**.

> *Unfortunately, the ActionScript Dictionary doesn't make much of a distinction between classes and instances – for example, `Array` is always described as an object. Okay, this isn't wrong, but it can make things confusing for us if we're using one word to talk about two different things! Since I'm all for keeping things clear, I'm not going to make any shorthand approximations.*

Let's take a closer look at what these things actually do for us.

Classes

A class is really just a template for a particular type of object, which defines how it should be constructed, what it should be able to do, and so on. In the same way as a physical building will always starts off as a blueprint on an architect's drawing board (or AutoCAD-enabled desktop), an object will always begin life as a class.

The class contains a list of the common characteristics that all objects constructed from it should have. For example, imagine we had a class called Plant – it might have a template that includes:

- Name of plant
- Height of plant
- Color of flower
- Flowering month
- Recommended soil type

This might not seem particularly useful in a Flash movie... Unless, that is, you suddenly landed a big contract with a international chain of garden centers, found yourself commissioned to design an interface for the 'create a garden' page on their website, and needed a way to keep track of all the different sort of plants they sold. You never know when this sort of thing might come in handy!

Take a quick browse through the Actions toolbox, and you'll notice that all the built-in ActionScript classes (Array, Boolean, Date, Function, and so on) are named with a capital letter at the beginning:

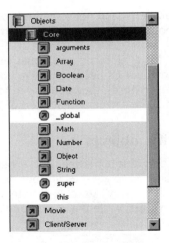

This is a helpful convention that reminds us whether we're dealing with a class or an instance in our script.

Instances

Just as a single set of blueprints can be used as the basis for lots of physical buildings, one class can be used to produce lots of distinct instances of Array class objects. Any object instance based on the Plant class would feature a corresponding list of **actual values**. So, you might have an object instance called myFirstFlower (of class Plant) that included the following values:

- daffodil
- 10cm
- yellow
- March
- normal

Now you could use this information to cover a virtual garden with daffodils and show them flowering in March (or dying if the soil turned out to be too acidic). Another instance might store information about sunflowers; another one, information about lilies and so on.

> In general, you use an object class to create a specific type of object instance; give it a name, and you can then use (and customize) this instance in (and with) your script.

Making a custom object

What if we want to set up this `Plant` object then? There's no `Plant` class in the Actions toolbox, so it won't do any good to charge in and say `myFirstFlower = new Plant()` or something similar! Well, we could, but it wouldn't do very much – here's what Flash's variable list has to say about the `myFirstFlower` variable:

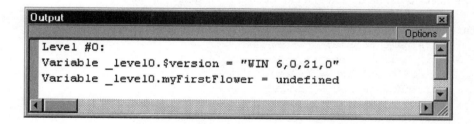

```
Output
                                                    Options
Level #0:
Variable _level0.$version = "WIN 6,0,21,0"
Variable _level0.myFirstFlower = undefined
```

One way we could make a start would be to write something like this:

```
myFirstFlower = new Object();
myFirstFlower.name = "daffodil";
myFirstFlower.height = 20;
myFirstFlower.flowerColor = "yellow";
myFirstFlower.flowerMonth = "march";
myFirstFlower.soilType = "normal";
```

Here, we've created another object from the built-in `Object` class – just like we did with the `Array` class before. We've then stepped through each of the properties we want, and told Flash what values to put in which slots – just like defining variables, only all the value containers are properties inside the `myFirstFlower` object.

`Object` is a totally stripped down class, which has the bare minimum of properties and methods – none of which we really need to know about at this level – to let us add in properties like those above. It therefore gives us a nice clean slate on which to build our own objects.

> In fact, `Object` is an extremely important class for ActionScript, as it's the class that all others are based on. It defines the basic rules for all ActionScript objects: and one of these is that it lets us add in properties as we go along. The great thing about working with `Object` is that it won't bog our `Plant` objects down with features that they don't need. It would be foolish to use the `Array` class as the basis for an object like this; there'd be no point in having `sort()` and `reverse()` methods for an object whose sole purpose is to describe a plant – what on earth would they do? No, the `Object` class gives us a lean, mean, instance that stores several pieces of associated data, ready for us to use further on down the line.

The only trouble with our code as it stands is that we've only really made an instance of the `Object` class – there's no way to create a second instance (called `mySecondFlower` perhaps) with the same set of properties without going through all of these lines setting up properties – and doing it again, and again, and again, for every new flower we decide to add in.

Instead, we need to define ourselves a Plant constructor function, like this:

```
function Plant(name, height, color, month, soil) {
    this.name = name;
    this.height = height;
    this.flowerColor = color;
    this.flowerMonth = month;
    this.soilType = soil;
};
```

You're probably wondering what all that business with `this` is all about – `this` is a keyword that refers to whichever object happens to have called our function. At this point it has no meaning, but as soon as we try Plan A again...

```
myFirstFlower = new Plant("daffodil", "10cm",
                              ➥"yellow", "March", "normal");
```

This time, Flash uses the `Plant` function to construct an object called `myFirstFlower`, with properties `name`, `height`, and so on. The arguments we've used make sure they're all given values to hold: "daffodil", "10cm", and so on. The advantage of doing it this way is that if we wanted to create another object instance of `Plant` (say `mySecondFlower`, a 15cm red tulip which grows in normal soil and flowers in June) we'd just need one more line to define it.

```
mySecondFlower = new Plant ("tulip", "15cm", "red", "June", "normal");
```

We can now read and write property values in `myFirstFlower` just as if it were any other object:

```
trace(myFirstFlower.name);      // traces "daffodil"
trace(myFirstFlower.height);    // traces "10cm"
myFirstFlower.height = "15cm";
trace(myFirstFlower.height);    // now traces "15cm"
```

Objects, objects, everywhere...

So far, we've seen how the `new` action coupled with the class name `Array` will make us an instance of the `Array` class. Likewise, we can pair up `new` with the class name `Object` to create an instance of the `Object` class, and even write constructor functions that `new` can use as classes from which to create custom objects. So is this `new` business the only way to create object instances?

Actually, no it's not. Most of the time, ActionScript does lots of work behind the scenes so that we can use objects without even realizing it. For example, it's pretty easy to create a variable:

```
myName = "Ben";
```

Well, you probably never realized it before, but variables themselves are based on objects! When you create a string variable, it inherits various properties and methods from a class called `String`, which you can find listed under Objects > Core again:

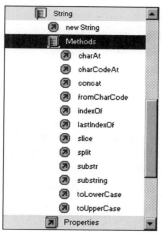

As you might be coming to expect, it has a constructor method `new String`, and a `length` property just like the one we saw for the Array class. It also has a bunch of methods that can be (and have been) used to manipulate the characters in the string. You may remember us using the `toLowerCase()` method as part of our password-protected movie back in Chapter 3. Well, this is where it started life – as part of the String class.

All the methods here are things that we might want to apply to the letters in a string. Many of them are similar (if not the same) as the Array methods we saw earlier, letting us mess around with letters in a string in the same way as we messed with elements in our array. However, there's no need for a method like `join()` here, because – unlike the elements in an array – all the letters in a string are *already* joined together.

That isn't to say an instance of the String class is exactly the same as a string variable; run one of each past the `typeof()` function if you want evidence! So how are they different? Well, I won't go into detail, because most of it is so subtle and low-level that it's enough to give me a headache! To give you a rough idea though, consider what happens when you take a string variable and change its value to 576. It automatically changes into a number variable (complete with a bunch of number-crunching properties and methods from another class called Number as it happens). String objects can't cope with a change like that – they just aren't that smart. As we'll see though, that's not always a bad thing...

It's about time we had an example or two, so let's put this String class to work and prove that the objects it creates don't behave so differently from those familiar old string variables we know and love.

Finding the length of a string

First of all, let's look at that one-off property the String class gives us: `length`. We're going to use the movie `input-output.fla` that we bolted together back in Chapter 2, so that we can get an instant result on the stage:

1.   Open up the file and select frame 1 on the timeline. Take a look in the Actions panel and change the second line so that it reads:

```
enter_btn.onRelease = function() {
    output1 = input1.length;
};
```

2.   Now test the movie, input some text, and press the button to see the result: it's the number of characters in your input string. As you can see, spaces are included in the count – as far as Flash is concerned, a space is a character just like any other:

9

3.   Now change your script to look like this:

```
myName = new String("Ben");
enter_btn.onRelease = function() {
    output1 = myName.length;
};
```

4.   Run the movie again, add some text if you like, and click the button; you'll see something like this

doesn't matter.... **Enter** :

3

The output is now ignoring our input (so it really *doesn't* matter what we type in!) and showing us the length of the text stored in the String-classed object instance called myName – the text is 'Ben', so the length is 3.

So, it doesn't make any difference here whether we create a bog-standard string variable or a String object – in this case, they do the same thing. So why use that long-winded new String constructor then? If myName = "Ben" does the trick, why bother with a longer version?

Let's do another example, and I'll show you why.

Choosing how to store your information

For this example, we're going to resurrect the simple calculator.fla movie, again from back in Chapter 2. Call it up and get ready to make some more script tweaks.

Here's how this particular movie looked when we left it:

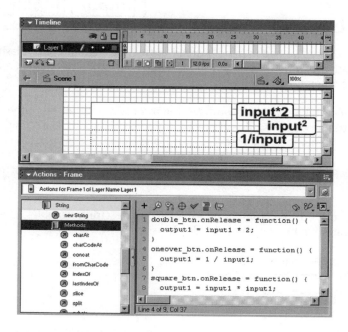

We had a button wired up to double the input, another to square it (that is, to times it by itself), and one more to figure out its reciprocal (or, in plain English, how many times it'll go into the number one).

So what about something simple like adding a number to our input? Sounds easy enough compared to all these other fancy calculations!

1. Start off by opening up the Library and dragging a new button instance onto the stage. Use the Property inspector to name it `addOne_btn`, and add some static text to label it as 'input+1':

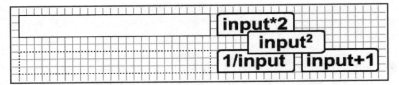

2. Now select frame 1 on the timeline and add the following to the end of the existing script:

```
addOne_btn.onRelease = function() {
   output1 = input1 + 1;
};
```

3. Run the movie and try out the new button:

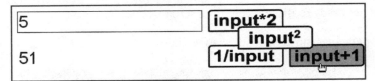

Ah... Not quite what we had in mind! Instead of treating 5 as a number, Flash assumes it's the string "5". We already know that + can be used to attach one string to another, and that's precisely what Flash has done here!

Hang on a minute! Why didn't we have this problem with all our other calculations? Well, an expression like `input1 * 2` doesn't make any sense if `input1` is a string, so Flash has to assume that `input1` is a number. Likewise `1/input1` and `input1 * input1`.

It seems we need to find some way of telling Flash that `input1` must *always* be treated as a number...

4. Well, just as the String class lets us explicitly create string variables, the Number class lets us explicitly create number variables. Try this for size:

```
addOne_btn.onRelease = function() {
   numberIn = new Number(input1);
   output1 = numberIn + 1;
};
```

5. Try the movie again, and you should find the new button works just fine:

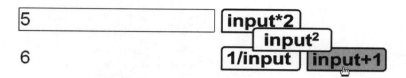

```
5
6
```

input*2
input²
1/input   input+1

Now that we've told Flash quite explicitly to create `numberIn` as a Number object, it has no excuse for misinterpreting it as a string!

Examining the content of a string

Let's use `input-output.fla` again (the original file, not the one we've just played around with) to look at another example of what we can with objects of the String class and all their methods.

If your movie's going to be good, robust, and immune to the violent whims of an unpredictable user, you must *always assume that the user will do the wrong thing*. For that reason, you need to be sure that your code is tolerant of all stupid answers.

For example, if you ask the user to respond to a question using a yes/no response, then the affirmative response might be "yes", or it might just be "y" (or even " y", complete with a leading space). What's more, you might also find any one of those responses in upper case. We could test for every one of these possibilities, but where on earth do we draw the line?

Let's say we'll treat the response as a 'yes' just so long as it contains the letter 'y' (in upper or lower case). We don't care if there are any other characters, so we just need to examine the input to find out whether it contains a 'y'.

Open up `input-output.fla` and prepare to script!

1. Before we do anything else, we need to make sure that we're only looking at lower case letters, so make the following changes:

    ```
    enter_btn.onRelease = function() {
        lowerCaseInput = input1.toLowerCase();
        output1 = lowerCaseInput;
    };
    ```

    Notice that the `toLowerCase()` method features opening and closing brackets at the end even though it doesn't take any arguments.

2. The next thing we must do to arrive at our desired output is to find a method that will check through our `lowerCaseInput` string variable and let us know if it found a 'y' character. This is a little less obvious, but if we use the tooltips in the Actions toolbox, we can find something appropriate:

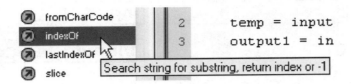

A **substring** is simply a part of a string, and the **index** is a number telling us the position of a letter within that string (like the position of an element in an array). We want to look for the substring "y", and although we aren't worried about the position of the letter within the string, we can check that it *is* there by looking out for a value that isn't -1.

Change the third line, either by typing or using the left-hand pane, so that it now reads:

```
enter_btn.onRelease = function() {
    lowerCaseInput = input1.toLowerCase();
    output1 = lowerCaseInput.indexOf("y");
};
```

This will search the `lowerCaseInput` string for an occurrence of the string "y". If it finds one, it returns the index of its position; if not, it returns -1. We're then going to relay our findings to `output1`, which will in turn display them for us on the screen.

3.   Test the movie, and try entering different text. Flash always starts counting index values from 0, so if "y" is right at the beginning of the input string, it'll return a value of 0:

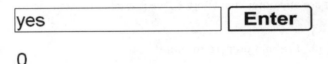

4.   All the same, as long as you enter something containing the letter 'y' (that covers "Y", "y", "yes", "Yes", and even "Oh, yes please!"), the number displayed will always be zero or greater:

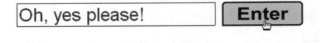

Note that Flash will only tell you about the *first* occurrence of the letter 'y' that it finds – if you enter "yay", it will still only return 0.

5. On the other hand, anything *without* a 'y' gives -1:

Now we can test whether output1 has a value greater than -1 to interpret the user's response... Unless they were especially polite and said something like "No thank you...", in which case our whole 'find y in the input' solution kinda falls down. Looks like this one will need a bit more work before it's ready for use in the real world!

Okay, we haven't solved the problem of robustness in one fell swoop here... In practice, it's often much more reliable if you limit what the user can do in the first place – 'yes' and 'no' buttons would be much more suitable if we were *really* intent on getting a yes/no response from them.

However, you've now seen how to apply the indexOf() method to a string variable. Because it's a fantastically smart ActionScript variable, it lets us use the properties and methods defined in the String class to perform various actions on the text inside it...

> *Hmm... using methods to perform actions? Something very peculiar's going on here!*

Lurking objects

There are certain ActionScript classes that, for one reason or another, we don't need to construct for ourselves before we go putting them to use.

One of these is called Math, and it's designed to work a bit like a simple calculator: it has methods that let you do complex mathematical operations (pow, sqr, sin, cos) and generate random numbers, and properties that store 'useful' mathematical constants... No, don't laugh! I assure you, when you start wanting to put 3D effects into your movies, you *will* find them invaluable!

Unlike most calculators though, Math doesn't have a memory, so in many ways, it's acting more like a library of math commands that you can use whenever and wherever you need them. Since all the properties are constants (that is, they all have values that can't be altered), it doesn't make much sense to construct instances of Math... They'd all be exactly the same, and you wouldn't be able to change any of their properties, so what on earth would you do with them?

The answer is, we don't. We access the class directly, like this:

```
output1 = Math.sqrt(input1);
```

This takes `input1` as an argument in the `sqrt()` method, which works out the square root of its value (that is, it figures out the number you have square to get `input1`). Here's how our calculator might look with a brand new 'square root' button...

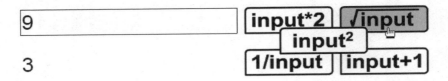

Apart from that one line above, there's nothing new here at all – I'll let you work out how to wire it all up for yourself!

Another object we access directly via its class name is Stage. There's a very different reason why this object doesn't have lots of instances: it's because it corresponds to the movie stage itself! We can only ever have one Stage object in a movie, so although it has properties that can change, Flash won't let us create any instances of our own.

So what use is this Stage object thing? Well, say we want to know the current dimensions of the stage, we can call up the width and height properties like this:

```
xDimension = Stage.width
yDimension = Stage.height
```

Big deal! We knew that from the Property inspector. But say, for example, you wanted to make a movie that showed a ball bouncing around on the stage – within the *confines* of the stage. Sure, you could set up a couple of variables (`xLimit=550` and `yLimit=400`) telling it where the far edges of the stage were... So what then if you *changed* the size of the stage, but *forgot* to update the variables? Bingo: busted movie! Much safer if you use `Stage.width` and `Stage.height` to set your limits – then they're both updated for you automatically!

You can find the Stage class listed in the Actions toolbox under Objects > Movie:

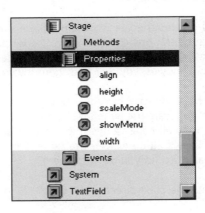

Alongside it, you'll see one or two familiar names...

It looks like these objects aren't content with meddling about behind the scenes! They're making a bid for freedom and starting to take over the stage itself... Is nothing sacred?

Yes, these objects really are *everywhere* – including the stage itself! Now that you've learnt how to work with purely ActionScript-based objects, you're all set to discover what objects have to offer us in the realm of the graphical...

Making a showreel

There are a lot of sites out there that use dynamic animation in a *functional* way. That's to say, the animation serves a purpose rather than just acting as eye candy. Navigation systems are perhaps one of the most useful things you can do with ActionScript. In this example, we're going to build an image gallery, using a sideways scrolling motion to navigate through our showreel. You could use it for anything you want, whether that's showing off your holiday snaps, or presenting an online portfolio...

In the process, we're going to use objects as a means of passing information to functions.

You can find the finished showreel in the download for this chapter, saved as showreel.fla. Copy it to a directory on your own machine and put copies of the three accompanying JPG files (cobblestones.jpg, planet.jpg, water.jpg) in the same directory.

Okay, I confess these aren't all my own work! Credit and thanks must go to Photoshop Masters Scott Hamlin and Scott Balay (and their awesome 'Power Effects' book) for the spiffing techniques whose end results you see here!

Load up the FLA and give it a test run to see what it does.

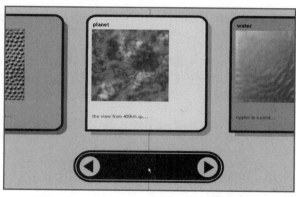

It's very simple to use: just move the pointer towards the left, and the showreel will scroll over to the left; move it towards the right, and the showreel will scroll back towards the right. The scrolling increases in speed as you move the cursor further from the centerline.

Remember the movies we made back in Chapter 1, when we looked at a tiny little script that could make various objects (including a car, a bat, and a Starfleet SpaceCruiser™) follow the *x*-position of the cursor? Well, this is essentially the same thing – just a little more elaborate. The original ball scroll was done with just two lines of ActionScript, and this one doesn't take that many more. This is the type of site navigation that had long-time ActionScripters gazing in awe when it was first used with earlier versions of Flash!

> *Another thing to note is that the images themselves aren't built into the movie. As long as you have files* `cobblestones.jpg,` `planet.jpg,` *and* `water.jpg` *in the same directory as the movie, Flash can pull them in when it needs them. It doesn't even matter what the images are: as long as you use the same file names, you can even replace them with your own pictures, and the movie won't miss a beat...*

Setting up the stage for the showreel movie

Let's start building the showreel movie for ourselves. First off, we need to prepare a few movie clips and give ourselves something to work with on the stage.

1. Create a new Flash document, and give it a total of four layers in the root timeline. You should call them actions, pictures, control bar, and center line.

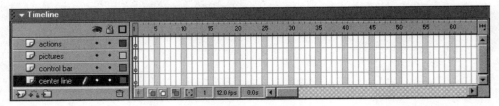

I've also made my stage a little smaller than the default (500 x 400 pixels) and given it a pale blue background (#CECFFF), so that it doesn't feel quite so stark...

2. Next let's add in the graphics that will help guide our users about the stage. I've used a vertical line to mark the middle of the stage (250 pixels across), and a chunky black bar to show which direction the showreel will scroll.

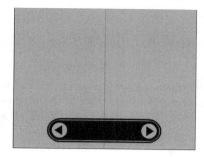

Neither actually *does* anything, so pop one onto each of the lower two layers and we can forget all about them!

Now for the important part: we're going to start building the showreel. It's going to consist of a long string of individual cells – each one will hold a single picture, and information about it.

3. Use Insert > New Symbol to define a new movie clip called cell, and give it four layers called content, border, background, and shadow.

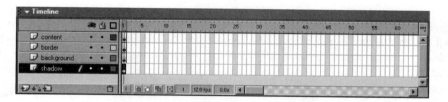

4. Select the background layer and add a white square with a 5pt black border – you can use the Round Rectangle Radius button 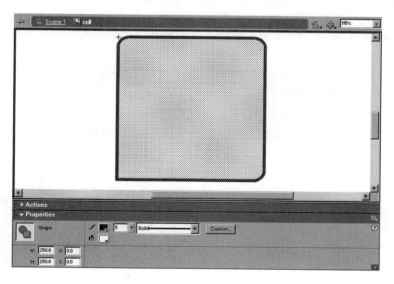 to give it curved corners if you like that sort of thing.

183

It should be 250 pixels wide, 250 pixels high, and positioned with its top left corner at X:0, Y:0.

5. Select the border, and use Edit > Cut *and* Edit > Paste in place to move it into the layer called border.

6. Select the background layer again, and make a *copy* of the white fill you left there. Paste it into the shadow layer, slightly down and to the right of the original. Use the Color Mixer to change its color to black, and set Alpha to 50% so that it's slightly transparent.

7. Select the background layer one more time, and hit F8 to convert its contents to a movie clip – we'll use this to give our showreel cells some color. Go straight back to the cell timeline, and you'll find an instance ready and waiting. Use the Property inspector to give it the instance name bgnd_mc:

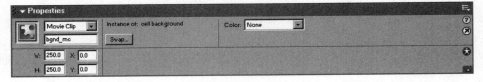

8. Now select the content layer and add a pair of dynamic text fields: one at the top and one at the bottom

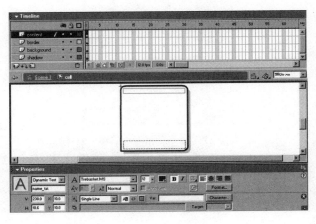

Use the Property inspector to name them as `name_txt` and `description_txt`. The lower one should also be set to Multiline, so that we can put in lots of nice descriptive text about our images.

9. Still on the content layer, add a black box in the space between the two text fields. Set its transparency (or Alpha) to 50% and press F8 to convert it to a movie clip. Head straight back to the cell timeline and set its instance name to `placeholder_mc`:

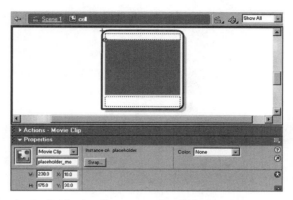

Now we've set up the individual cell as a movie clip, let's do the same for the complete showreel.

10. This bit's a lot simpler than the cell was. We just need to create a new movie clip called reel in the library, and stick in a single instance of the cell movie clip. You should call it `cell_mc`.

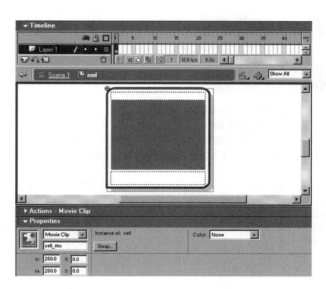

What – just one instance? Yes, just the one. We obviously don't want to run out of cells, but there's no point in making more than we need. So that our showreel movie stays as flexible as possible, I'm planning to use `duplicateMovieClip` to add more cells as and when they're needed. All the decision-making then goes on within the ActionScript, giving us a much more versatile movie! Neat, huh? Okay, you'll believe it when you see it.

11. There's just one more thing we need to do before the stage is all set up: add an instance of the reel movie clip to the main timeline, on the pictures layer. Use the Property inspector to name it `reel_mc` and position it at X:20, Y:20.

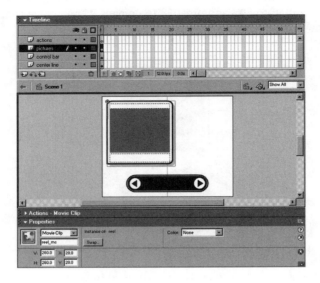

   All done!

Now the stage is all ready, it's time for us to add some ActionScript wiring behind the scenes and make all our movie clips perform some magic!

Scripting the showreel movie

Just like the Hangman example we saw in Chapter 4, there's quite a lot of script to get through here, but don't let that put you off! It all breaks down into very simple chunks, and we'll take them all quite slowly. Even if you don't understand every single line, you should still be able to get an idea of how the movie hangs together (and see how to tweak the important bits so that you can create your own variations!)

The first of these chunks controls the scrolling. It looks at where the mouse x-position is in relation to a centerline, and moves the `reel_mc` movie clip instance based on that distance. The direction (left or right) takes care of itself as long as we also consider the *sign* of this distance – whether it's positive or negative. We're not interested in the y position of reel, because we're only moving the movie clip from left to right. We're not moving it up and down at all, so it will always stay at the same y value.

Before we start working on the code for the scroll, we need to make sure that we're very clear on what we need to do – remember, if it won't work on paper, it won't work when you code it. We need a diagram, so here's a cleaned up version of the sketch I drew to figure out how this scroll movement should work:

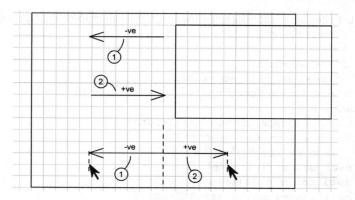

1. Here's the basic script, which you need to attach to frame 1of the actions layer:

```
center = Stage.width/2;
_root.onEnterFrame = function() {
    reelSpeed = (_xmouse-center)/10;
    reel_mc._x += reelSpeed;
};
```

Like I said before, it's not dissimilar from the stuff we did back in the first chapter.

According to our diagram, we need to relate the distance between the mouse and the centerline to the speed at which the reel scrolls. In other words, we want the reel to scroll faster the further away from the centerline the mouse gets. We've already defined center as the 'halfway across the stage' pixel value, so we get this line:

```
reelSpeed = (_xmouse-center);
```

We use reelSpeed to tell Flash how many pixels to move reel_mc across the screen every frame. Except, in the finished FLA, it's actually this...

```
reelSpeed = (_xmouse-center)/10;
```

The original line made it scroll too fast, so I just divided it by ten to make it scroll at a more sensible speed. Try running the movie now, and you'll see an instant result – the one-cell showreel moves from left to right under mouse control, just as we wanted it to.

When the mouse pointer is on the left of the centerline (case *1* in the sketch) _xmouse-center will be negative, giving us a negative speed and reel_mc moving further to the left with every new frame. If our mouse is to the right of center (as in situation *2*), we'll get a positive speed and the reel scrolls towards the right.

2. There's still a problem though. The reel doesn't stop when it gets to the edge, so it's quite easy to lose it off the side of the stage! In order to fix this, we need to put some limits on where reel_mc

can move. Let's set up a stop value at either end. We can stop changing `reel_mc._x` if it ever tries going beyond these values:

```
center = Stage.width/2;
cellWidth = reel_mc.cell_mc._width;
_root.onEnterFrame = function() {
    leftStop = 0;
    rightStop = Stage.width - cellWidth;
    reelSpeed = (_xmouse-center)/10;
    reel_mc._x += reelSpeed;
    if (reel_mc._x <leftStop) {
        reel_mc._x = leftStop;
    } else if (reel_mc._x >rightStop) {
        reel_mc._x = rightStop;
    }
};
```

Now, if the reel moves too far in one direction or the other, we stop it dead in its tracks!

Here, the left stop is at the left-hand edge of the stage, and the right stop is `cellWidth` pixels short of the right-hand side. The x-position of `reel_mc` tells us where its top-left corner is, but we want it to stop when its *right-hand* side hits the edge of the stage. We therefore take `cellWidth` off the value, which makes up the difference.

That's fine as long as we only have one cell in the showreel; but what about when we add some more in? With the stops as they are, we can't scroll anything off the left hand side of the stage, so we're never going to see a third or fourth cell, let alone a fifth, sixth, or seventh...

3. It looks like we need to rethink the stops. Ideally, we should be able to scroll far enough to see *any* one of the cells in the middle of the stage, no matter how many we have. The following should do the trick:

```
center = Stage.width/2;
cellWidth = reel_mc.cell_mc._width;
_root.onEnterFrame = function() {
    leftStop = center - reel_mc._width + cellWidth/2;
    rightStop = center - cellWidth/2;
    reelSpeed = (_xmouse-center)/10;
    reel_mc._x += reelSpeed;
    ...
};
```

The stops now ensure that the middle of the cell at either end of the showreel doesn't go past the center line. In the following screenshot from the finished application, you can see this. The cell is at the furthest right it can go – halfway across the center line.

If you run the movie now, you'll see that we've killed the scrolling movement! Our single cell is trapped in the middle of the stage – our new stops mean that it can't move either left *or* right...

Believe it or not, this is a *good* thing. The same cell occupies the left *and* right ends of our showreel, so the fact that it's confined to the center of the stage proves that our stops have worked. Of course, they'll be a lot more use when we've added in a few more cells!

At this stage, we have a perfectly good scroller. We just need to add in some pictures and text, and take it away! You could add some more instances of cell, import some graphics, add some static text fields, and so on. Great.

However, we're aiming a bit higher than that. Now we have some ActionScript power behind us, let's make it really work for us! Rather than hard-wiring cells and images into our movie, we're going to get ActionScript to figure out what we want and do it for us.

Next chunk then: we're going to write an ActionScript function that adds new cells!

4. We know how to write functions, and we know how to make duplicate clips, so lets put the two together. The function's going to define two arguments: num (telling it *which* cell we want to set up) and details (telling it *how* we want it set up). Here's the basic function declaration:

```
NewCell = function (num, details) {
    oldClip = _root.reel_mc.cell_mc;
    newClip = oldClip.duplicateMovieClip("cell"+num, num);
    newClip._x = num*300;
};
```

We start off by using oldClip to store a reference to the original cell instance, which is tucked away inside reel_mc in the root timeline. This just means we can now use the oldClip container in our script in place of the bulky _root.reel_mc.cell_mc, which is a bit of a mouthful in anyone's book!

Next, we use duplicateMovieClip to make a copy of the original cell. The new movie clip is called cell1, cell2, or whatever – depending on what value num has, and we store a reference to *that* in a container called newClip.

Now we tell Flash to set the _x property of newClip to num*300. Now newClip doesn't actually have an _x property, but it's pointing to something that does: the new movie clip. The end result is that our first cell (num=0) gets placed at X:0, while the second (num=1) goes to X:300, the third (num=2) to X:600, and so on.

5. Now just add a couple of function calls to the end of the script:

```
NewCell(0, "");
NewCell(1, "");
NewCell(2, "");
```

Run the movie and you'll see we now have a grand total of three cells, which scroll back and forth across the screen. All our new movie clips are created *inside* reel_mc, so the coordinates are relative to that. Our original script moves reel_mc, so all the cells move with it!

6. So, we've got lots of nice blank cells on the stage. They scroll okay, but they aren't much to look at. We need to pass our NewCell function some more information – a name, for example:

```
NewCell = function (num, details) {
    oldClip = _root.reel_mc.cell_mc;
    newClip = oldClip.duplicateMovieClip("cell"+num, num);
    newClip._x = num*300;
    newClip.name_txt.text = num+1 + ". " + details;
};
    NewCell(0, "Ben");
    NewCell(1, "Sham");
    NewCell(2, "Matt");
```

There's a new line in the function, which sets value of the name text field. We've used the details argument to pull strings out of the function calls:

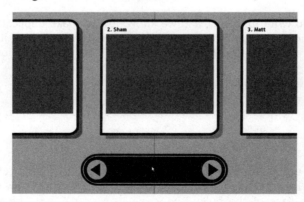

7. Alternatively, we could use details to pass information about what color we wanted to make the new cell's background – here's how we might do that:

```
NewCell = function (num, details) {
    oldClip = _root.reel_mc.cell_mc;
```

```
    newClip = oldClip.duplicateMovieClip("cell"+num, num);
    newClip._x = num*300;
    // Set color of cell background
    myColor = new Color(newClip.bgnd_mc);
    myColor.setRGB(details);
};
    NewCell(0, 0xFF9999);
    NewCell(1, 0x99FF99);
    NewCell(2, 0x9999FF);
```

This time, we've used the Color object to set the color of bgnd_mc inside each new clip:

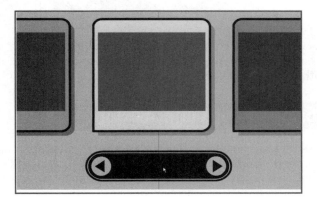

8. Most importantly of all, we want to tell Flash which images to use in each cell. There's a useful action called loadMovie(), which we can use to call up image files, but it still needs to know which file we want!

```
NewCell = function (num, details) {
    oldClip = _root.reel_mc.cell_mc;
    newClip = oldClip.duplicateMovieClip("cell"+num, num);
    newClip._x = num*300;
    // Set cell content
    content = newClip.placeholder_mc;
    content.loadMovie(details);
};
    NewCell(0, "cobblestones.jpg");
    NewCell(1, "planet.jpg");
    NewCell(2, "water.jpg");
```

This time, the new lines load up the image specified by details, and use it to replace the placeholder_mc movie clip instance in each new cell:

Of course, we actually want all three of these – and perhaps more! Of course, we could give the NewCell function a few more arguments, passing name in one, color in the next, and filename in the next. However, there's another option: we could send the details argument an object.

Objects for storing picture information

So far, we've always used simple variables as function parameters, passing strings and numbers to help the function do its job. But there's no reason why we can't feed it objects as well – then the function can pull out various property values as and when it needs them. We don't have to deal with lots of parameters, and we can define our object properties wherever we like.

1. Let's start by declaring a constructor function for a Picture class of object. Every Picture object will have four properties: name, link, color, and description, so it'll look like this:

```
Picture = function (name, link, color, description) {
    this.name = name;
    this.link = link;
    this.color = color;
    this.description = description;
};
```

2. Assuming we pass our NewClip function one of these Picture objects, via its details argument, we can use its properties like this:

```
NewCell = function (num, details) {
    oldClip = _root.reel_mc.cell_mc
    // Create a new cell
    newClip = oldClip.duplicateMovieClip("cell"+num, num);
    // Set cell position and text fields
    newClip._x = num*300;
    newClip.name_txt.text = num+1 + ". " + details.name;
    newClip.description_txt.text = details.description;
    // Set cell content
    content = newClip.placeholder_mc;
```

```
        content.loadMovie(details.link);
        // Set color of cell background
        myColor = new Color(newClip.bgnd_mc);
        myColor.setRGB(details.color);
    };
```

I've combined all our earlier cell customizations (plus a new one that sets the description text) into one version, which uses the four properties of the Picture object referred to by `details`. Of course, this relies on us calling `NewCell` with proper parameters...

3.   Here's the last piece in our jigsaw puzzle:

```
// Set up picture objects
pic0 = new Picture("cobblestones",
                   "cobblestones.jpg", 0xFF9999,
                   "from an English country lane...");
pic1 = new Picture("planet",
                   "planet.jpg", 0x99FF99,
                   "the view from 400km up...");
pic2 = new Picture("water",
                   "water.jpg", 0x9999FF,
                   "ripples in a pond...");
NewCell(0, pic0);
NewCell(1, pic1);
NewCell(2, pic2);
```

We create three objects, specifying properties as we go, and create the three cells quite separately. In fact, this would be even tidier if each Picture object was one element in an array – then we can simply loop through all the elements and create a new cell for each:

```
pics = new Array()
pics[0] = new Picture("cobblestones",
                      "cobblestones.jpg", 0xFF9999,
                      "from an English country lane...");
pics[1] = new Picture("planet",
                      "planet.jpg", 0x99FF99,
                      "the view from 400km up...");
pics[2] = new Picture("water",
                      "water.jpg", 0x9999FF,
                      "ripples in a pond...");
for (i=0; i<pics.length; i++) {
    NewCell(i, pics[i]);
};
```

Whew... I'm sure you'll be very pleased to hear that's the script all done! Try the movie out again, and you should get the full-on effect of a scrolling picture gallery...

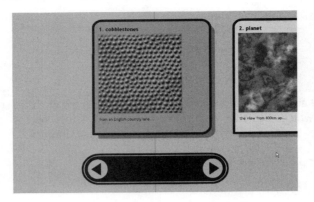

So, was all that hard work *really* worth it? We seem to have spent quite a lot of effort getting nowhere very much. The scrolling effect is pretty straightforward, and most of the script seems to just be mucking about with data behind the scenes. That's as may be, but thanks to all that mucking about, we have a showreel whose contents are completely defined by four lines of script.

> *Any time you want to change the content or appearance of one of our cells (or even add a completely new one) you can simply change (or add) an element in the* pics *array.*

Here's that script in full, complete with helpful comments:

```
// Initialize useful variables and picture array
cellWidth = reel_mc.cell_mc._width;
center = Stage.width/2;
pics = new Array();
// Handler to move showreel left and right across the stage
_root.onEnterFrame = function() {
    reelSpeed = (_xmouse-center)/10;
    reel_mc._x += reelSpeed;
    // Apply limits to reel position
    leftStop = center-reel_mc._width+cellWidth/2;
    rightStop = center-cellWidth/2;
    if (reel_mc._x < leftStop) {
        reel_mc._x = leftStop;
    } else if (reel_mc._x > rightStop) {
        reel_mc._x = rightStop;
    }
};
// Define constructor function for Picture objects
Picture = function (name, link, color, description) {
    this.name = name;
    this.link = link;
```

```
            this.color = color;
            this.description = description;
    };
    // Define function for creating cells in the showreel
    NewCell = function (num, details) {
        // Create a new cell
        originalClip = _root.reel_mc.cell_mc;
        newClip = originalClip.duplicateMovieClip("cell"+num, num);
        // Set cell position and text fields
        newClip._x = num*300;
        newClip.name_txt.text = num+1 + ". " + details.name;
        newClip.description_txt.text = details.description;
        // Set cell content
        content = newClip.placeholder_mc;
        content.loadMovie(details.link);
        // Set color of cell background
        myColor = new Color(newClip.bgnd_mc);
        myColor.setRGB(details.color);
    };
    // Create array elements to define cell details
    pics[0] = new Picture("cobblestones", cc
                          "cobblestones.jpg", 0xFF9999, cc
                          "from an English country lane...");
    pics[1] = new Picture("planet", cc
                          "planet.jpg", 0x99FF99, cc
                          "the view from 400km up...");
    pics[2] = new Picture("water", cc
                          "water.jpg", 0x9999FF, cc
                          "ripples in a pond...");
    // Loop through array elements, creating a new cell for each
    for (i=0; i<pics.length; i++) {
        NewCell(i, pics[i]);
    };
```

As I said before, don't panic if you don't understand every line in here – that's not the point. What you should be starting to appreciate is that it really pays to *structure* your scripts. Break them down into task-focused chunks, and the ease with which you can modify them later on should more than make up for the extra effort involved in writing them in the first place!

Summary

So, what have we learnt in this chapter? We've been introduced to objects, which are merely ways of grouping together related variables, constants, and functions so that they more closely resemble actual things that you might want to represent in your Flash movies.

As they represent real-life things, objects have state and behavior (they not only *are* things but they *do* things as well). In ActionScript, objects are described by their **properties** with their actions described by **methods.**

ActionScript has some built-in objects, which represent the sorts of standard elements that you'd want to include in your movies (such as numbers, strings, and math symbols) but you can also create your own objects to represent anything you wish. We've also learnt the difference between classes (which are general definitions of an object, such as Car or Tree) and **instances** (which are specific objects, such as Ferrari or Oak)

In the next chapter, we're going to tie the general concept of objects within code into something you've been using in Flash since before you'd heard of ActionScript – the movie clip – and we're going to see that you've been using objects all along, without even realizing it.

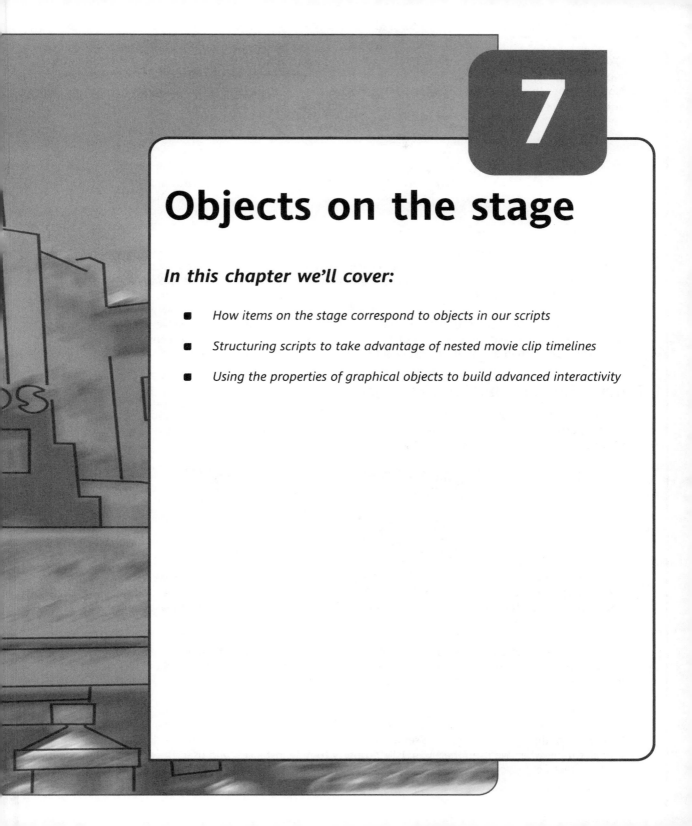

Objects on the stage

In this chapter we'll cover:

- *How items on the stage correspond to objects in our scripts*

- *Structuring scripts to take advantage of nested movie clip timelines*

- *Using the properties of graphical objects to build advanced interactivity*

Okay, let's not waste any time here. There's one main idea to wrap your brain around in this chapter: the movie clips, buttons, and text fields we've been using since way back when – well, *they're all objects too*. Not only does this fact make it a lot easier for us to explain a whole variety of ActionScript syntax, but it also opens up a lot of possibilities for what we can do to the things we see on the stage in the course of a movie.

> *The clues were all there, but credit to you if you spotted this already! If not, don't worry, because we're about to take a fresh look at these old friends.*

We already know that objects are useful for grouping together methods and properties that all have some sort of common theme. But what do the pure ActionScript objects (like Array and String) have to do with movie clips and things? Nothing at all, except that they all have things they **are** and things they can **do**. After all, that's what objects are good for!

Words like 'instance' and 'property' have already cropped up a few times when we've been talking about items on the stage, and whether or not you made a connection with the *object* instances and *object* properties we learned about in the last chapter, the connection's there sure enough.

Movie clips and buttons as objects

As we know, to control an item on the stage, we need to give it an instance name, and we can do this via the Property inspector. For example, say you've a movie clip called bat in the library; when you drag an instance onto the stage and select it, the Property inspector will look like this:

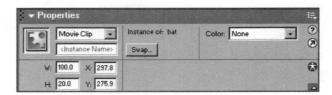

From here, we can set the instance name of this particular bat symbol, and also tweak its position, width, height, and even color. Any changes we make will only affect this particular instance (which we'll call bat_mc) and any other bat instances we decide to put onto the stage will have their own quite separate properties.

Once we've assigned an instance name to our movie clip instance, we can control these properties (and many more) from ActionScript. What's more, we do it in the same way as we controlled object properties in the last chapter – for example, we can set the *x*-coordinate like this:

```
bat_mc._x = 200;
```

So to control the bat's x-position, we set a property called _x for the bat_mc movie clip instance. We did a similar thing when we used the _visible property to hide instances, and used the text property of a dynamic text field to control what text appeared in it.

We also know that there are plenty of things a movie clip can **do**, so we expect to find at least one or two methods – for example, we can stop the bat_mc timeline like this:

```
bat_mc.stop();
```

But surely that's just the good old stop() action being applied to bat_mc? Yes, it is. But think for a moment about *what* an action really is – it's just an instruction to your movie (or to a movie clip) to **do** something. As far as ActionScript is concerned, there's no difference between notions of 'applying the stop() action to a movie clip' and 'calling a movie clip's stop() method'. They both mean the same thing: stop that movie clip!

> *When you're just starting out you can just talk about actions or commands and nobody will notice, but using their proper name, 'methods', will never fail to impress. Knowing how to apply methods in Flash is crucial if you want to make it as a top class ActionScripter.*

We've already seen a few other movie clip methods, such as duplicateMovieClip(), which we can use to make copies of a movie clip instance.

So, each instance (whether it's an input text field, a dynamic text field, a button, or a movie clip) has a set of **properties** that relate to its physical appearance. This is a movie clip, so the **properties** correspond to things like its position, size, visibility, and total number of frames, while the **methods** do things like play, stop, load, and duplicate it. A button instance has its own particular properties and methods, which (amongst other things) let us control whether or not it can be pressed. Text fields also have their own properties and methods, the majority of which determine how the text will appear on the screen.

> *If you look in the Actions Toolbox, you'll also see that the classes (MovieClip, Button, and TextField) behind each of these instances also contain lists of events. Yes, the events are part of the objects too – is anything safe? We won't talk about how they fit into the world of objects, since that's pretty advanced stuff, which you can safely get along without at this stage. It's useful to know they're there though, if only as a reminder of what events are available, and a place to start your own investigations.*

Using object properties

Let's have a quick reminder of movie clip object properties in action:

1. Draw a circle on the stage, and press F8 to make it a movie clip with the instance name ball01_mc.

2. Copy it, and paste in another instance called ball02_mc.

3. Create a new layer called Actions in the root timeline, and add the following script:

```
ball01_mc.onEnterFrame = function() {
    _x += 1;
};
```

Run the movie, and you'll see both balls move across the screen. Surely we've only defined a callback for the first ball, so why are both moving? Simple: when we specify _x in the event handler, we're actually working on _root._x, the x-position of the root timeline, which controls the *whole stage*! Both balls are on _root, so both balls move.

4. Now change the code like this:

```
ball01_mc.onEnterFrame = function() {
  ball01_mc._x += 1;
};
```

Now ball01_mc moves on its own. This is what we want: the onEnterFrame event handler for ball01_mc controls ball01_mc and nothing else.

5. Of course, that's not say we can't make it control something else:

```
ball01_mc.onEnterFrame = function() {
    ball02_mc._x = ball02_mc._x+1;
};
```

Now the ball01_mc event script controls the _x property of ball02_mc!

It's quite easy to get a feel for a movie clip object, because its properties and methods relate to its physical appearance. As you've seen, not all objects are so intuitive – in general, they can be collections of any number of properties and methods that may or may not have an obvious visual representation.

Behaviors

Behaviors are slightly different to methods and properties, and aren't so fundamental to how we *define* objects on the stage. However, they're very useful when we come to use library items, as they allow us to create instances of one symbol type from Library items of another type.

All symbols of a given type have a certain set of behaviors: a movie clip will behave like a movie clip (with frames, a play head, and a stop() method), while a graphic symbol has a distinct visual appearance and not much else. There's really not a great deal more to know about behaviors than common sense tells us.

One exception here is when we want to give graphic symbols properties that allow us to animate them – like the movie class has. To control a graphic symbol from ActionScript, you simply need to use the Property inspector to change its *behavior* to that of a movie clip:

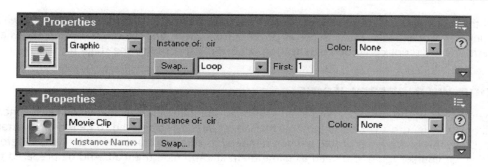

Now, despite the fact that cir is defined in the library as a graphic symbol, the movie itself will treat this particular instance as a movie clip. You gain use of the standard movie clip properties, and can begin to animate the symbol by writing ActionScript to modify them.

Hang on though! From what we discussed earlier, it sounded like bat_mc was an instance of a class called bat (as defined in the Library). But now we've seen a MovieClip class in the Actions Toolbox, and discovered it's possible to change the instance behavior without changing the library item. So what's going on?

Two sides of the same object

The first thing to get clear is this: the Library doesn't *define* object classes. Actually, it just serves as a place where we can collect resources for dropping into our movies – a library item won't normally have anything to do with the compiled movie unless we put an instance on the stage.

If the library item is set up as a button symbol, it will store resources that you'd expect to find useful in a button, such as four frames labeled Up, Down, Over, and Hit, which will be shown when the appropriate mouse events trigger them off. On the other hand, if it's set up as a graphic symbol, it only needs one frame.

So, if you drag a button symbol onto the stage, and tell it to behave like a graphic, Flash will create a graphic based on resources from the first frame of the button symbol. Likewise (as we saw just now), if you drag a one-framed graphic symbol onto the stage and tell it to behave like a movie, it won't suddenly acquire more frames – the resources simply aren't there – but it will take on the ability to *behave* like a movie clip. We're basically telling Flash to create a movie clip and use the (limited) resources of the graphic symbol to give it some kind of visual presence on the stage.

> This 'behaving like a movie clip' business is all down to the MovieClip class. Likewise, a button's behavior is defined by the Button class. The behavior of a graphic is notable by its absence – it just sits tight and (hopefully) looks good – so we've no need for a class to define what it can do.

So, is there any way to tap into these Library resources from our ActionScript? After all, we're trying to find out how to control as many things as possible from there, and we could save ourselves a lot of time and effort if the script could be made to drop all our instances onto the stage for us.

Working with library items

The good news is: this isn't very hard at all. Our main stumbling block is that when Flash generates a SWF, it will normally ignore any Library symbols that aren't already being used to help define instances on the stage. Okay, this isn't a great problem if you're happy to add an instance of every symbol before you start scripting. Of course, you'd also need to name them all. And hide them all. And be prepared to take a bit of a performance hit if there are lots of them. But, if you have lots of time on your hands and you're not fussed about making your movie efficient, that's just fine.

That's not me though, and I suspect it's not you either!

If you've never scripted before (and possibly if you have) this may be the first time you realized this was possible – let alone seen it done. With non-scripted movies, you *always* have to put stuff on stage manually.

What we're talking about here is quite different – we'll use ActionScript to take a movie clip **directly** from the library and put it onto the stage. Okay, at first this may seem like a minor thing, but you can make some really cool features with this technique: for example, you can let users pick what symbols are used to control a movie – even while it's running. You'll certainly find it lurking behind stacks of the awesome effects produced by famous Flash designers.

Let's cut the talk, and see how we can use ActionScript to pull symbols straight out of the library and onto the stage:

Making a swarm of particles

In this example, I'm going to create a small cluster of particles, each of which will move about in tiny, random steps, giving the appearance of a swarming mass of, well, who knows what! I hope you'll agree though – the end result sufficiently eye-catching to make the effort worthwhile.

1. Create a new movie (CTRL/CMD+N). Make sure the stage is active and use the Properties inspector to give it a black background. In the Timeline panel, rename Layer 1 as actions.

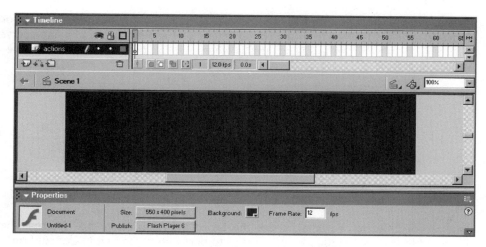

2. Use Insert > New Symbol to create a new movie clip called particle. Use the Color Mixer to set up a radial fill style fading from opaque white at the center to transparent white at the perimeter. Now add a circle to the particle movie clip (mine's about 70 pixels in diameter).

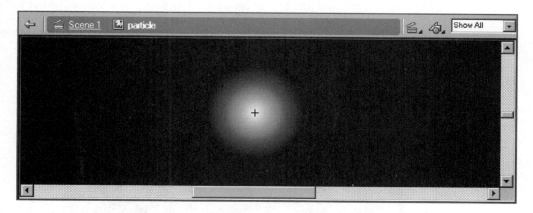

Now click on the Scene 1 link to head back to the main timeline. In a moment, we're going to write some ActionScript that will put several copies of the particle movie clip onto the stage for us. First though, we must first tell Flash to include it in the final SWF, and how to identify it.

When we create a symbol (graphic, button, or movie clip) in Flash, the name we give it in the library is really just for our benefit – a descriptive name to help remind us what it's for, and so that we can refer to it easily in text and speech. As far as ActionScript is concerned, that name doesn't exist. So, in order to call up a library symbol from ActionScript, we need to give that symbol a special codey name that ActionScript can see: this is called a **linkage identifier**.

As we've learnt, if there aren't initially any instances of a symbol on the stage (and this will certainly be the case for our particle movie clip), Flash won't normally bother including it in the SWF it generates. If this happened, our ActionScript would end up asking for something that wasn't there. Let's do something about that.

3. Call up the Library panel (press F11) and CTRL-click (right-click on PCs) on the entry for our particle movie clip. Select Linkage from the context menu that appears, and you'll find yourself presented with the Linkage Properties dialog. This is where we link our movie clip up to the ActionScript environment.

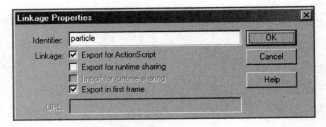

Set the Identifier to "particle", check the Export for ActionScript box (so that the movie gets exported to the SWF, ready for ActionScript to play with it), and hit OK to confirm.

In this case, we've used a Linkage Identifier that's the same as our descriptive library name, saving us from any possibility of a mix-up. Remember though: they're quite separate names (one for you, one for ActionScript) and could just as well be completely different if that was what you wanted.

4. Select Frame 1 of the actions layer (in the root timeline) and open up the Actions panel. This is where we're going to put all our ActionScript.

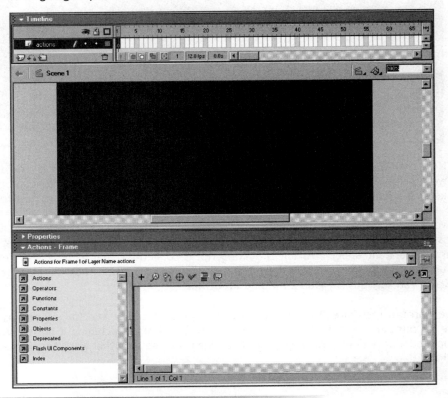

5. Begin by putting a single instance of the particle movie clip onto the stage, using the attachMovie() method:

```
_root.attachMovie("particle", "particle1", 1);
```

This will leave us with an instance of the particle movie clip (called particle1) on level 1 of the root movie timeline. If you test run the movie now, you'll see it sitting there, lifeless and still – let's do something about that and bring it to life!

6. Add the following lines to your ActionScript:

```
_root.attachMovie("particle", "particle1", 1);
_root["particle1"].onEnterFrame = function() {
    this._x += (Math.random()*4)-2;
    this._y += (Math.random()*4)-2;
};
```

These new lines define an event handler for our particle1 object: whenever it enters a new frame, it will change its own _x and _y properties (defining its position on the stage) by a random amount of up to 2 pixels in either direction. This will make it shuffle around randomly on the stage, as you'll see if you test run the movie again.

Math.random() generates a random decimal number between zero and one, such as 0.56478903454. By using Math.random()*4, we get a random number between zero and four, and then subtract two, giving us a value between -2 and 2.

If you want to be sure of getting a whole number (that is, 78, rather than 78.456734324), you can use Math.round(myVal) to round the value up or down to the nearest whole number, or Math.floor(myVal) to simply chop off the decimals and round down.

7. Note that we're using a timeline loop to animate the particles – it's only because the movie will, by default, repeat indefinitely, that they move at all. So what about the ActionScript loop?

Well, we actually want to put a whole lot of particles onto the screen. We could just cut and paste the above code (replacing each particle1 with particle2, particle3, and so on) but that would be rather a waste of time when we have the power of loops to fall back on. Add the highlighted lines below to your ActionScript:

```
for (counter = 0; counter<10; counter++) {
  _root.attachMovie("particle", "particle1", 1);
  _root["particle1"].onEnterFrame = function() {
    this._x += (Math.random()*4)-2;
    this._y += (Math.random()*4)-2;
  };
};
```

Here, we've set up a for loop, using the variable counter to keep track of how many loops we've been through; we use 'counter is less than ten' as its condition. Everything inside the brackets will be repeated again and again until the expression counter<10 turns out to be false. Fortunately, counter++ will add 1 to the value of counter every cycle – so, after ten cycles, counter will reach 10 and our loop will stop looping.

As you can see, the brackets also contain the code we used to create the particle1 instance of our particle movie clip (on level 1 of the root timeline). Now we're executing that code ten times, it should make us ten separate particles – shouldn't it? No, it won't, unless we make a few changes. Firstly, we need to give each instance a different name, so that ActionScript can tell them apart. Secondly, we can only attach one instance to each depth level – at the moment, they're all being attached to level 1, so each one gets wiped out when the next is attached. So we also need to change the depth number every time we call attachMovie().

We already know about one way to do all this – back in Chapter 4, we did a similar thing using the function duplicateMovieClip() and a counter variable called i:

```
duplicateMovieClip(particle_mc, "particle"+i+"_mc", i);
```

In fact, duplicateMovieClip is a MovieClip object method, so we could have written this is as:

```
particle_mc.duplicateMovieClip("particle"+i+"_mc", i);
```

This time, we don't have an instance on the stage to begin with, so we call attachMovie() from the root movie timeline. Apart from that though, the same basic principles stand.

> You may have already noticed that _root shares many similarities with the movie clips we put into it – in fact, you can almost think of it as a movie clip in its own right: it has a timeline, as well as properties and methods you'd expect from any movie clip. The main difference is that it's always there, so we don't need to create it ourselves.

So, here's how we can attach a brand new particle movie clip instance to the stage for each new value of counter:

```
_root.attachMovie("particle", "particle"+counter, counter);
```

We use '+' to add (or concatenate) the current value of counter to the end of the string literal "particle" to create a new, unique string for each loop.

8.   Let's put this in so that each of our instance names and level numbers stays unique – change the highlighted lines as shown:

```
for (counter = 0; counter<10; counter++) {
  _root.attachMovie("particle", "particle"+counter, counter);
  _root["particle"+counter].onEnterFrame = function() {
    this._x += (Math.random()*4)-2;
    this._y += (Math.random()*4)-2;
```

```
    };
  };
```

If you run the movie now, you'll see the gently pulsating cluster of particles we've been working towards.

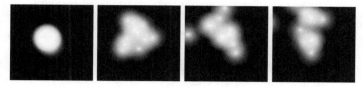

Navigating the timelines

Something we've seen rather a lot of here is the keyword this. I explained it very briefly at the end of the last chapter, but it's very useful, and has quite a subtle effect, so it's worth spending a little more time on.

Whenever you use ActionScript to define a variable, a function, or even an object, you're always defining it in the context of a particular timeline. If your script is attached to the root timeline (which it probably will be most of the time), a variable called myVar will have the full name _root.myVar (or _level0.myVar if you look in the debug variables – unless you're into heavy stuff like loading multiple movies, you can assume that _level0 is always equivalent to _root).

The _root bit on the beginning is called a **path**, and quite literally tells Flash what route it needs to take to get to the correct timeline. As soon as you have several instances of a movie clip in your movie, this becomes very important.

Different place, different variable

Say you defined a variable called igor in the timeline of a movie clip called castle. If you then added an instance of castle called glamis_mc to the main (_root) timeline, the full name of the thane variable inside would be _root.glamis_mc.igor.

> *Remember – since we address variables in the same way as we address movie clips in a path, it's always handy to include the _mc suffix on the end of the clip's instance name so you can easily tell them apart.*

So why go to this trouble – what's wrong with just calling it igor? Well, if you added another instance of castle (called cawdor_mc) to the root timeline, then you'd have another variable called igor sitting in there too. Its full name would be _root.cawdor_mc.igor, and the two igor variables would be quite separate.

> *A variable has a value and a name, but like streets with identical names in two different cities, a pair of like-named variables can be quite different beasts; if you pick the wrong one, you can get hopelessly confused! Say you were in Ealing, London, and asked a cab driver to take you to Broadway, you might be a little worried if he whisked you off to Manhattan for an audience with Liza Minnelli!*

So, most variables are **localized** to a particular timeline. Identically named variables in different paths are quite distinct entities, and can hold different values or types. Flash would recognize your two `igor`s as being different, no problem, but you would have to be very careful to make sure that *you* remember the difference!

Locating variables from inside a callback function

This seems obvious enough when you're placing your scripts within your movie clips and buttons; but I've already expressed a preference for centralizing code. Ideally, you should keep as much of it as possible on the first frame of your root timeline. So, how do you locate a variable when you're using it as part of a callback function?

Well, the normal place to define a callback is on the root timeline of the movie. Flash will assume that any variables you use inside the function are to be found on that timeline, and *not* in the button your callback references.

Say we want to model the changing bat population in each of our castles, and put the following code in the root timeline:

```
glamis_mc.onEnterFrame = function() {
  batCounter = batCounter + 1
};
cawdor_mc.onEnterFrame =function() {
  batCounter = batCounter - 1;
};
```

From this, we might expect to find Glamis's bat count going through the roof (no pun intended), with Cawdor quickly plummeting to zero. Actually, both callbacks are changing the same variable: `_root.batCounter` to give it its full name – and because one bumps it up while the other bumps it down every frame, its value never changes.

We need to make it more explicit that we want each event handler to work on a different variable `batCounter`, with one defined for each castle – so their full names are `glamis_mc.batCounter` and `cawdor_mc.batCounter`:

```
glamis_mc.onEnterFrame = function() {
   glamis_mc.batCounter = glamis_mc.batCounter + 1
};
cawdor_mc.onEnterFrame =function() {
   cawdor_mc.batCounter = cawdor_mc.batCounter - 1;
};
```

We now have two variables of the same name but in different places, so they can have different values and not interfere with each other.

Reusing callbacks

Let's suppose we introduce a third castle into our imaginary scenario. This one's called `rosslyn_mc`, and it has a bat infestation problem similar to that of `glamis_mc`. We might simulate it like this:

```
glamis_mc.onEnterFrame = function() {
   glamis_mc.batCounter = glamis_mc.batCounter + 1
};
cawdor_mc.onEnterFrame =function() {
   cawdor_mc.batCounter = cawdor_mc.batCounter - 1;
};
rosslyn_mc.onEnterFrame = function() {
   rosslyn_mc.batCounter = rosslyn_mc.batCounter + 1
};
```

Of course, that'll work fine; but between you and me, there's a simpler way to do it.

The event handler code we just added is almost exactly the same as what we wrote before for `glamis_mc`; the only difference is that one works on `glamis_mc`, while the other works on `rosslyn_mc`.

> *"So what?" you may think, "it's just a couple of lines!" Sure, it's no big deal in this case – but if you're writing full-blown movies with event handlers that go on for pages, it's a real pain if you have to duplicate everything and change all the names. As the environmentally conscious amongst you will appreciate, extra keystrokes make your keys wear out more quickly, which means more plastic key production and a swifter onset of global warming. Oh yeah, plus it makes your movie bigger and generates extra opportunities for code errors – both Very Bad Things™ as well!*

Well, the folks at Macromedia have thought of all this, and made it nice and easy to recycle callbacks. There are two steps involved:

- **multiple assignments** – writing one event handler to deal with several events

- **relative paths** – using `this` to refer to the controlling timeline

The first may sound a bit intimidating, but (as usual) it really isn't! When we write out a callback, the equals sign does the same thing as it does when we use it to set a variable: it takes whatever's on its right-hand side, and assigns it to whatever's on the left hand side. You may hear programmers refer to it as 'the assignment operator' for precisely this reason – 'equals' will do fine for us though.

The handy thing is that we can do this more than once. If we write:

```
myVar1 = myVar2 = "Sham";
```

we're setting the values of two different variables (myVar1 and myVar2) to the string literal 'Sham'.

Likewise, if we put...

```
glamis_mc.onEnterFrame = rosslyn_mc.onEnterFrame = function() {
   glamis_mc.batCounter = glamis_mc.batCounter + 1
};
```

...we're setting the same callback for the onEnterFrame events of both glamis_mc and rosslyn_mc; and we only have to write it out once!

Hang on though! If we do this we're in trouble, since the batCounter variable specified here is the one for glamis_mc; what about rosslyn_mc.batCounter? Well this is where the second step comes in.

We've already done a little with the this keyword. As you may recall, it always refers to the **source** of the event that's being handled – that is, the timeline that generated it. If we're handling the glamis_mc.onEnterFrame event, then this points to glamis_mc. Likewise, if we're handling the rosslyn_mc.onEnterFrame event, this will point to rosslyn_mc.

> Inside a callback, this in front of a variable name changes its scope from the timeline the code is attached to, to the timeline where the triggering event came from.

So, to make our callback recycling work properly, we just need to generalize the event handler like this:

```
glamis_mc.onEnterFrame = rosslyn_mc.onEnterFrame = function() {
   this.batCounter = this.batCounter + 1
};
```

Now we have two callbacks for the price of one!

To write an all-purpose handler, just scope your variables to the **controlling** timeline (by putting `this` in front of their names) rather than to the timeline to which they're **attached**. This is a fundamental concept to get to grips with. Once you have, you've made a major step forward in mastering Flash MX ActionScript!

So, we have a neat way to keep our code centralized, but still have it behave in the logical way that we want it to.

Same name, different variable

Let's see how we can put `this` to work.

1. Let's start off with our faithful friend, the `input-output.fla` movie that we saved away back in Chapter 2. Since we want to look at the effects of nesting variables inside a movie clip, let's change the behavior of our Enter button and use that. Just to remind us that we're now dealing with a movie clip, give it the instance name `enter_mc`:

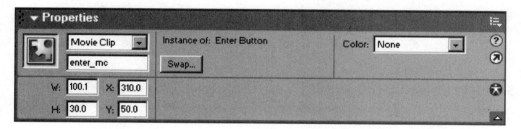

2. Select the first frame of the timeline, and use the Actions pane to change the script attached to it as follows:

```
enter_mc.onRelease = function() {
  input1 = "root";
  output1 = input1;
};
```

Test the movie and hit the button without typing anything. You'll see that both of the boxes display the word 'root':

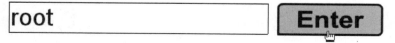

root

This is because we just told the button's `onRelease` event handler to do that! It sets the input box to display 'root', and then sets the output box to mimic the input box.

The extra line we added simply sets the value of `input1`. Remember that, unless we specify otherwise, a variable exists in the timeline it's created in. At this point, there are no explicit paths in our code, so `input1` is interpreted as `_root.input1`, and set to hold the string literal `'root'`.

3. Since we define `output1` for use by the dynamic text field (which is also sitting in the root timeline), its full name is likewise `_root.output1`. We can therefore make this whole callback more explicit by rewriting it as follows:

```
enter_mc.onRelease = function() {
  _root.input1 = "root";
  _root.output1 = _root.input1;
};
```

Since our script's attached to the root timeline, we don't actually *need* to do this. But what if we wanted to access variables or properties that *aren't* defined in the root timeline?

4. Add the following lines to the top of your script:

```
enter_mc.onPress = function() {
  this.input1 = "movie";
};
```

This sets up an event to trigger as soon as the movie clip is pressed, which creates a variable called `input1` *inside the movie clip*. It contains the value 'movie'.

5. Okay, now we can really demonstrate what's going on. At the moment, if you test the code you'll still get 'root timeline' showing in both boxes. Go back to the `onRelease` handler and change it like this:

```
enter_mc.onRelease = function() {
  input1 = "root";
  output1 = this.input1;
};
```

All we've done is to add a `this` path in front of the second variable, but if you test the movie, you'll see what a big difference this makes. The input text box is still being set on the root, so it still displays 'root'; but the output text box is now being set to display the variable we defined inside the movie clip (`enter_mc.input1`), so it reads 'movie'.

root

movie

Same action, different object

When you ran the movie, you'll no doubt have noticed the button cycling through all the different states we originally defined for the button symbol. Now that we've told it to behave as a movie clip, there's no built-in rollover behavior, because that's something a button does, and not something a movie clip does. Well, not unless we tell it to!

Let's write some event handlers that will make our movie clip behave like it's a button.

1. First, we can add some actions to our existing handlers. When we press the button, it should go to the down position at frame 2:

```
enter_mc.onPress = function() {
  this.gotoAndStop(2);
  this.input1 = "movie";
};
```

2. Likewise, when we release the button, it should go back to the up state at frame 1:

```
enter_mc.onRelease = function() {
  this.gotoAndStop(1);
  input1 = "root";
  output1 = this.input1;
};
```

Once again, we've used `this` to tell Flash what path to use. In both cases, we want to `gotoAndStop()` on the instance called `enter_mc`. Since that's the object on which we've defined the callback, we can refer to it using `this`.

3. We can finish this off by adding `mouseOver` and `mouseOut` event handlers, and making the movie clip stop at frame 1 automatically:

```
enter_mc.onRollOut = function() {
    this.gotoAndStop(1);
};
enter_mc.onRollOver = function() {
    this.gotoAndStop(2);
};
enter_mc.gotoAndStop(1);
```

Run the movie one more time, and you'll see the movie clip behave just as if it were a button.

So, a few lines of extra code to get the same effect as we had to begin with – what's the big deal? Well, apart from the fact that we've seen how `this` helps us make sure we're running actions on the right timeline, we now have the framework for a totally customizable button behavior, all written in ActionScript.

Using this script as a starting point, you can make up your own button rules from scratch. What's more, you can have as many complex transitions as you like on this movie clip button – not just the three frames and a hit zone you have with the normal button.

At this point, you might well be thinking one (or both) of the following:

- "I want to be good and include clear paths in my callbacks, but I really can't be doing with writing `this` out 100 times in my code."

- "Can't I just define a variable that *any* movie clip or button in my entire movie can talk to without having to mess around with remembering a path?"

Luckily, there are simple solutions to both of these problems.

Changing the default path

Instead of writing `this` in front of every variable in a callback, you can nest the handler code inside a `with` action. Here's an example:

```
enter_mc.onRelease = function() {
  with (this) {
    _root.input1 = "root";
    _root.output1 = input1;
  };
};
```

We use the `with()` action to specify a timeline when we start, and any variables we use in the `with` body that aren't specified with an absolute path (in this case, just `input1`) are assumed to be on that timeline.

We have to prefix the other variables with `_root` because we're now looking inside the `enter_mc` movie clip, but the text boxes are still on the root timeline. We don't need anything extra for the final `input1` variable because its path is already set as the `enter_mc` movie clip – thanks to the `with()` action.

> *Normally, if we use a variable without specifying which timeline it's on, Flash assumes it's on the current timeline. Inside a* with *statement though, Flash will assume it's on the timeline specified in the* with *action.*

The usefulness of this approach is a little more obvious if we have lots of `this.` variables to consider:

```
glamis_mc.onEnterFrame = function() {
    this.batCounter = this.batCounter + 1;
    this.visitors = this.visitors - 1;
};
```

becomes:

```
glamis_mc.onEnterFrame = function() {
  with (this) {
    batCounter = batCounter + 1;
    visitors = visitors - 1;
  };
};
```

Using paths to put functions where we need them

We can also use this technique to define functions in other timelines. Say we have a movie clip on the root timeline with the instance name `mathClip_mc`. If we want this clip to contain a simple `double` function, we'd need to use code like this:

```
double = function(result) {
    var result;
    result = result*2;
    return result;
};
```

Let's run through a quick example to see this in action, and use it to make a movie clip accelerate off the screen.

1. Create a new FLA document and create a simple shape on the far left-hand side of the stage. Convert this shape into a movie clip and give it the instance name `mathClip_mc`.

2. Attach the following code to the first frame of the root timeline:

```
with (mathClip_mc) {
    double = function (result) {
        var result;
        result = result*2;
        return result;
    };
    _x = 1;
}
mathClip_mc.onEnterFrame = function() {
    this._x = double(this._x);
};
```

You'll see here that we've used a `with` command to tie the two pieces of code (defining the function, and setting the `_x` property) to the `mathClip_mc` timeline. We've then used a callback to run the function every frame. If you test the movie, you should see the shape zoom off the screen.

Using functions as objects

There's another way to add functions to a movie clip (or any object for that matter). Just as all string variables are automatically able to use the methods defined in the String class, all functions have automatic access to methods in the class called Function. You can find it amongst the Core objects in the Actions Toolbox:

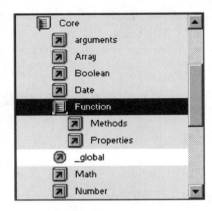

The method we're going to look at here is called `apply`, and this lets us to take a generic function and apply that to any movie clip we like.

1. Start a new movie, and draw a shape on the stage up in the top left-hand corner. Convert your shape into a movie clip, and give it the instance name: `ball_mc`.

2. Open up the Actions window and select frame 1 in the main timeline. Now type in the following movement function:

```
mover = function () {
    this.onEnterFrame = function() {
        this._x += (_xMouse - this._x)/this._width;
        this._y += (_yMouse - this._y)/this._height;
    };
};
```

Here, we've embedded an event within our main function, and just referred to the movieclip as `this`. One of the most powerful things about the `Function.apply` method is that it defines `this` as the object that you are applying the function to – making it totally generic. Now to call the function...

3. Add this line after the previous piece of code:

```
mover.apply(ball_mc);
```

As you can see, we're addressing our function as we would any other object, using dot notation to specify the method, and then passing our argument (the name of the movie clip that we want to apply the function to) inside the brackets.

That's it! Run the movie and you should see your shape follow the mouse pointer around the screen. For practice, create another couple of shapes on the stage and use the `apply` method to apply the function to them too. Depending on the instance names you used, your final code should look something like this:

```
mover = function () {
    this.onEnterFrame = function() {
        this._x += (_xMouse - this._x)/this._width;
        this._y += (_yMouse - this._y)/this._height;
    };
};
mover.apply(ball_mc);
mover.apply(shape1_mc);
mover.apply(shape2_mc);
```

Now that you've written the function, you could apply to any object at all: use it to move a ball, a tree, a dog, anything you like really.

You can see how powerful this feature is in creating concise and re-usable code, and what a benefit it will be to your toolbox. It can initially feel a bit strange thinking of a function as an object, but as with many of these things, the less deeply you think about it the more it makes sense, and one day you'll be innocently using it when it'll suddenly click into place and you'll wonder why you ever found it confusing in the first place. Flash is often like that, and ActionScript even more so. The secret is just to keep at it, and keep making the most inane Flash movies – trying strange and different things – until they no longer seem different or strange, just normal.

Global variables

To fully answer the second of our two questions from earlier on (I know – you thought I'd forgotten!) we need to introduce a new concept: the **scope** of a variable is the part of the movie in which it can be referenced. There are three different types of variable scope:

- Local – only available within the {} bracketed script block in which they're defined

- Timeline – variables available to any timeline (provided you use a target path)

- Global – variables available to any timeline (which don't need a target path)

We've already seen how `var` can be used to declare **local variables** inside a block of script. This is most commonly found when working with loops, which often recycle their counter variables. We don't want `counter` from one loop to interfere with `counter` from another loop, so we make each variable local to its own loop. They're both destroyed as soon as the loop's finished and neither has any idea of the other's existence.

As for timeline variables, we've already learned that their path is part of what makes them unique; their position in the movie is part of the thing that defines them. Whenever we define a plain old variable, we have to ask: *where* have we defined it? Say we define a variable in some ActionScript that we've attached to a movie clip – the variable's **location** will be the timeline of that movie clip, but its **scope** extends to all timelines in the movie. That's to say, as long as you know where to look path-wise, you can access it from anywhere you like!

What we really want to do is define a variable that has the entire movie as its scope, but doesn't need us to specify a target path. Before Flash MX came along, ActionScripters would often fudge their way around this one by storing commonly used 'global' variables in _root. That way, if they did have to specify a path, at least it was nice and short!

We can do things properly though, and creating a truly global variable in Flash is as simple as this:

```
_global.myVar = "This is available anywhere in the movie!";
```

If you were then to trace this from anywhere else in the movie, you could simply put:

```
trace(myVar);
```

And the correct value would be displayed in the Output window. Try it if you like and see:

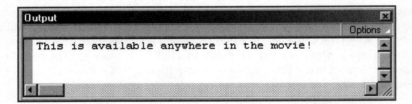

It's worth noting that you can only use the short name to *access* the variable, and not to set it. Say you now added the following code in the root timeline:

```
myVar = "Ben";
```

This would override the global value – that is, `trace(myName)` would give you 'Ben' – but *only* for the root timeline. Even then, you could still access the original, global value by simply using:

```
trace(_global.myName)
```

If you wanted to set the global variable to something else later on in the movie, then you'd have to do it as you did initially, by prefacing it with _global.

Summary

In this chapter we've covered a wide range of concepts and skills to do with objects, including:

- Movie clips and buttons as objects

- Object properties, behaviors and classes

- Utilising the library contents directly through your ActionScript

- Navigating timelines and using paths

- Using functions as objects

- Creating and using global variables

Congratulations – you're well on the way to mastering the scripting skills that will take your Flash work to new heights. You've learnt the basic ActionScript structures that underpin everything else, and we're now ready to start looking at the really amazing stuff that's possible when you start putting them to work. Time for a well-deserved rest!

In the next half of the book, we're going to look at building whole projects and adding in cool new features like sound and sprites. The visibility on this mountain is improving with every passing minute, and now it's time to really start focusing on the summit.

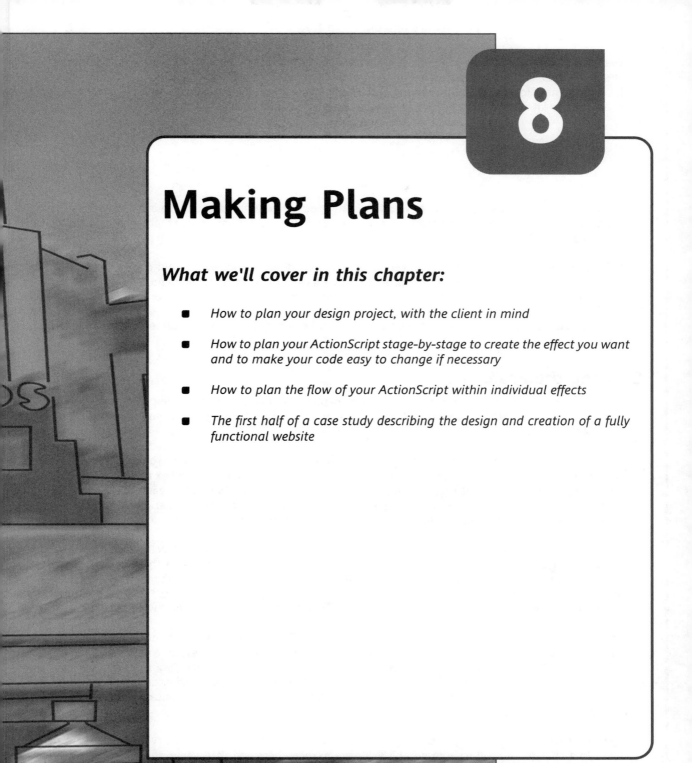

Making Plans

What we'll cover in this chapter:

- How to plan your design project, with the client in mind

- How to plan your ActionScript stage-by-stage to create the effect you want and to make your code easy to change if necessary

- How to plan the flow of your ActionScript within individual effects

- The first half of a case study describing the design and creation of a fully functional website

I've been involved in programming and design for some time now. My original discipline was engineering, and I have been close to computers in one form or another since the late 1980s. My engineering discipline has taught me a lot about computers and coding, and there is one fundamental rule that I have carried over with me into multimedia design:

> *If it doesn't work on paper, it won't work when you code it*

In this chapter, I'd like to show you how, as I'm setting out on a design project, I've learnt to define the overall problem, split it into manageable sections, and structure my ActionScript so that it gives me exactly what I need in a way that's easy to change if I need to.

I'll round off the chapter with a little reminder that web design is not just a cold-coding process. I'll introduce you to stun:design, a web site project that we'll work on as we go through the book. You'll learn how to plan usable interfaces and brew up cool vehicles to show off your cutting-edge ActionScript skills.

The best place to start is always the beginning, and that beginning is where you define what you need to do.

Defining the Problem

If this book were a textbook on writing novels, this chapter would be all about defining your **plot**. Without plot, your characters would have no motive and your audience would quickly realize your book was going nowhere.

The same holds true for ActionScript coding. If you don't have a good idea of what you want to achieve, you're stuck. Most designers love to play around with ideas and end up with a toolbox of little demos and cool effects that they can put together later to build up a full web site. Even this organic way of working (which is the way I work) requires you to think about how your effects will fit together and what your aim actually is for a web site. You should have a fair idea of direction before you start.

In real life you have a further complication that thwarts your ideas and clean, structured designs. That complication is **the client**. A good plan is a safety net that helps you guard against those little requests, "Can we just move everything half a pixel to the left", or "No, we can't use that, didn't I tell you we wanted an advertising banner to go on top?" (Uhh, no you didn't), and the all time classic, "That's great, and I know we go online in two days, but here's a list of 35 minor changes that Bob and I would like..."

The primary driving force of design must be managing the client's **expectations** and discussing their **real needs**. Formulating the project beforehand and getting agreement early on goes some way to solving this. All the same, I'd be making false promises if I told you that, in a typical project, your design objectives wouldn't change at least once! This is something you just have to live with, and make sure that your design is defined well enough to let you go backwards as well as forwards, and branch out onto a new path if the client (or technical problems) force you to do so.

Your plans will help you through this, so you can point to them and say things like, "Well, if you want to make that change, this will have to go, this will have to move here and that will go there, is that okay?", without having to take the time to actually do it first to see what it looks like. This is a fact of web design, and though you may not experience it until you've finished a few paid jobs, you'll be glad of your plans when you do.

Keep your ideas in a safer place than your head

Working in a field that requires me to think creatively doesn't mean that I am instantly creative. By the time I need some ideas, they're usually all gone. We all get good ideas, but most of us forget them with the passage of time. I now keep a hardbound book of lined paper for these transient ideas and a book of black card pages (black because it makes things much easier to scan into a computer), where I keep pictures that have caught my eye.

I have a real collection of images in my book now, from Polish Nightclub flyers to stylized text-less instructions for inserting camera film told through icons. It's all great reference material. For example, I kept the edge of an old pay slip from a few years ago: one that was obviously printed by a big fast industrial computer printer. It has those funny sprocket holes in it, some print registration marks and some optical character recognition numbers. I would normally have put this straight in the trashcan, but one day it struck me that it had a real made by computer feel, so I kept it. Several years later, I used it for the opening titles of a graphic novel I wrote and illustrated, which has an intelligent supercomputer as a main character.

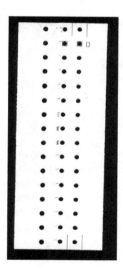

You can see the progress from the grubby bit of paper on the left to the finished article on the right. Download the book's support files and take a look at stundesign.swf to see how the final design turned out. You may think that it looks similar to the data animations from "The Matrix", but mine was based on a scrappy bit of paper and not a thousand-dollar computer animation!

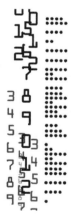

So, you've talked to the client, you've gathered a collection of ideas from things that you see every day, and perhaps any assets (sound, music, video clips) that will play a part in your final site design. The next step is to tie down these ideas, to form a concrete shape that shows you how you need to implement any ActionScript as part of the project.

There are a number of ways you can do this:

1. Write down the essence of the site in plain English.
2. Quickly code up a basic sample site and discuss it with the client if possible.
3. Storyboard the site, perhaps as a set of static Photoshop or Paint Shop Pro mock-ups, and present them for approval.

In fact, you'll most likely use a mixture of all the above. I find the storyboarding option the most useful, both in terms of communicating with the client, and for my own use, to see how the site develops stage by stage.

Storyboarding

Storyboarding is a good way of getting a preliminary feel for what you want. It allows you to define navigation, visualization and style early on in your site design. The term is a throwback to the film industry, referring to the sequence of pictures drawn by cartoonists to plan how characters would move during the animation.

Some people may ask, "Why waste time creating static sketches when you could just as easily start drawing in Flash?" I find that the little extra work I put into storyboarding really lifts a presentation and allows me to fully explore my creative ideas before I need to concentrate on developing and animating them in Flash.

If it doesn't work on paper, it won't work when you code it

A storyboard can be whatever you want: a sketch on the back of a beer mat, just for your own use, or a full-blown presentation of the site from beginning to end to show to the client. I've seen complex storyboards showing a full web site mocked up, with arrows and typed notes saying how everything will work. My advice is to find the middle road between those two. I rarely do more than a few sketches and perhaps a preliminary mock-up of one page in Photoshop to get the feel of the site. The client is paying you for the finished site and not the intermediate artwork, so make the storyboarding functional and don't go overboard; it isn't a finished product in its own right.

Assuming that the client hasn't requested to see it, you can see the kind of sketch that I begin my work with on the next page.

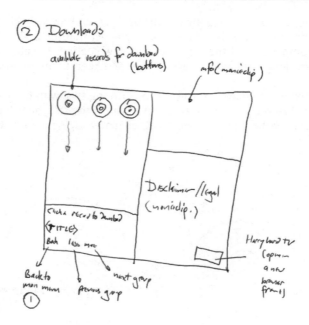

This one is for part of a site I designed where you can select from a number of different band names, and download available (and I hasten to add, legal) MP3 files. It probably took me a maximum of ten minutes to draw, but if you look at the final page based on this sketch, then you can see that the final interface is very true to the initial sketch.

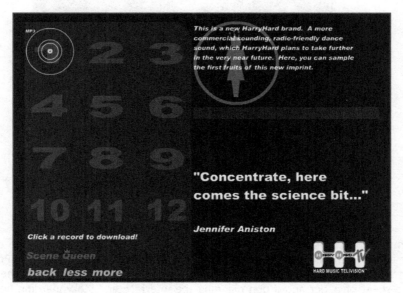

Trying to fit everything into Flash without an initial goal would have taken a lot longer, so you can see how this initial storyboarding saved time.

Storyboarding also gives you an opportunity to start figuring out how to begin coding effects for particular areas of the site. On the music site, I had to deal with the fact that the user might choose to skip the intro before the essential components of the main site had downloaded. To cater for this, I needed something to show the viewer how long they would have to wait and keep them amused for this short time.

I thought a VU meter would be quite a novel way of showing this, with the needle flickering up the scale to show the percentage loaded. As you can see, in this part of the storyboarding and sketching, I'm already starting to think about how the needle needs to be animated by ActionScript.

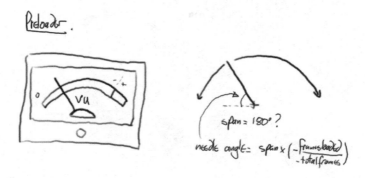

Here's the final work. Again, quite close to the initial three-minute scrappy sketch...

It's worth remembering that Flash isn't necessarily the best environment for you to develop your initial ideas. Playing around within graphics packages like Adobe Photoshop or Paint Shop Pro, along with making your own sketches, can be a much richer way of working. Twenty minutes at the beginning of your project with a sheet of paper and a pen planning the interface and storyboarding how the ActionScript will work is time well spent.

Once you've sketched what you want to do with your ActionScript, you can again save yourself a lot of time by staying away from your monitor just a little longer and not diving headfirst into that Actions panel. Take some time to plan in more detail how your code will be structured to fit with your designs.

Building your ActionScript

As you begin to think in ActionScript terms, you're always starting from the same point: you know how you want your designs to work. What you need to think about is the best way to get there. There are two main ways of breaking down programming problems: top down or bottom up.

Top down design routes involve looking at the overall task and breaking the problem down into smaller and smaller chunks, whereas a **bottom up** design would mean starting by looking at the basic building blocks, adapting them and building upwards towards the solution.

Thinking from the Top Down

The top-down method is called a **functional** method, because it looks at the functions that you have to carry out, or *what you have to do at every stage*, to perform the solution. You begin by looking at the aim in general terms, or **high-level requirements**. Then you break each of those general stages up into separate steps that become easier and easier to manage. These are the individual **requirements** that you can deal with in turn on your way to building the complete package.

Sounds strange? Let's say that we're looking at breaking down the high level requirement of making a cup of tea. If we took the top-down approach, we'd first define the top-level design statement, which is:

> Make a cup of tea

and then break it down by one level to its main stages:

1.0	Boil some water
2.0	Put some sugar and a tea bag into a cup
3.0	If the kettle has boiled, pour some water into the cup
4.0	After 2 minutes, remove the teabag, add some milk and stir

Breaking the task down to this level is called the **first iteration**.

We'd then look at each of these tasks and break them down even further:

1.1	Fill kettle with water, two thirds full
1.2	Switch the kettle on
2.1	Add one teaspoonful of sugar to the cup
2.2	Add one teabag into the cup
3.1	Wait until the kettle has boiled
3.2	Pour water from the kettle into the cup, until the cup is 3/4 full
4.1	Wait two minutes
4.2	Remove the teabag from the cup

4.3   Add milk to the cup until the cup is 7/8ths full

This is the **second iteration**.

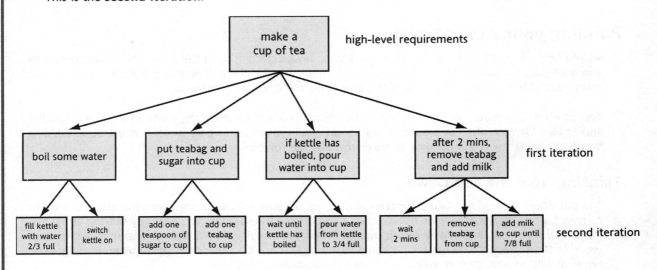

The top-down approach fits well when you're dealing with a tightly defined problem. A tight definition eliminates the need for too many iterations, or breaking the task down again and again, and makes each stage easy to change if necessary. For anything more complex, though, it throws up some pretty basic problems. The most important of these is that if the high-level requirement changes, that change must filter down through all the iterations, making you think about what you do at every stage all over again.

For example, if you preferred coffee, you'd have to start at the beginning all over again with a new top-level design statement:

Make a cup of coffee

and change all the instructions at every stage below that, changing **teabag** references to **spoonful of coffee**, take out that **wait two minutes** stage (because now we don't need to wait for coffee to brew), and so on. You may think that this isn't such big job in this domestic real-world example, but if your top-level design statement reads:

Build a navigation computer system for a combat helicopter with satellite position systems, radar, and weapons management facilities

you'd have a bit more of a problem changing things around when the boss changed his mind about what he wanted his helicopter to do. You'd have to look at all ten thousand of the requirements for the system and see what the impact of the change that your boss was asking for was on each requirement. This can take an extremely long time (I know, I've been there in similar civil projects!) and even longer if you have to prove that you did the analysis of the changes properly. This experience has taught me to go for the easier option when I can. Speaking of which...

Thinking from the Bottom Up

Making a change in a bottom-up design is nowhere near as difficult. Taking the bottom-up approach involves looking at the problem, splitting it up into very general areas and asking, "What are the basic building blocks here?" You look for basic structures within your problem and write general solutions for them, before adding specific details to these general solutions to make them suit the problem that you're dealing with.

Going back to our tea example, the general building blocks of the problem are:

- Moving things from one container (such as a sugar bowl) to another container (such as a cup)
- Measuring quantities
- Waiting for particular processes to complete (boiling the kettle)

If we were tackling this in ActionScript, we'd begin to create actions based around these general building blocks.

We could start with a **moving** action, adding details of whichever containers and substances were involved:

```
move(from_container, to_container, thing)
```

then add a **measuring** action, where we can display 'how much' of 'what substance' we want measured:

```
measure(quantity, substance)
```

a **switching on the kettle** action, using basic on/off commands:

```
kettle (on)
```

and a conditional structure like the one we saw in the last chapter to detect when the kettle has boiled, and switch it off:

```
if (water boiling) {switch kettle off}
```

We could then look at the problem and see how to build up to making a cup of tea using these structures. For example, to fill the kettle we'd want to use the 'move' routine to fill it with water from the tap, so:

```
from_container    is the tap
to_container      is the kettle
thing             is water
```

My thing is not just any amount of water, but two thirds of the kettle, so I can express it as:

```
measure(water, TwoThirdsOfTheKettle)
```

So my full statement to fill the kettle would be:

```
move(tap, kettle, measure(water, TwoThirdsOfTheKettle))
```

Taking it all in this way, my basic solution might look like:

```
move (tap, kettle, measure(water, TwoThirdsOfTheKettle))
kettle (on)
move (sugarbowl, cup, measure(sugar, OneTeaspoon))
move (teacaddy, cup, teabag)
repeat {
}
until (event (kettle_boiled))
move (kettle, cup, measure(water, measure(water, TwoThirdsCup)))
repeat {
}
until (event(tea brewed))
move (cup, trashbin, teabag)
move (milkBottle, cup, measure(milk,OneEighthCup)
stop
```

The two `repeats` will make us wait (repeatedly doing nothing) until the event we've specified has been detected.

This looks suspiciously like ActionScript already! We've lost the timings like 'wait two minutes' from the previous top-down version. Why? Because it doesn't matter! We moved away from the initial problem to the extent that what didn't really matter dropped out of the problem. We never even considered it.

This method can save us a little work and is also useful when the main problem or design aim is likely to change frequently, which could happen more often than you think. We used a move routine to fill the kettle with water from the tap. Once we've written that general routine, we can use it over again, with just minor changes for several other actions, including:

```
move (teacaddy, cup, teabag)
```

With our top-down solution, wanting coffee instead of tea caused us a major problem and we had look again at the whole process. If we're faced with that problem here, the basic building blocks stay the same – we just have to change a few minor details again:

```
move (coffeejar, cup, coffeepowder)
```

That's much easier. Because our bottom-up design didn't just look at the top-level problem (making tea), we generalized the problem, or **abstracted** it. So, we don't care whether it's tea or coffee or crude oil - we can still use our basic move() and measure() building blocks again, and won't have to change them when we do. Bottom-up design digs the foundations before building on top of them, while top-down just puts itself down in any old way. When the winds of change blow, you can guess which one stays standing longer.

This bottom-up design method can be much harder to understand than the top-down alternative because, as adults, I guess we all prefer to think **functionally**. Common sense says that bottom-up design shouldn't work, but it seems to work rather well. It really comes into its own with problems that can be reduced to a few types of building blocks, which means that it works particularly well with animation and graphic interfaces.

A while back, I provided technical support for another friends of ED book called 'New Masters of Flash', in which Flash designers like Yugo Nakamura wrote about their work, and showed how they'd put together some pretty impressive effects. It struck me that all the designers featured were, without exception, using a bottom-up approach to their ActionScripting. This was despite the fact that these were all creative people at the very front of their field, who'd taught themselves ActionScript – in other words, the type of people you might have expected to find using a top-down approach.

The work that we'll do in the final few chapters of this book will be based on a bottom-up approach, as it looks like a required skill for those of you who want to be in the future volumes of New Masters of Flash!

When you code in Flash, matters aren't usually as clear-cut as a straight choice between a top-down and bottom-up approach. Most ActionScript structures will require a mix of the two. We'll talk about what approach to take with different ActionScript structures later. The aim of this section is to enable you to look at a problem and start to think about the best way to code it.

> *Thinking and looking **before** you jump straight into coding will mean that your ActionScript changes from a 'keep coding until it works' mindset to something altogether more elegant in thought and design.*

We've just taken a look at the type of general approach you might want to take to your coding. Before we continue, we're going to have a look at a way of presenting a coding problem graphically that might help put you in a better position when you come to coding.

Flowcharting

You've got an ActionScript problem – not necessarily for your whole site, but probably just the ActionScript for a single frame. You can't describe what you want to do to, say, the first iteration of a top-down design process. Your problem can't be easily defined, so you might consider sketching the problem as a flowchart.

To build an ActionScript flowchart, I use three kinds of flow symbol:

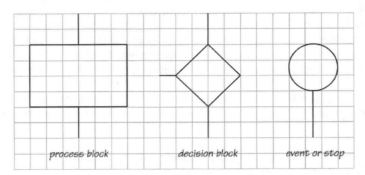

The **process block** represents a set of linear actions that occur one after another.

The **decision box** is like a junction: you can either go forward or turn, depending on whether the answer to your question is true or false (yes or no).

The **event/stop** circle represents the event that starts or finishes a particular flowchart.

Let's look at how this would work if we wanted to build a menu of buttons that allowed the user to control how a movie clip plays, just as if it were a videocassette in a video machine. Once we'd created a set of buttons a bit like these, we would want to attach some ActionScript to each of them. I'll show you how we could use flowcharts to help define what each button does.

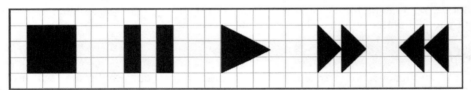

As we begin to plan, we'll make a note of some main points:

1. We're interested in two main properties of the movie clip: `_currentframe` and `_totalframes`.
2. The `_currentframe` property describes the frame that Flash is currently playing.
3. The `_totalframes` property is the total number of frames within the movie clip (which is, of course equal to the number of the last frame).
4. The first frame is when `_currentframe = 1`.

With these in mind, we'll build some flowcharts.

The Stop button is fairly straightforward. When the user presses it, we want the movie to stop. The flowchart shows that when a press event is detected on the Stop button, we need to have some ActionScript that stops the movie exactly where it is, at its `_currentframe`:

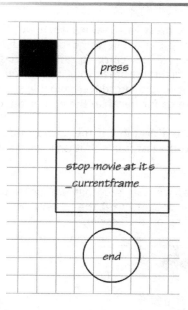

The Pause button is slightly more complicated. When the user presses it we need the movie to stop just where it is as if the Stop button had been pressed. But we also need to set the movie playing again when that Pause button is released. So, we have two events in our flow diagram:

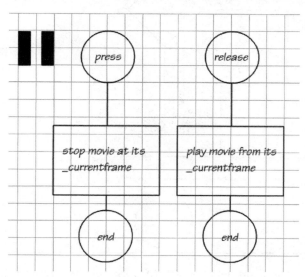

When the viewer presses the FastForward button we need the movie clip to advance at a much faster rate than normal. To make it move at, say, five times the normal rate, we would ask it to go to _currentframe + 5, every time the user presses FastForward.

Houston, we have a problem. If we press FastForward when we're within five frames of the end of the movie, that means that we're asking the movie to go beyond the last frame. Unfortunately, the Flash player won't let you do this. It will probably come to rest in the last frame, but introducing an anomaly like this is never a good idea, as it might just break your movie. You should always try to ensure that your code is free from quirks like this that could introduce avoidable glitches. We therefore need to make sure that we don't ask our script to take us further than the end of the clip.

So, our ActionScript needs to make a decision: if the _currentframe is within five frames of the last frame, we want the movie to go to the last frame. If it isn't, we want it to go to _currentframe + 5 as normal.

If we draw a flowchart for this, we can see that we need to build in code to check whether _currentframe is greater than or equal to (>=) the _lastframe - 5 and create two routines to tell the movie clip what to do depending on the answer:

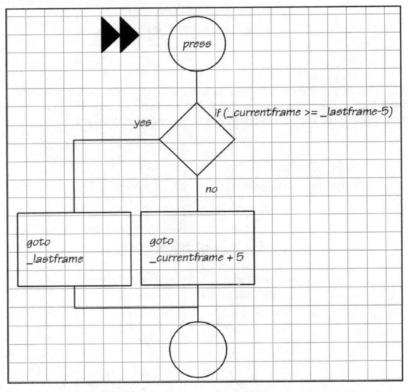

These diagrams show how you can help yourself to work out the advanced level of logic that the final code must have, using a simple graphical tool. You could very quickly sketch these diagrams on a piece of scrap paper before you begin to build the ActionScript behind each button to give yourself some pretty useful visual clues.

You may find it helpful to try sketching your own flowcharts for the other two buttons: play and rewind.

Don't go overboard though. Flowcharts are useful, especially for designing a single event handler that consists of lots of decisions or loops, or both, but they do have their limitations. If you try to flowchart really long sections of ActionScript, you'll quickly run out of paper. You may even discover the flow diagrams become more difficult to produce than the code itself!

I use flowcharts to get a simplified bit of ActionScript going. Then, once it's working, I forget about flowcharts and slowly start building up the ActionScript itself. For example, with our FastForward button the simple structure that we saw in the flowchart is fine as a beginning, but if things were left this way, the user would find that they had to click the button over and over again to keep the movie playing FastForward.

The solution for this would be to build a **toggle** mechanism into the button, something that makes it continuously alternate between two actions each time it's pressed. The first time the user presses, it's set to run on FastForward and carry on running until it's pressed again, when it's set to stop.

Of course, I could have flowcharted the solution to this; but taking the skeleton that we've seen here, coding it and then adding this additional function would be quicker.

Let's put some of this theory into practice – it's time to introduce our case study...

Section 1 - Introducing stun:design

Let's begin putting some of our newly acquired ActionScript skills into practice, by creating the interface for the stun:design site.

In the download section for this chapter, you will find a HTML file and a SWF. Place these in the same directory (or on your desktop). Open the HTML file in a browser. As long as the SWF is in the same place as the HTML, you will see this in the browser – the stun:design site.

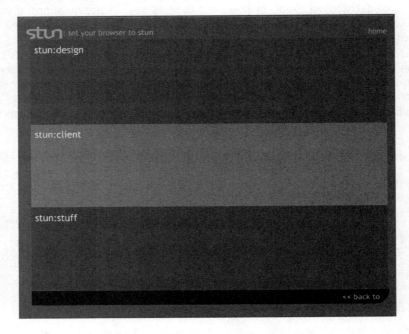

There are three areas to look at. The top right text indicates where you are now. As you move through the site, it keeps track of your current position in the site hierarchy.

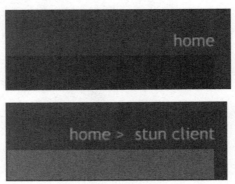

At the bottom is a *visual* representation of the same thing. The pages change color as you move through the site, and this is reflected in the lower black strip, the **back button strip**. It is sometimes also referred to as a **breadcrumb trail** because it's reminiscent of a person dropping breadcrumbs to mark out their trail, so that they can retrace their path.

This contains a small icon of the pages you have visited. Clicking on any of the icons will take you back to a previous page with the same color scheme.

The back button strip shows an important feature of the compact or integrated UI; not only are the colors pretty, they are also a critical part of the UI interface! The color-coding is used to allow you to recognize the back path. There are no bells and whistles in a compact UI design; everything has something to do with navigation, and put together, all these little cues and pointers (hopefully) create that elusive beast – a web site that needs no instructions because its interface is totally stripped down and **intuitive**.

Finally (if you haven't worked it out yet), the navigation is performed simply by clicking on the strip you want to go to next. The selected strip zooms and pans to fill the browser window, and if there are further pages to visit in the current navigation, it will split into strips again. It's one of those sites that is far more difficult to describe than to actually use. Click once or twice on the navigation and it should all immediately (and intuitively) make sense.

Not mentioned here is the *way* it moves. The navigation transitions are smooth, as are the color fades and transformations.

Right, that's what we will design from scratch. The next question is *how do we start?*

Deconstructing the problem

The first thing in any competition is to know your enemy, and the next thing is to know how to beat them, and the best way to do that is to divide and conquer. That's exactly what we will do.We will:

- Work out what the problem actually is, so we know our enemy.

- Subdivide the problem into easy to beat parts, so we can tackle each one on its own, something that gives us a much better fighting chance.

We can think it all through, but that tends to hide practicalities. Let's instead construct the method behind what the stun: design site does, manually, but within Flash, to make a working sketch of what we need to achieve.

The walk though below is an 'edited highlights' that traces exactly how I worked out how the final site should operate before I coded it up, taken from my design notes.

1.   Open a new Flash document. Select View > Rulers to show rulers. Click-hold-drag on the horizontal and vertical rulers to drag out four ruler guidelines as shown.

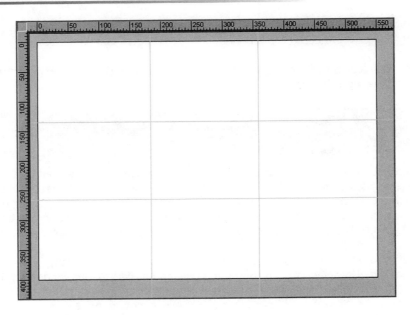

2. The middle square represents our viewable browser area. In this area, draw out a rectangle as shown below, making it cover about a third of the inner square. (Because we are only doing a rough 'Flash sketch', it doesn't need to be totally accurate, so turn off Snap and Show Grid if you have them enabled, via View > Grid**...**).

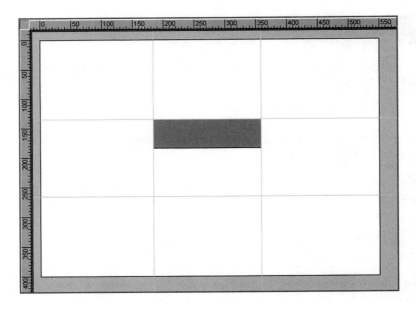

3. This is one of our three strips. Select it and make it a movie clip with F8. Call it strip.

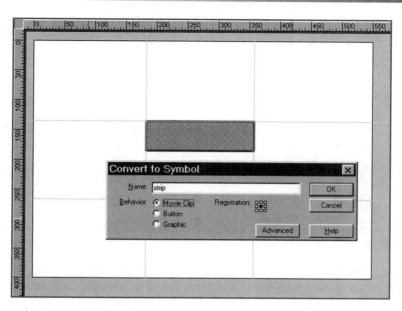

Why did I make it a movie clip? Why not leave it as it was? Well, the UI uses color changes as part of its operation, and this only works for a movie clip, as only a movie clip can be made to have a variable attribute called **color**. That is because the movie clip is an object, but if you want to see proof that you can't change the color of a raw graphic, here's the lowdown:

4. With the movie clip strip selected, open the Property inspector

The **color** dropdown currently says None. Change it to Tint. By varying the sliders that will now appear, you can vary the color of strip.

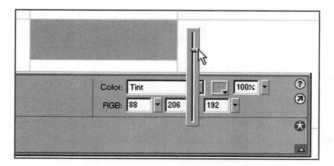

In the final site we'll have Flash varying the color via the Color object we saw in action back in Chapter 6, and use it to create all those funky but subtle color transitions. For now though, convince yourself that the Color object cannot be used with a raw graphic by drawing another square, this time not making it into a movie clip, and seeing that when you select it, the Property inspector does not show the color dropdown menu. This is because the raw graphic doesn't have the properties that allow the color function to work on it.

5. Delete the graphic so you end up with our movie clip only on the stage. Select the movie clip and return the **color** dropdown on the Property inspector to *None* to bring the clip back to its original color

> *The ball, tennis racquet and Starfleet Space Cruiser™ in Chapter 1 were movie clips for the same reason – they had properties and an instance name, which Flash needs before it can control them with ActionScript. Flash just doesn't have the capability to control raw graphics in this way, and that is why ActionScript sites use movie clips all the time.*

We have our strip movie clip, and are happy that there is a reason for it to be a movie clip and not anything else.

6. Now open the library window (CRTL/CMD+L) and drag another three instances of the strip movie clip onto the stage to emulate the stun:design site's tricolor. If your strips are too big or too small, you can either scale them to fit, or simply change the ruler lines around them.

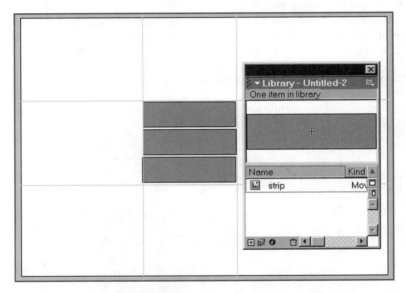

So how do we scale this lot? Well, suppose we clicked on the bottom strip. Flash would scale it, and the other strips, up as it zoomed into it. Let's try it manually.

7. Select the Free Transform tool. Now let's see if we can get some insight of how Flash will do the zooming. Select the bottom strip, scale it up a little (with the Transform tool).

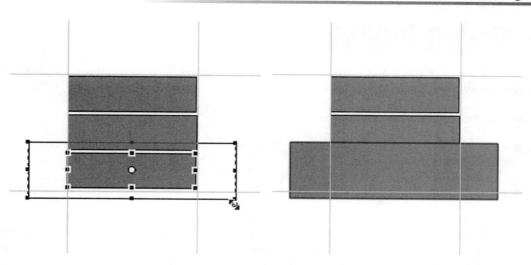

Whoops. There are two problems straight away.

One problem is that as the page starts to grow, it goes off screen. The final site always keeps the selected strip on screen as it grows. That's something our code will have to watch; *the selected strip must never be allowed to go off screen*. Rather, it has to 'push' the unselected strips off screen to make room.

The other problem is that only the selected strip does anything. The other strips just sit there, and the selected strip will eventually cover them.

Now, these issues are actually the two critical problems of the whole site UI, because the site navigation relies on them.

> *How do I know that this is the critical problem? Some of you might be thinking 'You knew because you're a programmer, and I wouldn't get that insight because I'm not'. Well, that does my ego a lot of good, but isn't actually the truth. I'm as good as you are. The truth is that I realized this 'insight' by thinking about the design for a day. A whole day!*

There is no magic point where you become a New Master of Flash and just know. The thing about New Masters is that they have the courage and conviction to keep thinking about the problem until it is solved. As you progress, you will of course realize that there are routes that tend to work in Flash and those that tend not to (and you get a feel for what is a problem and what is not), but all creative design is about taking leads and following them until one works, using judgment, creativity and cunning in the process. Time and thought is the main resource, though.

Solving problem #1

Let's have a look at the '*the two strips do not move when I scale the third*' problem first. There are three possible solutions:

- Some sort of collision detection.

- Move all three strips proportionally so that they always keep the same relative distance apart and so they will never overlap.

- Cheat.

All the existing similar sites use point 1 or 2, but I always have a soft spot for item 3 when I see a problem like this. I know that this is one of those problems that is a *performance bottleneck*. Moving all three strips together in some controlled way will be a brain-wringer for Flash because it has a lot of things to do. Better if it all worked in some automatic way that required no coding.

The following step is *so* simple in hindsight, and it solves our problem with no coding at all.

1. Press undo (CTRL/CMD+Z) until you get back to the three equally sized strips. Select them all. (Hold down SHIFT while you select).

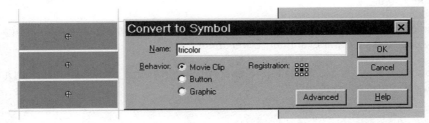

Call the movie clip *tricolor*, because that is what it is, a movie clip with three pages in it.

Okay, now try to scale the bottom strip. See that? This time all the other strips scale as well *because they are embedded in the same movie clip!*

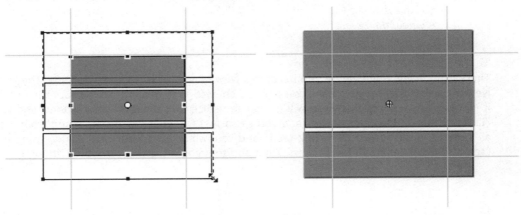

Cool! So now the movie clips never overlap, and we don't have to do anything highfalutin like collision detection to achieve this!

Solving problem #2

We want the bottom strip to stay on screen as it scales (zooms) by moving it so that it never overlaps the ruler guide lines. This will keep it on screen by *panning* so that it always stays on the visible screen. The best way to make something do *what we want* in programming, if the solution isn't immediately obvious, is to look at *what we don't want to do.*

What makes our strip go off screen? Well, we drag with the cursor and the tricolor moves off all four edges. If you look at the finished site, you will see that we don't seem to care about the right edge; it's the left, top and bottom edges that concern us. A strip scales when you select it, and grows off the right hand side of the screen. It doesn't go off screen on the other three edges as it grows. Once it has filled the screen, it stops.

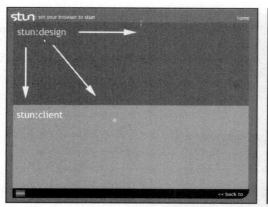
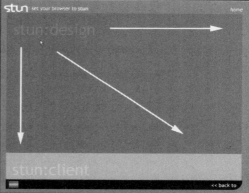
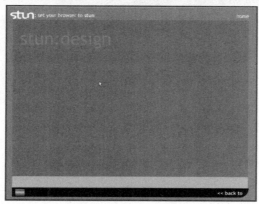

So the final site does something different; it scales the tricolor, but at the same time moves the selected strip so that its top, left and bottom left corners never go off screen

You can model this by doing it yourself with our little Flash sketch:

1. Starting with the original tricolor, suppose the bottom strip is pressed. We need this strip to scale up so that it fills the screen, but as soon as we begin to scale it, we get the situation shown below, where the whole tricolor goes off-screen on all four edges. Try this yourself, scaling the tricolor by a small amount...

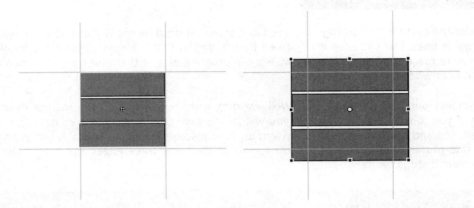

2. What we actually want to happen is this. Move the tricolor so that it occupies a position as shown. The left edge is kept at the screen edge, and the selected strip is prevented from going off the bottom.

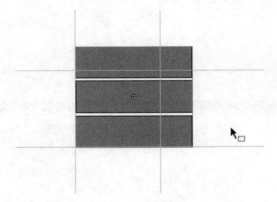

3. If you keep doing this, you will eventually end up with the strip hitting the top edge of the screen. Its color now fills the screen.

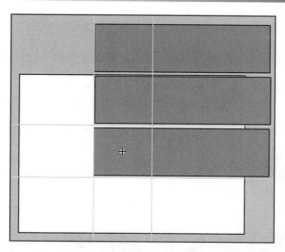

So that's how the final code does it! The three strips are actually a single movie clip that forms a tricolor. In addition to this, because the three strips are still separate movie clips within the bigger tricolor, we can still access them individually to make color changes.

Okay, so what happens next? We have one strip that now fills the screen, and two strips that are off screen and can't be seen. Although the non-selected strips are off screen, Flash still has to draw them, so we need to do something about them, or we have another performance bottleneck looming.

We also need to change the one strip, so it changes into the three-color tricolor again. We're stuck!

Although we are seeing lots of problems in our little walkthrough here, this is a good thing, because we know about all the pitfalls up front when we come to code it all up! If we saw this new problem after we had already coded up the zoom/pan functionality, we may find we have to discard the coding so far to overcome the new problem.

A good programmer always plays about with the ideas before committing to coding because it uncovers the potential problems further on.

A good motion graphics programmer will do a bit more, and dry run the animations manually like we are doing, because it uncovers issues that would be missed if we drew sketches or just thought about it in our head. Doing it for real has several advantages, the main one being that it injects reality into our ideas!

Time to look at the options:

- Split each strip into another tricolor, so our original tricolor has further tricolors already embedded in it.
- Redraw the pages using the drawing API (that you may have heard about, and we'll look at in more detail in chapter 12) so that they can be redrawn to look like 3 strips again... or something intense like that.
- Get Flash to somehow physically delete the extra off-screen strips.
- Cheat.

All the options are actually either inflexible or difficult, except my favored way forward. Guess which option I chose?

Solving problem #3 and #4: cheating

In all the best detective novels the culprit is someone that was innocuously introduced early in the story. Nobody suspects the blind flower girl in the opening chapter, but that was the fatal mistake, for it was she who killed the countess!

We've introduced the solution early on as well: changing color. Use the by now oversized tricolor from the last part.

1. To see how this is done, we have to make our little test look more like the final site. We need to make sure there are no gaps between the strips within tricolor. Edit tricolor in place to move all the strips so they just touch:

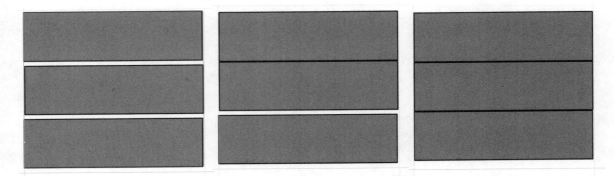

2. Change the color of this strip instance via the Property inspector as we did before, to blue. Note that you still have to be inside the tricolor clip editing in place, or you will tint all four pages.

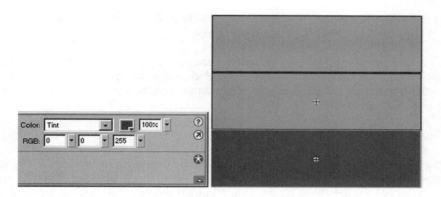

3. Give the other strips different colors. You can choose them yourself – the values are not important as long as none of them are blue, for reasons which will soon become evident.

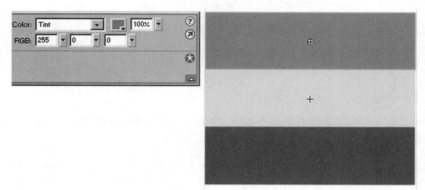

Let's recap. Only the blue strip is on screen at the moment, and we want to somehow get rid of the other two strips that are off-screen. The cheat is that we don't get rid of them. We bring them back on screen.

4. Change the color of all the non-blue strips to the same blue as the bottom strip.

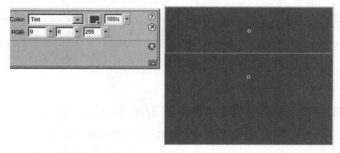

5. Now, here's the really cunning part. Get out of edit in place and *scale the tricolor* back to where it was at the start of the whole thing. Because the three strips are all the same color, the user will

not notice this, *and will not see the fact that you have brought the missing strips back on screen* because they can't see what is going on off-screen.

All we do now is fade the blues towards the colors of the next page in the hierarchy, and the user thinks we have gone to a new page by zooming in to a strip, and then splitting it into three new strips. We have done no such thing! What we have actually done is zoomed out, and then sneakily zoomed back to the *same tricolor,* but with different colors!

We don't constantly zoom in at all – it's a trick!

This is the difference between motion graphics programming (including things such as PlayStation games and film special effects as well as Flash web design) and other forms of programming – *we are always cheating.* The 3D in Quake is not really 3D (it's on a 2D monitor screen for a start) and the X-Wing fighters in Star Wars are really twelve inch models or nothing but data in a computer. We cheat like hell. In fact, the bigger and more subtle the cheats, the better the programmer!

Of course, others call this *approximation* but I know different.

Have another look at the stun:design site to get a feel for what is *really* happening when you click on a strip and 'zoom in' to a new page. Play about with it until you can see all the wires and mirrors and how the lady is really not sawn in half at all.

Parting shots

We have learned the first important rule in Flash motion graphics: *know what you want to code up before you start.*

We have addressed all the problems in the navigation we will be using, and have solved them in principle by running through the animations and transitions *manually.* You are much better off doing this by manually updating the graphics in real-time than just dry running it on paper, because motion graphics is, by definition, about *animation.* By doing it this way, you get some insight into what Flash has to do, and some shortcuts and approximations that you can make in your motion graphics whilst still maintaining the desired effect.

This is what creative ActionScript is all about. So far in our project, we haven't touched ActionScript at all, but I hope that already you are beginning to see something important: the *mindset* that creates all that cool and impossible Flash stuff on the web.

Best of all, Flash problem solving and coding is not about math. It's about creating cool effects and stuff for other people to see, and I hope you are beginning to see the fun of it all.

Section 2 - Preparing static graphics for stun:design

Now it's time to create the basic graphics for our stun:design site. The final FLA is included as `stun_setup1.fla` if you get stuck.

What we are going to do...

We are going to create the final versions of our basic site graphics. Although there are not many of them (we are going for a minimalist style), they have to be precisely placed for our ActionScript to work. We only have to be out by a few pixels after all, and the audience will see through the trick.

You will need the file `stunLogo.fla`. This includes the stun logo that we will be adding as part of the incidental graphics on the page. You can of course decide to use your own logo, rather than ours, at some point, but it is probably better that you use ours for now so that we are all on the same page.

Setting up the FLA

1. Open a new FLA with File > New. Select Modify > Document... to access the Document Properties window. Change Dimensions: to 800 x 600 and the Frame Rate: to 18.

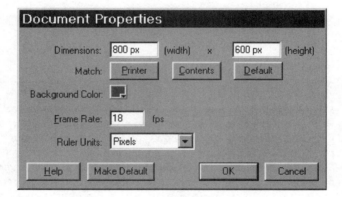

Click on the Background Color tab and change it to the third gray down from the top, leftmost column (#666666).

Animation in ActionScript requires precise measurements, so we had better have a think about these next. This is a cleaned-up version of the site layout sketch I created for this site.

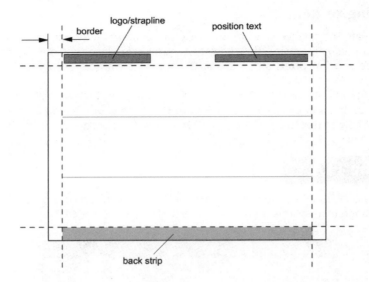

It is always a good idea to create a rough plan of what you want your UI to look like, so that, at the very least, you can fit everything in. Also, drawing the UI first allows you to decide on how much space you want for the actual content. It is sometimes obvious when a Flash designer has gone all out for designing a cool never-seen-before interface, and has forgotten about the content placement – you end up with an overpowering interface and little space for the actual content!

Adding layers

1.   Rename the existing layer Layer 1 to actions and create two layer folders called frame and UI. The frame layer will contain all the symbols in the border area (or 'the frame'), and the three strips (as discussed in our walk through earlier) that form the main interface itself will be in the folder UI.

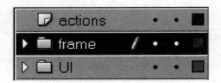

2.   The actions layer will be reserved for the code that will later actually animate our site. To make sure we do not inadvertently put graphics in this layer, lock this layer now.

Adding some construction lines

1. Create two new layers in the layer folder frame and call them guideHoriz and guideVert. **Hide the grid** (View > Grid > Show Grid) if it is being displayed.

2. In layer guideHoriz, draw out two thin horizontal lines that span the width of the stage. Now, using the Property Inspector, give one line a y: value of 30.0 and the other one a value of 570.0.

3. In layer guideVert, draw out two vertical lines in the same way, this time giving them x: values of 30.0 and 770.0.

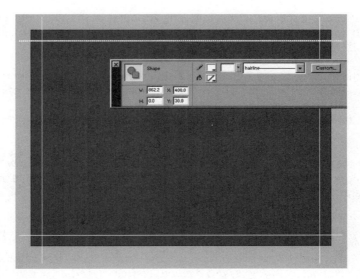

> Note that the reason we are not using ruler guides is that you cannot place them accurately with the Property inspector. We want a greater accuracy than just doing it by eye. It's not that I am just being really fussy here – I know how particular ActionScript can be!

4. Make both of these layers guide layers (right-click / CTRL-click on the layer title and check guide on the pop-up menu that appears). We now have our border clearly marked on our screen. Lock both these layers.

Adding the position text

1. Still in the frame layer folder, add a new layer called mainTitle. In this layer, add a dynamic text field. Using the Zoom tool if you have to, place it in the border area of the top right hand corner of the frame area. Extend the text field area so that it is about 450 pixels long (you can read its width from the Property inspector).

2. Change the font to Trebuchet MS 16 point (see introduction for more details), or use _sans (or an Arial, Helvetica, or Humanist font of your choice with a Regular style).

3. Using the Property inspector set the following attributes of the text (noting that if you are not sure which field does what, just hold the cursor over the Property inspector and wait for the help text to pop-up).

   - In the Instance Name field (it's the field on the far left that will initially have the grayed out text <InstanceName> in it) give the text box the instance name of main_txt

   - Set the Line type pull down menu to Single Line and enter mainText in the field marked Var:

   - Hit the Character… button and in the Character Options window that will appear, check Only and Lowercase letters (a-z). In the And these characters field at the bottom, add a '>' character.

   > *We are telling Flash to save the font outlines for these font characters. Flash has two methods of drawing text on screen. One is as a bitmapped version of the font, and the other is as a true vector. ActionScript can only animate text that is printed as a true vector, because it needs to know the fill and point information to rotate, fade, and move it accurately. This is what we are telling Flash to do, but we have to be careful to tell Flash to only save the outlines of text we will be actually using because such information has to be saved within the final SWF, and adding too many font characters can increase the final download size of your site.*
   >
   > *Another reason why we are specifying Trebuchet as our font – its simple outlines make it a low download when compared to more complex fonts.*

4. Change the font color to light blue (#00CCFF) and click on the Right/Bottom Justify icon (it is just above the Format… button).

5. Finally, position the text field as shown below, being careful to not go out of the frame area marked out by our lines. Type in the phrase 'title text' in the box and it should appear exactly as shown in the screenshot.

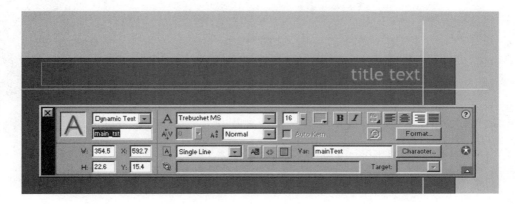

Adding the stun logo and strap-line

1. In the layer folder frame, add a new layer called graphics. We will use this layer to place all our static graphics on. If they're not already locked, lock all other layers.

2. Select File > Open as Library and open stunLogo.fla from the download for this chapter. The library for this FLA will open. Drag the stunLogo graphic onto the stage, and position it in the top left corner of the border area as shown. With the stun logo still selected, use the Property inspector to tint the logo to light blue.

3. Change the Color: drop down from None to Tint. Change the Tint Amount to 100%, and the RGB: sliders to 0, 204, and 255.

4. Next, add some static text immediately after the stun logo as shown on the next page:

The text reads ':set your browser to stun' and has the following attributes:

- Font - Trebuchet 16 point
- Color – #00CCFF
- Alignment – left/top

Creating the back strip

1. On the stage, draw out a long black oblong with no stroke. Don't worry about the size or position too much, we will set this precisely in a moment.

2. Bring up the Info panel (CTRL/CMD+I or Window > Info). Select the oblong and set the registration point on the Info panel (via the little matrix arrowed in the diagram below) to the top left. Set the width W: to 740.0 and the height H: to 30.0. Set the position of the oblong to X: 30.0, Y: 570.0.

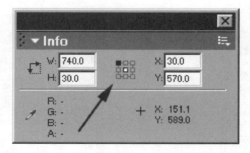

This will move and scale the oblong so that it fills the lower edge of the border as shown on the next page.

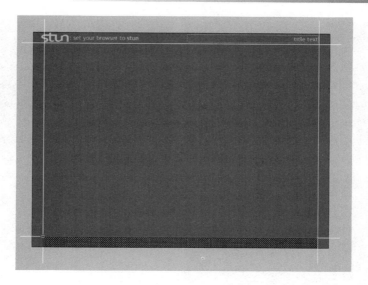

> *The more observant will have wondered why we didn't just go ahead and use the value boxes in the Property inspector. The reason is that the Property inspector does not include the registration point matrix. This specifies where the measurements are taken from, and it is set to the center point of the shape. I wanted to measure from the corner point, and so had to use the Info panel, because only that window contains the registration point matrix.*

3. Hit F8 to change this graphic into a symbol, calling it backStrip. Double-click on it to edit in place.

4. Let's create a little curve on the far right corner to break up all those straight lines with a bit of curvature. Zoom into the far right corner, and select the Oval tool. Select no fill and a hairline stroke. Then, in a blank bit of the stage, drag out a circle outline (holdSHIFT down to force Flash to create a circle and not an oval). Use the Property inspector to give the circle a height and width of 60 (we want it to be twice the height of our oblong, which we know has a height of 30).

5. Now drag the circle over to the right-hand edge of the oblong, as shown below. Position it so that when you select the bottom right corner, only the portion highlighted becomes selected.

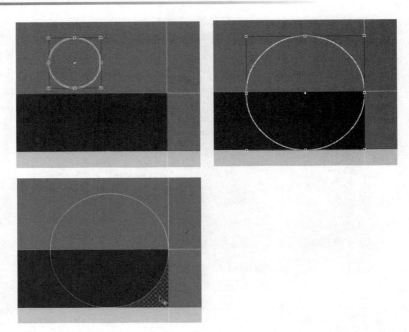

You will find you may have to try a few attempts to get the circle correctly positioned. Remember the Undo shortcut is CTRL/CMD+Z. (I know I had to!)

6.   Erase the selected corner, to give you the smooth curve as shown below left. Add a new layer above the existing layer (Layer 1) and call the new layer text. Add the '<< back' text as shown below, using static text, and our old friend Trebuchet 16 point, color #00CCFF. I have actually changed the color of the '<<' to yellow because I though it looked good that way, but you can leave it blue if you think I'm being too fussy.

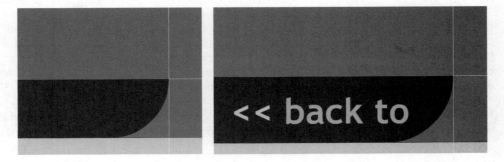

Phew! That's an awful lot of close-up screen work in one go. Don't worry, almost done!

This is what your timeline should look like on the main stage (hit the Back button to get out of 'edit in place').

7. In the layer folder frame create our final layer frame.

> *This next excercise will contain a symbol whose raison d'etre may not be immediately obvious, but if you look at the finished site (which we introduced earlier), you will notice that the colored strips don't show up as they pan off stage. That's because a border the same color as the stage background hides them. We have done this instead of a Flash mask, because our way is much less processor-intensive.*

Adding the frame cut-out

The frame cut-out will hide the parts of the main interface as it slides off screen. If you don't understand how this will work just yet, bear with it, because we shall see how it works in a while when we start to animate the interface.

1. Lock and hide all the layers (if you lock or hide a layer folder, all layers inside it are also hidden) except the two guides and layer frame.

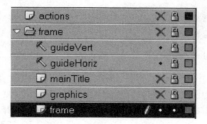

2. Select the Rectangle tool with no stroke and a fill color that contrasts with the background (such as bright green).

3. Make sure View > Snap to Objects is checked and draw out a rectangle starting from the top right corner and off stage, down towards the bottom right, making sure that it covers the border gutter and some of the area off the stage. See the diagrams below. As you get close to the guide lines we added, the cursor will snap to them. You want the rectangle to go up to (but not beyond) the guide lines, so that they only cover the border.

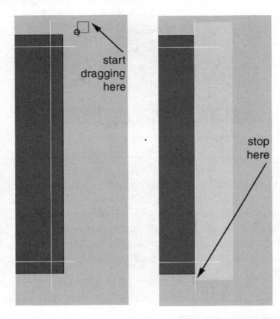

start
dragging
here

stop
here

4. Repeat this until you have got a frame shape that covers all the border areas and extends beyond the stage edges on all four sides.

5. Group the frame with itself (select it and hit CTRL/CMD+G). That may seem a little strange – why group a graphic when there is only one of them? Well, if we were to later inadvertently draw over the frame with other graphics, they would tend to split our frame or cut shapes out of it, unless we group it or make it into a symbol. There's no need to make it into a symbol because there will only ever be one of them (and making symbols when we don't need to only clutters up the library). So instead, I have just grouped it with itself!

6. Finally, use the Fill tool with the fill color set to the background color (#666666, or use the Eyedropper tool to sample the background color) and then change the frame color to this color. The frame will merge with the stage, which can be a bit confusing, so make the layer show outlines only by clicking on the colored brick arrowed to the right, so that it turns hollow. Your frame will now show up as a hollow rectangle on the stage.

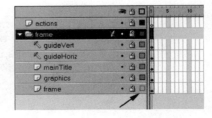

Finally, here's a picture of our final version (`stun_setup1.fla`), and yes, I took the precaution of tidying up the border frame (that we just drew).

Section 3 - Preparing dynamic graphics for stun:design

In this section we are going to finish building the raw graphics for our site in readiness for the star of the piece – the code. We will add the parts of the interface that Flash will control directly, or the **dynamic part** of the interface.

The final FLA for this chapter is included as `stun_setup2.fla` if you get stuck or need to compare notes.

You will remember the diagram to the right from earlier in the chapter. The three strips in the middle are missing so far, and we will add them now. We will also build the little icons that appear on the back strip at the bottom. Be warned though, neither of them will look anything like the colorful funky things we see on the finished site. We need some additional ActionScript magic to be added before they start looking anything like that!

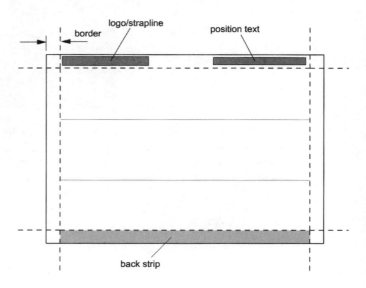

First, a bit of housekeeping...

1. Earlier on, we created the contents of the frame layer folder. We can safely close and lock that folder now, because we will not be adding anything to it, and want it out of the way. Also, if it isn't already, lock the actions layer, because that will be reserved for our ActionScript.

2. Inside the UI layer folder, add a new layer called page. At this point, all layers should be locked except the new layer.

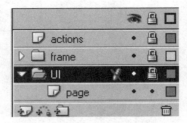

Making the strip movie clips

1. Select the Rectangle tool with fill color #999999, no stroke, and draw a rectangle on the screen in any free area.

2. With the rectangle selected, use the Property inspector to give it a width W: of 740.0 and a height H: of 180.0. These numbers have come from our sketch above. Last chapter, we made the border area 30 pixels thick all round the perimeter of the stage, so given our 800x600 stage, each strip must be (800-30-30) x ((600-30-30)/3), or 740x180.

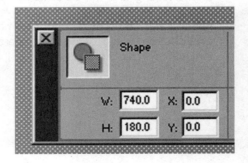

3. Select the rectangle and hit F8 to make it a movie clip. Call it pageStrip and make its registration point the top left corner (via the little 3x3 matrix to the left of Registration: as shown below).

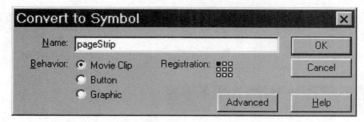

4. Using the Property inspector, move this movie clip to position X: 30.0, Y: 30.0. This will move the instance to the top left hand edge of the inside frame area. Name the instance strip0_mc.

5. Copy the rectangle (CTRL/CMD+C) then paste it twice (CTRL/CMD+V), or alternatively drag two instances of it from the library. Either way, position and name the new instances as follows.

Copy 1 -   X: 30.0
                    Y: 210.0
                    Instance Name: strip1_mc

Copy 2 -   X: 30.0
                    Y: 390.0
                    Instance Name: strip2_mc

You should now see this, with the central area totally covered by our three instances of pageStrip. There should be no gaps between any of the page instances, given that they fit perfectly within the available space.

With none of the pageStrip instances selected, you should see what appears to be one solid rectangle. If you don't (you may see the odd line at a page intersection), zoom into the line to make sure – Flash may be fooling you, and the line might disappear when you zoom in rather than get bigger.

Forming the tricolor clip *page*

1. Select all three instances of pageStrip (SHIFT+click to select multiple symbols) and then hit F8 to make the three strips into a single movie clip. Call this movie clip page and change the registration point to the center point as shown below (this last step is important because we will check our measurements from the center point in a moment).

    Now go back to the Property inspector. The page movie clip should have the dimensions shown below.

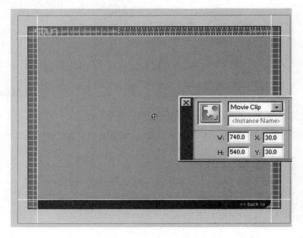

2. Give this an instance name `tricolor`. Although it doesn't look like a tricolor right now, it will do later when all the strips have different colors.

3. Double-click on the page movie clip so we can edit it in place. Rename the current layer (Layer 1) to back and create two new layers called guide and text above it. Lock layers back and text.

4. In layer guide, we will add some construction lines to show that the big rectangle is really three smaller page clips. Add some lines to do this as shown on the next page. I have made my lines green to contrast with the grays, and have given them a thickness of 3 to make them highly visible.

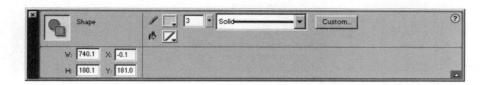

5. Make layer guide a guide layer by right-clicking (or CTRL-clicking for Mac) on the layer title and checking Guide. We will add our text next. Lock layer guide and unlock text.

Adding the strip titles

We want to add a dynamic text field over each strip, close to the top edge, as shown below. Unlike the other movie clips, Flash will not be directly animating these, so we can place them by eye.

1. Place one text field on strip0_mc and drag it out so that it is two lines long and covers the general position shown. Inside the text field, type 'title text' so that we can see how the text will show up.

The text should have the following attributes in the Property inspector:

- Instance name: strip0_txt
- Font: Trebuchet MS, 20 point
- Alignment: Left/top
- Line type: Multiline
- Var: title0

The height, width and X, Y values are 'don't cares' – as long as the placement and general shape looks like the image above, it's fine (although you can just put in my values if you want to be sure).

2. Hit the Character... button on the Property inspector (with the text field still selected) and check Only and then Lowercase Letters(a-z). This will include font outlines for the text characters we will be using.

3. Copy this text three times, placing the copies in the same positions over strips 1 and 2. The only thing that will change is that the instance names should be `strip1_txt` and `strip2_txt` and the Var: fields should be `title1` and `title2`.

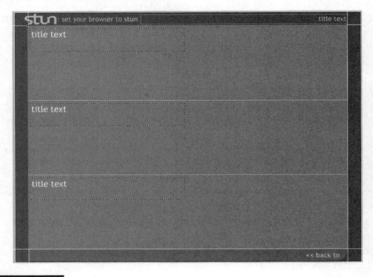

Creating the icon

The final interface has a set of icons that show little versions of the last visited page on the back strip. These icons are really just smaller versions of our main pages, and work in much the same way. In fact, we will use almost exactly the same movie clip.

1. In the Library panel, make a duplicate of page (right-click/CONTROL-click on page and then select Duplicate), and call the new clip icon. Edit icon, and delete all layers except back.

2. We now have a fair few symbols in the library. Time for a tidy up! Here's my library folder following a bit of a spring clean. It's good practice to keep your library neat and tidy because it will help you keep track of things when projects get big and complicated.

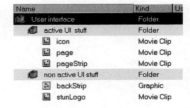

Before we move on...

We have now built up all the graphics for our interface. Almost unbelievably, it consists of nothing more than a few drab rectangles and odd bits of text, plus one real graphic (the stun logo). Where is all that cool movement and the funky colors coming from?!

Well, obviously, that's the real subject of this book. We have been slowly building up the graphical side of our site in readiness for the real star of the piece; *ActionScript,* and that is the missing piece that will turn this ugly duckling into the finished site you have already sampled.

Section 4 - Getting ready for action

So far we have concentrated on the graphics and design of our site. We haven't really done any coding, but have been building up the main non-script parts of the site. In this section we will do three things.

- First off, we will be doing very little with the graphics, timeline or stage, so we will customize the Flash environment for some serious scripting!
- Next, we will initialize our site. This consists of setting the variables that our site will use to their initial values.
- Finally, we will set up our basic code structure. As our site develops, we will add to this structure, but it will largely remain unchanged in terms of major building blocks.

The final FLA for this section is included as `stun_initialize_end.fla`, and the starting point is included as `stun_initialize_begin.fla`.

Getting ourselves comfortable

Although you may be used to designing sites with heaving Libraries full of lots of symbols, the stun:design UI actually now has everything it needs. All we need to do is add the content, but we will do that once the UI itself is completed. Since we will not be touching either the timeline or stage for some time, we may as well re-arrange the furniture for the job of coding.

The following environment is what I used to develop the site. I wrote it on a PC with a 1280x1024 sized screen. You may want to make minor changes if you are on a Mac or if you have a different screen resolution, but barring those who are set in their ways, I would advise that we are probably going to end up with the longest ActionScript listing you have ever seen, and YOU will be the one writing it! The days of three-line button scripts and ten-line `onEnterFrame` scripts are well behind you. We will have developed a 300+ line script by the end of this book, and you need a totally different environment to the one you have been used to for tween-based sites!

1. At the moment, you will have a timeline that looks like the one shown on the next page. Close the frame and UI folders if yours are still open, unlock the layer actions and select frame 1 of this timeline. Open the Actions panel and press the Pin icon, pinning the focus of the Actions panel to frame 1 of layer actions.

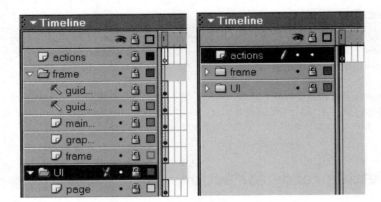

2. Mimimize the Timeline panel.

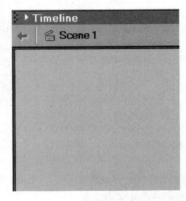

3. Dock the Actions panel to the lower middle area and, by pulling the top edge of it upwards, extend it to cover the stage area as shown below.

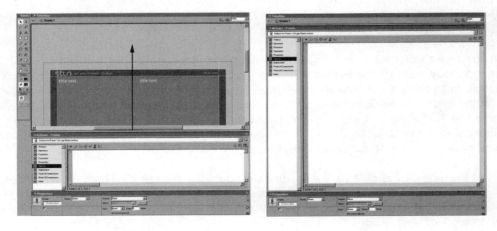

We have replaced the big wide stage area with a big wide scripting area!

4. Finally, you may consider changing the font we are using to show lines of code. The default font is cool for short scripts, but as the lines get longer, it can tend to make everthing look really cluttered. Whilst writing this site I changed the font to **Trebuchet MS 10 point**. You can change the font to the same thing (or something similar such as Helvetica or Arial) by clicking on the Actions panel's drop down menu (top right icon) and selecting Preferences. The Preferences panel will appear, with the ActionScript Editor tab showing. Select the font you want in the Text area of this tab.

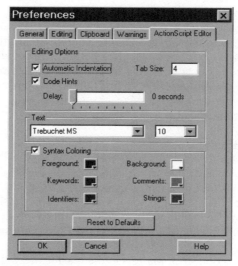

Initializing the site variables

Before we can intialize our variables, we need to think about which variables we actually need. Time for another diagram.

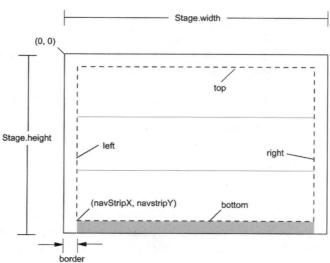

There are a number of points on the screen that our scripts will need to know about. They are:

- The height and width of the stage area, because most of our measurements will be based upon the stage size, `Stage.height` and `Stage.width`.
- The thickness of the border area or 'gutter' that encloses the main content, border.
- The position of the top, bottom, left and right edges of the main UI, top, bottom, left and right.
- The position of the back naviagation strip, navStripX, navStripY, because to place our icons on it, we need to first know where it starts.

To capture the stage dimensions, we can simply read them from the Document properties window (Modify > Document). That's cool, but it would be better if we could get the stage dimensions from Flash during runtime, because we may later decide to change the stage size. Remember that the Stage object allows us to get the stage dimensions directly from the Flash player during runtime.

1. Add this in the Actions panel.

    ```
    trace(Stage.height);
    trace(Stage.width);
    ```

    Test the FLA. This will not give us the values 800 and 600 for width and height. It will give us the width and height of the current window that is showing the SWF. On the web, this window will be the browser window. To fix this, we have to tell Flash to show the movie in the ExactFit mode (these are the same display modes that you can set in File > Publish Settings > HTML).

2. Since we are Flash ActionScript Masters in the making, we will make the change via scripting rather than via the Publish settings. Add the following line as shown:

    ```
    Stage.scaleMode = "exactFit";
    trace(Stage.height);
    trace(Stage.width);
    ```

    If you test the FLA now, you will find that you see the correct dimensions. However, this is *not* the display mode we want! Whilst in test mode, hit CTRL/CMD+B to bring up the bandwidth profiler to see why! Worse still, make the bandwidth profiler bigger (click-drag its lower edge)- the stun:design site is scaled to fit in its newly resized window, but doesn't maintain its proportions... urgh!

3. Not to worry, if we can change the display mode, we can change it back! Add the following line:

    ```
    Stage.scaleMode = "exactFit";
    trace(Stage.height);
    trace(Stage.width);
    Stage.scaleMode = "noScale";
    ```

    That's better!

    Okay, we now have almost all the values to base our site measurements on except one - the border. It is actually 30 pixels from the stage edge all the way round, and this is how we tell Flash this.

    ```
    border = 30;
    ```

4. Simple! Delete all the code you have added so far and add the following script:

```
// Define screen extents for later use...

Stage.scaleMode = "exactFit";
border = 30;
bottom = Stage.height-border;
top = border;
right = Stage.width-border;
left = border;
Stage.scaleMode = "noScale";
```

This defines all our important screen measurements in terms of the three primary measurements height, width and border. Have a look at the sketch we saw two pages ago if you are unsure about any of them.

I have not included the two measurements that show where the back strip is yet. We will do that separately later – it will require a major bit of code in its own right.

The next thing we want to add is the initial colors of the strips. I have chosen some colors for us: #993333, #119922 and #005577. You can get an early look at these colors by entering them into the Color Mixer panel. You can change them more to your liking if you violently disagree with my choice later, but leave them as they are for now so that we all develop the same site.

5. The site will use these colors to tint the first set of strips, and will base all further page colors on them. They therefore define the colors of **all** the backgrounds in the site. Add the following script to what you have so far...

```
// Define initial screen colors (further colors will
// use these colors as their seed)

color0 = 0x993333;
color1 = 0x119922;
color2 = 0x005577;
```

color0 to color2 are the three variables that hold our Hex color values.

6. We will add our navStripX and navStripY measurements now. Add the following code to the end of the script so far:

```
// Define navigation strip variables...

navStripX = border;
navStripY = bottom;
```

We have now initialized all the main variables that define our graphic UI. Flash now knows where everything is.

Defining the code to drive our UI

Our three strips within the instance `tricolor` are still the dull looking slabs of grey they have been for some time. I think that has gone on for long enough – time to add some color into their lives.

We also need to start adding some code to get them moving. Our animation code will be totally event-driven in this site (in keeping with the preferred way of writing Flash MX code). To set up the events, we will have to attach all the functions we will be using as event handlers as well.

The code associated with the strip and tricolor functionality will get quite involved, so it is better to separate it all out into functions that we can write separately. We will call the function that sets the tricolor page up (unsurprisingly) `stripPage`.

As we have seen earlier in the book, the `apply()` method of the Function object applies a function to a timeline. The functions will still run from `_root`, but rather like callback event handlers, they will be associated with `tricolor`, so within the functions, `this` will mean `tricolor` and not `_root`.

1. Type this code in below the definition of the `navStrip` variables

    ```
    // Initialize UI...

    stripPage.apply(tricolor);
    ```

We now need to write this function. Where do we write it? Well, the temptation is to write it *after* the code we have so far, but the convention is to define all functions at the top of your code.

We will therefore add the functions *before* the main code we have written so far.

There are two main things our function `stripPage` needs to do:

■   Define the code that *sets up* the ability to change color, and also includes the *ability* to change the colors. We have to *initialize* this ability as well as *include* this ability, because the thing that allows us to change color (the `Color` object) is not part of the movie clip – we have to add it separately.

■   Define the event handler scripts that change position. As we shall see later in the case study, there is not just one event handler to perform the animation, but a sequence of them, each handling a particular part of the animation before handing over control to the next event handler in the sequence. We will start the ball rolling by adding the first one in this sequence, `navigate`.

Writing the code to set up the events and function hierarchy

We could make `stripPage` a massive piece of code that did all our code setup but there is a much easier way to keep all our code manageable – make `stripPage` refer to two other functions:

■   One that defines the color changing abilities
■   One that defines the movement (animation) abilities

The problem with calling two new functions is *speed*. It's a bit like me trying to talk to you through a third person because we don't speak the same language. I say 'hi!' to Frank, and then Frank says 'hi' to you. Then you say 'hi Sham!' to Frank, and Frank says it to me. Not good. It would be far better if I learned your language, and then I could just say 'hi!' directly!

The function-based version of this is **inheritance**. Rather than *call* another function, we can make stripPage *assimilate* these other functions into itself. That's cool because we can still write the functions separately, but at runtime, we just call stripPage, and stripPage contains all the other functions we need without having to go and ask.

1. Here's the code. You need to add it above the code so far as shown:

```
// DEFINE MAIN SETUP SCRIPTS

stripPage = function () {
  // note use of Function inheritance
  this.inheritEvents = stripEvents;
  this.inheritCols = stripCols;
  this.inheritEvents();
  this.inheritCols();
};
```

This calls out two new functions called stripEvents and stripCols. There are a few things to notice here.

The way inheriting a function is written differently to calling it:
This line of code means *make me the same as another function called myFunction:*

```
MyInheritedFunction = myFunction;
```

This code is saying *run myFunction and make me equal to the result it returns:*

```
MyReturnedValue = myFunction();
```

The implied target of this:
What does this mean in stripPage? Well, we have applied stripPage to the movie clip tricolor, and so this means the instance tricolor.

Inheriting a function does not mean that it is executed:
When you cause a function to inherit another, it doesn't mean that you also run it. So as well as inheriting the functions stripEvents and stripCols, as inheritEvents and inheritCols, we also have to run the newly inherited functions. This is something you don't have to do for functions that act as event handler callbacks, as we shall see below.

2. Okay, so now we've written the stripPage function, but now we have two other functions to write. Here they are. You need to write them above stripPage but below the DEFINE MAIN SCRIPTS comment.

```
// DEFINE MAIN SETUP SCRIPTS

stripEvents = function () {
  // attach button events to the 3 pages...
  this.strip0_mc.onRelease = navigate;
  this.strip1_mc.onRelease = navigate;
  this.strip2_mc.onRelease = navigate;
};
stripCols = function () {
  this.colStrip0 = new Color(this.strip0_mc);
  this.colStrip1 = new Color(this.strip1_mc);
  this.colStrip2 = new Color(this.strip2_mc);

  this.setCol = function(col0, col1, col2) {
    var col0, col1, col2;
    this.colStrip0.setRGB(col0);
    this.colStrip1.setRGB(col1);
    this.colStrip2.setRGB(col2);
  };
};
stripPage = function () {
  // note use of Function inheritance
  this.inheritEvents = stripEvents;
  this.inheritCols = stripCols;
  this.inheritEvents();
  this.inheritCols();
};
```

Lets look at these functions in turn.

The stripEvents script attaches the onRelease button events to our three strip instances inside the bigger tricolor instance. Notice the way we have done this. Rather than using an anonymous function...

```
MyClip.onRelease = function() {
  // do this
};
```

...we are this time actually using a *named* script called navigate. To do this, we again omit the () at the end of the function (in much the same way as we did with inheritance before). So why did we then have to do the extra step of executing the inherited functions, but this time we don't? Well, when we are attaching to an event, Flash *knows that the function has to be run each time the event occurs*. When it is not an event, there is nothing to actually run the script, so we have to do it ourselves at least once.

The second thing to notice about the stripEvents function is how it is referring to the individual instances inside the tricolor movie clip. The stripEvents function takes tricolor as its subject because the function that called stripEvents, (stripPage) also had tricolor as its subject. That's quite powerful if you think about it – functions can *pass on the memory of the movie clip (or more correctly, the timeline) that called them to other functions*.

Although the `this` of `stripEvents` is `tricolor`, look what happens next: we have three lines that refer to the embedded instances `this.strip0_mc` to `this.strip2_mc`.

Eh?

Well, what we are saying here is that inside `this` (`tricolor`) you will find another movie clip called `strip0_mc` (or one of the other two)

That's okay, but the *really* cool thing is when you look at the full line:

```
this.strip0_mc.onRelease = navigate;
```

We are no longer calling `navigate` with the subject `this` as `tricolor`, we have *changed it* to the three movie clips *inside* tricolor! The function `navigate` will not take `this` as `tricolor`, but each of the movie clips `strip0_mc` to `strip2_mc`.

As our functions work back from the first function, `stripPage`, they are fanning out to cover more and more of the stuff that needs defining, *and they are doing this on their own!* All we do is say 'set up tricolor', and we have written the functions further down to know that `stripPage` consists of three new movie clips, and those need defining as well.

The `stripCols` function is also something new. If you look carefully it does something strange – it defines a function *within itself* called `setCol`. It's rather like those Russian dolls where you open the big one to find a smaller one inside. This is another structure in our code that is following the tendrils of our problem up through the trunk and out to the branches. Our initial function only has to apply itself to the single trunk, and the code will split and redefine itself as it encounters the problem branching out!

So why have we done this? Well, in the case of the color functionality, we don't need to just define the function, we also need to define some other stuff, and the function `stripCols` does just that.

So we have an insight to the structure of this bit of code, how about what it actually does?

Well the first thing we need to do is set up a color object in each `stripn_mc` clip. This is an object with methods that allow us to change the color of a movie clip. Once we have done that once for each strip, and *only then* can we actually use the line that does the color change. Lets have a look at the embedded function.

```
this.setCol = function(col0, col1, col2) {
  var col0, col1, col2;
  this.colStrip0.setRGB(col0);
  this.colStrip1.setRGB(col1);
  this.colStrip2.setRGB(col2);
};
```

This function actually takes some arguments; the three colors we want the three strips to be, `col0`... `col2`. We then use the `setRGB()` method of the color object to apply the color transition.

There's one final subtlety here, and you need to be aware of it. The lines that are actually executed when we call `stripCols` and `setCol` are different. When we call `stripCols` from `stripPage` the following lines are actually executed:

```
this.colStrip0 = new Color(this.strip0_mc);
this.colStrip1 = new Color(this.strip1_mc);
this.colStrip2 = new Color(this.strip2_mc);
```

`setCol` is then *defined* but not *executed*.

If we make a call to `setCol` (as we will in the main code at the end), only the function `setCol` is run. The rationale for this is obvious if we step back and have a think. The `stripPage` function is setting everything up, and to do that it has to set up the color objects and define `setCol`, but not execute `setCol`. When we actually use the interface, we will be changing colors and actually want `setCol` to set colors to create our transitions. In that case, we will call the *embedded* function `setCol`.

If you are having trouble with this, think of `stripCols` as a two-stage rocket. `stripCols` is the first and second stages that together make the complete rocket. When you launch (initialize) the rocket, you want only the lower first stage to burn (execute). Once you are up in orbit, you want the smaller second stage to actually do stuff, and that part is called `setCol`. At this point, you don't need the first stage to run (the part that initialises the color objects) and to achieve this you have split your rocket (`StripCols`) into two stages (`StripPage` and `SetCol`).

Okay, where are we up to?

We have set up the part of the code that sets up the event handlers, but haven't yet set up the event callback function that we refer to, `navigate`. Our color functionality is complete though, because there are no more outstanding functions to consider.

Setting up the event handler callbacks

We will not actually finish the `navigate` code sections yet. They require some decision making capabilities that we won't put in yet, but we can set up something called a **stub.** This is an incomplete program section that is acting as the placeholder to some code that we will write later. It will prove that we are on the right track, but it will not yet animate anything. You need to put it above the code so far, at the top of the Actions panel. Here it is.

```
// DEFINE EVENT SCRIPTS

navigate = function () {
    // intitialize navigation event handler here
    trace("");
    trace("you pressed me and I am"), trace(this._name);
    trace("but you need to fully define me");
    trace("before I start doing anything else!");
};

// DEFINE MAIN SETUP SCRIPTS
```

```
stripEvents = function () {
   // attach button events to the 4 pages...
```

The function `navigate` will output some text when we press a strip, but we are almost ready to run our FLA, so we will leave what it actually does for you to find out in a moment!

Invoking the color change code

So far, we have only *set up* the color changing code, `setCol`. We will now add the code to run it. The code is part of the main script (the stuff at the very bottom of the listing). And here it is.

```
// Initialize UI...

stripPage.apply(tricolor);

// Set UI colors...

tricolor.setCol(color0, color1, color2);

// now sit back and let the event scripts handle everything ;)

stop();
```

The active part here is the line

```
tricolor.setCol(color0, color1, color2);
```

This line calls the `setCol` function that we placed within `tricolor` to allow us to make color changes to the individual pages. We are passing the three color values we defined earlier.

Okay, we are ready to test the FLA...

Running the FLA

Did it work? With a script as long as this, there are bound to be errors, so if it doesn't work as expected, here's a quick run through of potential problems:

- Check that all your instance names are correct on the movie clips `tricolor` and `strip0_mc` to `strip2_mc`. If you used `stun_initialize_begin.fla` as your starting point, you don't have to worry about this.
- Check that all the variable and function names are correct. A good way of doing this is using the Find icon at the top of the Actions panel. If searching for a variable doesn't stop at every line you expect it to, then the missing line has a typo!

Here's what you will see if all has gone according to plan:

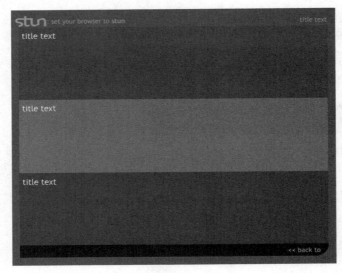

First off, we have color! The three color variables color0 to color2 have been applied to our three strips strip0_mc to strip2_mc. You can play about with the values we have equated with the color0...2 variables if you wish. For example, you can design alternative colors in the Color Mixer and replace one or more of the values used in our code here:

```
// Define initial screen colors (further colors will
// use these colors as their seed)

color0 = 0x993333;
color1 = 0x119922;
color2 = 0x005577;
```

For example, try changing color2 as follows:

```
color2 = 0xAAAA22;
```

This will give you a yellow instead of the blue. Change the color back to its original value when you're finished.

Secondly, mouse over any of the three strips, and the mouse will turn to a hand icon. This means that the strips are now acting as buttons. If you click on any of them you will see the following text appear in the Output window:

```
you pressed me and I am
strip1_mc
but you need to fully define me
before I start doing anything else!
```

The name will change depending on whether you press strip 0, 1, or 2. This shows that the site is aware of where you are asking to go because each strip returns its own name.

Before we move on...

You may not think we are very close to a fully working site here, but we have a lot of important features covered in the code so far.

- We have set up the variables that tell Flash what the UI looks like, and where all the important points are on the screen. If we ever need to change the stage size or position of any of the major parts (something you will have to do when you come to customize the site for your own ends), we know that these will be the only variables we will have to redefine. This makes our design *flexible*.
- We have defined a structured code hierarchy early on in the project. This makes our code easy to *modify*.
- We have initialized the main functions that define our UI, and attached all the main events.

We will be back to complete the site later, but for now, prepare yourself for Chapter 9, where we will be looking at how to make hyper-efficient code that can be repurposed and re-used over and over again – modular ActionScript.

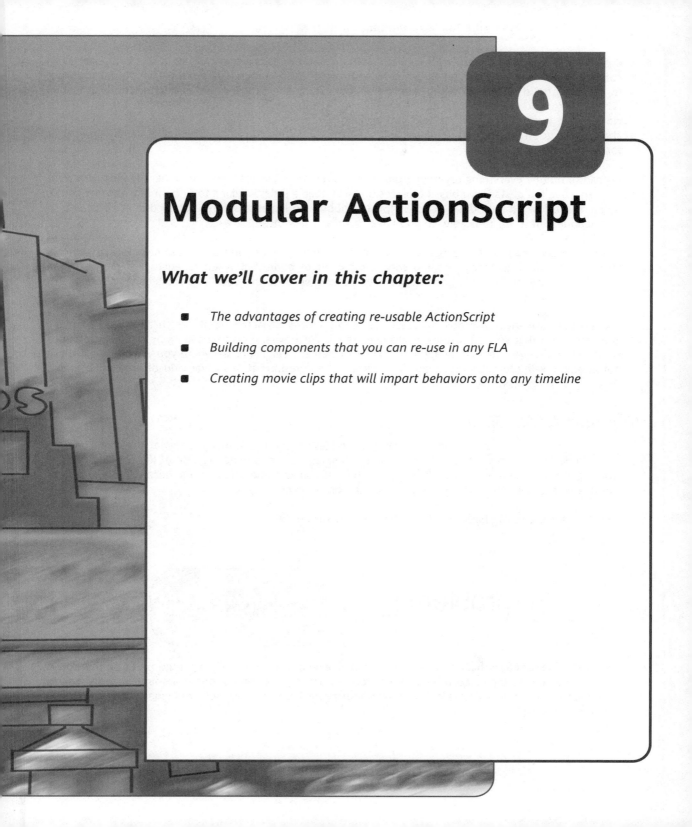

Modular ActionScript

What we'll cover in this chapter:

- *The advantages of creating re-usable ActionScript*

- *Building components that you can re-use in any FLA*

- *Creating movie clips that will impart behaviors onto any timeline*

If you're anything like me, you want to learn anything and everything that can help make your Flash skills commercially valuable – so that you can get something back for all the hard work you've put in! You want to get doing stuff in the minimum amount of time, using the simplest and easiest methods available. What's more, you don't want to get bogged down with irrelevant stuff that you'll never use in the real world. Well, I wrote this book to help you do just that, and this is where we start getting really serious about those good returns – this chapter holds out the tantalizing prospect of being paid many times over for a single piece of code!

Instead of bolting everything together from scratch every time you start work on a new project, you want to keep a bag full of standard bits and pieces that just need a little tweaking to fit right in with what you're doing. This is just what modular ActionScript is all about: writing efficient, re-usable code. It's efficient, so you need less of it. It's re-usable, so you have to write it less often.

Yes, you've guessed it. I *like* being paid twice for the same piece of coding. You can have lots of identical little movie clips following the same short simple bit of code, but when taken together, the overall behavior is *complex*. This is a good concept to explore because the code you actually need to write to create this apparent complexity is *short* and *simple*.

This chapter will show you how to create re-usable blocks of ActionScript, which allow you to make graphic effects that you can use over and over again. We'll expand on that theme by creating **behavior movie clips** that you can use to apply particular movement behaviors anywhere you want to. As if that's not enough, we'll look at a new Flash MX feature: the **component**, a special kind of movie clip that is specifically designed to be re-usable.

Modular ActionScript

There are many functions and effects that require Flash to be doing many things at the same time. In order to do this, you need to work with several timelines, each one handling a bit of the problem, and all working at the same time. You can't do that with what you've come across so far, because you're used to working with a single timeline (usually `_root`) to control everything.

This diagram shows the basic single-timeline project structure:

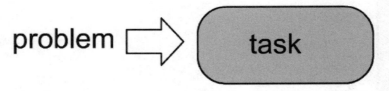

You have a big problem that you throw at the timeline, and have an equally big multi-part task that solves it, sprawling all over the place in the process. You may end up with an enormous amount of code, making it difficult to properly structure or document your project, and heaven help you when you want to add new functionality!

This diagram shows the modular approach:

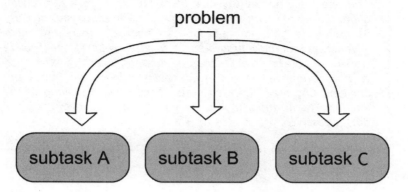

This way, you have separate timelines (in movie clips or loaded SWF levels), and each tackles a **subtask** – that is, a well-defined and self-contained part of the overall problem.

Each subtask is now more compact, with a better-defined problem to solve, which makes it easier to read and code. Furthermore, since you've broken down the specific task at hand into smaller (and probably more generic) subtasks, you're more likely to find these subtasks coming in handy elsewhere. If a similar problem arises in future, you can either re-use your existing subtasks in a slightly different context, or tweak them slightly to fit the bill. Either way, you'll wind up spending much less time on development than if you were to write the whole project from the ground up.

Black box programming

In programming, a black box is a piece of code that you can re-use without necessarily knowing all the details of how it works. You can't see inside the box because it's black, but you don't need to. The black box approach stipulates that all code must be *self-contained* and distinct from any other code.

You're only interested in two things:

- What it *does* to the outside world (its function, method or behavior)

- What it *needs* from you and *gives* back to you (its interface)

One example of a black box that should be very familiar is the remote control for your television. While you may not have the faintest idea of how it works or what goes on inside, you can still use it to change the channel. You provide it with an input (by pressing buttons), it does some processing and talks to the TV, and you get a nice predictable response: the channel changes.

> *Aside from the* **portability** *of a black box (and we're not talking about the remote control here, but the ease with which you can carry its usefulness from one situation to another), there are other advantages that make programming in this way beneficial. If you're working as part of a team of programmers for a given system or site, each programmer doesn't need to know how the others are implementing their allocated parts of the project, so long as the interface specification (that is, the inputs and outputs of the black box) is observed.*

So how does this black box relate to what we're doing?

The first rule for us is that, to make code self-contained it really should be within a movie clip and not on the main timeline. The main timeline isn't portable in the same way that a movie clip is because it's not self–contained and is consequently not a library item. To integrate the movie clip into our site, we simply have to add it to our library and make minor modifications to integrate it into its new environment. We've already seen examples of this, but we haven't really looked at how to create them for ourselves. That will change when we look sound control sliders in a moment.

So, self-containment is an important feature of modularity, and the movie clip captures this requirement beautifully. But... (there's always a *but* isn't there!) Unless a movie clip controls itself (we'll be looking at this possibility in the next chapter), it isn't totally self-contained. It might come into contact with the world outside in two ways:

- By addressing other timelines in Flash
- By receiving or outputting data

The black box approach has ways of dealing with these areas of contact. You might think that it's impossible for a movie clip to address other timelines while still being totally self-contained and distinct from any other code. As soon as you address another timeline, you're setting up a relationship with something else in that particular FLA that won't be there in another FLA. Our black box movie clips must only access what we know will be there in any situation, so any actions we use in them should be independent of what the target is called and where the movie clip has been put.

The solution is to use a special path called `_parent`, which refers to whichever timeline the movie clip has been attached to. You can think of the hierarchy of movie clips inside a movie as being like a big matriarchal family tree: the movie itself is the head of the family who has several daughters; each of them may (or may not) have daughters of their own, and so on, and so on... If you ask anyone in the family who their parent is, they'll point to whichever woman is one up the tree from them – assuming none of the men in the family are about, of course!

`_parent` always refers to a movie clip relative to itself, so we describe it giving us as a **relative path**. We've already seen one relative path: when `this` is used inside a function definition, it points to whatever it was that called the function. Now that we're attaching script directly to movie clips, it's useful to know that `this` can also refer to the movie clip your script is attached to – just as `_parent` is like a path to 'my mother', `this` is like a path to 'me'.

It goes without saying that black box code should be well documented so that we know what interactions to expect when we use it. This is important normally, but when we're writing code so that we can re-use it later it becomes absolutely vital. You'll never remember the intricacies of something you wrote when you come to re-use it while chasing a deadline six months later. Even if it seems like a waste of time now, document it!

You don't learn these techniques by reading about them. You learn by *doing them*, which is exactly what we will do in the next section. When looking at the particular examples, see if you can spot how I am adhering to the rules above.

Creating a component

In this first example, we're going to create the Flash MX version of a black box: a **component**. This is a special kind of movie clip, which is completely self-contained and comes with lots of features that will prove very useful when you start writing modular movies. As we'll see, you can't actually edit a component whilst it's on the stage, but you *can* modify what it does by simply changing parameters in the Property inspector.

There are a good few cartoons and other full-length features on the web at the moment, and it would be a good idea to have the sort of control over some of them you get with a normal video. In this exercise we will create a modular set of video controls that you can drop onto any timeline containing tween type animations.

If you get stuck at any point, you can get my finished version `videocontrols.fla` from this chapter's download file.

1. Create a new FLA document. The first thing we'll need is the video control buttons. I got mine from Window > Common Libraries > Buttons and then selected the playback folder, where you'll find a set of buttons complete with all the play, rewind symbols. Drag your buttons from the common library onto the stage and arrange them in a strip like this, giving them instance names (from left to right) pause_btn, play_btn, rewind_btn, fastforward_btn and stop_btn:

   This strip consists of five buttons. The Pause button should freeze the target timeline at the current frame. Then, every time it's pressed, it should advance to the next frame. The Play button should undo any other button and start to play the movie from the current frame. The Rewind and Fast Forward buttons should work like standard video fast-search buttons: they will cause the movie to play at a faster rate (say x4) either backwards or forwards. The Stop button should stop the movie at its current frame.

2.   Select all of your buttons (either drag a selection box around them all or hold down the SHIFT key and click on each in turn) and press F8 to convert them to a movie clip called videocontrols. Now double-click the movie clip to enter 'edit in place' mode. Rename the layer containing your buttons as buttons, and create a brand new layer called actions:

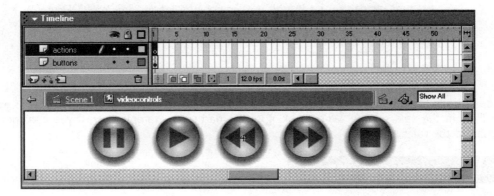

Let's start defining actions for these buttons. The Play and Stop buttons sound like they should be relatively painless, so we'll look at them first.

3.   The Play button simply has to make the timeline on which our video controls sit (which will be their _parent timeline) start to play. All we need to make this happen is an onRelease event handler containing a _parent.play() command.

Pin the Actions panel to frame 1 of layer actions, and add the following script. All further scripts will be added as a continuation of this script so there is no need to unpin for a while yet.

```
play_btn.onRelease = function() {
    _parent.play();
};
```

4.   The Stop button isn't much different from Play, only this time we need a _parent.stop():

```
stop_btn.onRelease = function() {
    _parent.stop();
};
```

Now we have a little functionality to play with, let's try our controls out. We're going to add a simple motion tween so that we can see when the timeline's running and when it's not.

5.   Go back to the main timeline, rename the existing layer as controller, and add a new layer called tween. Select frame 20 in both layers and press F5 to insert frames:

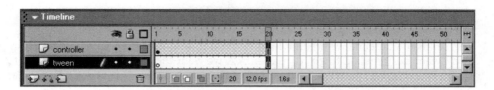

6. Select frame 1 on the tween layer and draw a circle just below the Pause button. Select frame 20 in the same layer, select Insert > Create Motion Tween, and press F6 to insert a keyframe:

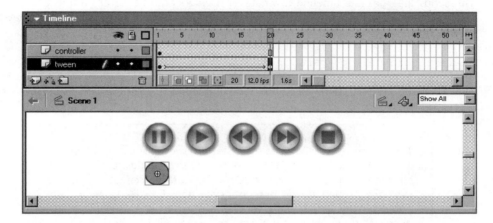

With this frame still selected, SHIFT-drag the circle over to the right until it's directly below the Stop button. That's the tween created – now run the movie to see it in action, and try clicking the Stop and Play buttons to check that they work.

Now we come to some slightly trickier ones. The Pause button needs to do one of two things: if the movie's playing, pressing it should bring the movie to a halt, just as stop does. However, if it's pressed when the movie's *already* paused, it should do what many video recorders do – something called *single stepping*. Every time you hit the button after the initial pause, the movie sneaks forward by a single frame and then stops again.

Let's say we're sneaky about this, and just enter the *single step* mode right away (that is, we just 'go to the next frame and pause' for *all* Pause button presses); how many people will actually notice? How many people have ever noticed that video recorders do two different things on the first and second press of the pause button? That's right. None, because the frame rates are too fast for anybody to realize that's what's happening.

The `onPress` action for the Pause button is actually the same as the Stop button: a simple `_parent.stop()`. The `onRelease` action is a little harder. We want the `_parent` timeline to `gotoAndStop` on its next frame. If you think back to earlier in the book, you may remember a movie clip property that tells us which frame a movie is currently on: `_currentframe`. To go forward one frame we just do a `gotoAndStop` to the parent's `_currentframe+1`.

There are three possible ways to write this command, but two of them won't work. Here they are:

```
gotoAndStop(_parent._currentframe+1);
```

This sends the timeline we are in (videocontrols) to whatever the _parent timeline is plus one. We don't want *our* timeline to go to _parent+1, we want the _parent timeline to go to _parent+1. If _videocontrols timeline pauses, the movie on the parent timeline is going to carry on playing and not a lot will happen!

```
_parent.gotoAndStop(_currentframe+1);
```

This sends the _parent timeline to whatever is videocontrol's current frame, plus one. This isn't a runner either – we still end up on the wrong timeline, and we've got nothing to play for the user on this one...

```
_parent.gotoAndStop(_parent._currentframe+1);
```

This sends the _parent timeline to the frame immediately after the one it's currently on; precisely where we want it.

> *This one really bothered me the first time I met it. You may be aiming an action like* gotoAndStop *at a different timeline through a pathname, but, unless you explicitly say otherwise, Flash assumes that any properties you describe, such as* _currentframe+1, *are based on the actual timeline that the action is attached to. This means that you **must** put a path to* _parent *in for both the* goto *command **and** the property.*

Now that we've got that sorted out, let's give the Pause button these onPress and onRelease actions that we've just worked out.

7. Add the following code to frame 1 of the actions layer

```
pause_btn.onPress = function() {
    _parent.stop();
};
pause_btn.onRelease = function() {
    _parent.gotoAndStop(_parent._currentframe+1);
};
```

The Fast Forward and Rewind buttons are also a little tricky because we want them to change the speed of the movie for as long as they're held down. The trouble is, Flash doesn't give us anything like a setTimeline method to change the frames per second. If we want to play the movie at three times normal speed, we must do it by playing just one frame out of every three.

We can achieve this by writing event handlers for the onEnterFrame event in the video control timelines. Every time the play head enters a frame, it should kick the parent's timeline on to the next frame but two (if we're fast-forwarding) or the last frame but two (if we're rewinding). These behaviors should kick in when the relevant button is pressed, and switch off as soon as that button is released.

This gives us three possible tasks for the onEnterFrame event handler:

- Normal mode – do nothing

- Fast Forward mode – go to current frame plus 3

- Rewind mode – go to current frame minus 3

As you know, we can't define multiple event handlers for a single event, so how do we make onEnterFrame behave properly in each circumstance? Well, we could define a variable to specify which mode we're in, use our button events to set it, and write an all-purpose handler (perhaps using a switch...case structure) that picks appropriate actions based on its value.

Then again, why not cut out the middleman? We want to use button events to modify what the handler does, and there's no overlap between the different modes and what they do. Let's just get our button event handlers to completely *redefine* the onEnterFrame handler as required.

There's an important distinction to note here: onMousePress and onMouseRelease are both user-generated 'one-shot' events, whereas onEnterFrame is generated by the timeline and fired for every frame. You can think of them as manual and automatic events; by using one to control the other, we're producing some pretty complex behavior.

We define each of the onPress button event handlers so that they set up a handler for onEnterFrame that will fast-forward or rewind the parent timeline. The buttons' onRelease handlers then delete the timeline's onEnterFrame handler by making it undefined.

> *If you've read the previous version of this book, you may recall that we had to get round not being able to do this in Flash 5 by creating frame-based loops. These tend to spread your code out all over the timeline, making the code all but impossible to follow. The MX version lets us keep all the code on one keyframe, making it far more readable.*

8. Add the following in the Actions panel:

```
fastforward_btn.onPress = function() {
    onEnterFrame = function () {
        _parent.gotoAndStop(_parent._currentframe+3);
    };
};
```

This script defines an `onEnterFrame` handler for the current timeline, making the parent timeline advance at three times normal speed. This behavior will continue indefinitely until we redefine or remove the `onEnterFrame` handler.

> *You may have noticed that the Actions panel doesn't show* `onEnterFrame` *in dark blue as you might expect it to. This is because the part of the Actions editor that colors keywords expects there to be a movie clip name (or* `_root`, *or* `this`) *before the* `onEnterFrame` *before it will recognize it as a method. We are not adding anything because we want to attach the* `onEnterFrame` *to the timeline of the* videocontrols *movie clip. Adding* `_root` *would not do this, and more subtly, neither would* `this`.

Notice that `this` states the `_parent` path for both method and property, just as we did for the Pause button. We decided earlier that x4 would be a good approximation of a faster rate for a fast-forward or rewind function. When we're calculating this, we need to bear in mind that Flash advances at the rate of 1 anyway, so for a Fast Forward button, we want Flash to advance at this rate +3

9. To stop us fast-forwarding, we need to delete the `onEnterFrame` script, and the instant we will do this is when the Fast Forward button is released:

```
FastForward_btn.onRelease = function() {
    onEnterFrame = undefined;
};
```

10. We need to do the same for the Rewind button.

```
rewind_btn.onPress = function() {
    onEnterFrame = function () {
        _parent.gotoAndStop(_parent._currentframe-5);
    };
};
rewind_btn.onRelease = function() {
    onEnterFrame = undefined;
};
```

Now that we've defined actions for all our buttons, we can use our videocontrols movie clip to control any timeline it's thrown at! Here's the full code listing:

```
play_btn.onRelease = function() {
    _parent.play();
};
stop_btn.onRelease = function() {
```

```
        _parent.stop();
    };
    pause_btn.onPress = function() {
        _parent.stop();
    };
    pause_btn.onRelease = function() {
        _parent.gotoAndStop(_parent._currentframe+1);
    };
    fastforward_btn.onPress = function() {
        onEnterFrame = function () {
            _parent.gotoAndStop(_parent._currentframe+3);
        };
    };
    FastForward_btn.onRelease = function() {
        onEnterFrame = undefined;
    };
    rewind_btn.onPress = function() {
        onEnterFrame = function () {
            _parent.gotoAndStop(_parent._currentframe-5);
        };
    };
    rewind_btn.onRelease = function() {
        onEnterFrame = undefined;
    };
```

There's one more thing to do before we finish off: we can make our movie clip into a component.

11. Open up the Library panel (F11), click on the button to create a new folder called videocontrols assets, and drag all the gel buttons into it. Now right-click (or CTRL-click) on the videocontrols movie clip and select Component Definition

12. Tick the Display in Components panel check box and give it the tool tip text of Video Controls. OK all this and the movie clip should now appear in the library as a component .

You can now use this set of controls on *any* timeline that consists of tween animations anywhere in any FLA. All you have to do is drop it into the target timeline! So how have we achieved this feat of coding?

Well, our video controls don't refer to any *specific* timeline, but to _parent (that is, whatever timeline videocontrols finds itself placed on). The controls don't need to know anything about this timeline, not even how many frames it has. Since the controls are completely self-contained, you can drag them onto *any* timeline, and they'll work.

The fact that we've wrapped the whole thing up as a component means that we can drag videocontrols from its place in the library and onto any other timeline, whether it's in the same movie or not. All its assets (that is, the bits and pieces it needs, in this case the gel buttons) are automatically copied across with it.

We now have a completely self-contained building block, so we should be able to re-use it elsewhere. Let's try this out.

Re-using a modular movie clip

A couple of years ago, when we were all still on Flash 4, people were beginning to use Flash for e-greeting cards. Most of them were pretty saccharine, so I came up with an altogether darker example that used some photography I came across on the Internet by a man called Martinus Versfeld. I asked him if I could use some of his pictures for one of my pieces, and like most people on the Web tend to (if you ask nicely), he said OK. You can find the results of this in the download file for this chapter as darkMX.fla. This exercise will show you how easy it is to drop those video controls onto another timeline.

1. Open darkMX.fla and create a new layer called control in the root timeline. This is where we're going to put our controls, so make sure that it's the topmost layer; otherwise they could be obscured by stuff on a higher layer moving in front of them:

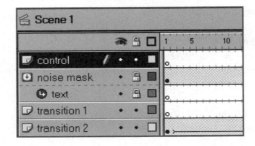

2. Now use File > Open as library to open videocontrols.fla, giving us access to the videocontrols component in the library window. Make sure the control layer is selected and drag the component onto the stage:

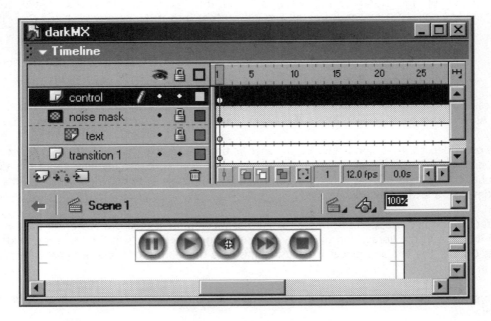

3. If you now press F11, you'll see the library for darkMX.fla, in which you'll see videocontrols listed along with its assets folder (containing definitions for all the gel buttons):

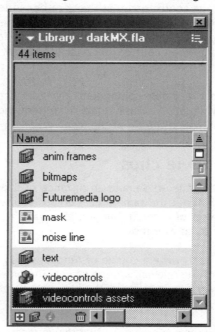

Yes, a tidy library is always a good idea in a document as complicated as this, and you don't need me to tell you why! If you run the movie now, the video controls will operate as you would expect.

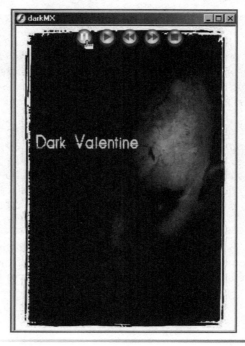

Of course, this set of controls will only act on a single timeline. If your animation consists of other movie clips as well as the timeline that holds videocontrols, it won't control them, just the timeline that it's placed on. You could modify the controls so that they can be hidden. You could even add a drag bar or use the _alpha property to make them semi-transparent when they're not in use. You could build up a whole site navigation system using a little TV remote control unit for your navigation; press the channel buttons to move about, and the video controls to control the movies. Enough of my ideas – I'll leave you to experiment.

We've now seen how to build a re-usable component, giving us a convenient timeline controller that we can use in all sorts of different situations. This has lots of consequences for how we write our Flash movies in future; but so far you've only seen the tip of the iceberg...

Modular control of movie clips

Imagine you have a movie clip called blob, and an instance of it on the stage called blob_mc. Say you want to make it do several things at the same time. Perhaps you want it to move about the screen in a particular way (based on one set of criteria), but you also want it to change its appearance (based on a completely separate set of criteria) as it moves.

The simplest solution would be to write a couple of functions that referred specifically to blob_mc, and trigger them whenever each of the relevant criteria is met. The only problem is that you'd have to create a new set of functions for every new instance of the blob you wanted to control, referring to blob2_mc, blob3_mc, and so on.

Of course, we could define the same functions so that they refer to _parent, build them into movie clips, and embed those movie clips into blob. Every instance of blob would then have these behaviors applied automatically.

> *A movie clip that has no content but scripts that act on its _parent is often referred to as a behavior movie clip (since that's what the Macromedia Director versions of the same thing are called). This is what Flash 4/5 users were stuck with in the past, embedding these behaviors inside movie clips they wanted to control.*
>
> *A behavior movie clip doesn't need to know anything about its parent other than the fact that it's a movie clip with the usual properties a movie clip possesses. We can do anything to it because we know what general properties the parent will have. For example, we don't need to know in advance how big it is, since we can always use the _xscale and _yscale properties to find out.*

The trouble with using _parent to refer to the timeline we're sitting in is that it can really tie our hands. Say you want to control some (but not all) instances of a particular movie clip. If we embedded a movie clip (or component) in the library definition of the movie clip, we're stuck with an identical component in *every* instance.

Fortunately, components let us control things in a much more flexible way. One of the neatest things about components is that you can attach them to specific *instances* of a movie clip. What's more, you don't even need to edit the movie clip to apply the component – you can just drag-and-drop your component onto the instance you want it to control, and hey presto!

How to simulate realistic movement

Before we look at building one of these amazing drag-and-drop behavior components, we're going to take a quick detour. We're well on the way to the top of the ActionScript mountain, and so we won't settle for just *any* behaviors here – we'll go for the big one: **real movement**. This is motion based on real physics, and takes into account the fact that objects in the real world have mass, and therefore move in a fairly complicated way. Let's work out what number-crunching code needs to go into our component before we start building it.

Don't panic though! There's very little math involved here; there's just a lot of common sense, along with some precise observations that you may need to think about carefully. If you find it hard going, just take it nice and slowly. It's not difficult, just a bit different, and it's well worth knowing about if you want to go on to build the kind of sites and effects that have everyone else gaping in awe!

Creating realistic motion isn't that different from what we've already done in Flash, but it can seem quite a challenge, simply because we have to account for little things like the laws of physics! Okay, come out from behind the couch. It may sound scary, but it's not. Really.

Real objects have **mass**. This is what makes them feel heavy, and also makes it hard to start and stop them moving. Just think about how much less effective your accelerator and brake pedals are when your car is loaded full of people. For a more dramatic example, just think about pushing a massive oil tanker along a flat stretch of road with your bare hands – or worse still, trying to stop it!

> *Objects have mass, so they can't start (or stop) moving immediately. When they start to move, it takes time for them to build up speed. When they stop moving, it takes time for them to come to a halt - this is call* **inertia**.

You'll be pleased to know that this is all the physics we really need for our simulation. Of course, if we let it, this could still start getting all mathematical and tricky on us. We don't really want that, so let's break it down into some common sense steps. (Common sense is well known as an ancient and powerful approach to problem solving!)

Let's look at our blob movie clip again. Say we place an instance of it (called `blob_mc`) on the stage at coordinates x=100, y=100. We want it to move across to x=200, y=100 in a realistic way.

```
if (blob_mc._x < 200) {
    blob_mc._x += 10;
}
```

Don't worry about where we'd put the code for now – the important thing is that it runs for every frame, and controls the position of the blob.

In this case, every time we enter a new frame, we check that the blob's x-coordinate is less than 200, and add 10 if it is. When the movie starts playing, the x-coordinate is 100 (where we originally put the blob). After one frame it's 110, after two it's 120, and so on. After ten frames it's 200 and it stops moving.

Well, that was easy! If you try it out though (and you can if you run `blob1.swf` from the download), you'll see that it moves quite unnaturally – it moves at the same speed throughout and stops abruptly; this makes it look fake!

So how can we fix this? Let's pause for a moment and think about what we're trying to do. We'll keep it simple for now: make the blob slow down before it reaches the target. At the moment, it moves at the same speed throughout. The line that does this is

```
blob_mc._x += 10;
```

which moves the blob by 10 pixels for every frame. What if we change '10' to something else? Well, changing it to '1' would slow the whole thing down, and changing it to '20' would speed the whole thing up, but neither would actually do what we want and give the blob different speeds at different times. What we want is something that can vary – a variable!

Let's say we use a variable called speed to tell us how fast to change the position:

```
blob_mc._x += speed;
```

Now we just need to figure out what value to give speed. Well, we know where to start looking: the blob begins at x=100 with a speed of 0, and ends up at x=200 with a speed of 0. Of course, we can also guess that it needs some more speed in between; otherwise it won't ever *get* to x=200!

We need to find a value that starts positive (when the movie starts) and then drops away to zero as the blob approaches its destination. That's easy: we use the distance between the blob and the target! We can work this out by finding the difference between `blob_mc._x` (the blob's current x-coordinate) and target (the x-coordinate of the destination). When we do the sums, we find it starts off at 100 (200 - 100 = 100) and finishes as 0 (200 - 200 = 0), which is just what we need.

We know where the blob's heading for, so the last bit should be easy:

```
target = 200
speed = target - _x;
blob_mc._x += speed;
```

So, if x is less than 200, the speed is positive and the blob moves to the right. If x is 200, the speed is zero; just what we wanted – isn't it? Not quite. You see, the first time your movie works out the value of speed, it'll be 100. Add that to x, and it'll take you straight to the end, before you have time to blink!

Okay then, let's scale down the `speed` a little:

```
target = 200;
speed = target - _x;
speed = speed / 10;
_x += speed;
```

Now the `speed` value will start out as 10, and get smaller as the blob closes in on its target. This approach gives great results – check out `blob2.swf` to see this simple example in action.

Let's consider what we've done here. As we get closer to our destination we want to slow down – or to put it in terms we can describe in ActionScript, we want to travel less and less every frame. We use `speed` to control how far we move for each frame, and by making it a specific fraction of the distance remaining.

That figure of 10 I used to scale down the speed was actually very important. If you're adventurous, you may already have tried plugging in some different values here; it's not like I gave you any good reason for using 10 after all! Say we used 2 instead, and traveled half the remaining distance in each frame – it would work just as well, only quicker:

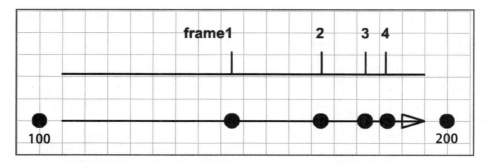

In fact, this value directly controls how quickly the blob slows down (or **decelerates**, for the more technically minded among you – engineers would say it controls the **stiffness** or **feedback** of the system). If it's a large number, the blob will take ages to reach its destination because the speed falls off too quickly. If it's a very small number (between 0 and 1), the blob will overshoot because the speed doesn't fall off quickly enough.

> How do I know all this? Well, it's down to a bit of math beyond the scope of this book, but for the interested, go and find out about **Control Theory**.

In fact, we can generate very specific behavior by carefully picking our value:

- If it's less than 0.5, the blob accelerates past the target and never stops.

- If it's equal to 0.5, the blob will overshoot by exactly the original distance, overshoot back again, and so on, and so on, **oscillating** around our target forever!

- If it's greater than 0.5 but less than 1, the blob will overshoot slightly, but come back and stop on the target after a few 'bounces'.

- If it's exactly 1 (or we simply leave it out) the blob goes straight to the target, as we saw earlier.

- If it's between 1 and 2, the blob slows down and stops at the target without overshooting.

- If it's over 2, we'll never *quite* reach the target.

Of course, the easiest way to find something you like is to play around with the numbers and see what happens; but hopefully these pointers will help give you some idea of what to expect. I personally find a value between 1.8 and 2 gives the most aesthetically pleasing result.

We can sum it up like this – for each frame we work out the blob's new position as follows:

New position = current position + ((target position - current position) ÷ constant)

Why is this important? Well, it's the simplest, most processor-friendly equation we can use to add realism to movement in our Flash movies. This is because it simulates acceleration, which suggests our blob has a whole host of real physical properties and processes acting on it (such as weight, viscosity, friction, inertia, and more besides).

> *Although this equation is about motion changes with time, it has no explicit reference to time. That's because our movie is based on frames, and it's the frame interval that creates our time-based motion.*

We've now spent a little while looking at some fairly heavy concepts behind simulating real movement, but we haven't really tied it in with modular programming. It's surely about time we did – after all, that's what the chapter's all about!

We're about to use this equation in three particular types of movement behavior, and you'll see how we can build on it to create some complex-looking motion. More importantly, we'll see how to define the behavior separately from the object it's acting on, so that we can effortlessly re-use it time and time again. Let's make some movies to practice what we've been talking about!

Trailing the pointer

In this example, we're going to create a component that will control a separate movie clip and make it chase the mouse cursor. Remember our equation:

New position = current position + ((target position - current position) ÷ constant)

In this case, our target will be the mouse pointer, whose position coordinates are stored in `_xmouse` and `_ymouse`. The movie clip instance will be called `trail_mc`, and we'll use its properties `_x` and `_y` to maneuver it about the screen. We therefore need to use our equation twice: once for the x-coordinates, and once for the y-coordinates:

```
_x = _x + ((_xmouse - _x) / n)
_y = _y + ((_ymouse - _y) / n)
```

Note that I've used a variable called `n` to denote the constant. We'll need to remember to define that somewhere in our code.

Just in case you get stuck at any point, you can find a complete version of this exercise saved as `inertia.fla` in the download file for this chapter.

1. In a brand new Flash document, open the library and create two movie clips called trail and inertiaFollower. The first will be the 'blob' we use to follow the pointer, while the second will define the actual trailing behavior. The idea is, we'll eventually turn inertiaFollower into a component so that we can simply drop it on *any* movie clip to make that movie clip trail the pointer... Cool, huh?

2. Open up trail (double-click on its entry in the library) and draw a black circle about 50 pixels across in the center of the stage. All done there.

3. Now open up inertiaFollower. Add a new layer, and rename your two layers as actions and icon.

4. In the icon layer, draw a small red square. This is purely so we can see that the inertiaFollower is there.

   Now we want to make our inertiaFollower a behavior component that we can drag-and-drop onto objects on the stage. To do this, we have to make it a component and define a special component parameter called `_targetInstanceName`.

5. Right-click (or CMD-click) on the inertiaFollower movie clip in the library, and select Component Definition. Now press the '+' button at the top of the dialog that appears. This adds a parameter in the panel below it. In the Name field, enter `myTarget`, and set Variable to `_targetInstanceName`. Be sure to type this exactly, complete with an underscore at the beginning, or the feature will not work. Also, make sure you hit ENTER following each entry

   While we're at it, you can check both the Options checkboxes (at the bottom of the window) and enter "mouse follower behavior with inertia" in the Tool Tip Text field.

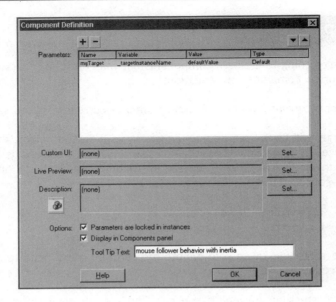

What have we done?

Well, we turned our inertiaFollower movie clip into a component for a start! _targetInstanceName is a special component property that changes to reflect the name of the movie clip we drop it onto during author time – we'll be making use of this in a moment. We'll also be making our component appear in the Components panel, and this is what the tool tip text and the two checkboxes are all about.

Let's test the drag-and-drop feature. For this to work, 'Snap to Objects' mode has to be enabled. You can do this by either pressing the magnet icon in the Main toolbar (top of screen, above the timeline), or via View > Snap to Objects.

6.   Place an instance of the trail movie clip onto the stage and give it the instance name trail_mc. Now drag a copy of inertiaFollower from the library and onto trail_mc.

7.   Take a look in the Property inspector, and you should see the following:

This means our component has read the name of the instance you dropped it on. 'Um... so what?' you may be asking. Well, since we know the name of the instance, *we can control it*.

Okay. It's time for some scripting. Remember though: you can't edit a component in place. The only way you can get inside it is via the version in the library.

8. Open up the inertiaFollower component from the library and select frame 1 of layer actions. Add the following code:

```
// Set target movie clip...
myTarget = _targetInstanceName;

// Define behavior event...
_parent[myTarget].onEnterFrame = function() {
    // Capture mouse positions
    targetX = _root._xmouse;
    targetY = _root._ymouse;
    distX = targetX - shapeX;
    distY = targetY - shapeY;
    // Apply inertia equation...
    shapeX += (distX/5);
    shapeY += (distY/5);
    // perform animation...
    _parent[myTarget]._x = shapeX;
    _parent[myTarget]._y = shapeY;
};
```

The first two lines take the _targetInstanceName property and equate it to a variable called myTarget. So, we know that the instance name of the clip we want to control has a name held in myTarget; but do we know *where* it is? Well, since we just placed our component on top of it, it's a fair assumption that they're both on the same timeline. In this particular case, that's _root; but to keep things general, we access it as _parent. That's all we need to form a general path to the thing we want to control: parent[myTarget].

The rest of the code is simply the inertia effect, continuously applied via an onEnterFrame command. Our target is the current mouse position, and where we are now is (shapeX, shapeY).

> *Note the use of square brackets to enclose the variable (or dynamic) part of the path. Without it, Flash would assume that the path was the literal string "parent.myTarget" and go looking for a movie clip called myTarget. In actual fact, we want it to look for the movie clip instance trail_mc, whose name was stored in the property _targetInstanceName (and copied to the variable myTarget). The brackets are how Flash knows that this is what we want to do.*

9. Once you have entered this code, test the FLA. This time, you'll find that the ball follows the mouse.

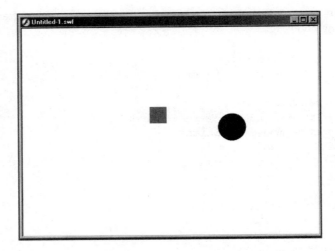

There's only one slight problem now: the icon for our behavior is still visible. That's an easy one to fix.

10. Just below the first line of code, add the following:

```
this._visible = false;
```

This will make our `inertiaFollower` instance invisible.

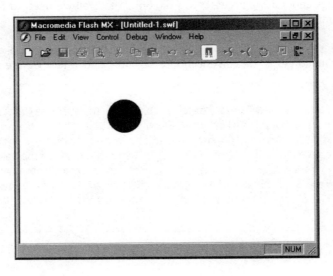

> *Be careful when using* `_visible`*; not only does it make your movie clip invisible, it also disables all scripts on it from the next frame onwards! We're okay in this case because we are attaching our* `onEnterFrame` *to the target movie clip directly.*

There's one last thing we can do with our follower behavior before we finish: customize the inertia of the effect for each instance.

11. Right-click (or CTRL-click) on the inertiaFollower component in the library, and add a new parameter via the '+' button again. Give this new parameter the name `inertia` and the variable name `inertiaValue`. Change the type field from `default` to `number` and change the default value to 5.

12. We now need to use our new parameter in our script. Change the lines I've highlighted below in frame 1 of the actions layer:

```
// Apply inertia equation...
shapeX += (distX/inertiaValue);
shapeY += (distY/inertiaValue);
// perform animation...
_parent[myTarget]._x = shapeX;
_parent[myTarget]._y = shapeY;
```

13. Now delete everything from the stage, and add four instances of trail. You don't need to give them instance names (as mentioned earlier, Flash gives them instance names itself if we don't, because all objects must be named).

14. Drop an inertiaFollower component on each circle, and use the Property inspector to give them `inertia` values of 2, 4, 6, and 8.

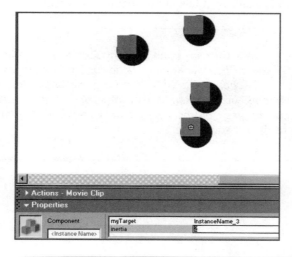

15. Now test the FLA. By giving each instance a slightly different value we have built up an altogether more complex animation. This is all happening through modular clips and code re-use.

Let's develop what we've done in the last exercise to create a swarm. We will also leave components for a moment and use a different approach to modular code: *functions*. You have been using functions all along so far when we have been defining functions as part of the event handler structure, but you can also use functions in a number of other ways...

Embedding movie clips

Our next example may look daunting from a distance, but it's based quite closely on inertiaFollower, and only took me half an hour to put together. Of course, I've had a bit of practice with Flash, but I guarantee that you'll be doing the same within six months if you stick with it! All I've done with Swarm is to start off with a simple set of premises, and build it up from there. The story doesn't end here either: there is much more I could do with Swarm and we'll talk about that in a moment.

> *If you go away with one thing from this section, remember that Flash allows you to quickly visualize behavior-based changes under the control of ActionScript. Once you have the basic ingredients, it is easy to build up to a stunning, dynamic and re-usable effect. This is not easy to grasp, but bear with it, because it is important, and once you see it, it is easy to do.*

Swarming behavior

We're going to look at modeling a swarm of flies – the swarm as a whole will follow the mouse about (like our last example), but individual swarm members have slightly different destinations. Why? Because in real life it is difficult to occupy the same place as something else! So a swarming fly will land slightly to one side of its neighbor. That is the nature of **swarming**. The individual members of a swarm are actually trying to all go to the same place, but they can't, and are always trying to maintain a position in an area with limited space.

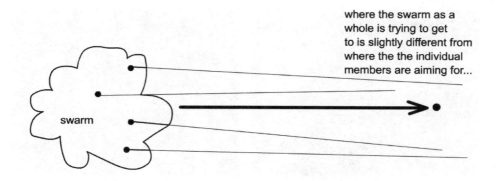

where the swarm as a whole is trying to get to is slightly different from where the the individual members are aiming for...

swarm

There is also the *type* of motion. A swarm in motion will tend to be more spread out when it's traveling because each member needs space to fly. When it's at rest, the swarm can become more tightly packed, because speeds are now much lower, and some of the members may be just stationary and hovering rather than actually moving. There is something here about the *density* of a swarm.

Where did I get all that information? Nowhere. No books on flies or queuing theory, chaotic motion or fluid dynamics. I just used my observations of two inertiaFollower balls moving around following my cursor, and combined that with the memory of walking down a canal path with my partner last summer, having to dodge past the odd congregation of flying insects.

swarm is exactly the same as inertiaFollower except for a few things:

- I've added two new terms – flockX and flockY – which denote a random position around the target destination (which is again the cursor), where the _parent heads for. Since it's random, it's different for each member of the swarm.

- This 'flock' position also changes according to whether the cursor is moving or not: if it's moving, the swarm is traveling so the spread gets bigger; if not, the swarm is stationary, and won't be so spread out.

- I've used the variables oldTargetX and oldTargetY to determine whether or not the cursor is moving. If the current target is the same as the old target, then it's safe to assume the cursor is stationary.

- Every now and again, there's a chance that each swarm member changes where it wants to get to, due to its neighbors getting in the way. We therefore want to simulate this.

- I've tweaked swarm so that it can be applied to multiple instances.

Although the code looks quite a lot bigger, these really are the only changes I've made. If you want to really kick-start the swarm, increase the frame rate from 12fps to 18 or 24fps (Modify > Document > Frame Rate). The faster you make them, the more they feel like an angry swarm... I can almost hear the buzzing!

You can see the final FLA as `swarmMX1.fla` if you hit trouble at any point.

swarm is a one-frame clip that initializes itself and then creates an `onEnterFrame` script to run continuously (every frame) to animate it. Why haven't we created this as a component? Well, there's the small matter of practicality. If you look at the screenshots above (or if you've already run `swarmMX1.fla`) you should appreciate that it would be difficult to drag and drop a component onto every one of our flies!

It's always important to remember that components are only one of the ways to create modular code – albeit a very powerful one! There are actually a number of different ways, and these can include:

- Using embedded timelines

- Using functions as re-usable code

- Using functions as objects (callbacks)

We will start off with the embedded timelines way of writing this code, but will go up to using callbacks, modifying our code to fit in with each different approach.

Creating a swarm

1. Open a new FLA and create a new movie clip called swarm. Click on the first frame of this movie clip and open the Actions panel. Pin the panel to this frame, and add the following code:

```
// initialize parameters
shapeX = _parent._x;
shapeY = _parent._y;
targetX = 0;
targetY = 0;
oldTargetX = 0;
flockX = (Math.random()*200)-100;
flockY = (Math.random()*200)-100;
```

Notice the addition of the `flock` variables I mentioned just now and the `oldTargetX` variable. We're setting the `flock` variables to a random number between -100 and 100.

The next thing we need to do is set up an `onEnterFrame` script to constantly animate our fly movie clip. Here's the trick; the fly movie clip is not this one... this one is simply the brain that causes the fly to move. The thing that we see on screen will be the movie clip that `swarm` is embedded in – that is, its `_parent`.

2.   Add the following lines to the end of your code:

```
// set up onEnterFrame script to animate _parent...
this.onEnterFrame = function() {
```

3.   We now need to fill in the body of the `onEnterFrame` handler function. The first part needs to pull in our target position (that is, the current mouse position) and work out how far we are from it:

```
// Capture mouse positions and distance from mouse
targetX = _root._xmouse;
targetY = _root._ymouse;
distX = targetX-shapeX+flockX;
distY = targetY-shapeY+flockY;
```

To make sure the whole swarm doesn't head for exactly the same position, we've added the `flock` offsets, which we have already defined as random numbers. This offset is not only random, but a *different* random number for each member of our swarm, so they will all head for the mouse position plus or minus a bit. This will mean that we will see our swarm not actually head for the mouse itself, but *swarm around it*.

Our next bit is completely new – we need to let the flock variables change value depending on whether the cursor is still or moving.

4.   There are two motions the swarm will take up, based on this code. If the current mouse position is the same as it was last time, the mouse hasn't moved, and the flock variables have a one in ten chance of flock movement, otherwise leaving them to settle:

```
if ((targetX==oldTargetX) && Math.random() > 0.9) {
    // add small scale random darting if mouse is still
    flockX = (Math.random()*100)-50;
    flockY = (Math.random()*100)-50;
```

So if the mouse stays still, the swarm gets closer, as if it is about to settle. If the mouse has moved, we make the swarm bigger by increasing the flock variables:

```
} else if ((targetX != oldTargetX) && Math.random() > 0.8) {
    // add large scale random darting if mouse is moving
    flockX = (Math.random()*400)-200;
    flockY = (Math.random()*400)-200;
}
```

5. Finally, we apply our motion equation. We are currently at shape and need to travel a distance dist. I have set the inertia constant to 20, so we travel one twentieth of the remaining distance in each frame, which is quite slow (in keeping with the speed of a swarm of bees or similar small creatures). The new bit here is keeping a record of the previous targetX mouse position to help us decide whether the mouse is moving or stationary:

```
// Apply inertia equation
shapeX = Math.round(shapeX+(DistX/20));
shapeY = Math.round(shapeY+(DistY/20));
// perform animation
_parent._x = shapeX;
_parent._y = shapeY;
// remember the current mouse pos so we can tell if
// it has moved next time around
oldTargetX = targetX;
}
```

Notice that we do not animate this but _parent:

6. We now need a movie clip that will swarm around the mouse pointer. In my FLA, I've set my background to black (do this with Modify > Document), and created a movie clip called bug, which is just a small white cross:

7. Still inside bug, rename the current layer (the one the cross is on) to graphics and add a new layer called behavior. Drop an instance of swarm (our fly's brain) into it, placing it near to the cross.

8.   Now return to the main stage and drag several instances of the bug movie clip onto the stage. How many you drag out will depend on the size of your original 'bug' graphic symbol – as you can see here, I made my crosses quite big and only used a few so you can see them clearly in the screenshot.

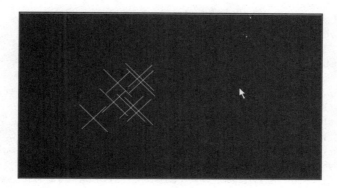

9.   Test the movie. If you leave the mouse still, you'll see the swarm bunch up and flit around it as a dense swarm. If you move the mouse, the swarm gets less dense as its members move apart to enable them to move for the journey. Here's a happy bonus - leave the cursor still for a bit and then move it slightly. It's almost as if the swarm has been disturbed and is getting angry! Funny how when you model simplicity, complex behaviors seem to just emerge...

Okay. Let's recap. So far we have created a modular movie clip called swarm. This can be dropped onto the timeline of any movie clip (and not just bug) and that movie clip will start to act like a fly. Try it! We've created modularity via the _parent path, just as we did in our first example with the video controls. The only differences are that in this case we've defined a behavior (so no interface) and applied it to a movie clip (and not the main timeline). The code can be re-used because it works by controlling a *general* movie clip _parent. This means that you can use it with any movie clip.

That's cool, but notice that we tell a movie clip it is a fly by manually dropping a 'fly brain' into it via swarm. Once the movie clip has this brain inserted, the deed is done, *and you can't easily change this at runtime*. This makes the code rather inflexible. The next way of implementing our swarm FLA overcomes this feature; we will use the function object.

Using function as an object

Yes, that harmless looking function keyword we've been using to make event handlers – don't forget that it's an object too! As we saw back in Chapter 7, it has a particularly useful method called apply(), which will apply it to any target you care to specify. So, if we defined a function called fly() and wanted to apply it to an instance of our bug movie clip called _root.bug_mc, we could do it like this:

```
fly.apply(_root.bug_mc);
```

Have a look at swarmMX2.fla. This code does exactly the same thing, but applied with functions. The main code is now on frame 1 of _root, and looks like this:

```
fly = function () {
    this.shapeX = this._x;
    this.shapeY = this._y;
    this.targetX = 0;
    this.targetY = 0;
    this.oldTargetX = 0;
    this.flockX = (Math.random()*200)-100;
    this.flockY = (Math.random()*200)-100;
    // set up onEnterFrame script to animate _parent...
    this.onEnterFrame = function() {
        // Capture mouse positions and distance from mouse
        this.targetX = _root._xmouse;
        this.targetY = _root._ymouse;
        this.distX = this.targetX-this.shapeX+this.flockX;
        this.distY = this.targetY-this.shapeY+this.flockY;
        //
        if ((this.targetX == this.oldTargetX) && Math.random()>0.9) {
            // add small scale random darting if mouse is still
            this.flockX = (Math.random()*100)-50;
            this.flockY = (Math.random()*100)-50;
        } else if ((this.targetX != this.oldTargetX) &&
                    ➥Math.random()>0.8) {
            // add large scale random darting if mouse is moving
            this.flockX = (Math.random()*400)-200;
            this.flockY = (Math.random()*400)-200;
        }
        // Apply inertia equation
        this.shapeX = Math.round(this.shapeX+(this.DistX)/20);
        this.shapeY = Math.round(this.shapeY+(this.DistY)/20);
        // perform animation
        this._x = this.shapeX;
        this._y = this.shapeY;
        // remember the current mouse pos so we can tell if
        // it has moved next time around
        this.oldTargetX = this.targetX;
    };
};
//
//
for (i=0; i<20; i++) {
    _root.attachMovie("bug", "bug"+i, i);
    fly.apply(_root["bug"+i]);
}
```

Whoa! This looks much more complex! The lines are much longer for a start, but closer inspection reveals that the only thing that has really changed is that every variable name and path is now preceded with this. That's because the code has been even further generalized than the last example – the **scope** of our code has changed.

Last time round, although the thing we were controlling was a general movie clip _parent, the code variables were on a *specific* timeline, and that was the timeline of each swarm instance. This time, the code variables will be on the same timeline (_root) unless we define them to be otherwise.

That's where this comes in: it tells Flash to place the code on 'the timeline the function is scoped to'. That may seem a little complicated, but bear with it, because you always do the same thing, and once you have tried this method a few times, it comes naturally to keep adding this.

> *The only things that aren't preceded with* this *are the mouse position (we still use* _root._xmouse *and* _root._ymouse *because we want the position of the mouse relative to* _root, *and* **not** *relative to each bug) and globals such as the* Math *object.*

The other thing to notice is that the script is no longer controlling _parent, but this – each bug instance ends up controlling itself! The code looks more complicated, but it is actually *easier* because there is no longer a hierarchy of control.

There's one more big advantage to this apparent complexity: all our code is now in frame 1 of the _root timeline. This makes it much easier to add or subtract bits of code rather than having to mess about on a hunting expedition through the library to work out which timeline each bit of code is, and how it is related to other bits of code (as you progress in Flash, and start looking at other peoples' code, you will find that this can become very confusing).

With this 'function as an object' style of coding, you don't have this difficulty. The only problem is with remembering to add this to everything.

Also, notice that there are no longer any bug instances on the stage. The loop at the end of the script populates the stage with the bugs for us.

```
for (i=0; i<20; i++) {
    _root.attachMovie("bug", "bug"+i, i););
    fly.apply(_root["bug"+i]);
}
```

This gives us 20 bugs, called _root.bug0 to _root.bug19. Each one has a fly() function applied to it. Look back at the main code, and you will see that this function includes the initialization script *plus* an onEnterFrame script.

So what are the advantages of this way of doing things? Well, as a beginner, you will be thinking 'wow that all looks a bit daunting!' That's understandable: the nested timeline way is much easier to get your head around. Believe me though – this method is *much better*. The reasons for this are:

- It makes code both **target-independent** (that is, you don't need to know where the thing you are controlling is) and **position-independent** (so you don't need to know where your code will end up). Nested timelines that use the `_parent` trick are only target independent. The code in `swarmMX2.fla` is *totally* independent of the application you wind up using it for, and that makes it more re-usable.

- You have more control of the final effect. For example, change the `i<20` part of the `for` loop at the end of the script to 50 and rerun the script. Now think how long it would take you to do the same thing manually! The way we have written the code makes it easier to tweak because all the controls are software parameters rather than manual 'put 50 of these on the stage' deals.

- You can define event handlers *before* the movie clip you're applying them to exists. If you think about it, we've defined an `onEnterFrame` handler without having anything to attach it to. That makes for flexibility. We can choose to *not* attach the swarm event, or allow the user to control the effect, and select from different events at runtime. For a good example of this, change the `for` loop at the end of the script as follows:

```
_root.onMouseDown = function() {
    for (i=0; i<20; i++) {
        _root.attachMovie("bug", "bug"+i, i
        fly.apply(_root["bug"+i]);
    }
    _root.onMouseDown = undefined;
};
```

This will not attach all the script to the instances (in fact, it won't even create the instances) until we click the mouse. We have taken the generation of script away from a linear path and made them **conditional**. This not only leads to increased flexibility, but also allows more complex structures to be built up that support cool things like adaptive behavior – and that's not too far from the programmer's holy grail: **Artificial Intelligence**.

Taking things forward

Let's say I want to develop this further. Instead of swarms chasing the cursor, I want them chasing food. The food would be a plant called "spore" growing on a distant planet. The user could cause spore to grow or die out by changing the climate. The behaviors of the swarm aren't fixed but can mutate in response to the changing conditions. The members can be grazers that eat spore or evolve to be stronger and eat other grazers, or become scavengers, eating spore but keeping an eye on the weaker grazers. There are all sorts of other possible behaviors I have written down, like pollution, growth and aggression – and I might well call this game "Ecology".

So far, I've managed to get as far as modeling the spore growth – maybe you'll see this game in another book! For now though, you can see that each iteration in this exercise is just another step to something more complex. Where will *you* end up with this?

Summary

In this chapter we've taken a look at some seriously professional ActionScript techniques. We've covered:

- Best practice for modular, black box programming

- Creating modular movie clips

- Building ActionScript to create real movement

- Creating behavior movie clips

- How to create a swarming effect and how to improve it using functions as objects

This far in the book, our movies have been silent affairs. In the next chapter, we'll cover how to get your movies to make noises.

Sound

What we'll cover in this chapter:

- *Importing sound clips into the library*

- *Converting a sound clip into a sound object that ActionScript can control*

- *Using sound object event handling to synchronize sounds*

- *Adjusting sound objects to pan and change the volume of a sound effect*

- *Creating a soundtrack for stun:design with interactive graphics for controlling the volume*

This chapter is about using sound to enhance your Flash movies, a feature that will really start to open up the world of Flash multimedia in your designs. Multimedia web sites, in HTML for example, have usually separated the sound content from the rest of the site. However, the introduction of sound in previous versions of Flash has dramatically improved the overall user experience. Clever use of music and sounds in your designs allows for a high degree of interactivity and usability, and at the very least goes towards producing a pleasant atmosphere within your site. With Macromedia Flash MX we can now begin to push the limits of using sound in our web sites, from streaming sound in parallel with video, to actually sequencing and mixing completely new pieces of music online.

At the moment, I think sound is somewhat ignored by many Flash designers. So much so, in fact, that when I come across a site which uses sound well, it sometimes blows me away more than a site with good visuals, because it's that much rarer.

In the past, sound on the web has been problematic, but then MP3 came along. Before the advent of MP3 there were very limited options for the web designer: **MIDI** (Music Instrument Digital Interface), which is not a universal standard and tended to be of variable quality depending on your hardware, and **sampled sound files** of various formats (like WAV, SND, and AIFF), which could be rather bulky – a major headache during download!

MP3, on the other hand, is a sound format that compresses sounds intelligently via several different filters to give a much smaller file size for a given quality than any other sound compression system. It is now *the* standard for music files on the web, in the same way that Macromedia Flash is the standard for high-impact, highly interactive web sites. It therefore comes as no surprise that Flash now supports MP3.

OK, that's enough background details for now; let's start, quite naturally, with the very basics – importing and using sounds in Flash MX.

Adding sound to Flash movies

Compared to what we've covered so far, working with sound in Flash can be quite complicated. In fact there are so many options to choose from that even advanced Flash users often don't know when to use one over another. Don't worry though – we're going to start from absolute basics, and build things up nice and gently from there. We won't go into every detail, but by the end of the chapter you should have a good enough grasp of the basics to confidently start exploring the more advanced options for yourself.

Attaching sounds to a timeline

The simplest way to add sounds to a Flash movie doesn't involve using any ActionScript at all! It's also fairly limited in terms of what it lets you do, but we'll use it as a starting point so that you can see what's going on.

1. Open a new document in Flash MX and select File > Import to import some sound files. You can find a small collection of sound effects in this chapter's download folders, which I sampled from an analog sound generator – remember to select All Formats so that you can 'see' these MP3 files.

Once you've imported all the files, press CTRL+L to call up the library panel:

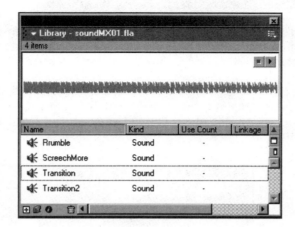

The image shown for each item depicts the sound wave it contains, which shows you roughly how the sound's volume varies over time. You can listen to the selected sound right away by simply clicking on the play button  in the top right corner.

2. We can attach these sounds to any keyframe we like. Select the item called Transition and drag it onto the stage. You won't see anything appear on the stage itself, but take a careful look at frame 1 on the timeline, and you'll see a small horizontal line running through the middle

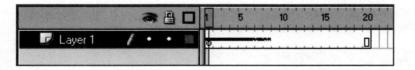

Now insert a frame (F5) at frame 20, and you'll see that this horizontal line runs right across the first eight frames – it's actually a tiny picture of the sound wave we just added in:

The sound will play whenever the play head hits the keyframe it's attached to. As you can see from the timeline, the Transition sound will begin playing when frame 1 is entered, and finish playing by frame 9. Test the movie now, and you should hear the sound repeated every couple of seconds as the movie loops around its twenty frames.

Attaching sounds to button keyframes

We're not just limited to putting sounds on the root timeline: you can just as easily attach them to keyframes on a button, so that a sound plays every time a particular button state occurs. Say you attach a sound to the *down* state: it will play every time the button is pressed.

1. Open a new document and import the two transitions sound files (or just take a look at `button.fla`). Now open the Macromedia buttons library (Window > Common Libraries > Buttons) and drag an instance of any button that takes your fancy onto the stage – I've used the blue arcade button

Double-click on the button to edit it. Add a new layer called sounds, and insert keyframes in the over and down frames on the new layer

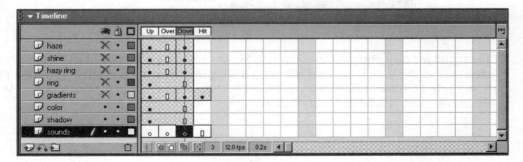

At this point, we could easily drag sounds from the library straight onto the stage – like we did before – to attach them to selected frames. However, there's another way to do it, which is well worth knowing about!

2.   With the over keyframe selected, take a look at the Property inspector, and you will see a dropdown menu labeled Sound. Click on it and select transition to attach our 'transition' sound to the keyframe. Repeat for the down keyframe using the transition2 sound.

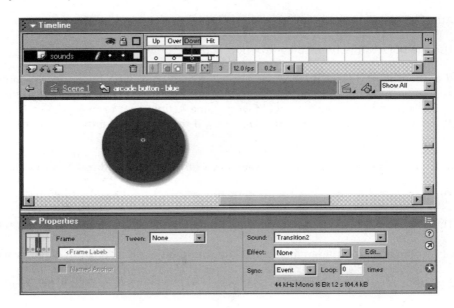

Now test the movie – you will hear the sounds play as you roll over or press the button.

Note that it's not normal practice to add sounds to the up state, while attaching sounds to the hit state is effectively just the same as attaching sounds to the down state (so you only need to attach a sound to one or the other, and not both).

Have a look at the file moreButtons.fla for an example showing several buttons, with sounds attached, in action.

None of this should really be new to you, but it does serve to emphasize an important concept: sounds must always be attached to something. Attaching sounds to keyframes on a timeline is a cool and pretty simple way to put them in your movies, but it's fairly inflexible.

ActionScript gives us a powerful and much more versatile approach: we can attach sounds dynamically at run time, and attach sounds to non-timeline-based events (such as the pressing of a key or a mouse button) or any more complex events that your code has been wired up to recognize (such as 'site has finished loading' or 'spaceInvader12 has just been hit'). Let's start making some noise with ActionScript.

Using a sound object

This is where we really step into new territory, and start using sound objects so that we can truly program our sound effects. Sound objects are the fundamental building blocks that we use to work with sound in ActionScript, and there are three simple steps involved in using one in your movie:

- Define a sound object

- Attach sound data to the object

- Use the object's methods to control how and when the sound is produced

As you'll see very shortly, these methods give us some pretty neat ways to control the sound. For instance, you'll see that we have enough control to produce a stereo soundscape, so that if you had a car moving from left to right on the screen, you could write some ActionScript to make the car's engine sound pan from left to right at the same rate. In the same way, if the car moved into the distance, ActionScript can make the sound fade.

All of this is possible in Flash MX, and we even have some other sound features to play with:

- The `onSoundComplete` event – for detecting when a sound has finished playing.

- The `loadSound()` method – for loading sound files directly into movies at run time.

All of these commands are used to manipulate the **sound object**. Creating this object is actually very easy, but can also be very fiddly, and you can easily forget what you are doing if you blink in the middle of the process! We'll now see how to create a sound object and use it to vary sounds dynamically.

Playing sounds from ActionScript

Just as we can with movie clips, we can add and manipulate sounds in our movies at two distinct stages:

- At design time (that is, using the Flash authoring tool to drag, drop, import, and so on)

- At run time (writing ActionScript that will do all this hard work while the finished SWF is running)

When there's no ActionScript involved – as was the case in our examples so far – it's fairly safe to say that all the hard work's been done at design time. Play the movie and it hums. Click the button and it beeps. All safe, all predictable... all pretty boring! Add a little ActionScript into the mix and things get interesting quick.

With ActionScript, we can make all sorts of subtle changes to our sound, perhaps in response to user input, *while the movie's running*. That doesn't mean we don't have to make any design decisions; quite the contrary in fact. It means that we can design complex, flexible soundtracks that can adjust themselves to all sorts of different situations.

The possibilities are truly fantastic – in fact the only way to really convey the scope of what this means for your movies is to show some of those possibilities being put into practice. So, once we've walked through all the basics, that's precisely what we'll do.

Attaching sounds to the sound object

In the last example, we attached sounds to keyframes on the timeline. This time we must attach them to a sound object, so our first step must be to create that sound object.

1. Create a new document, and rename Layer 1 as actions (or alternatively take a look at the FLA file soundObject1.fla, where you'll find the completed code for this example). Select frame 1 and open the Actions panel (F9). Pin the Actions panel to this frame and place the following ActionScript on the first line:

   ```
   mouse_sound = new Sound();
   ```

2. Next, we must attach some raw sound data to this object. There are two ways to do this: the first is to load an item from the library with the attachSound() method; the second is to load sound directly from an external file using the loadSound() method. We're going to concentrate on the first approach for now, as it's very similar to what we did with movie clips in the last chapter.

   > Don't panic – we'll take a look at the second approach (which is a very cool feature of Flash!) later on when we come to look at ActionScript and streaming.

3. Remember that an item's name (as shown in the library) is invisible to ActionScript, so once we've imported it, we'll need to give it a **linkage identifier** before we can call it up from our code.

   Use File > Import to pull in the transition sound effect, and press CTRL+L so that you can see it in the Library panel:

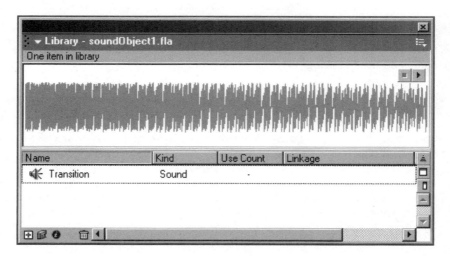

4. Now right-click (CTRL-click on a Mac) on the new Transition sound clip and select Linkage. Check Export for ActionScript in the Linkage Properties dialog, and the text Transition will appear in the Identifier text box (as well as the Export in first frame box becoming checked):

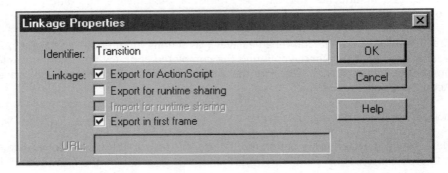

Accept these changes by clicking OK. We can now use the name Transition to refer to this sound clip from within our ActionScript.

> *Remember – for every sound clip you use, there are three names to consider: the name of the file it came from, the name it's given in the library, and the linkage identifier it's given so that we can refer to it from ActionScript. If you mix any of them up, your ActionScript may not work! The bad news is that they're all completely independent, so there's nothing to stop them being completely different. The good news is that Flash is on your side, and – as you've seen – it will normally default them all to the same thing (based on the name of the original file), in this case* Transition*.*

5. Next, we attach the Flash library's sound clip to the ActionScript sound object. In line 2 of your code, add the following:

    ```
    mouse_sound.attachSound("Transition");
    ```

    The argument for attachSound is a literal string (we know this because it is in " " marks), and this means it must be *exactly* the same as the linkage identifier we just defined in the Linkage Properties dialog.

6. Now we need to add some code that will make our sound play. To this end, we use the start() method specifying two arguments: the first indicates how far through the sound (in seconds) it will start playing, and the second indicates how many times the sound will repeat. Add the following lines to your code:

```
_root.onMouseDown = function() {
    mouse_sound.start(0, 1);
};
```

Note that in this case we want to play the complete sound once, so we've set the first argument to zero (starting at zero seconds) and the second to one (playing it once). Since we're using the onMouseDown event to trigger it, you just need to click the mouse to hear some results. Now would be a good time to check your syntax and auto-format.

> *Note that each time the sound repeats (assuming you tell it to) it will play from the same start point. If, for example, you were to call* mouse_sound.start(0.5,5), *you'd hear the same section played five times, but you'd never hear the first half-second of the original sound.*

7. Press CTRL+ENTER to test the movie. Although there's nothing on the stage, you should hear the Transition sound played whenever you click your mouse button. If you do multiple clicks very quickly, you start to hear a number of different versions of the sound. Flash has eight channels of sound, so although it can play a new version of the sound each time you click, it can only play eight at any given time. Once there are eight sounds playing, it will ignore any new commands to play sounds.

    This can produce some cool and unexpected effects, but it isn't really ideal for our purposes: the purpose of the sound is to indicate that someone's pressed the button, so it really ought to sound every time that happens. The simplest way to fix this up is to make sure there's only one sound playing at a time. How? We stop each sound just before we start the next one.

> *Remember that you'll need to have the main toolbar activated – otherwise, you won't see these options. To activate the main toolbar, choose the* Window > Toolbars > Main *menu option.*

Controlling sounds via the sound object

We can stop the sound with the ActionScript command mouse_sound.stop("Transition"). You could be forgiven for wondering why we can't just use mouse_sound.stop(), as we're simply telling Flash to stop playing sound from the mouse_sound object. Since we already told it that mouse_sound is attached to Transition, why should we have to specify it again? Well, it may seem pointless, but that's how it works:

- If you do add the linkage ID in a sound.stop() then only that sound object is stopped.

- If you don't add the linkage name, then all sound is stopped in the SWF.

1. Add the new line shown below in the onMouseDown event handler:

```
_root.onMouseDown = function() {
    mouse_sound.stop("Transition");
    mouse_sound.start(0, 1);
};
```

Any sounds associated with mouse_sound that are currently playing will be stopped, ensuring that we don't fill all eight sound channels with duplicates. If mouse_sound isn't producing any sound for us to stop, the extra line will have no effect.

2. Test the FLA again, and you'll find that you no longer get that odd echo effect. The stop() command now prevents you filling up every available sound channel with a new version of the same sound.

    What if we want to make sure that the triggered sound plays right through before it can be triggered again (instead of restarting every time the event occurs, whether or not the sound has finished). You might want to do this, for example, when you want the user to actually hear the full sound (if it's a voice giving some information, for instance). It also feels more professional, because you don't get that awful 'scratching' interruption effect. Fortunately, Flash MX gives us the onSoundComplete event, which occurs whenever a sound completes all the loops specified in sound.start().

3. So, to make our mouse-driven sound play right through following a mouse click (and ignore subsequent clicks until it's done) we need to modify our script to look like this:

```
// set up the sound object
mouse_sound = new Sound();
mouse_sound.attachSound("Transition");

// set up the sound finished flag
soundFinished = true;

// set up a handler function for the onSoundComplete event
mouse_sound.onSoundComplete = function() {
    soundFinished = true;
};

// set up a handler function for the onMouseDown event
 _root.onMouseDown = function() {
    if (soundFinished) {
        mouse_sound.start(0, 1);
        soundFinished = false;
    }
 }
};
```

As you can see, our code's really started to expand. I've started adding in comments so that we don't forget what each bit does.

I've used a Boolean called `soundFinished` to indicate whether the `mouse_sound` sound is currently playing, and it should always be true if that's the case. The only thing that can set it to false is the `onMouseDown` event, which (as we know) also triggers the sound.

As soon as `soundFinished` becomes false, the `onMouseDown` event can no longer trigger new sounds because the main event handler is inside an `if` statement that will only run if `soundFinished` is true.

This situation will continue until the sound runs through the specified number of loops, whereupon our `onSoundComplete` event handler sets it back to true, allowing the `onMouseDown` event to start new sounds.

*This is a **very** useful bit of code because it contains a very common advanced coding structure (known as an* interlock, semaphore, *or* inhibit flag – *depending on the context in which it's being used). Essentially, we're using one event (*onSoundComplete*) to modify a value (*soundFinished*) that governs what actions are triggered by another event (*onMouseDown*).*

In fact, this is the same sort of structure that your operating system uses in multi-tasking. For example, when two programs want to access the same hard drive, the first will lock the second out until it has finished. The fact that each program limits its usage to very short periods of time gives us humans the impression that both are actually using the same hard drive simultaneously... sneaky, huh? As you can probably imagine, it's possible to set up some very sophisticated responses to user events when you organize things in this way.

Creating dynamic soundtracks

While we're looking at the `onSoundComplete` event, let's do something fun with it. We now have a way to spot when a sound finishes playing, so why not use that event to trigger another sound! We should be able to link several sounds together quite seamlessly, and create an ongoing soundtrack that can jump from one sound clip to another (in response to the user, or whatever's going on in the movie) without any audible joins – a dynamic soundtrack.

Dynamic soundtracks are becoming a big talking point in the video games market, particularly in first-person shooters such as Quake™, Half-Life™, or Jedi Knight™. You'll often hear the background music change as you move from one area to another (or when a load of Stormtroopers appear round the corner) to reflect the changing mood of the game.

In the past, you'd often have to put up with having one piece cut off halfway through as an Imperial March or some up-tempo rhythms kicked in to signify ACTION! Nowadays you'll be much harder pushed to spot the joins, as game designers create soundtracks in lots of tiny sections that can be played together in a whole variety of different sequences, but nevertheless sound like a continuous piece of music.

Creating dynamic soundtracks from scratch can be a very tricky process, mainly because you need to find (or create) a number of sound clips that will sound okay together, no matter what order you play them in. Fortunately, I've done the hard bit for you – check out the following files in the download.

- `beats01.wav`

- `beats02.wav`

- `beats03.wav`

- `beats04.wav`

The actual ActionScript isn't too hard: we basically just need to trigger each new sound with the `onSoundComplete` event that's generated by the last sound finishing. Let's start putting together our movie.

1. Create a new document in Flash (this exercise is `dynamic.fla` in the download). Use the Property inspector to set the document size to 250 pixels by 150 pixels. Now use File > Import (or press Ctrl+R) to import the four sound files listed above into the library:

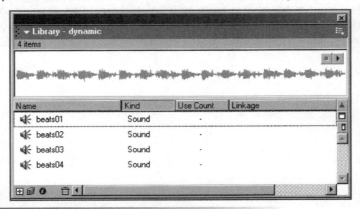

2.   Now right-click on each item in turn to set its linkage properties, exactly as we did for the transition clip in the previous example:

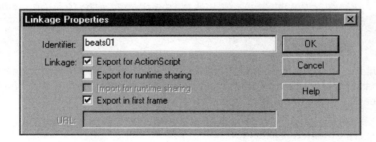

3.   Use the default identifier for each one. When you've finished, the Library panel should look like this:

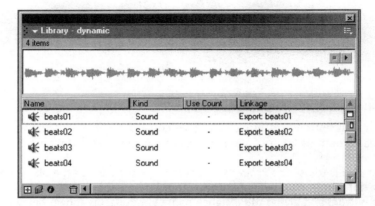

4.   Now it's time to set up the root timeline. We need two layers: actions and interface – you should be able to guess what we're going to do with them! Use F6 to insert keyframes on frame 5 of each layer:

In fact, we're going to put everything into frame 5, and not into frame 1 as you might have expected. There's a very good reason for this: some SWF players may still be running initialization routines during frame 1 of a SWF, and since our movie depends on very accurate sound timing, we want to make sure that the player doesn't compromise this accuracy.

> *Here's a useful rule of thumb: if your movie relies a great deal on the accurate timing of events, it's always a good idea to start coding from a few frames in.*

5. Let's build up the interface now. This will consist of four buttons (for selecting sound clips) and two dynamic text fields (to show which sound is currently playing and which one is up next) with a label each (simple static text fields). Here's how frame 5 of your interface layer might look:

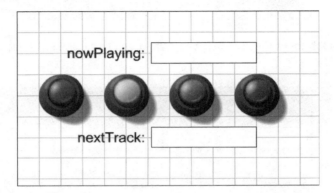

Note that the buttons I'm using here have come straight out of the Push Buttons folder in the Macromedia buttons library (Window > Common Libraries > Buttons).

6. The next step is to use the Property inspector to name each of the objects we'll want to use in our ActionScript. Let's begin by naming each button after the sound clip we want it to trigger. Select the first button, and give it the instance name beats01 (as shown below):

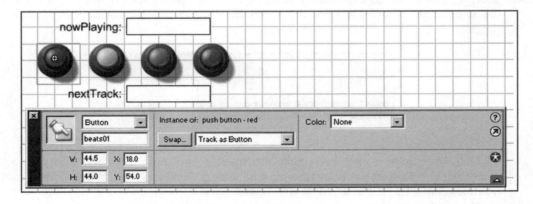

Repeat for each of the other buttons, naming them beats02, beats03, and beats04 respectively.

So what's going on here? Why aren't we calling them beats01_btn, beats02_btn, and so on, as recommended by Macromedia? Well, there's a good reason for this: we're going to be using a sneaky shortcut to keep our code to the minimum. We'll use an ActionScript variable called soundNext to indicate which track we want to play next – we therefore want it set to beats01, beats02, beats03 or beats04, depending on which button was last pressed. The simplest way to do that is to name the buttons beats01, beats02, and so on, and set soundNext to the name of the button each time. Don't panic if you're not quite following just yet – all should soon become clear!

7. We must now do the same for the dynamic text fields: name them nowPlaying_txt and nextTrack_txt:

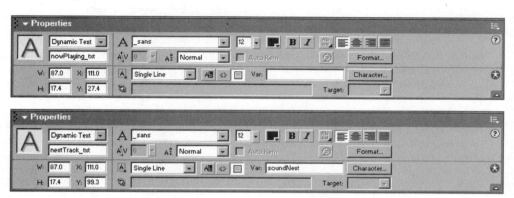

Note that I've given the second one a Var setting: soundNext. This is essentially just a hangover from previous versions of Flash, back when text fields weren't really objects, and the only way to manipulate them from ActionScript was to link their text to a variable. Now that we can use the text property this isn't strictly necessary, and in some circles it's actively discouraged.

In this case however, it's going to help make our code a lot simpler to follow: since soundNext indicates which track to play next, it's only common sense to wire it up directly to our Next Track display.

8. OK, now that the stage is set, let's write the ActionScript that'll bring it to life. All the following code needs to go into frame 5 of the actions layer:

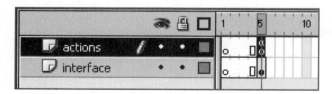

We begin by initializing the soundNext variable, which (as we've already noted) we'll be using to indicate which track we want to play next:

```
// initialize starting track
soundNext = "beats01";
```

9. Next, we create our sound object, attach the specified sound clip, and tell it to play through once. We also update the nowPlaying text field with the name of the clip:

```
// set up dynamic sound object
dynamic_sound = new Sound();
dynamic_sound.attachSound(soundNext);
dynamic_sound.start(0, 1);
nowPlaying_txt.text = soundNext;
```

10. Now we wire up the buttons with a rather strange looking event handler:

```
// define handler for button events
beats01.onRelease = beats02.onRelease = beats03.onRelease =
➥beats04.onRelease = function(){
    soundNext = this._name;
};
```

Actually, all this does is assign the same handler function to the onRelease events for each of the buttons. We could have written it out as four identical event handlers – one for each button, like this:

```
beats01_btn.onRelease = function(){
    soundNext = "beats01";
};
beats02_btn.onRelease = function(){
    soundNext = "beats02";
};
beats03_btn.onRelease = function(){
    soundNext = "beats03";
};
beats04_btn.onRelease = function(){
    soundNext = "beats04";
};
```

Clearly, the first technique saves a lot of repetition. I know which way I'd rather do it!

But what about the function itself?

```
soundNext = this._name;
```

Well, this is how we refer to 'whatever generated the event that called this function'. For instance, if the function got called because the beats02 button generated an onRelease event, then this refers to the beats02 button. In that case, this._name gives us the instance name of the beats02 button (beats02 – logical, huh?), which is precisely what we want to update the soundNext variable with.

So pressing any of the four buttons makes nextSound equal to one of four string values. These string values are the same as the four linkage names for our sound clips, so we can safely feed soundNext into the attachSound method on our sound object:

```
dynamic_sound.attachSound(soundNext);
```

Now we just need to bundle this together with a `start(0,1)` method call and a command to update the `nowPlaying` text field, and specify how they should all be triggered.

11. Let's see what effect our earlier approach – using the `onMouseDown` event – has. Type this ActionScript in below the earlier code:

```
// trigger next sound
_root.onMouseDown = function() {
    dynamic_sound.attachSound(soundNext);
    dynamic_sound.start(0, 1);
    nowPlaying_txt.text = soundNext;
};

// stop the timeline
stop();
```

Try this out (CTRL+ENTER) for a taste of what can happen when Flash sound goes wrong! The `stop()` command is vital, because without it your movie will loop around frames 1-5 with the interface flashing on and off and sound clips being added one on top of another.

12. Well, we know what needs to be done. The whole point of this exercise was to put the `onSoundComplete` event through its paces, so let's see that put into practice. Change the line I've highlighted below in the final event handler:

```
// trigger next sound
dynamic_sound.onSoundComplete = function() {
    dynamic_sound.attachSound(soundNext);
    dynamic_sound.start(0, 1);
    nowPlaying_txt.text = soundNext;
};
```

Test run the movie again, and you'll hear quite a difference! When you listen to it, you'll understand why it's so ingenious: the sounds won't just change as soon as you click one of the buttons – they'll only change after the track that's currently playing has finished. This means that our little techno tune stays in a musical beat sequence no matter what we do!

When you first click one of the buttons, you'll see the nextTrack text field updated immediately, but no change to the nowPlaying field and, more importantly, there will be no change in the sound. However, once the current clip has played right through, both will change to match the clip shown in nextTrack.

This is sequencing to the nearest beat in a 4 beat sequence. A dance DJ would call this 'mixing in on the beat', and most other musical types would call it a sequencing loop. I'm currently working on a Flash-based emulation of a classic analog synthesizer – by scanning in images of the original synthesizer's buttons and dials, the thing even looks like the original. Best of all, it's all based on the techniques you've seen here, and the code behind it all really isn't that dissimilar to what we've been using!

Controlling sounds from ActionScript

Thanks to the sound object, we can use ActionScript to manipulate our sound clips in more subtle ways than we've looked at so far. In particular, we can alter two aspects of the original sound: the volume (how loud the sound is) and the panning (the balance of sound we hear in each ear). The ActionScript sound object has two methods that allow us to make the changes that we want:

setVolume()

This method allows you to vary the total volume produced by a sound object. The values that change this are pretty obvious:

- `sound.setVolume(0)` - gives you 0% volume (silence)

- `sound.setVolume(100)` - gives maximum volume, which largely depends on your speaker setup

setPan()

The sound object's `setPan()` method allows you to vary the sound level in each speaker, that is, the *balance* between them. The values that we can apply to it alter the sound accordingly:

- `sound.setPan(0)` - gives an equal balance in left and right speakers

- `sound.setPan(-100)` - gives the full current volume in the left speaker, and nothing in the right

- `sound.setPan(100)` - gives the full current volume in the right speaker, and nothing in the left

Let's put this information to use and design a simple sound control system.

Building sound controls

Take a look at the figures below, and imagine the black square is a stage as viewed from above. The black dot is you sitting in front of the stage, and the white dot is a musician on the stage. As the user drags the white dot around the stage area, we want ActionScript to dynamically alter the stereo image, or panning, and the volume of the music to reflect the performer's movement around the stage.

Say the musician was standing right in front of you by the footlights; you would hear the sound at a maximum volume, in your left and right ears equally.

If they then moved towards the back of the stage – assuming of course that they're not using an amplifier – and played at the same level, the sound would become equally faint in both ears.

Finally, if the musician moved down and across to stage left, you would hear more sound in your left ear than in your right ear (and vice versa if they moved to stage right):

Let's go to work.

1. This example is called `controls.fla`. Once again, set up two layers called actions and interface, and use File > Import to import the `percussion.wav` sound file into the library. Right-click (CTRL-click on a Mac) to call up Linkage…, and set the sound clip to Export for ActionScript. Your library should then look like this:

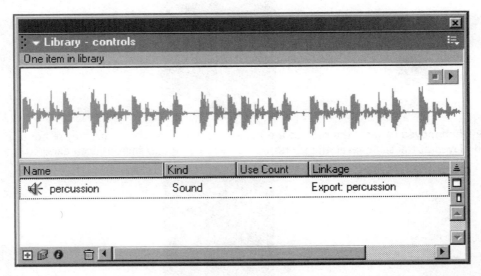

2. Create a movie clip called puck, and add a white circle with a black border. It should have a diameter of roughly 15 pixels, and be centered on the coordinate x=0, y=0. This will be the control we use to drag the virtual musician around on the stage.

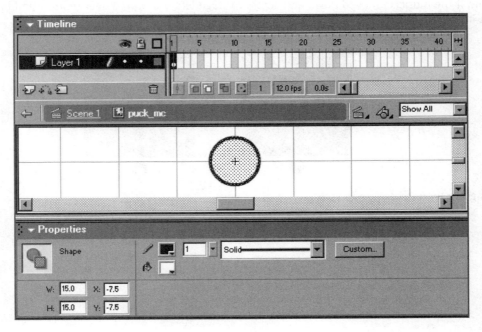

3. Now create a second movie clip called controller, and place a borderless black square, 100 pixels across, in the center of the stage. You can use the Property inspector to fine-tune its size and position. Add a small black circle just below it (to indicate where you're listening from at the front of the stage), and make sure it's placed centrally. Now rename the layer it's on as back.

   Add another new layer called dragbutton and drag a copy of the puck movie clip out of the library, placing it center stage and giving it the instance name of puck_mc.

   Create one more new layer called text (still on the timeline for controller) and add a pair of dynamic text fields. Their Var settings (specified in the Property inspector) should be set to pan and vol, and you should label them (using static text fields) accordingly.

   Here's how the controller_mc movie clip should look when you're done:

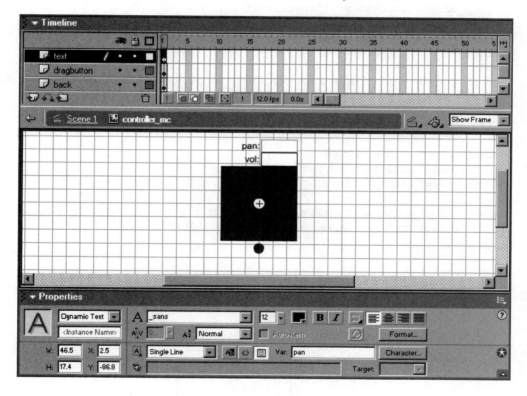

4. Back in the root timeline, drag the controller movie clip from the library into frame 1 of the interface layer, giving it the instance name of controller_mc.

5. Select frame 1 in the actions layer and use the Actions panel to add in a simple stop() action. Your root timeline will now look like this:

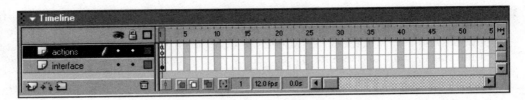

6. We now want to make the percussion sound start playing and loop forever (actually, the maximum number of times that Flash will let you loop a sound is 214748, so for a sample that's only a second long, this amounts to almost 60 hours of looping! – easily enough for most purposes). Add the following code to set up a sound object and start it looping:

```
loop_sound = new Sound();
loop_sound.attachSound("percussion");
loop_sound.start(0,1000);

stop();
```

If you test the movie now, you will hear the sound playing, but have no control over it. Let's fix that.

7. Our next step is to wire up the puck, so that we can use the mouse to drag it about:

```
loop_sound = new Sound();
loop_sound.attachSound("percussion");
loop_sound.start(0,1000);

controller_mc.puck_mc.onPress = function() {
    this.startDrag(false, -50, -50, 50, 50);
};

stop();
```

This constrains the mouse drag to a rectangle like this:

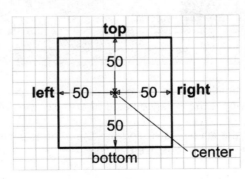

The values I've used represent distances from the center point (which is the position the puck initially starts off at on your stage). Remember that the *y* direction is measured such that *down is positive* (as is the stage).

> *A draggable button will drag **everything** on the timeline it's placed on. So if you put it on, say, the root timeline, it will drag the whole SWF. By contrast, a movie clip has its own timeline, so when we make it draggable, only the clip itself will be dragged along with the mouse.*

8. Since the puck control is constrained within this area, it will get left behind when the user drags the cursor outside of the bounding box. With this in mind, we need to stop the drag action as soon as the mouse moves outside the box. We can do this by including the usual `onRelease` condition with the `stopDrag()` action:

```
loop_sound = new Sound();
loop_sound.attachSound("percussion");
loop_sound.start(0,1000);

 controller_mc.puck_mc.onPress = function() {
     this.startDrag(false, -50, -50, 50, 50);
};
controller_mc.puck_mc.onRelease = function() {
     this.stopDrag();
};

stop();
```

OK, the puck now works properly, but makes no difference to the sound we hear. Nor does it give us values for volume and pan in the dynamic text fields. Hold on though, we're nearly there! We just need to do a little elementary math first...

We need to evaluate `setVolume()` and `setPan()` values for our sound object, from the x- and y-coordinates of the drag button.

Our button can be dragged 50 pixels to the left and 50 pixels to the right from its initial starting position. We need to scale this to -100 to +100 for use in the `setPan()` method. This is simply a question of doubling the *x*-coordinate of the button:

(-100 to 100) = (-50 to 50) x 2

So, more generally:

pan level = (button x-coordinate) x 2

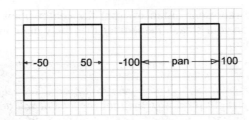

Likewise, we can drag the button 50 pixels up and 50 pixels down from its starting position. This must be translated to a range of 0 to 100% for use with the setVolume() method. To do this, we just need to add 50 to the button's *y*-coordinate:

(100 to 0) = (50 to −50) + 50

That is:

volume level = button y-coordinate + 50

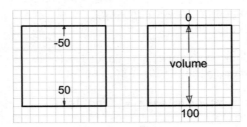

Now we're ready to start producing the effects we want.

9. The final section of code is a handler function for the controller movie clip's onEnterFrame event. We've already taken care of stopping the main timeline – if we didn't, we would end up reinitializing the loop_sound object twelve times every second! The movie clip's timeline goes on unabated though, and every time its play head enters a new frame, we need to update its pan and vol variables according to the puck's latest position – this is where our math comes into play. We then want to use these variables to update the loop_sound object, calling its setPan() and setVolume() methods to manipulate it. Here's our finished code:

```
loop_sound = new Sound();
loop_sound.attachSound("percussion");
loop_sound.start(0,1000);

controller_mc.puck_mc.onPress = function() {
    this.startDrag(false, -50, -50, 50, 50);
};
controller_mc.puck_mc.onRelease = function() {
    this.stopDrag();
};
controller_mc.onEnterFrame = function() {
```

```
        this.pan = 2*this.puck_mc._x;
        this.vol = 50+this.puck_mc._y;
        loop_sound.setPan(this.pan);
        loop_sound.setVolume(this.vol);
    };

    stop();
```

Try the movie once again, and you should find it works a treat! Drag the puck around the stage and you'll hear the sound move from side to side, rising and falling in volume as you move it up and down.

These sound variations are occurring in real time, in response to how you drag the button. This is a template for creating a dynamic soundscape for your web sites or Flash games. As the sound source moves around the screen, you can create the appropriate sound effects on the fly with the sound object and ActionScript.

Dealing with large sound files: compression and streaming

You've probably noticed it by now, but most sound files tend to weigh in on the heavy side – a lot of information goes into making just a little snippet of sound, and the size of your audio files will most likely reflect this. If you're making local movies for a local audience (or you're blessed with clients who all have limitless bandwidth) then this might not be a problem.

However, if you're designing anything for the wider realms of the Web, you've got to think very carefully about the size of files you work with. Most folks simply aren't going to stick around long enough to see the fruits of your labor if those fruits take twenty minutes to download. This is one reason why sound on the Web hasn't been as common in the past as it might have been.

In recent years though, two technologies have started to help change things for the better: compression and streaming.

Compression

Compression is just a process of squishing big files into smaller files, figuring out what information's important and what can be thrown out, so that you end up with a version of the file that's still adequate for the job, but isn't so large! The best-known form of audio (sound) compression is MP3, which typically squeezes sound files down to a tenth (or less) of their original size without much audible loss of quality.

As we mentioned at the start of this chapter, Flash MX can work with MP3 files – along with many other compressed sound formats too numerous to discuss here – in just the same way as uncompressed WAVs and AIFFs. However, generally there are very few times you would use anything else other than MP3 because the others are really just legacy formats, included for backwards compatibility.

Here are some points to keep in mind when thinking about compressing your Flash files that include sound:

- Flash has the option to compress the whole SWF (File > Publish Settings > Flash), and this takes up performance bandwidth of the player for other things during streaming. If the SWF content is already compressed (that is, it consists of lots of sound) then you should consider not compressing it.

- You will typically use high compression rates (for small file sizes) for sound, and should consider using sound files that compress well. Generally, low, bassy sounds compress much better than high frequency sounds.

- Rather than accept the default settings, you should look at each sound file separately, and find the best compression settings for each. Sound is bandwidth-heavy, and can be the biggest part of your SWF file, so take every precaution to minimize the file sizes.

So, there are things we can do to bring down file sizes using compression – but that's only one part of the solution.

Streaming

Streaming is another way to tackle large file sizes, by which the files (whether they're sound files, movies, or even SWFs) are able to start playing well before they're fully downloaded. Your browser won't stop and wait for the complete file to be loaded in, but will store individual frames as and when they become available, and play them back in sequence when it has a large enough collection to make it worthwhile.

If we used a system of placing our entire soundtrack into a movie clip we, or rather our viewers, wouldn't receive the benefits that streaming has to offer because *Flash doesn't start to play a movie clip until the whole movie clip has loaded in.* This is unacceptable for the end user; waiting extra time for a 200 KB soundtrack to load in before the site appears is bad design. So, the first rule of Flash sound is that, unless you expect all the end users to be in possession of high bandwidth connections, you should avoid placing your complete soundtrack within the manacles of a movie clip.

This makes streaming look like a good option all round. However, if you're thinking of using ActionScript *and* streaming, there are a few caveats to bear in mind:

- A continuous soundtrack requires us to stream in sound continuously; this will cut down the bandwidth available for doing other things.

- A streaming source locks itself to the timeline: if the timeline can't keep up, the Flash player will miss out frames to catch up. This is fine for a timeline full of tween animations, but it could be disastrous for your ActionScript: any ActionScript attached to those lost frames could easily be lost too, causing all sorts of errors.

- Streaming sound is not really conducive to a typical timeline under the control of ActionScript, where we could be jumping about all over the place.

So streaming sounds and ActionScript don't mix. Is there any hope?

The best way, and really the only sensible way to add a substantial soundtrack to a Flash ActionScript site (without running up massive download times) is to use `loadMovie()` to load it up as a new SWF.

This has a number of advantages:

- The sound loads up quite separately from the main site, so you can easily discard the soundtrack (based on user preference) and free up any further unwanted sound download.

- Unlike Flash's streaming sound type, you can re-use the sound once it's been downloaded because the soundtrack consists of event sounds.

- SWFs containing just sound are transparent because they will have nothing on the stage, so there are no issues with loading a soundtrack and obscuring lower levels of SWFs.

Controlling our soundtrack across multiple SWFs may sound a little daunting, but is actually perfectly possible and easy as long as you use the right path to your soundtrack. Funny how most things in Flash tend to hinge on an understanding of the correct path!

So far in this chapter we've taken a look at how the new Flash sound object can give us pretty efficient control over individual sound movie clips to create some cool effects. But wait a minute, I'm sure we can take what we've learnt even further. Forget click sounds attached to buttons or the odd incidental effect – as ActionScript experts, we should settle for nothing less than making that sound object control a full, life-sized soundtrack. In the latter half of this chapter I'll show you how I did this for the stun:design site.

The stun:design web site

The process for creating a soundtrack for the stun:design site fell into three stages:

- Creating the soundtrack to overlay over our web site with `loadMovie()`

- Creating the controls to modify the soundtrack's volume and pan levels from the stun web site

- Creating the sound object to control our soundtrack from the main web site

Let's begin with a little background, and then we'll round off with a hands-on demonstration, where you can test what we did for yourself.

I created the stun soundtrack with the help of a good friend (if you've read *Foundation Flash* you'll no doubt have met him already and seen some of our previous joint efforts). The file for my soundtrack is called `soundtrack.fla`, and the raw MP3 files that we used to create it are contained in `stunsounds.zip`.

A word of warning before you download it: The FLA file is about 7.5 MB, because, although we imported the six sound files as MP3 into Flash (and they were 192 KB each at this point), once they're in the FLA, it seems that Flash balloons the file sizes up by converting them to raw sound data. The final SWF, though, contains compressed sound data. When you come to test the soundtrack, be aware that there's a lot of sound compression for Flash to do before it can create the SWF file, so there will be a long pause while compiling.

If you want to bypass all this trouble, just download the readymade `soundtrack.swf`, which is all you will really need for this demo anyway. You could even just load up the separate MP3 files via the more download-friendly `stunsounds.zip`, which is 1.5Mb or so, and build up your own soundtrack. Don't forget the kicker streaming sound at the start of your composition though. The sounds have been normalized to sound OK together, so you can safely maintain them at their current levels when you play them all at once without overdriving the overall sound level (aren't we good to you, considering this is a programming book, not one about music!).

> As a side note, if you want to get into music composition for the web using Flash you may want to look at the `soundtrack.fla` file, because it contains a lot of tips and tricks (most of which are beyond the scope of this book).

Anyway, back to business. Here's a view of the soundtrack's timeline and library:

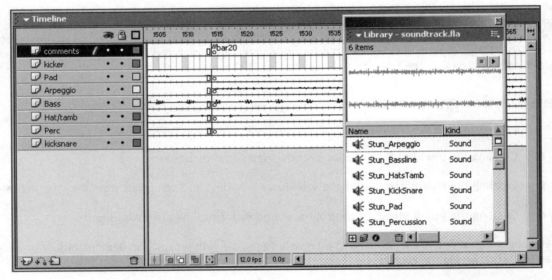

There are six sounds, all of which are loopable and last for two bars each. Using loopable sounds means that we can splice them together on the Flash timeline to create a soundtrack (or, if we're lacking imagination, we could just loop them forever).

We arranged these on the main timeline to form a musical composition. The track has been made to last just under five minutes, which is as long as I would expect a casual visitor to listen to a piece of music that was nothing more than the constant recycling of six basic samples. If music was to play a much more prominent part of the site, I would have considered using several different compositions that the user could select maybe by clicking on a little DJ's bag full of records. (I should stop giving away all the ideas I am using on my own web sites!).

Of special note is the bandwidth profile for the soundtrack. The track has been arranged to stream in satisfactorily on a very low bandwidth, and will work even on a 28 KB modem. Notice that we're using streaming on the soundtrack timeline, which consists of event sounds. To confuse the issue, there *is* a type of sound in Flash called *stream sounds* (which we're not using).

The upshot of using event sounds that stream in is that it only needs to load in once. After the initial 16 KB preload, the soundtrack will happily stream in without crossing the limit line of the 28 KB modem (which took some arranging!). This is achieved by copious use of the bandwidth profiler. You can see here that we've made sure that we don't go over the 200 bytes per second bandwidth limit of a 28 KB modem, following initial download. That way, we can be sure of uninterrupted streaming on even low bandwidths:

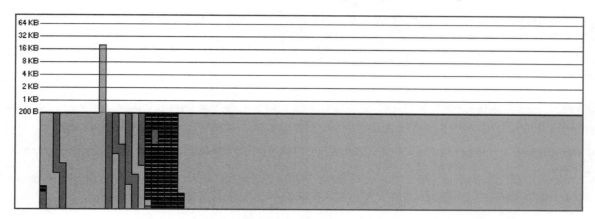

At the time of writing, a bug has been found in the Flash MX player that causes Flash SWFs to continue loading in even if the user no longer requires the content. The only way to stop a partial SWF streaming in to completion is to close the browser window. The following example has been developed with this bug in mind (we are not using `unloadMovie()` because it does not currently work as it should). We will release a revised version on the errata page for this book when the Flash player is cured of this bug.

Now for a little (well, actually quite a lot!) of that hands on experience I promised earlier. I thought it would be cool to show you in detail how I created some slider controls for the volume and pan of the sound object on stun:design. I'll take you through quite thoroughly so that you can take these away to use on your own sites.

You should create this control in a separate FLA from the soundtrack because that way it will load in the soundtrack and play that. This is a useful technique to use in general when your Flash site consists of bandwidth heavy multimedia.

It's worth emphasizing this point: load your multimedia separately so that it doesn't affect the main site loading time!

Creating the sound controls

The sound controller will be based around the scrollbar component. We will alter it such that it is no longer used to scroll a text field, but instead is used as a slider (sometimes also called a 'spinner') that varies a value.

We have provided a starting point for our sound controller as soundControlStart.fla. This includes the basic graphics for our FLA. The final FLA is included as stun_soundControlFinal.fla. To try out the FLA so that you hear the soundtrack, you need to run it from a directory that also includes soundtrack.swf (included with this chapter's source code download).

In soundControlStart.fla we have two layers, actions and graphics. Layer actions just has some code to change the style format, but we're not concerned with that so that layer is locked, and we're going to concentrate on the graphics layer.

I've dragged an instance of movie clip soundController from the library onto the stage in layer graphics. Double-click on this movie clip instance to have a look inside it - you'll see two layers, icon and back. These contain our core graphics. There are three frames of graphics, the first and second of which contain the graphics shown below left and below right respectively:

The first one is what the user will see when there is no sound. Pressing the icon loads up the soundtrack, and a new icon will appear  to allow the user to vary the soundtrack volume and pan settings.

The third frame contains the basic graphics for our fully opened controller:

Remember, this is unfinished – the sliders will occupy that big bit of space in the center, and the x icon allows you to close the slider window and get back to the ? icon.

OK, I don't like the word 'unfinished' – let's get to it! The first thing we will need is an *invisible* button.

Adding the invisible buttons

An invisible button is simply a button that has no Up, Over, or Down states – just a Hit area. This means that your button is invisible to the user, but they can still detect when they pass the mouse over the Hit area (sometimes called the hotspot).

Invisible buttons will obviously never replace the usual buttons that we see every day for navigation – can you really imagine a user hunting around the page, waiting for the cursor to change to tell them that they've found the button to take them to your portfolio page? – although some sites will use invisible buttons for all their navigation by placing them over graphic symbols that just look like buttons (but don't actually do anything). When the user clicks on them, they're using an invisible button without knowing it. Other designers drop invisible buttons over static button shapes and add audio so that the user receives some musical reward when they roll over, rather than a visual effect.

Flash also allows you to use invisible buttons for something completely different: to create a **draggable area**. This is where the button is used not as a user input device, but rather as a handle with which to drag a movieclip around the screen, in much the same way as we drag a heavy bag around the airport by its handles – but with less effort.

1. We'll first make an invisible button. Do this by creating a new button and call it invisible. Put a keyframe in the Hit frame.

2. Draw a simple filled-in square on the stage.

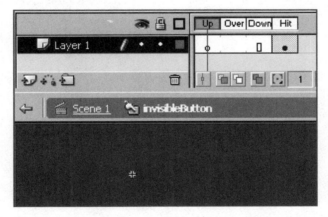

3. Next, we'll create a draggable bar graph, or a slider, for the sound and pan controls. First, however, let's briefly highlight how it will work. We will set up our scrollbars such that they *think* they are controlling a text field, but in fact they are controlling *nothing*. What we will do though is read the scrollbar positions and convert their positions to variables, which we will use to control our volume and pan values.

   Create a new layer folder within soundController called buttons. Inside it, create three new layers called play, stop, and toggle:

4.   Lock all layers except play while you're working. In frame 1 of this layer, drag an instance of the invisible button onto the stage, and scale it so that it fits over the speaker icon as shown below:

5.   Give this button an instance name `play_btn`, and delete frames 2 and 3 of this layer. Ultimately, this button will make Flash load up our `soundtrack.swf` and cause it to start playing.

6.   Next up is layer stop. Again, lock all the other layers and select frame 2; make it a keyframe. Still on this frame, drag 1 instance of the invisible button onto the upper icon (the speaker), like this:

Call this button `stop_btn` – this button will stop the soundtrack once it is playing. Delete frame 3 of this layer.

Sanity check – this is what you should see on the timeline so far:

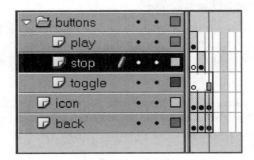

8. Last but not least, we will add something to layer toggle. Create a keyframe on frame 2 of this layer, and drag into it our third and final invisible button. You should resize it so that it covers the ⑦ icon, as shown below:

Name the new button `toggle_btn`.

Another sanity check and a quick recap is now in order. The timeline so far should look like this:

So now you have the `play_btn` on frame 1 (you can check this by hiding all layers except this one), the `stop_btn` on frame 2, and the `toggle_btn` on frames 2 *and* 3. Obviously, what we need to do next is pull everything together with some clever ActionScript.

Adding the button scripts

We will not be adding the code for this movie clip on the main timeline, but on the sound controller itself. It has been built to be modular, so that we can simply drag and drop the finished sound controller directly into our web site (or your web site if you like the soundtrack!), and it will work as long as it can find the soundtrack.swf file.

1. Add a new layer actions above all the others, giving it keyframes on frames 2 and 3. Give frame 1 a label init, frame 2 a label closeMenu and frame 3 a label openMenu. Select keyframe on frame 1 and pin the Actions panel to it.

2. Add the following code to frame 1. This is our initialization script, and it runs when we release the play_btn instance:

```
play_btn.onRelease = function() {
  // start streaming in the soundtrack
  loadMovieNum("soundtrack.swf", 1);
  // initialize sound object...
  soundtrack_sound = new sound(_level1);
  // initalize scrollbar positions...
  soundPan = 50;
  soundVol = 75;
  play();
};
stop();
```

This script does 4 things:

- When we press and release the button, it will load up our soundtrack.swf as a new level above _root (notice that we can point the sound object to a timeline as well as to a movie clip).

- It will create a new sound object, soundtrack_sound, to control the sound on this level.

- We also define two new variables: soundPan and soundVol. We will be using these later to give the user control over the (you guessed it) volume and panning levels.

- Finally, the play() at the end makes us go to the next frame.

Outside the event handler, we have a stop(). Unless the button is pressed, we will stay on this frame because of it. The soundtrack will be loaded in, and the sound object and variables will be defined only when the button is pressed.

On to frame 2 – unpin the actions window, and pin it to frame 2. Add the following script:

```
stop_btn.onRelease = function() {
    soundtrack_sound.stop();
    _level1.stop();
    gotoAndStop("init");
};
toggle_btn.onRelease = function() {
    enabled = true;
    gotoAndPlay("openMenu");
};
stop();
```

This contains the button scripts for our two buttons stop_btn and toggle_btn. The stop_btn simply stops the currently playing soundtrack (and something must be playing for us to get to this frame, as to get here we must have pressed play_btn), and returns us back to the start frame just in case the user has a change of heart and decides the soundtrack isn't just bandwidth-stealing *muzak* after all.

The toggle_btn sets a variable enabled to true, and then jumps to the next frame. This will cause the slider window to open.

As long as neither button is pressed, the stop() at the end of this script keeps us parked at this frame.

4. On frame 3, we only have the toggle_btn instance left. The user will press the x button (or rather, the invisible button over it) to close the slider window. To do that, we need to go back to frame 2, and that is what the new script we will attach here does (don't forget to unpin, and then pin frame 3):

```
toggle_btn.onRelease = function() {
    enabled = false;
    gotoAndPlay("closeMenu");
};
stop();
```

The FLA up to this point is included with the download files as stun_soundInProgress.fla.

We are now ready to test it. To hear any sound, copy the file soundtrack.swf to the same place you have the currently open stun_soundInProgress.fla (or your equivalent). Remember, you need to do this because that is where Flash will look for it when you hit the play_btn.

When you hit the icon the first time, you will hear the sound start to play (wait a few moments, because the soundtrack has a quiet beginning). Hitting the button a second time will turn the soundtrack off. Hitting the 🛈 icon when the soundtrack is playing will reveal the slider menu (without a slider at the moment), and hitting the X will close it.

So far so good! Next we'll be adding the missing controls.

Adding the slider controls

1. Create two new layers, text and sliders, below the actions layer, as shown below (note that we've closed the buttons layer folder to make our timeline less cluttered):

2. Lock all the other layers, and add a keyframe on frame 3 of each of the two new layers. We will now add our slider controls. Drag a scrollbar from the Components panel (Window > Components) onto the stage. Whoops! Two things are wrong straight away:

    ■ I've left space for a horizontal scrollbar, but ours is vertical.

    ■ The style of the scrollbar just doesn't go with our design.

    The second point has already been covered: the scrollbar will conform to the global style changes we have made on _root. The first point, however, is important. We *can* change the scrollbar orientation, but the most obvious way to do this (rotate and scale it via the Free Transform tool) is exactly what you *can't* do!

    > *Although you may think you can just treat a component as a graphical symbol, scaling and rotating as you wish, the default components are actually software objects, and you must change their appearance by talking to the code via property changes. If you do otherwise, you will tend to break them. The only time you can scale a component is when the component is embedded within a movie clip, and you transform the movie clip.*

3. So here's the correct way to change the size or orientation of a component. With the scrollbar selected, select the Parameters tab in the Property inspector and change the Horizontal parameter to true. Move the scrollbar so that it is orientated within the window as shown. If you need to change the size of the scrollbar, you must do so via the W: and H: fields of the Property inspector, and *not* via the normal graphic tools (that is, the Transform tool). Give the scrollbar an instance name `vol_slider`.

4. Drag another instance of the scrollbar from the Components panel and do the same thing, this time placing the scrollbar as shown below the first one. Give it an instance name pan_slider.

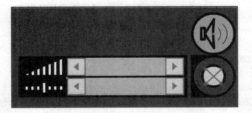

5. Finally, add some static text as shown in frame 3 of layer text. I have used 22 point Trebuchet MS in keeping with the stun:design site:

We are now done with the graphics.

6. Time for another of the sanity checks that I'm so fond of – your timeline should now look like this:

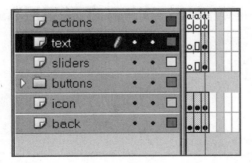

There is one last thing we need to do; we need to add some sly ActionScript trickery to fool the scrollbars into 'thinking' that they are in fact controlling text fields, whilst at the same time getting them to do what we really need.

7.   In frame 3 of layer actions, add the following script to what is there already:

```
toggle_btn.onRelease = function() {
     enabled = false;
     gotoAndPlay("closeMenu");
};
vol_slider.setScrollProperties(50, 0, 100);
vol_slider.setEnabled(true);
vol_slider.setScrollPosition(soundVol);

pan_slider.setScrollProperties(50, 0, 100);
pan_slider.setEnabled(true);
pan_slider.setScrollPosition(soundPan);

this.onEnterFrame = function() {
     if (enabled) {
             soundVol = vol_slider.getScrollPosition();
             soundPan = pan_slider.getScrollPosition();
             soundtrack_sound.setVolume(soundVol);
             soundtrack_sound.setPan((soundPan*2)-100);
     }
};
stop();
```

Before we explain this code, let's describe what we have done in more general terms. Firstly, we need to tell the scrollbar what the size of the text field it is supposedly controlling looks like. We then need to convince it that the text field is full (such that scrolling is required), and that it should be active. Finally, we need to initialize the scrollbar positions so that they reflect the current volume and pan values.

After we have initialized the scrollbars to believe all this, we need to constantly convert the scrollbar positions into the values that will drive our sound object setPan() and setVolume() methods.

In the following subsections we'll take a more detailed look at the methods and the event that we used in the previous script:

■   setScrollProperties()

■   setEnabled()

■   setScrollPosition()

■   onEnterFrame

setScrollProperties()

The `setScrollProperties()` method of the scrollbar is written as follows:

```
setScrollProperties(pageSize, minPos, maxPos)
```

A scrollbar has three main scroll related properties:

- `pageSize` – the amount of the text field that is currently viewable. A scrollbar slider changes to reflect the portion of the current window that is viewable. For example, if a scrollbar is showing 30% of the total text in the textfield it will look something like the scrollbar to the left, whereas if it is showing something closer to 5% of the available text in the window, it will look more like the right scrollbar.

- `minPos/maxPos` – the maximum and minimum scroll positions. We can give the scrollbar a value of the top and bottom of the scrollbar range. Usually, we would use this range as an indication of where we are within the text, but we can also use it to tell us *where the slider is along the scrollbar*.

The `minPos/maxPos` values of our sliders have been set to `0/100` to give us a 0 to 100 scale:

```
vol_slider.setScrollProperties(50, 0, 100);
pan_slider.setScrollProperties(50, 0, 100);
```

> *It's worth noting that although* pan *is measured from −100 to +100 by the sound object, you cannot enter a negative position for a scrollbar. We could have made the pan scrollbar go from 0 to 200, but we decided to stick with 0-100 for consistency with the other scrollbar (which makes for easier debugging).*

setEnabled()

This merely tells the scrollbar whether it should be enabled (active) or not. When attached to a text field, the scrollbar can automatically decide whether it should be enabled, but you can override this via `setEnabled`. We have overridden the scrollbars to be `true`, and this makes them act as if they are attached to a scrollable text field:

```
vol_slider.setEnabled(true);
pan_slider.setEnabled(true);
```

setScrollPosition()

This defines the current scroll position. By setting it for a scrollbar that is actually targeting a text field, you can make the text scroll up and down on its own (rather like the closing titles of a movie). We have set ours to the starting volume and pan values, soundVol and soundPan:

```
vol_slider.setScrollPosition(soundVol);
pan_slider.setScrollPosition(soundPan);
```

onEnterFrame

Finally, the onEnterFrame event constantly reads the current scrollbar positions and applies them to the sound object:

```
this.onEnterFrame = function() {
    if (enabled) {
        soundVol = vol_slider.getScrollPosition();
        soundPan = pan_slider.getScrollPosition();
        soundtrack_sound.setVolume(soundVol);
        soundtrack_sound.setPan((soundPan*2)-100);
    }
};
```

One thing to note is that we only make changes if enabled is true. This is only true if the scrollbars are in view. It is possible for this script to run when the scrollbars have just disappeared, and this will return the soundVol and soundPan values as undefined, which is why we had to have an enabled condition.

The final version of this example is included as stun_soundControlFinal.fla. You can test everything by playing this FLA from a location that includes soundtrack.swf.

The use of dynamic sound control can dramatically enhance a web site by adding sound cues to what's happening on screen. This is a powerful ability, because many home users now have fairly advanced audio equipment attached to their computer's audio-out ports. The use of the sound object with soundtracks offers the user fairly advanced sound control options, which are very easy to implement in ActionScript, once you've overcome the very precise steps that need to be taken to set up a sound object in the first place.

Pump up the volume!

Summary

This chapter has taught you something that a lot of people seem to be struggling with: how to totally tame and understand the sound object. Believe me, this took me some time, so you're benefiting from my late nights, and you can use the time you've saved building your own Oscar award-winning soundtracks.

In this chapter we've covered:

- Creating a new sound object and controlling it with ActionScript

- Adding pan and volume controls

- Creating the stun:design sound control interactivity

In the next chapter we'll look at how to give your movie clips autonomy so they are self-contained and can look after themselves. We're getting to a pretty professional standard now!

Sprites

What we'll cover in this chapter:

- *Investigating what a sprite is*

- *Creating sprites and assigning movement and collision behaviors*

- *Detecting a collision*

- *Creating the stun:zapper game*

In this chapter we'll go over what we mean by **sprites** and tie them into the related building blocks that you have already learnt about in the last two chapters. Then we'll look at basic sprite functionality and how to create it, before deconstructing an entire game so that you will know enough about sprites to go away and start making your own games.

In reading this chapter, you are entering a new level of advanced ActionScript programming. This isn't the steep cliff-face at the top of the mountain it may seem at first, but is rather the integration of the concepts you have been looking at in isolation in earlier chapters. We're going to take the separate areas of ActionScripting and put them together to create something that is much bigger than the sum of the parts. The glue that holds advanced ActionScripting together is your ability to see through the problem with forward planning and be totally familiar with the separate building blocks.

What is a sprite?

A sprite is a screen-based object whose behavior and actions are controlled by dedicated code that is integral within itself. This means that our main code can let the sprite get on with whatever it's doing in terms of movement, collision, appearance and so on, safe in the knowledge that it can look after itself.

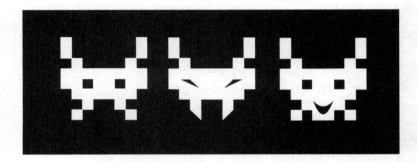

It can be a space invader, or a happy little spider that follows you around the web site helping you when you get into difficulty. The sprite should be able to do three things without you having to keep an eye on it, none of which should be new to you. It needs to:

■ Move

■ Detect collision

■ Act independently

The first point is that a sprite should be able to move around the screen in an intelligent way, and know if it's moving into areas where it shouldn't be (such as off the visible screen area), and take its own remedial action.

The second point involves collision detection. A sprite should be able to detect when it's hit another sprite, and take the appropriate action - move away, explode, or cause what it's hit to explode. This is a new way of using old techniques – collision detection is just a new *method* that's applied to the movie clip object.

The last point involves the programming techniques we learned in Chapter 9. Our sprite should keep the main program informed of what it's doing and what its status is. This strongly implies that our sprite routines should be designed using a *black box* or *modular* approach. The main program shouldn't have to bother with taking care of the sprite's movement or collision detection, and only needs to know what is necessary. The sprite is really just a self contained movie clip that has methods that it applies to itself to control its own behavior.

In Chapter 9, we covered the principles of something that went beyond animation, and moved into the realm of **simulation**. Simulation is a cornerstone for all that's related to advanced behaviors and specifically the behaviors' interaction with each other. To create a believable game world, we define rules for it, and everything in the world has to conform to them. The interaction of the game sprites with each other is the difference between creating real-time games and creating separate advanced animated effects for web sites.

We've already covered the principles that underpin the basic elements of sprite construction – it's just that you never knew you were a games programmer. There are three basic factors we need to consider for sprite construction:

- Control

- Movement

- Collisions

Let's take them one at a time.

Control

Control is all about simulating intelligence and giving the impression that the sprite is aware of what's going on around it.

Control is just a *behavior*. For our game, we'll steal the behavior for the aliens from the behaviorSwarm we looked at in Chapter 9. We have to modify it to control itself so that it doesn't talk to Flash unless it has to. This is quite easy. At the start of all the paths, we remove `_parent` and replace it with `this`.

For example, the behaviorSwarm movie clip (in `swarm.fla` from Chapter 9's download files) uses the following lines to move its parent:

```
_parent._x = shapeX;
_parent._y = shapeY;
```

To make them apply to the current movie clip itself, we change the lines to:

```
this._x = shapeX;
this._y = shapeY;
```

Rather than controlling another movie clip with `_parent`, we're controlling our own movieclip with `this`. Although that looks like a small change, it's a big change in scope. The behavior is now controlling its own actions rather than those of a separate movie clip.

Now that we're giving the sprite some independence, we need to remember that it has to be aware of its own surroundings and their rules. It's not talking to the main program any more, so it needs to know this itself. It's a big boy now, it's moved out into the real world and it has to do its own washing. As well as knowing about what is going on around it, our sprite also needs to be aware of its own internal status. These are two separate *levels* of influence: local and global.

Global and Localized Data

Think of sprites as people. As people, we have internal influences, such as our own thoughts and emotions. We also have information coming to us, say, what's going on in the immediate environment, or television news about what's going on in another country. Our internal influences are the most important, but we need to be aware that we may have to adapt them in reaction to what's going on around us.

Sprites are the same. Their internally generated behavior controls them in the same way that our emotions control us. At the same time, though, the sprite must also look to see whether its actions are beginning to break the external rules by looking at the immediate environment. The sprite doesn't have the same level of complexity that we do. Its repertoire of interaction is:

1. Set my next movement as per my behavior.
2. Check whether I'm breaking any rules.
3. If I'm breaking no rules, modify my behavior as per the rules of my environment, otherwise move me as per my behavior (and keep repeating the three steps).

The simplest way to illustrate these steps is to look at **boundary violation**.

The sprite in the diagram has a behavior that causes it to move off the visible screen boundary. How do we tell it not to do that? One option would be to put something about the size of the screen into the sprite behavior itself, but that's not true to life. In real life, how far we travel depends on the circumstances surrounding us. If it's raining, we won't walk so far. Putting the size of the screen in the behavior also makes the behavior less adaptable. In future, we might want the behavior to change depending on a different external factor, something else that's happening. Having to build everything again doesn't really fit in with the modular lessons that we've been learning.

In real life, we don't carry around information about our environment with us – we perceive the *environment itself*. An easier and more consistent way to tell our sprite not to move off the visible screen is to realize that the screen boundary positions are a *worldwide* set of attributes, or something that everything in our world should know about. In other words it's a **global** piece of information that every sprite needs.

The contrast to this is **local** information that's contained within the sprite's immediate environment and not in the wider world. As an example, once the sprite moves, it would look at where its environment ends by looking outside of itself and onto the global (or `_root` timeline). It would check global variables on the external timeline that tell it that it's violating a global rule and modify its behavior. In the same way, the internal thoughts of the sprite (I'm getting rather close to this other sprite) are only required by the sprite itself, and if anything else wants to know this information, it should have to ask the sprite.

We can see that information in our game world is also in two *levels*. The global information about the world is the lowest level, and as we get more and more specific, it gets less centralized and more concerned with individuals within the world. One sprite on one side of the screen doesn't really need to know that two sprites on the other side of the screen have just collided, it might put him off trying to kill the evil human at the bottom of the screen!

The key word here is *levels*, because it's something that Flash has already and something that we've been talking about in this book. We've seen that `_root` is the highest level, and that the individual movie clips or embedded behaviors (if any) have their own level, which is their own timeline. So, to know global information about the world, any movie needs to look at the lowest or shared timeline, `_root`. If it needs to talk to or know anything from an inhabitant within the world, it looks at the movie clip timeline owned by that inhabitant's movie clip. Our world data is therefore structured around levels, and these levels are based on timelines.

There are actually three definite levels that a sprite can access, and they are;

- `_global`

- `_root`

- `this` (the timeline of the sprite itself)

So what do we use each for? I have made global constants (such as the screen boundaries) live in `_global`, with the shared data (which I define as 'global data that is also dynamic or open to change') live in `_root`. Finally, local data lives on the local timelines, or `this`.

It is important when reading the scripts in this chapter to recognize which level each piece of information is on. The way to do this is:

- Global data is preceded by a 'g'. This is not something that Flash requires; it's a naming strategy I have used to avoid confusion.

- Shared data has no path (and will be therefore placed on `_root`, because it is where the scripts are). Many of you may be thinking 'why don't you put it on `_global` instead?'. The reasoning is actually a little tricky, but see the focus point below if you want to be let into the secret.

- Local data is preceded by `this` (which means that it will be placed on the timeline scoped by the current function, and this will usually be the timeline of the sprite itself).

> *The reason why I haven't used* `_global` *for 'global data that varies' (I've used* `_root` *instead) is that although you don't need a path to access a global, you do when you come to write to it. Unless you specify* `_global` *at the front of the variable name when you write to it, the variable will be created on the timeline you are on.*

Here's an example:

If I create a variable

```
_global.gMyVariable = "foo";
```

I can read it from any timeline like this:

```
something = gMyVariable;
```

`something` will equal `"foo"`.

If I now want to change `gMyVariable` to `"foobar"` from the same timeline, then

```
gMyVariable = "foobar";
```

will not work because it will not access the global variable gMyVariable. It will instead create a *local* variable, so now you have two variables called gMyVariable. You have to specify the global path when you write to a _global (unless you are writing a function that you have placed in _global). To avoid confusion, you should always specify the _global path when writing to a variable on _global.

```
_global.gMyVariable = "foobar";
```

We'll see how to apply this in the next section when we'll have a game world that consists of a section of deep space. Its inhabitants will be SwarmAliens and our courageous Lone Crusader© in his Starfleet SpaceCruiser™.

Our next issue surrounding sprite construction is a vital one: movement.

Movement

Movement is the most important attribute to the gamer, but to the programmer it's merely a consequence of control. We've already seen this in things such as the *swarm* behavior, which wasn't a movement so much as a section of code that controlled properties of a number of movie clips. The fact that these properties were actually associated with position is how the movement occurred, but we could just as easily have applied it to size or color, and so on.

We don't need to say much more about movement. Movement is a visual property that we think is important in real-time applications, but to us as programmers, it's really just a consequence of all the control and relationships that we've set up in our game world. Talking about movement in isolation isn't meaningful. Instead, we'll be concentrating on the control we define that creates this movement in the first place.

If we want to create movement, we have to say, "What's the behavior that is causing that movement, and what are the important features that I have to simulate to reproduce it?"

We did exactly this with our *swarm* movement, by breaking down the swarming *behavior* by deconstructing its movement back to a set of rules that are followed to create the movement in the first place.

Now to our last point: collision.

Collision

Collision is a vital ingredient in a believable game world because most sprites have to know something is near them before they can interact, or change their behavior in some way. In the game we'll be looking at, collision means just that. In other, more sedate, games it may mean something more fundamental: the initiation of complex interaction between the two sprites. In other words, sprites don't necessarily have to try to blow each other up!

In the *Ecology* game I mentioned at the end of Chapter 9, collision would mean that two creatures that are in significant proximity start interacting. The two sprites would have to be able to signal to each other and retrieve information about exactly what type of creature the other one was. This information would allow the sprite to decide whether the other sprite was a potential mate, or food, a predator, or just another like-minded creature with which to swarm with for safety.

Collision is something new, so we'll show you in practical terms how it works in Flash. The file for this FLA is in the download file for this chapter as collisionMX.fla.

What is collision? Two things are in collision if their boundaries intersect. This is almost the same as real life collisions. In real life, the boundary is the shape's outline but in the virtual world, this boundary can be bigger or smaller than the sprite outline, so two circles can 'collide' (when their boundaries intersect) without their sprite outlines ever touching each other.

In this exercise we'll create some basic collision detection. We'll create two circles and set up some dynamic text to tell us whether or not Flash sees a collision between them. We need to move the 'hitter' circle towards the 'target' circle somehow, and the easiest way to do this is by making it draggable.

Detecting a collision

Firstly we want to create two movie clips.

1. Create the first movie clips, which will be our target and call it hitarea. It has to be a single frame movie clips that has a definite shape, so make a new graphic symbol called circle and draw a circle on the stage. Drag an instance of circle onto the stage of the hitarea.

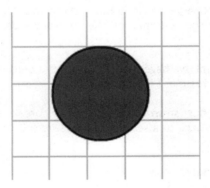

Next, we want to create the 'hitter'.

2. Create a new movie clips called hitter. Name layer 1 circle and drag an instance of circle from the library into the movie clip.

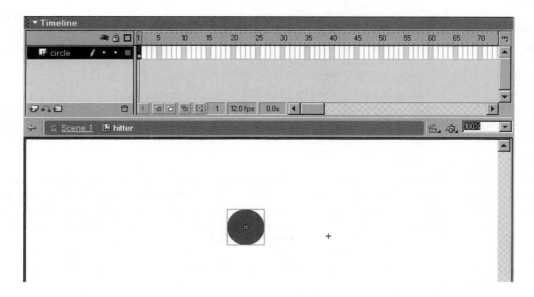

3. Still in hitter, create a layer and call it text. Put a dynamic text box just underneath the circle. This will contain a bit of dynamic text set up to display a variable coll (as in *collision*) so enter coll into the Var box in the Property inspector. Select the Show Border Around Text button so that the text has a border we can see. Unselect the Selectable button:

4. Back in the root timeline, create a new layer and call it actions. Rename the original layer as graphics. We now need to add some ActionScript to frame 1 of the actions layer. Enter the following code into the Actions panel.

```
hitter = function () {
    this.onPress = function() {
        this.startDrag("");
    };
    this.onRelease = function() {
        this.stopDrag();
    };
    this.onReleaseOutside = function() {
        this.stopDrag();
    };
```

The functions are fairly self-explanatory. Pressing the mouse button on the hitter will grab it to enable it to be dragged and releasing the button stops the dragging, whether the pointer is inside the hitter or not.

The following section of code is where the interesting things happen. Type this in directly under the previous code.

```
this.onEnterFrame = function() {
    this.coll = "";
    if (this.hitTest("_root.hitarea")) {
        this.coll = "hit";
    }
};
};
```

This script checks whether this movie clip (the one that contains our ActionScript) is touching our hitarea instance (which is the target of our hitter). The expression is **true** if an overlapping is seen, and **false** if it isn't. If it's true, our if will set coll to "hit", and we'll see this in the dynamic text field. If it's false, coll will be nothing (note how we set coll to be nothing, rather than leave it as undefined) and so the text box will remain blank.

This bit of code simply applies the hitting action to both hitters, so you can use either of them to trigger the hit.

```
hitter.apply(circle01);
hitter.apply(circle02);
```

> Remember, if at anytime you get lost or just want to check you're doing things correctly, open up collisionMX.fla to check against the original file I created.

5. Drag two hitters and one hitarea onto the stage. Give the circle an instance name hitarea with the Property inspector, and give the two hitters (circles with text boxes) instance names of circle01 and circle02. Test the movie.

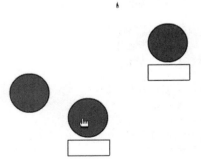

You can drag either of the two hitters around. If you drag either one over the hitarea instance, you'll see the dynamic text change to tell us that a collision has taken place between the two.

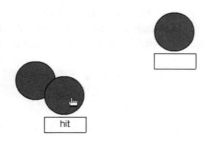

This would make a nice drag-and-drop interface. You could have the user physically drag and drop products (which would be the equivalent of our circles) into a shopping basket, for example, or have a MP3 downloads page where the user chooses the music they want through record icons dropped into a DJ's record bag.

There are some factors to note here. Before we continue I should draw your attention to a couple of things. You have to name the item you want to detect the collision with, so you must know its instance name. This means that you can't just detect a collision with anything. To do this would require a loop that looked at all available instances, which would mean that you have to know the names of all available instances at any time. We've got out of having to know what the instance name of the `hitter` is by simply calling it `this`.

Why did we drag two instances of `hitter` onto the stage instead of just one? We did it so that we could see that `coll` could be true for one `hitter` and not necessarily true for the other. The two variables have the same name but a different path, which makes them unique. Each instance's local variables are *unique*, even though they share the same names, because they are in different movie clips.

Notice also that we used a general function `hitter` and then made it specific to each instance by applying the function to `circle01` and `circle02`. We didn't need to write separate code for each hitter, saving ourselves some typing. This is also a good example of structured coding.

The hit detection sometimes gives a true when the circles are close but not touching. This is because we're checking whether the **bounding boxes**, which are the little outlines that appear when you select a movie clips on the stage of the movie clipss, are touching:

Bounding box ⟶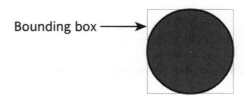

You can modify the command to check for outlines rather than the bounding box, but this is a bigger job, and might slow Flash down in a video game.

There is one final area to consider in interactivity – performance. At the moment, the circles are updated at 12fps, and this is a little slow. There are two ways around this. One is to increase the fps to something higher, but this makes Flash do *everything* faster, and is a little inefficient. Good programming doesn't rely on making things better using speed (because you will soon find out that you can never have enough), but on making your code *more efficient*. The Flash action `updateAfterEvent()` will add an extra screen redraw whenever it is invoked. You can only use this action inside (and at the end of) an event script, as the name of the action itself suggests. That kind of sounds useful, but where do we want to use it?

What we actually want to do is add extra frames only when the user is dragging a circle. We know when that occurs, because the circle in question will have been pressed *and* the mouse is currently moving. So here's what we want to do.

Once the mouse is pressed over a circle, we want to start looking for mouse movement, and use `updateAfterEvent` every time we detect this. In ActionScript, this converts to *create an onMouseMove event that simply updates the screen when an* `onPress` *event is seen.*

If the mouse button is released, then the user has stopped dragging. We no longer need to force Flash to use `updateAfterEvent`, and the easiest way to do that is to simply undefine (or delete) the `onMouseMove`. Have a look at `collisionMX2.fla` for an example of this in action. The updated definition for the `hitter` function is shown below, with new lines in bold.

```
hitter = function () {
    this.onPress = function() {
        this.startDrag("");
        this.onMouseMove = function() {
            updateAfterEvent();
        };
    };
    this.onRelease = function() {
        this.stopDrag();
        this.onMouseMove = undefined;
    };
    this.onReleaseOutside = function() {
        this.stopDrag();
    };
    this.onEnterFrame = function() {
        this.coll = "";
        if (this.hitTest("_root.hitarea")) {
            this.coll = "hit";
        }
    };
};
```

If you run this FLA, you will see a marked improvement in the animation speed.

*Increasing the frame rate to silly values because 'it seems to run better' is a common technique. Its okay for little animated effects, but if you are building serious Flash applications, you only need to accelerate **some** of the things in the FLA. Accelerating them all makes the Flash player work harder, and leads to posts on the Flash boards with questions like, 'Why is Flash so slow?' The answer is of course that the developer is expecting Flash to cover over inefficient code by running just that bit faster if the fps is set higher. If only everything was this easy!*

We've had a look at fairly simple examples thus far. Now it's time to delve into a bigger example, something more like the sort of projects you will want to create yourself.

Planning stun:zapper

We'll create a space invaders type game, with swarming aliens at the top, and the player's ship at the bottom. This is a pretty well known setup, so I won't waste your time by showing you a design breakdown of a game that's been in the public domain since the late seventies.

But this doesn't mean I haven't thought it through! To shape my initial concept and develop an idea of what would happen, I thought of all the arena games I've played and broke down all the functions. I will live and die by my statement that introduced this book: "If it doesn't work on paper, it won't work when you code it."

For simplicity's sake I've decided that the player will only be allowed one life and one bullet (so that there's only ever one bullet on screen). Also, we won't have the invaders attacking by firing on the player. This is entirely possible, but I feel a little uneasy about defining a game with too many sprites on the screen at the same time. Instead, the aliens will perform some form of swooping or diving attack, which calls for fewer sprites and therefore a faster game.

One of the major reasons that Flash is disadvantaged is that it's forced to play its game inside a browser window and can't control the screen attributes, such as what size the full screen will be. Unlike dedicated consoles which actually play games on fairly small screens, usually no bigger than about 600x400 pixels, Flash has to play on a screen of unknown bit depth. This could be a screen size of 1280x1024, on which currently only the highest specified desktop computers can render acceptably fast games, and then only with some form of graphic hardware support. Flash has to do this on a platform that wasn't built for speed - the browser. The Flash player itself doesn't do us any favors either, as it doesn't grab all the available processor time for itself as most video games do. So, we'll keep things simple for the moment.

In the early arcade machines, they always made the games last a calculated amount of time for the average player. The difficulty level was graded so that the player would think they had got their money's worth. An important consideration at the planning stage, and one often overlooked by Flash games, is how long do we want an average game to last? This affects all sorts of usability issues like 'is it too challenging?', 'does the game last long enough?', and 'does the player see enough of the game on the first turn to want to have another go?'. I generally assume that a good web game should last no more than one minute for the first go, have immediately obvious controls, and have no long preloads that break up the game. The player should also be able to get better from their abysmal start by practising.

The next step is to plan how the game will work from a programming perspective. The block diagrams that you see here all relate to different aspects of the game and are taken directly from the three pages of handwritten notes and sketches that I scribbled down before I wrote the game.

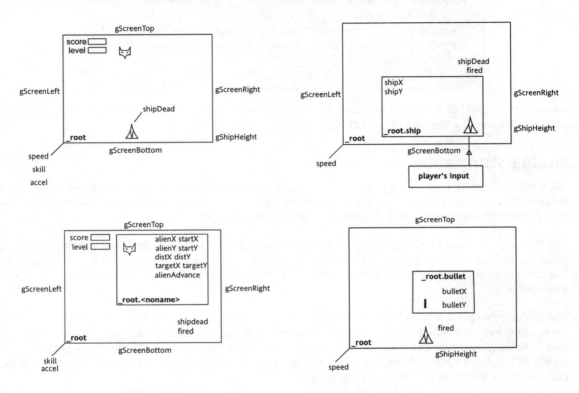

We'll come back to look at each of these in more detail as we look at the ActionScript behind each section. I wanted to show them to you here so that you could see how they're as useful as the flowcharts that we looked at in Chapter 8, but on a slightly higher level. Flowcharts would be more concerned with the detailed logic while these block diagrams are high-level overviews that helped me to mesh together a game world with no logical flaws. Once I had these, I dropped down a level and began flowcharting the smaller ActionScript cogs of that world.

I found that these were a lot more useful than flowcharts because they imply *relationships* rather than logic and are easier to formulate. They really show objects and their interfaces, which is useful for getting an overview of what each game piece can see and interact with in the game world, and what in the game world will influence its behavior.

It took me half an hour to create these, and by the time I had finished I knew I could complete this game, because all the information was in front of me. This is the way you need to work if you want to reach this level of ActionScripting, and it's more or less mandatory if you expect to do it commercially. I wrote this game in around eight hours, including planning, which isn't far from the timescale that you'll be used to in the real world. To turn ideas around that quickly you must plan everything out first in the same way that I've done. At first it may seem like something that is slowing you down, but with time you'll be able to home in to the important bits very quickly, and you'll find that the time spent reaps massive savings when you come to code it all up.

I don't propose to go through the whole program as a tutorial in this section, because you should have developed far enough in ActionScript at this stage to be able to see what's happening. I'm guessing that you're probably more interested in seeing how our plans are converted to ActionScript so you can go away and do the same thing with *Missile Command* or *Defender*. I'll do a breakdown of the code and tell you what each bit does and my reasoning at every stage.

As I've said, you need to plan all aspects of a game before coding it. What I'm going to do here is show you the plans and the code separately for each section so that you get a clear view of what the ActionScripting is doing in each section. Don't think for a moment that I only planned one section at a time!

The Game World (the root level)

One of the important issues in designing your game world is *approximation*. You want to concentrate only on those things that are important in your game. Deep space has all sorts of things that we are not interested in, such as temperature, radiation intensity, even gravity (which we are simulating indirectly). They won't affect anything in our game world, so we don't need them. This is an important thing to have a feel for, and it is one of the defining features of good simulation; knowing what to leave out and what to leave in...

The things I think we need to look at, the things that define the world in which our sprites will live and play are shown here in the finished game, followed by the first block diagram that I showed you:

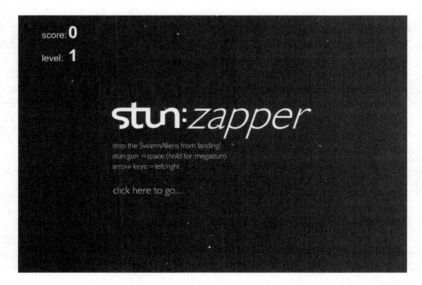

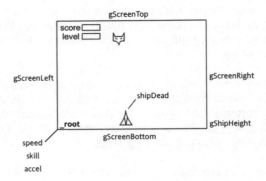

The variables outside the box are defined as true global parameters (and live in `_global`). The variables inside the square are all non-constant, and so I have kept them on `_root`. I'll define each one in turn and in a little more detail.

gScreenTop, gScreenBottom, gScreenRight, gScreenLeft

These are the game world limits and represent the visible screen area. We'll see later that the game actually allows some sprites to start off outside the game world, but their behaviors will force them to move back into the game world.

score

`score` is really there for the player and represents the carrot that keeps the player wanting to have another go. In the final game, I've never got more than 600 points. So now you have an incentive. As we'll see, `score` also feeds into the `level` parameter.

level, skill, accel

`level` is an important world parameter, because it controls how well the *SwarmAliens* will play. It's derived from the `score`, and the higher the score, the higher the level gets. The longer the player survives, the harder the game gets. `level` works by feeding into several other parameters that control the alien behavior; `skill` and `accel`(eration). As the aliens get more skillful, they will attack more, and as the `accel` parameter changes, they will get to their top speed faster, and therefore get from A to B quicker.

speed

`speed` is how fast things move in pixels per frame. The aliens will have a slightly different movement strategy, based on the equation in the last chapter, but the stars and player's ship will have movement based on this parameter.

shipDead, fired, gShipHeight

These are some parameters about the player's ship that will be needed by the other sprites, so I decided it would be more convenient to make them global. `shipDead` represents whether the player has died or is still fighting the good fight. `fired` tells us whether a bullet is in the process of being fired. `gShipHeight` is an odd one. I put it in because I could see it being important for at least some other sprites. One of these would be the bullet, which needs to start off at the top of the ship because that's where it's fired from. I thought it might also come in useful if the game runs too slowly.

The aliens can't hit the ship until they are `gShipHeight` above `gScreenBottom`. We don't really need to test for collisions between the aliens and the ship until then. As it happens, the game ran fast enough and I didn't need to do this, but if you decide to develop the game further – and I hope you do – then you have this option to consider.

Let's go and have a look at how I have coded this. Dealing with global issues involves the main timeline, so open `stunzapperMX.fla` from the download file for this chapter and have a look at the main timeline.

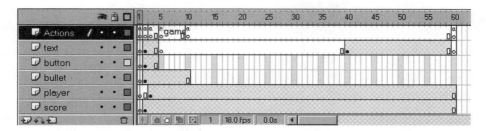

Oddly enough, it's frame 2 of the Actions layer that shows the start screen:

Frame 1 of the Actions layer initializes the global parameters that we've just discussed:

```
// set up screen extents
_global.gScreenLeft = 20;
_global.gScreenRight = 530;
_global.gScreenTop = 20;
_global.gScreenBottom = 380;
_global.gShipHeight = 40;
```

Frame 2 initializes the variables that need resetting at the start of every go.

```
speed = 10;
skill = 0.04;
accel = 20;
score = 0;
level = 1;
fired = false;
shipdead = false;
```

The script then waits for you to click on a button to start the game.

```
invisible_btn.onRelease = function() {
    play();
};
```

> *The Flash movie can be one of several things in a browser window, so when you press anything on the keyboard, the browser doesn't know which plug-in or textbox or whatever the key press is supposed to communicate with unless you give the browser a hint by selecting the target by clicking on it. Waiting for the user to click to start a game tells the SWF that we want to select it as well as starting our game.*

Frame 2 also starts up the starfield. Note that you can change the number of stars (any number from 1–100) by altering the argument of makeStar.

```
makeStar(15);
stop();
```

Once the player has clicked the invisible button behind the click here to go... text, the game proceeds to frame 3 and the script that sets up the ship and aliens.

```
starShip.apply(ship);
makeAlien(10);
```

As with the stars, you can make the game harder or easier by changing the number of aliens (again, from 1-100).

The game then proceeds to the loop in frames 5 to 10.

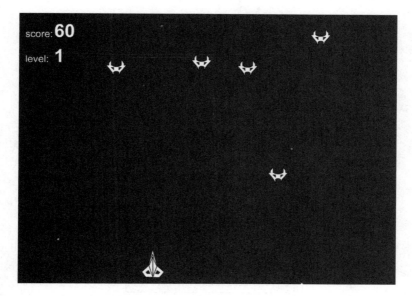

The game loop continues until the player has died, signified by `shipDead` being true. A check is also constantly being made during this loop to see whether the score is above `score x level`. If so, then the skill level of the aliens is doubled and the level increased by one. The first time this will happen is at score=200, and it will then occur every 200 points thereafter. The script that does this is attached to frame 10 of layer Actions, and it looks like this:

```
if (score>(level*200)) {
    skill = skill*2;
    accel = accel/1.5;
    level = ++level;
}
if (shipDead==false) {
    gotoAndPlay ("gameLoop");
}
```

This will continue to loop back to frame 5 (`gameloop`) if the player is still alive.

Frame 40 is the Game Over screen and, in true video game tradition, there's a short pause between frames 10 and 40 before it appears. Frame 60 simply sends the game back to the start so the player can try again.

The Player (the ship object and its interfaces)

The player's sprite has no intelligence or behavior of its own, but rather takes its movements from the player's keypresses. All it really has to do is move left and right, and fire on demand from the player. It also has to check that it's always within the game world.

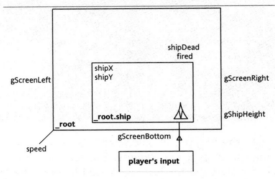

The ship code is split into a number of different functions (both of which are within the main function starShip).

When doing anything with code, it's always a good idea to initialize, so an initialization function makes sense (shipInit). This function initializes the ship position so that it starts at the bottom center of the screen. It also defines the keycodes that represent the three keys that control it.

The onEnterFrame script (which, like all event handlers, is really an anonymous function) is the main controlling script. This runs every frame and takes inputs from the user and moves the ship accordingly. When the ship is destroyed (shipDead = true), this event undefines itself. This erases the controlling script, and no further actions take place (which is why the ship stops moving when it explodes). The explosion sequence is on the ship timeline itself, and this is initiated by the this.gotoAndPlay("explodeMe") towards the end of the onEnterFrame script.

In the starShip() function in frame 1 of the main actions layer I've defined two local variables, shipX and shipY, that tell me the current position of the ship. By looking at the players inputs, I'll know whether the player is asking for the ship to move left (shipX = shipX-Speed) or right (shipX = shipX+Speed). I also want to check that I'm not going too far to the left (shipX<gScreenLeft) or to the right (shipX>gScreenRight).

The ship movie clip needs to control the firing of the bullet. If the user has *just* fired (and a bullet is already on the screen) we need to set `fired==true` so that they can't fire. Once the shot is complete, we need to make sure `fired==false` so that they *can* fire again.

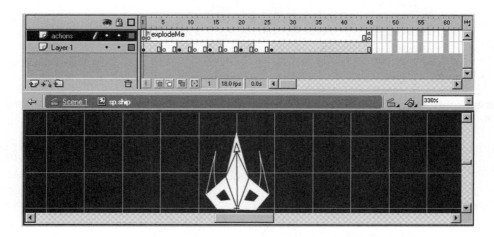

If you look in the ship's timeline, you'll see that it contains three action frames. The timeline will jump to that label `explodeMe` to make the ship blink and explode if it's hit (which means that `shipDead==true`). The three action frames are really where it all happens, so we'll look at those in detail.

The key codes are the values used by the **Key** object, which you haven't met yet. The Key object is very simple to use, and to detect a particular keypress all you have to do is find the key code for the key you want to detect. Use the action `Key.isDown(key code)` to detect whether the key is currently down. Placing it in an `if` statement's argument is usually the best way of handling the detection.

> *The codes for each key are listed in the Macromedia documentation for each particular key, look in the* Keyboard Keys and Key Code Values *section of the help files. It's also in Appendix B of the ActionScript Reference Guide if you have the printed material.*

I've defined the codes for the keys we use in the game – the left arrow, the right arrow and the spacebar:

```
// define key codes
this.leftArrow = 37;
this.rightArrow = 39;
this.space = 32;
```

Frame 1 initializes the sprite: the initial position of the sprite is to be the middle bottom of the screen, which equates to half way between `gScreenRight` and `gScreenLeft`, and at `gScreenBottom`:

```
        this.shipInit = function() {
            this.leftArrow = 37;
            this.rightArrow = 39;
            this.space = 32;
            this.shipX = (gScreenRight-gScreenLeft)/2;
            this.shipY = gScreenBottom;
            this._x=this.shipX, this._y=this.shipY;
            this.gotoAndStop(1);
        };
```

The main controlling code is in the `onEnterFrame` script inside `starShip` and I've done this for each of the three keys.

For the left arrow, we want to reduce the ship's x coordinate by `speed` as long as it won't take us past `gScreenLeft`.

```
        // user inputs
        this.onEnterFrame = function() {
            if (Key.isDown(this.leftArrow) && (this.shipx>gScreenLeft)) {
                this.shipX -= speed;
            }
```

For the right arrow key, we want to increase the ship's *x* position by `speed` as long as it doesn't take us past `gScreenRight`.

```
        if (Key.isDown(this.rightArrow) && (this.shipx<gScreenRight)) {
            this.shipX += speed;
        }
    }
```

The spacebar allows us to fire the bullet but only if there is no bullet currently in the process of being fired. If we are okay to fire, then we need to make the bullets x position the same as our ship's x position so that it fires from the same position that the ship is at.

```
        if (Key.isDown(this.space) && (!fired)) {
            fired = true;
            bullet.bulletX = bullet._x=this.shipX;
            bullet.bulletY = bullet._y=this.shipY-gShipHeight;
        }
```

Next is a looping action that looks to see whether the ship has died (through `shipdead`) and either causes the ship to carry on moving or explode, depending on the outcome:

```
        if (shipDead) {
            this.gotoAndPlay("explodeMe");
            this.onEnterFrame = undefined;
        }
```

If the ship is dead (`shipDead` is true) we undefine `onEnterFrame` and set the ship timeline (pointed to by `this`) running to the explode sequence. If it's false, then we keep the `onEnterframe` as it is.

Finally, we need to move the ship. Notice that I'm only changing the ship's *x* position. I don't need to change the *y* position because the ship doesn't move up or down, just sideways.

```
// ship movement
this._x = this.shipx;
```

All of the above script is useful as a template for anything that's required to move or happen as a result of keyboard inputs, so we have re-usable code again. The function can be used to control any sprite that moves in the same way.

The SwarmAlien (the alien1 object and its interfaces)

In many ways, the *SwarmAlien* is the only thing in the game with intelligence. Its movements are based around a real motion that uses acceleration, and it defines its own behavior, attacking or swarming based on a fairly advanced script. It also advances down the game world as time goes on, getting closer and closer to the hapless player. It is only a matter of time...

The *SwarmAlien* makes all the collision detections in the game, which is fairly impressive considering it is the main target. Altogether quite an intelligent lifeform!

In logical terms, in our game the aliens are hitting the bullets rather than the other way around. It's actually easier to do it this way because each alien has to make one check for one bullet, rather than the single bullet having to check for all aliens. This seems a bizarre way to model our 'bullet hitting' detection, but it actually results in less code.

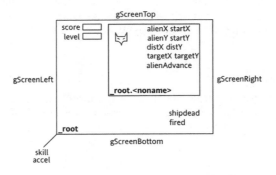

Before we look at the detailed code, lets have a look at what each of the functions that control the aliens are (they are all to be found within the spaceAlien() function).

> *Some of you may be getting a little confused as to why we are defining all our controlling functions as functions within another function. Well there are two reasons:*
>
> *We eventually need to apply the functions to movie clips. We can do that two ways. We can either apply each individual function separately, or we can just put them all within a larger function and then we only have to apply the one function. By defining all our alien functions in one larger function, we can later just apply them all by simply applying the function that contains all the others.*
>
> *The second reason is to do with something you may have heard about, but haven't yet seen; a prototype. When, in your later career as a Flash coding whizzkid you get to the point when you want to write object-oriented code, you will recognize the prototype structure as nothing new. It will look very much like what we are doing now; a function that contains other functions. By forcing you to code in the style we are using now, we are priming you for the next big step in your career (and we expect great things!). At the moment we are calling these big 'superfunctions' templates, but that's just a primer for what they really are the basis of once your coding gets to the next level; prototypes that define the methods of your custom objects. But you don't have to worry about prototypes at this stage of your coding career.*

alienSpawn()

This function initialises the alien when it first appears on the screen, and every time it reappears after being shot.

onEnterFrame()

The onEnterFrame() event initially calls alienBrain(), which is the main alien controlling script. When the alien dies however, this script is overwritten by alienReincarnate(). This second script is what the dead alien does; it simply waits until it can be respawned.

alienBrain()

This script is the main script that controls the alien. It is a modified version of the swarm behavior script, so although it looks a little complicated, you have already seen most of it. It consists of a few distinct phases:

It first applies the inertia equation to the alien's movement, moving towards the target point (`targetX`, `targetY`) in much the same way as the swarm FLA does. If the alien has reached the current target position, function `alienInitialize()` is called to decide on where the alien will move to next.

It also checks to see whether this alien has been hit by the player's bullet

        (this.hitTest(bullet) && fired)

... and whether this alien has managed to hit the player's ship.

        this.hitTest(ship)

alienReincarnate()

This function runs when the alien has been hit. It basically hides the alien and waits for a random amount of frames (it actually waits until `Math.random()<0.005`, or put another way, has a one in 1/0.005 (1 in 200) chance of respawning from the top of the screen every frame after it has died. On average, each alien will therefore reappear 200 frames after it has been hit.

To respawn an alien, the `alienReincarnate()` function calls `alienSpawn()` (to reinitialize the alien) and then reattaches `alienBrain()` to the `onEnterFrame()` event, causing the reincarnated alien to start living and breathing again. Spooky!

alienInitialize()

This function does the decision making of the alien. It decides whether the alien will swarm to a random position or whether it will swarm towards the player's ship. The latter is when the alien seems to dive towards the player's ship, and the former is when the alien mills around (swarms) at the top of the screen.

The aliens become more aggressive as time goes on because the deciding factor between dive and swarm is made based on the current skill level.

        (skill<Math.random())

As skill goes up, the aliens are more likely to dive towards the ship.

alienLanded()

If an alien dives past the bottom of the screen (an event which becomes more likely as the game progresses), the alien will stay at the point it landed, thus blocking part of the available area for the player to move. With the current difficulty settings, this is actually very unlikely to happen (the difficulty is such that the player will find it very hard to score above about 600, and aliens will not have reached a landing position by this score). I've included this function in case you play about with the difficulty settings, or if you are a much better gamer than I am and last long enough to see aliens landing!

alienHit()

This function handles the alien being hit. It updates the score and changes the `onEnterFrame()` script from `alienBrain()` to `alienReincarnate()`. This has the effect of changing the behavior of the alien from 'living' to 'dead'.

makeAlien()

`makeAlien()` is a function outside the main `spaceAlien()` template. It is used to ... well... make aliens. It takes an argument `quantity` which changes the number of aliens in the game. Setting this higher will give you more aliens.

An important (but subtle) point to notice is that this function will *not* be attached to each instance of the alien sprites. This is because it is outside the `spaceAlien()` template. Instead, this function is on `_root`, and there is only one of them.

Okay, back to the detailed code.

The first surprising thing to notice about the alien is that it has no instance name. This is because it doesn't need one – it doesn't divulge any information to the other sprites so there's no need to reference it.

The alien has a scary number of local variables. `alienX` and `alienY` are its position on the screen, and `startX` and `startY` are its starting positions. The starting positions are used because the alien never actually really dies. Once it's been hit it waits a short time and respawns at the original start position, which is just off screen (actually 500 pixels above the visible screen). There are *always* the same number of aliens about at any one time.

`distX, distY` are variables that we've met before; they are the *where we are* terms in our real motion equation from Chapter 9. `targetX, targetY` are our *where we want to go* terms. The `alienAdvance` variable is a modification to the *swarm* behavior we saw in Chapter 9, which the aliens will be using. It represents the distance from the top of the screen that the alien is allowed to swarm in. As the game progresses, this variable gets higher and the alien swarms lower down the screen, making it closer to its target, the ship.

As soon as the alien has been shot, the respawned alien has to start again from the top, and `alienAdvance` is reset to its start value to make this happen. The secret of the game is to shoot at the lowest aliens, because they will, on average, have the highest `alienAdvance`, and therefore give you the biggest headache.

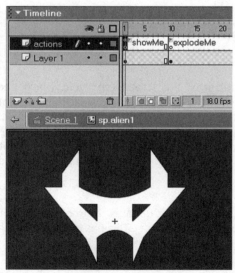

The first function initializes the alien. I've looked at its _x, _y properties and equated alienX, alienY and startX, startY to them. The alien acts rather like a salmon in that when it dies, it is respawned at its original birthplace, the positions off-screen you saw earlier. It's important to keep a record of the start position, because it is different for each instance.

The last line sets alienAdvance, which is a measure of how low the alien is allowed to swarm.

```
this.AlienSpawn = function() {
    this.alienX = this._x = this.startX;
    this.alienY = this._y = this.startY;
    this.alienAdvance = 4;
};
```

The alienInitialize() function is one of two large scripts (don't worry, there's only one more). The first if looks at skill and compares it with a random decimal number between 0 and 1, as supplied by the Math object's random() method. If skill is higher than the random number, the alien will perform a diving attack motion, and if it's lower, the alien will simply swarm. As skill gets larger, there becomes an increasing chance that the alien will attack rather than swarm aimlessly. In other words, it will become more *skillful*.

So how does it attack? Well, we'll be using the behaviorSwarm behavior that we defined in Chapter 9. That had a *target* set of variables which was our *where we want to go* term.

If the alien decides to swarm, our target is a random position somewhere in the top 1/alienAdvance of the screen. alienAdvance is 4 to start off with, so we're initially looking at the alien swarming somewhere in the top quarter of the screen, well away from the ship and posing no real threat (the words 'sitting' and 'duck' come to mind).

```
this.alienInitialize = function() {
    if (skill<Math.random()) {
        this.targetX = Math.random()*(gScreenRight-gScreenLeft);
        this.targetY = gScreenTop+Math.random()*
        ➡ (gScreenBottom/this.alienAdvance);
```

If the alien decides to attack, we set the target to be the ship's position, plus or minus a small random value. This means that the alien will now attempt to swarm to a position that's very close to the ship, but not directly *at* it! These lines will cause the alien to switch from the benign swarming motion into a kamikaze dive bomb...

```
    } else {
        this.targetX = ship._x+((Math.random()*100)-50);
        this.targetY = ship._y-5;
    }
```

The second if caters for the fact that there's no bottom limit to how far down the aliens can advance. If the alien intended to go lower than the bottom of the screen, it's constrained to just above the bottom of the screen. In this way, if the alien actually intended to move across and behind the ship, it will actually now sweep towards the ship on a collision course:

```
        }
    if (targetY>gScreenBottom) {
        targetY = gScreenBottom+10;
    }
```

The alienBrain() function is the big one. Here's where our modified behaviorSwarm comes in. You can really see code reuse at work here, because it is essentially the same idea with a few tweaks. The first five lines are almost the same as the ones you saw for behaviorSwarm except we have added a '*1/constant*' term that is now 1/accel. As accel gets smaller, the aliens will get quicker and more efficient.

The first block of code works out how far away the alien is from where it wants to be and stores this distance as the dist variables. This is then used in the movement equations to create a new position part way towards our target, alien.

```
    this.alienBrain = function() {
        this.distX = this.targetX-this.alienX;
        this.distY = this.targetY-this.alienY;
        // Apply inertia equation
        this.alienX = Math.round(this.alienX+(this.distX/accel));
        this.alienY = Math.round(this.alienY+(this.distY/accel));
```

The first if checks whether our alien has reached the bottom of the screen, or 'landed'. If so, the code jumps to the alienLanded() function.

```
    if (this.alienY>gScreenBottom) {
        this.alienLanded();
    }
```

The second if looks at whether we are close to our target. If we've reached our destination (or rather, are within 10 pixels of it), we allow the alien to swarm a bit further down the screen in recognition of its bravery in getting so far.

We then jump to alienInitialize(), which will set a new target for the alien to move to. This will, on average, be slightly lower down the screen and closer to the ship. In this way, the alien will slowly advance down the screen towards the hapless ship. Notice that I've reduced alienAdvance. This variable decides which fraction of the screen the alien can swarm in, and reducing its value will increase that fraction (sanity check: a third is less than a half; as the bottom number decreases, the fraction goes *up* in value).

```
    if ((this.distX<15) && (this.distY<15)) {
        this.alienAdvance -= 0.05;
        this.alienInitialize();
    }
```

The final part of this block of code performs the sprite movement, and checks to see whether in moving, our alien has hit either the bullet or ship. If the bullet has hit our alien, we jump to the alienHit() function and set fired to false (which allows the user to fire again).

If we've hit the ship, we want the ship to die (and we communicate this by setting `shipDead`). For added realism, you could also make the alien explode as well by going to `alienHit()` as before, but I kinda think the alien deserves a break for its bravery.

```
// perform animation
this._x = this.alienX;
this._y = this.alienY;
// check for collisions
if (this.hitTest(bullet) && fired) {
    fired = false;
    this.gotoAndPlay("explodeMe");
    this.alienHit();
}
if (this.hitTest(ship)) {
    shipDead = true;
```

`alienLanded()` is the function we jump to if the alien lands. In this case, the alien just freezes where it is. This means it's now level with the ship, the ship has less room to maneuver, and so it's not something you want to happen too often. The initial version of the game ended when this happened, but this felt a bit unfair, so the final version of the game lets the player soldier on.

```
this.alienLanded = function() {
    this._y = gScreenBottom;
    this.onEnterFrame = undefined;
    this.stop();
};
```

The `alienHit()` function is called when the alien is hit. This is a simple script that adds the points for this kill to the score (10 for each alien, multiplied by the current level, so you get more points the longer you last), and sets `alienAdvance` back to its initial value. Although it's not obvious by looking at the timeline picture, the alien graphic is replaced by an explosion at this point, and disappears after the explosion has faded.

```
this.alienHit = function() {
    score += level*10;
    this.onEnterFrame = function() {
        this.alienReincarnate();
    };
};
```

The alien sprite stays at the position it died at for approximately another 95 frames, and the final frame in the timeline sets the alien up for another attack, respawning it off screen at its original birthplace.

So the aliens never really die, but wait a while and are respawned behind the scenes! Killing them is really a bad policy, because they just come back stronger (but it's fun trying).

The Bullet (the bullet object and its interfaces)

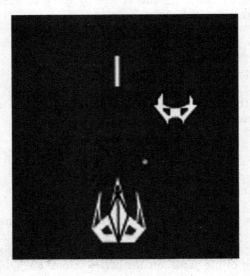

The bullet is the thing that comes out of the player's gun. There is actually only one bullet in the game - you are actually always firing the same one, although it's no less potent with each use. I hope for humanity's sake that your aim is better than the joker in the picture… miles away from the target! (well, OK, it was me).

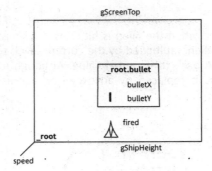

You can tell that the bullet is a simple object just by looking at its object diagram. At the instant it's fired, it takes on the *y* coordinate of the ship (bulletX=_root.ship.shipX). It continues up the screen until either it hits an alien on the way up, or it reaches the top of the screen (bulletY==gScreenTop). While it's traveling up the screen, it moves at 2*speed. Obviously, our bullet has to travel faster than the other elements in the game to be believable, and making it travel at twice the game speed is how we're achieving this bit of reality.

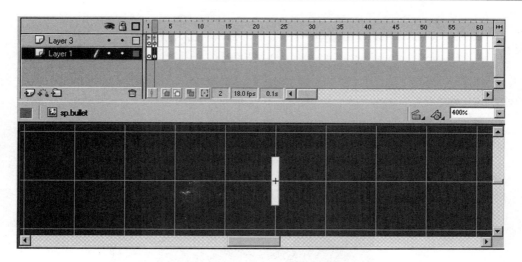

The bullet has two states. It can either be 'not being fired', or 'being fired'. If it's not being fired, we want it to be invisible. If it *is* being fired, we want it to be visible and move up the screen until it either reaches the top of the screen, or it has hit an alien.

The first two frames in the top layer of movie clip sp.bullet are labeled hideMe and showMe respectively. Layer 1 is empty, so the bullet movie clips is empty. The corresponding ActionScript for these two frames keeps looking for the bullet is 'being fired' condition.

As long as the gun has been fired (if (fired)), we switch to frame 2 (showMe) of the bullet movie clip via the code below (which is part of the bullet onEnterFrame() script), and the bullet becomes visible. The code animates it such that it starts moving up the screen via the last two lines of this snippet, which change the _y property of the bullet at a rate speed*2.

```
if (fired) {
   this.gotoAndStop("showMe");
   this.bulletY = this.bulletY-speed*2;
   this._y = this.bulletY;
}
```

Unless the bullet happens to hit an alien (and this is detected by the aliens themselves, so is not part of this code), the bullet has finished being fired when it hits the top of the screen. The next bit of code detects this and sets the bullet back to 'not being fired and ready to be fired again' (fired = false). The code also places the bullet back at the bottom of the screen once it has been fired, in readiness for the next shot.

```
if ((this.bulletY<gScreenTop) || (fired == false)) {
   fired = false;
   this.bulletY = gScreenBottom-gShipHeight;
}
```

Finally, if the bullet is not currently been fired, we hide it via the else branch of our code (which is only reached if fired = false)

```
    } else {
      this.gotoAndStop("hideMe");
    }
```

The debris of war

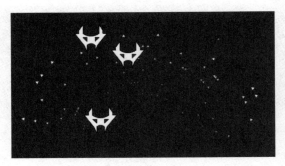

As well as the combatants, no laser battle in space is complete without some level of pyrotechnics. This game includes separate explosions for the aliens and the ship. The picture above shows the *SwarmAliens* victoriously moving through the expanding plasma cloud that was once my spacecraft.

This is all about the scrolling starfield that is the backdrop to the battle. No space game is complete without one.

The starfield is controlled by the `starDot()` and `makeStar()` functions. These are actually just very dumbed down versions of the alien scripts.

You might also want to look at an additional file, `stunZapperSound.fla`, which shows the game, plus the sound that goes with it.

Now you've had a look through the code for the stun:zapper game, take a few minutes to play the game. Go on, pretend you've got a stack of quarters in your hand and you're back in the arcade hall you used to spend all your time in when you were a kid. Once you've done this, think about how relatively simple the ActionScript that made all this possible is.

Summary

Once you've got your head around the way ActionScript works, you'll see that even quite complicated looking projects (like the stun:zapper game) are quite simple when you break them down into their constituent parts.

The main point that I'd like you to take away from this chapter is that *you can now do this stuff yourself*. Think how far you've come since I first showed you the `stop()` command at the beginning of the book. This is the beauty of ActionScript – it's not really that difficult, and yet you can achieve the most amazing things with it.

Drawing API

What we'll cover in this chapter:

We will use Flash MX's drawing API to dynamically create:

- *lines*

- *curves*

- *fills*

- *a kaleidoscope effect*

One of the new features of Flash MX is the **drawing API** (Application Programming Interface). This allows you to create totally new content within your movie clips. We can now get straight to the engine room of the movie clip and produce new sketches *on the fly*. In fact, there are three things you can create:

- Lines
- Curves
- Fills

Although you could emulate lines in Flash 5, you couldn't control the movie clip with clever scripting to create controlled curves or fills, so this feature is totally new. As we'll see in the next section, it all started with a turtle...

Turtle graphics

The drawing API of Flash is based around something called **turtle graphics**, so we will have a quick look at what that is before we get down to business, because it can get a little complicated.

Turtle graphics is an old graphics language that was used way back to control a little robot with a pen attached to it. The turtle was the robot – it typically looked like a little upturned bowl on wheels, hence the name, and it could do a few basic things:

- Lift the pen up (*penUp*)
- Put the pen down (*penDown*)
- Rotate without moving forward
- Travel forward (but not at the same time as rotating, so it could only travel in a straight line)

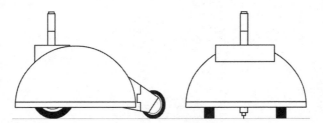

I can't swear on the details because I'm sketching from memory here (and I was young when I first saw one – I'm a lot older now), but I think it kind of looked like the one above. The pen fitted between the middle of two big wheels at the front, and the wheel at the back was like that of a shopping cart – it could twist on a hinge allowing the turtle to turn on the spot. Because the pen was situated at the center of rotation between the two front wheels, the turtle could rotate without moving the pen tip, and if the turtle moved forward with the pen down, it left a line describing its path.

You had two basic commands:

- *move(x, y)* – this was a *penUp* followed by a rotate until (x, y) was directly in front of you, and then move forward in a straight line as far as (x, y). It didn't result in a line being drawn.

- $draw(x, y)$ – this consisted of rotating until (x, y) was in front of you, followed by a *penDown* and move forward in a straight line as far as (x, y). It resulted in a line being drawn from your *start point* to (x, y).

Sometimes they put software on it that allowed you to enter angles and distances, so you could say 'rotate 90, move 5, rotate 45, move 6', and so on, but that was for the nursery kids. We used it with the Cartesian (x, y) scale. The deal was you put a piece of paper under the turtle and did stuff like working out how to draw a cube, or (even harder) an equilateral triangle. If you got that one, they even let you attempt to write your name with it. 'Sham' was the shortest name in class, so I aced it, but the surname was going nowhere!

Turtles were really cool in the early 8-bit computer days. Kids actually ran to math class to use them, and they only found out later that the turtle had fooled them into learning Cartesian geometry.

So anyway, what's this got to do with Flash? Well, Flash uses something that is recognizable as turtle graphics. In fact, most vector graphics actually *are* turtle graphics at the most basic level, and thinking in terms of the little turtle trundling around on cheap paper in real-time is easier than imagining the Flash graphics engine drawing stuff with scripts and events firing off, running at 12 fps. Indeed, the turtle makes it easy to visualize – they had kids doing Pythagorean theory at the age of five with these things, so it must be true!

Lines

Flash has a virtual turtle that controls the drawing API. It can move to a point (x, y) and then draw to a point (x, y). To draw a line from (50, 50) to (100, 100) you would:

- Move to (50, 50)
- Draw to (100, 100)

Easy huh? Let's get some practice by looking at an example.

Drawing lines

1. In a new movie, we'll add a script on frame 1 of the timeline. You don't have to rename the layer or anything. We're going to do everything in ActionScript, and we only need that one layer and that one key frame.

   The first thing we need is some paper. Let's create some virtual paper, a movie clip to be precise:

   ```
   _root.createEmptyMovieClip("paper", 100);
   ```

   This creates an empty movie clip called paper at depth 100. I chose 100 in case you want to go and add some other stuff on screen later.

   Where is this clip? Well, it's at (0,0) on the stage (because the _x and _y properties of a newly created clip are zero), which equates to the top left. Now here's an important point: as long as you leave it there, the coordinate space of the main timeline is the same as the local coordinates of the movie clip. As soon as you move it, however, the position of a turtle on the piece of paper called _root becomes different relative to a turtle on the piece of paper called paper, even if they head for the same point (x, y). As shown below, the internal coordinates of paper will show a different origin (0,0) to that of _root after being moved:

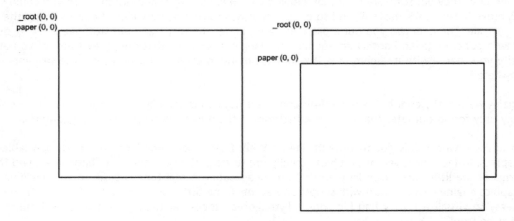

There are times when having the paper in a different place is a good thing, but not while we are getting to grips with the drawing API, so leave it where it is for now.

> *Don't forget that the y-axis is 'down' in Flash, not 'up' as it is in math. This is because web design is based around web pages, and they read from top to bottom.*

2. Next, we want to define our pen. A turtle could draw different lines depending on which pen you had in it, and the drawing API is no different. You select the linestyle of the turtle on the movie clip myClip by doing this:

```
myClip.lineStyle(thickness, color, alpha);
```

We will have a thickness of 3, a color of red (0xFF0000), and an alpha value of 100% for our turtle on paper, so type the following line in under the script we already have.

```
paper.lineStyle(3, 0xFF0000, 100);
```

3. We now have to move to our start point. The method to do this is moveTo(x, y). So if we wanted to move to (50, 50), we'd use this line:

```
paper.moveTo(50, 50);
```

4. The turtle is now in position at the start of the line. It now needs to put the pen down and draw a line as it travels to (100, 100). The method we use to draw is lineTo:

```
_root.createEmptyMovieClip("paper", 100);
```

```
paper.lineStyle(3, 0xFF0000, 100);
paper.moveTo(50, 50);
paper.lineTo(100, 100);
```

5. On testing this code, you should now see your line, a short diagonal in the top left corner that points at the bottom right corner. That's fine, but there's not much happening after the initial elation. Time for a little interactivity. Instead of `moveTo` a fixed distance and then `lineTo` to another fixed distance, we will use `lineTo (_xmouse, _ymouse)`, and we will do this every time the mouse moves. Change your script to the one shown below (the second line is new, and the `moveTo` and `lineTo` arguments have changed), which you'll find in the source code folders as `lines1.fla`:

```
_root.createEmptyMovieClip("paper", 100);
paper.onMouseMove = function() {
   paper.lineStyle(3, 0xFF0000, 100);
   paper.moveTo(275, 200);
   paper.lineTo(_xmouse, _ymouse);
};
```

Wow, an explosion in a paint factory!

6. Notice that this script gets slow if you allow a large number of lines to be drawn. We should really clean up the excess lines every now and then. We can't *undraw* lines, but we can *clear* the whole movie clip with `myClip.clear()`. Try this (`lines2.fla`):

```
maxLines = 100;
lines = 0;
createEmptyMovieClip("paper", 100);
paper.onMouseMove = function () {
   lines++;
   if(lines<maxLines) {
      paper.lineStyle(3, 0xFF0000, 100);
      paper.moveTo(275, 200);
```

```
            paper.lineTo(_xmouse, _ymouse);
        } else {
            paper.clear();
            lines = 0;
        }
    };
```

Here we are limiting ourselves to a maxLines of 100. As long as lines<maxLines, we do the original moveTo/lineTo actions in our clip paper. As soon as we see more than 100 lines, we clear our paper movie clip with paper.clear() and reset lines back to 0.

7.   We can also make our lines into one continuous line simply by commenting out or removing the moveTo action. You'd then see something like this:

If you can't visualize what is happening here, think back to our turtle. Rather than go back to the center of the screen after every mouse move, the turtle just waits for us to move our mouse, and then goes to the last position we were at *from where the turtle was on the last mouse move*. It is effectively following us. If it does it fast enough, all our straight line segments get short and therefore start to look like curves.

You may see the path the turtle makes being rather blocky. This is a function of the frame rate; the mouse movement is only being sampled at 12 fps. Try 18 or 24 fps if your machine is up to it (or reduce the stage size or quality if your machine is not).

We almost have the beginnings of a drawing tool here, and we'll develop this idea in a while. First though, we need to think about curves.

Curves

The curve functionality of the drawing API is best described by demonstration – time for another script! Add the following script to the first frame of a new movie. We are again going to use ActionScript only, so you only need the script and a single frame:

```
createEmptyMovieClip("paper", 100);
paper.onMouseMove = function() {
    paper.clear();
    paper.lineStyle(3, 0xFF0000, 100);
    paper.moveTo(100, 200);
    paper.curveTo(_xmouse, _ymouse, 400, 200);
};
```

This script can be found in the file `curves1.fla`. Note that we're now using a new method, `curveTo`, in place of our `lineTo`. We are moving our turtle to a point (100, 200) – center-left of the stage – and then drawing to (400, 200) – center-right of the stage. But something happens to the turtle in between. It's almost as if our mouse was some sort of turtle magnet; the turtle tries to get to the point (400, 200), but it is attracted to our magnet, and gets pulled away towards the mouse – the turtle's new path is a *curve*:

Notice that we are also clearing the paper every time. This means we delete the previous line and draw a new line every frame, and the resulting curve looks animated. Comment out the `paper.clear()` command to see all the individual curves that are making up our animation. Isn't that pretty... I have a feeling that lots of geometrical screen savers and 'Please Wait... loading' screen eye-candy are on the cards!

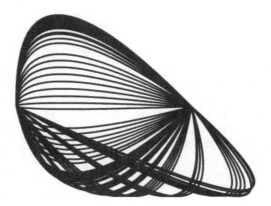

Looking at the difference between the `lineTo` and `curveTo` arguments we can see what is going on:

```
moveTo(100, 200);
lineTo(400, 200);

moveTo(100, 200);
curveTo(_xmouse, _ymouse, 400, 200);
```

The first two lines of code will cause a line to be drawn. Our turtle moves to (100, 200) and then draws to (400, 200). The second pair of lines contain our curveTo action, which also has the (400, 200) point specified, but also has a new set of control points (_xmouse, _ymouse). That explains why the mouse is doing stuff to the curve – its position is being used somehow.

So we have:

```
curveTo(controlPointX, controlPointY, x, y);
```

The curveTo is just like a lineTo in that it causes the turtle to go to (x, y) with the pen down, drawing a line as it goes. Unlike the lineTo, however, curveTo has a control point made up of (controlPointX, controlPointY) that affects the path the turtle takes. The turtle seems to want to go through the control point, but doesn't do it, so it *tends towards* the control point. OK, that's fine, but we really need more information than that to know what the control point is well enough to actually create a curve we can predict.

There are two ways I can tell you about this: one is to talk about quadratic Bezier curves and stuff like that for a couple of pages (and probably alienate half of my readership in doing so), and the other is to tell you what it actually does in non-mathematical words and pictures. Well, the pretty pictures option wins hands down every time for me – let's look at a quick example.

Create a fresh movie and attach this script to frame 1 of the main timeline (or just open up the file curves2.fla):

```
red = 0xFF0000;
blue = 0x0000FF;
createEmptyMovieClip("paper", 100);
paper.onMouseMove = function() {
    paper.clear();
    // draw curve...
    paper.lineStyle(3, red, 100);
    paper.moveTo(100, 200);
    paper.curveTo(_xmouse, _ymouse, 400, 200);
    // draw control point tangent...
    paper.LineStyle(0, blue, 100);
    paper.moveTo(100, 200);
    paper.lineTo(_xmouse, _ymouse);
};
```

This gives us the picture we want, and it's interactive as well! The thin line is the control line. It is a line joining the start point to the control point and the curve forms itself so that it is *tangential* to it:

A simple tool for drawing lines and curves

We now have everything we need to construct a simple interactive drawing tool. I've been working on a few test scripts in my attempt to create an 'all-singing, all-dancing' Flash-based drawing application that uses drawing layers in the same way as Photoshop, and has a floating toolbar, zoom in/out, snap, and a component driven UI. It will no doubt find its way into a later *friends of ED* book (unless one of you clever people creates it first), but as a starter, here's a beta script for the embryonic line/curve elastic band tool. You need to attach it to the first frame of a new movie as before, or just open up the file elasticBand.fla:

```
// INITIALIZE DATA
// Initialize Objects...
keyboard = new Object();
// Initialize variables...
endX = end2X=_xmouse;
endY = end2Y=_ymouse;
penToggle = false;
red = 0xFF0000;
blue = 0x0000FF;
black = 0x000000;
// END INITIALIZE DATA
//
//
// INITIALIZE GRAPHICS
// Create clips...
createEmptyMovieClip("paper", 100);
createEmptyMovieClip("pen", 101);
// END INITIALIZE CLIPS
//
//
// DEFINE EVENT HANDLERS
// keyboard listener and function...
keyboard.onKeyDown = function() {
  endX = end2X=_xmouse;
  endY = end2Y=_ymouse;
  penToggle = false;
};
Key.addListener(keyboard);
// pen events...
pen.onEnterFrame = function() {
  this.clear();
  if (!penToggle) {
    // if penToggle is false, use line pen...
    this.lineStyle(0, blue, 100);
    this.moveTo(endX, endY);
    this.lineTo(_xmouse, _ymouse);
  } else {
    // penToggle must be True, so use curve pen...
```

```
                  this.lineStyle(0, red, 100);
                  this.moveTo(endX, endY);
                  this.curveTo(_xmouse, _ymouse, end2X, end2Y);
               }
            };
            //paper events...
            paper.onMouseDown = function() {
               if (!penToggle) {
                  //first press...
                  // toggle to curve pen
                  // and set second endpoints of curve...
                  penToggle = true;
                  end2X = _xmouse;
                  end2Y = _ymouse;
               } else {
                  // second press...
                  // Draw the curve to the paper...
                  this.lineStyle(0, black, 100);
                  this.moveTo(endX, endY);
                  this.curveTo(_xmouse, _ymouse, end2X, end2Y);
                  // reset pen back to line pen...
                  penToggle = false;
                  endX = end2X;
                  endY = end2Y;
               }
            };
            // END DEFINE EVENT HANDLERS
```

There are two movie clips: paper and pen. The pen clip is where the cursor lines sit, that is, where curves and lines in progress are drawn. When you are ready to fix a curve, it is transferred to the movie clip paper. We have to do this because to animate our lines in progress (our 'pen') we have to constantly clear the pen movie clip. This means that we cannot draw anything permanent in it as well, so the movie clip paper is where we place our lines once we want them to be indelible.

> *Notice that if you were to split the paper into several movie clips* paper01, paper02, paper03, *and so on, you have the beginnings of drawing layers straight away with no fuss.*

To draw a line you move the blue line around to the first point you want to draw to. Click when you have your mouse at the right place:

The line will then turn red. If you click again without moving the mouse, you will get a permanent black line. If you actually want a curve, move the cursor while the line is red to form a curve:

Once you are happy, simply click again and the red curve will become a permanent black curve.

So, double-click to make a straight line single-click, bend the line, and single-click again to make a curve. Also, to move your cursor without drawing, just press and hold any key while you move. By doing this you can easily make a simple drawing consisting of lines and curves:

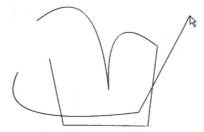

Not quite enough to make Picasso jealous, but pretty neat anyway.

How does it work?

As it stands, the basic code works as follows: all lines are drawn from point endX, endY to either the mouse position (_xmouse, _ymouse) for a line, or to (end2X, end2y) with the mouse position as the control point for the curve:

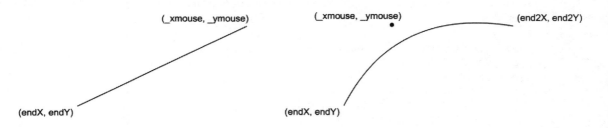

When drawing the current line style permanently to paper, the pen has two states: you've either clicked once (and the pen will draw a blue line) or twice (so the pen now needs to draw a red curve). This is controlled by the variable penToggle.

Fills

Okay, we're on to the final bit of the drawing API now – **fills**. Obviously, our poor virtual Flash turtle can only draw lines, so how do we visualize it drawing a fill? The answer is that it trundles around the **perimeter** of the area we want to fill and then politely asks the drawing API to fill the area it just defined. This perimeter is called the **fill path**, or just **path**.

Although the detail of the fill part of the drawing API is a little hairy, the fundamental principle is easy – as usual, we'll go straight to an example to show you how to use it.

Filling shapes

1. The first thing to do is to create a movie clip object to draw into. In a new FLA, attach the following script to frame 1:

```
createEmptyMovieClip("paper", 100);
```

2. Now that we have something to draw into, we want to draw round the edge of our shape. Here, we'll draw the square shown below:

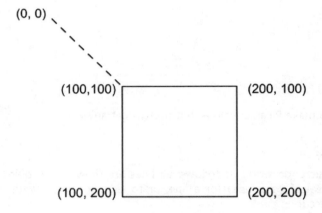

We have to move from the origin (0, 0) and draw out our square path. To do this, add the following lines:

```
paper.lineStyle(3, 0x000000, 100);
paper.moveTo(100, 100);
paper.lineTo(200, 100);
paper.lineTo(200, 200);
paper.lineTo(100, 200);
paper.lineTo(100, 100);
```

We have given our turtle a pen of thickness 3, black color (0x000000), and alpha 100%. Our turtle then moves from the start position to (100,100) and proceeds to draw round our perimeter in a clockwise direction. If you run the movie you will see the finished path drawn:

An important point to notice is that you must get the order of the corner points that you make the turtle visit correct. If they are out of sequence it will draw incorrectly, as the script below demonstrates:

```
createEmptyMovieClip("paper", 100);
paper.lineStyle(3, 0x000000, 100);
paper.moveTo(100, 100);
paper.lineTo(200, 200);
paper.lineTo(200, 100);
paper.lineTo(100, 200);
paper.lineTo(100, 100);
```

This looks like an hourglass or a rotated bow tie - clearly not what we want! Flash would still fill the path if we asked it to, but it would fill out the two enclosed triangles rather than the square we want filled.

3.   To fill our square, we first need to define our fill color. This is done via the beginFill method.

```
myClip.beginFill(color, alpha);
```

The color refers to the color of the fill, and you can also set the alpha. The beginFill also tells Flash one other important thing: essentially it says to the drawing API, 'I'm setting my turtle off on the path I want you to fill.' To tell Flash that the turtle is done, you simply include an endfill(x, y). Enter the following code in now:

```
createEmptyMovieClip("paper", 100);
paper.lineStyle(3, 0x000000, 100);
paper.beginFill(0xFF0000, 100);
paper.moveTo(100, 100);
paper.lineTo(200, 100);
paper.lineTo(200, 200);
paper.lineTo(100, 200);
paper.endFill(100, 100);
```

This script tells Flash that we have started to define around our path. It also tells Flash to fill with a red pen (0xFF0000) with 100% alpha. We then continue round our square as before (in the right order) to define the area to be filled. The last `lineTo` is now replaced by an `endFill`. This tells Flash to draw to the point (100, 100) and to fill the path defined by the turtle since the initial `beginFill`. You will see the red square with black border shown below if you run this FLA (or open up `fillSquare.fla`):

You can also make it out of curves instead of lines.

```
createEmptyMovieClip("paper", 100);
paper.lineStyle(3, 0x000000, 100);
paper.beginFill(0xFF0000, 100);
paper.moveTo(100, 100);
paper.lineTo(200, 100);
paper.lineTo(200, 200);
paper.lineTo(100, 200);
paper.curveTo(50, 150, 100, 100);
paper.endFill(100, 100);
```

This creates the shape below:

Notice that because we have to end our path definition with an `endFill`, and the line we want to end with is now a `curveTo`, we are a little stuck with the `endFill` since there are no more lines to create in our path. Instead, we simply `endFill` to the point we are already at (100, 100).

4. We can of course animate our filled shapes using `clear()` and redrawing a transformed version of the same shape every frame. You'll find the following code within the file `fillCartoon.fla`:

```
createEmptyMovieClip("paper", 100);
vertexX = new Array(100, 200, 200, 100);
vertexY = new Array(100, 100, 200, 200);

paper.onEnterFrame = function() {
  for (i=0; i<4; i++) {
    vertexX[i] += (Math.random()*10)-5;
    vertexY[i] += (Math.random()*10)-5;
  }
```

```
paper.clear();
paper.lineStyle(3, 0x000000, 100);
paper.beginFill(0xFF0000, 100);
paper.moveTo(vertexX[0], vertexY[0]);
paper.lineTo(vertexX[1], vertexY[1]);
paper.lineTo(vertexX[2], vertexY[2]);
paper.lineTo(vertexX[3], vertexY[3]);
paper.endFill(vertexX[0], vertexY[0]);
};
```

This time we're assigning the four points of our square to a couple of arrays. Our points are now (vertexX[0], vertexY[0]) to (vertexX[3], vertexY[3]), and we are varying their positions by a small random value every onEnterFrame (try different random increments for vertexX and vertexY, and different frame rates to find a nice organic animation).

Flash also allows you to define gradient fills. We would recommend that you don't use this for dynamic animation until you are fully up to speed with the solid color fills. It uses a number of objects to define the gradient, and, as with gradient fills generally, is a little slow if you try to animate your shapes as we have just done with solid fills.

Now that we have an idea of how the drawing API works, let's get our hands dirty and start playing. One of the cool things about the drawing API is that you can build up a generalized bit of code to draw something (the 'draw engine'), and then just go ahead and start playing about and experimenting. That's what the experts do in the recent *Flash Math Creativity* book, and we will do something similar, although we will keep the math rather closer to the ground, so don't worry!

First though, we need a starting point.

Kaleidoscope

My partner has a little kaleidoscope on a string. You twist it around and it creates lots of pretty patterns. It's all done with mirrors of course. In a kaleidoscope only one segment (the grayed out one in the following diagrams) actually contains the colored beads. The others are just reflections of it. I thought maybe I could do something similar, though to keep the math simpler, I'll base it on quadrants, rather than the kaleidoscope's eight-fold symmetry.

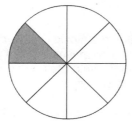
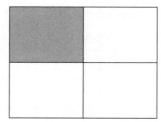

Lets go with this and have a look at the math.

Kaleidoscope math

To set up a kaleidoscope, we first need to understand how a real kaleidoscope works. Well, a kaleidoscope works via *reflections*. In math-speak, a reflection is simply a *copy*. There is a difference between the original and the reflections in a real kaleidoscope - the reflections are *rotated*. We rotate the original segment to create copies that form a circle. To do the same thing in Flash, we will need to perform a similar operation.

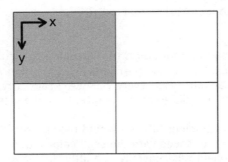

So, if the original segment has the orientation and position as shown, we need to *rotate* the other three copies. Generally, we need to rotate by 360/number of segments per segment. So if we have four segments, we need to rotate the first copy by 90 degrees, the second by 180, and the third by 270.

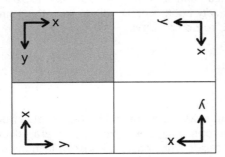
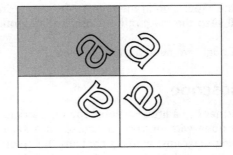

The next thing is to put that all into code...

Building the kaleidoscope engine

We will start off by drawing a simple shape (a rectangle) in a movie clip. To do that we need to select a line style and a fill color, and then move between the corner points within a `beginFill... endFill` set of actions. To define the corner points, it would be wise to hold them in an array, because we can then easily add more corner points later if we want to extend our code.

This function will draw out a general rectangle as shown. It will draw it within a movie clip specified by the argument `clip`, with a white border and a fill color defined by argument `color`.

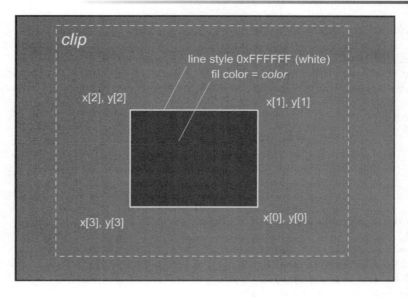

```
function drawQuad(clip, color) {
      path = _root[clip];
      path.lineStyle(0, 0xFFFFFF, 100);
      path.beginFill(color, 100);
      path.moveTo(x[0], y[0]);
      path.lineTo(x[1], y[1]);
      path.lineTo(x[2], y[2]);
      path.lineTo(x[3], y[3]);
      path.endFill(x[0], y[0]);
   }
```

It's not obvious how to create a rectangle without a border. To do this you can either set a linestyle with zero alpha, but this means that Flash will still draw a border (it's just that you can't see it). That's cool, but means that it still slows Flash down, and when you get to the heady heights of creating a 3D vector engine, you will want all the performance you can squeeze out of the Flash player. A better but somewhat obscure way to do it so that Flash doesn't even draw the lines is to set a linestyle of undefined. If you replace the line

```
path.lineStyle(0, 0xFFFFFF, 100);
```

...*with*

```
path.lineStyle(undefined, 0, 0);
```

Flash will not draw the lines at all, and your code will run faster because of it.

Okay. Let's use this function in a bit of code.

```
function drawQuad(clip, color) {
  path = _root[clip];
  path.lineStyle(0, 0xFFFFFF, 100);
  path.beginFill(color, 100);
  path.moveTo(x[0], y[0]);
  path.lineTo(x[1], y[1]);
  path.lineTo(x[2], y[2]);
  path.lineTo(x[3], y[3]);
  path.endFill(x[0], y[0]);
}

// Define screen extents for later use...

Stage.scaleMode = "exactFit";
middleX = Stage.width/2;
middleY = Stage.height/2;
Stage.scaleMode = "noScale";

// Define colors

color1 = 0x993333;
color2 = 0x119922;
color3 = 0xAAAA22;
color4 = 0x005599;

// create clip...

_root.createEmptyMovieClip("quad1", 100);
quad1._x = middleX;
quad1._y = middleY;

// Initialize points...

width = 100;
height = 100;
x = new Array();
y = new Array();
x[0] = 0;
y[0] = 0;
x[1] = 0;
y[1] = -height;
x[2] = -width;
y[2] = -height;
x[3] = -width;
y[3] = 0;
drawQuad("quad1", color1);
```

The additional code will create an empty movie clip called quad1 and place it in the center of the screen. It will then draw out a rectangle of height `height` and width `width`. This listing is included as `pattern01.fla`.

Okay, that's one static square. We are in the game of creating motion graphics though, so how do we make the drawing API create animated content? Well, we can clear all the content in a movie clip and redraw it. Change the function to include the `clear` line as shown here:

```
function drawQuad(clip, color) {
   path = _root[clip];
   path.clear();
   path.lineStyle(0, 0xFFFFFF, 100);
   path.beginFill(color, 100);
   path.moveTo(x[0], y[0]);
   path.lineTo(x[1], y[1]);
   path.lineTo(x[2], y[2]);
   path.lineTo(x[3], y[3]);
   path.endFill(x[0], y[0]);
}
```

This will clear the movie clip quad1 before we redraw. Now add the following code directly below the drawQuad() function:

```
_root.onEnterFrame = function() {
   for (i=0; i<4; i++) {
      x[i] += Math.random()*4-2;
      y[i] += Math.random()*4-2;
   }
   drawQuad("quad1", color1)
};
```

Also, delete this line from the end of the listing:

```
drawQuad("quad1", color1);
```

So what does this new code do? Well, it draws a new rectangle every frame, changing the position of the corner points every time, producing a 'wibbly' square.

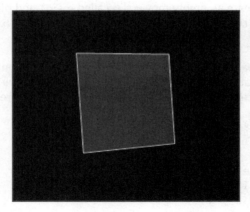

To create our kaleidoscope pattern, we need to create another three rotated versions of quad1. That's actually very easy. Change the 'create clip' section of code as follows:

```
// create clip...

_root.createEmptyMovieClip("quad1", 1);
quad1._x = middleX;
quad1._y = middleY;
_root.createEmptyMovieClip("quad2", 2);
quad2._x = middleX;
quad2._y = middleY;
_root.quad2._rotation = 90;
_root.createEmptyMovieClip("quad3", 3);
quad3._x = middleX;
quad3._y = middleY;
_root.quad3._rotation = 270;
_root.createEmptyMovieClip("quad4", 4);
quad4._x = middleX;
quad4._y = middleY;
_root.quad4._rotation = 180;
```

We also want to draw content into the new clips, so let's change the onEnterFrame:

```
_root.onEnterFrame = function() {
  for (i=0; i<4; i++) {
    x[i] += Math.random()*4-2;
    y[i] += Math.random()*4-2;
  }
  drawQuad("quad1", color1)
  drawQuad("quad2", color2)
  drawQuad("quad3", color3)
  drawQuad("quad4", color4)
};
```

Instead of just drawing in quad1, we are now drawing in all four quadrants, using different colors.

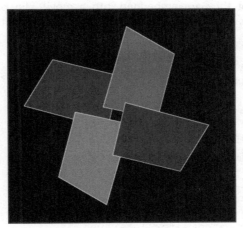

By changing the alpha values of the (now skewed) rectangles we are drawing via the function drawQuad, we can create some pretty overlapping patterns.

```
function drawQuad(clip, color) {
  path = _root[clip];
  path.clear();
  path.lineStyle(0, 0xFFFFFF, 40);
  path.beginFill(color, 70);
  path.moveTo(x[0], y[0]);
  path.lineTo(x[1], y[1]);
  path.lineTo(x[2], y[2]);
  path.lineTo(x[3], y[3]);
  path.endFill(x[0], y[0]);
}
```

Have a look at `pattern02.fla`, which develops this train of thought further, except this time we create our four quadrants so that they are embedded into a movie clip page4. This allows us to perform additional animation effects on our flower pattern. In this case, I have rotated the flower, by rotating the page4 clip.

```
function drawQuad(clip, color) {
  path = _root.page4[clip];
  path.clear();
  path.lineStyle(0, 0xFFFFFF, 40);
  path.beginFill(color, 70);
  path.moveTo(x[0], y[0]);
  path.lineTo(x[1], y[1]);
  path.lineTo(x[2], y[2]);
  path.lineTo(x[3], y[3]);
  path.endFill(x[0], y[0]);
}
// Define screen extents for later use...
Stage.scaleMode = "exactFit";
middleX = Stage.width/2;
middleY = Stage.height/2;
Stage.scaleMode = "noScale";

// Define colors

color1 = 0x993333;
color2 = 0x119922;
color3 = 0xAAAA22;
color4 = 0x005599;

// create clip...

_root.createEmptyMovieClip("page4", 100);
page4._x = middleX;
page4._y = middleY;
page4.createEmptyMovieClip("quad1", 1);
page4.createEmptyMovieClip("quad2", 2);
page4.quad2._rotation = 90;
page4.createEmptyMovieClip("quad3", 3);
page4.quad3._rotation = 270;
page4.createEmptyMovieClip("quad4", 4);
page4.quad4._rotation = 180;

// Initialize points...

width = 100;
height = 100;
x = new Array();
y = new Array();
x[0] = 0;
```

```
y[0] = 0;
x[1] = 0;
y[1] = -height;
x[2] = -width;
y[2] = -height;
x[3] = -width;
y[3] = 0;
page4.onEnterFrame = function() {
   for (i=1; i<4; i++) {
      x[i] += Math.random()*4-2;
      y[i] += Math.random()*4-2;
   }
   page4._rotation++
   drawQuad("quad1", color1);
   drawQuad("quad2", color2);
   drawQuad("quad3", color3);
   drawQuad("quad4", color4);
};
```

> Note that we have moved our onEnterFrame *event script to the end
> of the listing. We have to do this because I am now attaching the
> event to* page4, *and can only do that if* page4 *actually exists by the
> time the event script is seen by Flash. If I left the event script at the
> beginning, this would not be the case.*

We have something that has its moments, but it is just too slow and random. Have a look at pattern03.fla. This time, we have not only defined corner points, but given points 1, 2 and 3 a *speed* value (sX, sY) as well. Each quadrant moves around the screen area, and if it goes beyond border or width, it is bounced back by having its speed reversed (so that it changes direction back towards the inside of the allowed area).

```
// Initialize points...

width = 100;
height = 100;
x = new Array();
y = new Array();
sX = new Array();
sY = new Array();
x[0] = 0;
y[0] = 0;
x[1] = 0;
y[1] = -height;
x[2] = -width;
y[2] = -height;
x[3] = -width;
y[3] = 0;
```

```
    for (i=1; i<4; i++) {
      sX[i] = Math.random()*2+2;
      sY[i] = Math.random()*2+2;
    }
    page4.onEnterFrame = function() {
      for (i=1; i<4; i++) {
        x[i] += sX[i];
        y[i] += sY[i];
        if (Math.abs(x[i])>width) {
          sX[i] = -sX[i];
        }
        if (Math.abs(y[i])>height) {
          sY[i] = -sY[i];
        }
      }
      drawQuad("quad1", color1);
      drawQuad("quad2", color2);
      drawQuad("quad3", color3);
      drawQuad("quad4", color4);
    };
```

You don't have to constrain yourself to just four quadrants either. The file `patternBonus.fla` shows our kaleidoscope engine modified to handle 16 segments, and it begins to look like a true kaleidoscope.

Notice how this listing uses a `for` loop to draw each of the 16 quadrants (as highlighted):

```
    // create clip...

    _root.createEmptyMovieClip("page4", 100);
    page4._x = middleX;
    page4._y = middleY;
    for (i=0; i<16; i++) {
      page4.createEmptyMovieClip("quad"+i, i);
      page4["quad"+i]._rotation = i*(360/16);
    }

    // Initialize points...
```

```
[code we've seen before omitted]

page4.onEnterFrame = function() {
  for (i=1; i<4; i++) {
    x[i]  += sX[i];
    y[i]  += sY[i];
    if (Math.abs(x[i])>width) {
      sX[i] = -sX[i];
    }
    if (Math.abs(y[i])>height) {
      sY[i] = -sY[i];
    }
  }
  for (i=0; i<16; i++) {
    drawQuad("quad"+i, 0x0);
  }
};
```

The final two files in the download for this section start to move away from the concept of the kaleidoscope (but use what is essentially the same code) to create a totally new effect that users of Windows may recognize as similar to the **mystify** screensavers that ship with their operating system. There are two versions, **stunMystify**, which uses filled curved shapes, and **stunMystifyRetro**, for those who (like me) enjoy the old school stuff, complete with simple vectors...

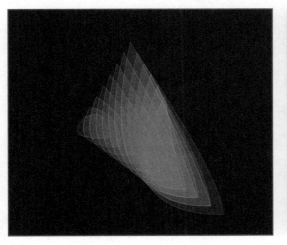 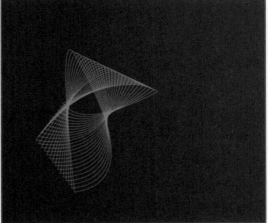

This sort of experimentation with Flash to create new effects is one way of creating code that may one day be re-purposed as part of a new site navigation. By making such experimentation open source, designers like Joshua Davis made a name for themselves early in Flash's history.

Summary

We've seen in this chapter that by using the drawing API, it's possible to *create* motion graphics via ActionScript, not just manipulate graphics that you've previously created in Flash.

It is somewhat ironic that you started out with Flash working in a purely visual way – it was all tweens with no code. And yet here we've produced quite impressive visual effects purely by using ActionScript – there's nothing else in the FLAs. I bet that when you began this book, you never thought you'd end up here...

In the next chapter we'll be going back to the stun:design website we began in chapter 8, and put some of the advanced techniques you've been learning over the previous chapters into practice.

Coding the stun:design site

What we'll cover in this chapter:

- *Creating our UI animation*
- *Adding forwards and backwards functionality*
- *Adding sound and content to our site*

You've nearly reached the end of the book, and have learned an awful lot – I hope you realize just how far you've come. In this chapter, we're going to finish coding the stun:design site we started building in Chapter 8. By the end of this chapter you'll have a framework into which you can slot content to produce a truly stunning, modern, and cool website.

Section 5 - Adding the basic UI animation

In the last section of Chapter 8 we ended our work on the DEFINE EVENT SCRIPTS part of the listing with a simple script that returned which strip we had pressed. We'll have a look at extending this and creating the first, very basic, event-driven animation to actually start animating the UI.

In doing this we'll take a look at how I started planning this via **UI storyboards**, little sketches that gave me an idea of how the interface should move, and how to achieve this. The storyboards are the actual FLAs I used early on in the design to visualize how to convert the ideas I had in my head into code. Here's a complete example.

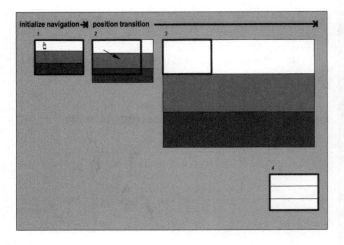

This proves that coding is a visual process. My code was written to a set of drawings, and this is true of commercially written code in anything from long-range missile global position/navigation systems with low level flying (Map Of Earth/MOE) digital autopilots, to all but the simplest web scripts

Without looking at the diagrams, and going straight to the code for stun:design, you'd just look at it and go 'Whoa! Where do I start with this?'. With the diagrams, you start to see the intent, and more importantly, you see how the code is just a symbolic representation of our drawings that the computer can understand. Coding and drawing are closer than most graphic designers may suppose, it's just a well-kept secret!

So far we have the three strips outputting a message when we click on them. What we actually want to do is something like this. When we click on a strip, we need to **initialize the navigation**. This is what the current navigate function will eventually do (it is step 1 in the storyboard). We then need to animate the navigation. We can split this into two separate parts.

The first transition is the zoom/pan **position transition**. This is where the selected strip zooms and pans so that it fills the screen (step 3 above). There's actually a trick at the end where the three strips flick back to their original positions as well, and this involves a color change so that all three strips take on the selected strip's color, and look the same as a single strip on its own (step 4). This step needs us to be really sneaky, because the user isn't supposed to see it!

After this, we need to fade our strips into three new colors via a **color transition**, and this takes us back to step 1. If we actually want to display content at step 4 rather than present further navigation options, we simply leave the three strips as the same color, as shown in step 4 above.

Let's build the core events that will handle these transitions. Navigate is our initialization event script, and it's attached to the button scripts via the function we have already looked at, stripEvents. posTransition will do the zoom and pan part, and finally, colTransition will do the final color transition if we need to present further navigation options (we'll look at colTransition in the next section, and concentrate on building the first two functions in this section). The additional lines you need to add to get to this point are shown below. Alternatively, have a look at stun_section5_part1.fla.

```
// DEFINE EVENT SCRIPTS

navigate = function () {
  // intitialize navigation here
  trace("");
  trace("you pressed me and I am"), trace(this._name);
  trace("I am initializing this navigation...");
  // then start navigation graphical transition...
  this.onEnterFrame = posTransition;
};
posTransition = function () {
  // now do the actual animation...
  trace("I am now animating the zoom and pan effect");
  // we have now done the position transition...
  this.onEnterFrame = undefined;
  // we next do the color transition...
  tricolor.onEnterFrame = colTransition;
};
colTransition = function () {
  // We finally do the color transition that makes the tricolor
  // split back into 3 here
  trace("I am now animating the color transition");
  // finally, remove all event scripts...
  trace("I have finished this navigation");
  tricolor.onEnterFrame = undefined;
  trace(""), trace(""), trace("");
};
```

If you test this FLA, you still won't see any animation, but all the steps in our storyboard are being output to the screen in the order we want them to. Each event handler runs and then calls the next one in the sequence...

```
you pressed me and I am
strip1_mc
I am initializing this navigation...
I am now animating the zoom and pan effect
I am now animating the color transition
I have finished this navigation
```

We've arranged our *events in the correct order before we start adding the actual functionality.* This is an important feature of using functions; you can add them as placeholders to define the structure. Once you have that right, you can go ahead and look at each function in isolation, fleshing out the code.

The next step is to define each event so that it starts actually moving things. In each function, the process is the same.

- Draw or otherwise visualize what it is you want to happen

- Convert it into code

navigate and posTransition

Navigate has to initialize the animation. It has to define the start and end position of our animation. Let's call the start position x, y and the end position targetX, targetY. To initialize, we have to know what x, y and targetX, targetY is in terms of (1) things we understand and then (2) in terms of things the computer understands.

For (1), we're out with the pencil and paper again.

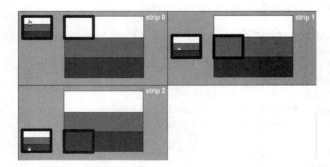

In each strip, the small image is what the site looks like before we click on a strip, and the large image is what the site will look like after the **position transition** has occurred. The solid black frame is the visible screen area. Looks like an IQ test, and that's what it probably is:

Q1 – What is the relationship between the three small images and the three big images next to them, expressed in terms of anything you can see in the picture?

No peeking! You have one minute... Okay, time's up.

A1 - When you click on any strip, the top left hand corner of the strip moves to the top left hand corner of the visible screen area. As it does this, the tricolor **clip also trebles in size.**

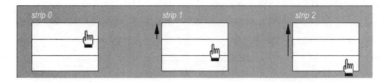

Q2 - For an extra 3 points (and the game), express the transition mathematically in terms of what you already know.

Now it gets a bit more tricky!

At the risk of stating the obvious, we know the transition is a position-based one, but less obviously, we also therefore have to express the answer in terms of positions only.

The starting position of `tricolor` is the top left hand corner (`border, border`).

At the risk of stating the obvious again (I have to, because I'm simply reiterating my thought processes in designing this site to give you an insight), the final position must be *related* to something that's to do with the three strips, because that is the only known thing that changes. I knew half the answer fairly quickly by looking at the existing drawings so far; the tricolor has to move a distance equal to the distance l shown below;

- If you hit `strip0`, the distance l (shown as l0 in the diagram overleaf) is zero.

- If you hit `strip1`, the distance is l1, and it's l2 if you hit `strip2`.

This distance is always actually the same; it's the *distance the selected strip is away from the top left corner*. It took me a while to work this out, because one of the lengths was actually zero; the top strip is already at the top left corner point, which threw me.

> *The moral of this is that zero is never a special case; it's a number just like any other, and if your logic assumes it is a special case, it's probably because your logic is flawed.*

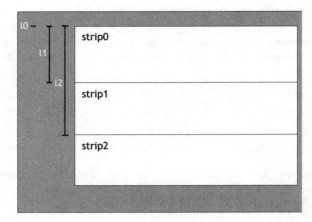

The distance of the center point of any given strip to the corner point you want to move it to is *always*

    -this._y

where this is the strip you have selected *inside* tricolor, and we're taking into account the *direction* you have to move as well (that's what the – sign does). However, the tricolor is also scaled up by 300% so that a single strip grows enough to fill the screen. We therefore also have to increase this length by the same amount.

    -3*this._y

We'll use this to move tricolor rather than the selected strip (so that all three strips move rather than just one), and we also need to take into account the fact that we don't want to move to the top left hand corner of the screen, but to the border:

    (-3*this._y)+border

Or, more simply:

    -3*this._y+border

Note that we don't need to worry about the x position – the elements are already at the required x position. A number of variations on this navigation require changes in x as well as y, and we'll consider these at the end of the project.

So we have our answer.

A2 – We already know which strip we've selected from the last chapter, because the script prints this in the Output **window every time we press on a strip. If we call this strip** this, **then the position we want to move to, relative to the center point, is**

    -3*this._y+border

and we also need to scale the movie clip containing the 3 strips, tricolor, **from 100% to 300%.**

Now replace the navigate function with this:

```
navigate = function () {
    // set up target for animation transition...
    s=100, x=border, y=border;
    yTarget = -3*this._y+border;
    sTarget = 300;
    // attach the animation transition to the
    // strip that has just been pressed...
    this.onEnterFrame = posTransition;
};
```

... and the posTransition function with this:

```
posTransition = function () {
    s = sTarget
    y = yTarget;
    tricolor._y = y;
    tricolor._xscale = tricolor._yscale = s
};
```

Alternatively, just have a look at stun_section5_part2.fla.

When you press a strip, that strip fills the screen. You can only do it once at the moment (as soon as you press a strip, the other strips disappear off-screen, so run it three times, pressing one of the three strips each time).

> To keep things simple, we are only developing the forward navigation to start with; you will not be able to go back yet. At this stage you will have to run the FLA again if you want to test navigating forward from a different starting point. To create the ability to go back through the navigation requires us to be able to store the path we take when moving forward, and this means that we really need to make sure we have the forward bit sorted out first.

So now we have run this (as yet still very basic) animation, let's have a look at the code we just added. Navigate sets up our starting position (y) and size (s) and our target destination (yTarget) and size (sTarget). Navigate is our onRelease event, and this starts up the posTransition animation. posTransition simply makes tricolor go to the final destination in one go.

Let's slow it down a little. We'll divide the distance between where we want to get to (yTarget, sTarget) into a number of steps, and call this number of steps step. We''ll then move towards where we want to be by this amount every onEnterFrame until we've done this step times, by when we'll be at our target position. Change the navigate and posTransition functions as shown (or for the lazy, have a look at stun_section5_part3.fla):

```
navigate = function () {
  // set up target for animation transition...
  s=100, x=border, y=border;
  yTarget = -3*this._y+border;
  sTarget = 300;
  step = 15;
  yStep = (yTarget-y)/step;
  sStep = (sTarget-s)/step;
  // attach the animation transition to the
  // strip that has just been pressed...
  this.onEnterFrame = posTransition;
};
posTransition = function () {
  s += sStep;
  y += yStep;
  tricolor._y = y;
  tricolor._xscale = tricolor._yscale=s;
  step--;
  if (step == 0) {
    this.onEnterFrame = undefined;
  }
};
```

Getting better! You may be getting a bit worried about the fact that you can see the other pages in the final state when the animation stops. If you test the FLA in a browser (CONTROL + F12), you'll see that the off screen stuff is not displayed, and that as the pages travel off screen they are hidden by that border we added earlier.

The final site uses a slightly different movement. Rather than linear motion, it uses an **inertial** motion. This creates a faster transition that can also appear smoother. To add inertial motion, change the functions as shown.

```
navigate = function () {
  // set up target for animation transition...
  s=100, x=border, y=border;
  yTarget = -3*this._y+border;
  sTarget = 300;
  // attach the animation transition to the
  // strip that has just been pressed...
  this.onEnterFrame = posTransition;
};
posTransition = function () {
  s -= (s-sTarget)/4;
  y -= (y-yTarget)/4;
  tricolor._y = y;
  tricolor._xscale = tricolor._yscale=s;
};
```

If you've taken our advice and installed the really useful 'center in browser' extension way back in the intro, you'll be able to publish the site as per the final stun site on the web, www.stundesign.com. In the HTML tab of the File > Publish Settings dialog, set Template: to Flash only (centered) and the Dimensions: to Match Movie.

> *The Flash only (centered) option is not available on the standard Flash MX install.*

Okay, we now need to do our little trick to 'put the tricolor back to the starting position without anyone knowing' sneakiness.

In function `posTransition`, add the following lines:

```
posTransition = function () {
   s -= (s-sTarget)/4;
   y -= (y-yTarget)/4;
   tricolor._y = y;
   tricolor._xscale = tricolor._yscale=s;
   if (Math.abs(s-sTarget)<5) {
      // if so, disconnect this function from onEnterframe...
      this.onEnterFrame = undefined;
      // then place tricolor back at start position...
      tricolor._y = border;
      tricolor._xscale = tricolor._yscale=100;
   }
};
```

This returns `tricolor` to its original position, but it's a little obvious to say the least! What we need to do is find out the color of the selected strip, and apply it to all three strips.

The color of each strip, `stripn_mc` where n = 0, 1 or 2 is held in variable `colorn` where n = 0, 1, 2. Obviously then, n is the key. To get n from the name of the selected strip, we use the following method of the `String` object:

```
substring(5, 6)
```

We apply that to the name of the current strip:

```
selectedStrip = this._name.substring(5, 6);
```

This will return 0, 1, or 2.

To form the required `colorn` variable (or more specifically, `_root.colorn`), we do this:

```
selectedCol = _root["color"+selectedStrip];
```

If `selectedStrip` is 2, `_root["color"+selectedStrip]` will give us `_root.color2`.

Okay, we're almost there. Add the following code to `posTransition`:

```
posTransition = function () {
   s -= (s-sTarget)/4;
   y -= (y-yTarget)/4;
   tricolor._y = y;
   tricolor._xscale = tricolor._yscale=s;
   if (Math.abs(s-sTarget)<5) {
      // if so, disconnect this function from onEnterframe...
      this.onEnterFrame = undefined;
      // then place tricolor back at start position...
      tricolor._y = border;
      tricolor._xscale = tricolor._yscale=100;
      selectedStrip = this._name.substring(5, 6);
      selectedCol = _root["color"+selectedStrip];
      tricolor.setCol(selectedCol, selectedCol, selectedCol);
   }
};
```

If you test the FLA now, you'll see the color of all three strips change on the snap-back. We're calling our previously defined function `setCol`. We used this in the last section to turn the gray strips to the three colorful ones.

The text gives the game away a little, but we can soon fix that by hiding it.

We'll fade the text whilst the transition occurs. To do this we need a value that goes from 100% alpha to 0% as the transition takes place. We already have one that goes from 100% to 300%, and that's the `s` value that controls scale. It's a good idea to follow the scale value, turning it to what we want, because then our text fade will be in synch with the transition itself.

To change the 100% - 300% of `s` to 100% - 0 of our new variable (say `fadeAlpha`) we do this:

```
fadeAlpha = 300-s;
```

We also need to change all three text fields' `_alpha` values to this, so let's create a function to do this. If we are hiding the text, we'll more than likely have to unhide it again later, so we might as well make our code re-usable!

Add the following new lines in function `posTransition`:

```
posTransition = function () {
   s -= (s-sTarget)/4;
   y -= (y-yTarget)/4;
   fadeAlpha = 300-s;
   tricolor._y = y;
   tricolor._xscale = tricolor._yscale=s;
   fadeText(fadeAlpha);
   if (Math.abs(s-sTarget)<5) {
      // if so, disconnect this function from onEnterframe...
```

```
        this.onEnterFrame = undefined;
        // then place tricolor back at start position...
        tricolor._y = border;
        tricolor._xscale = tricolor._yscale=100;
        selectedStrip = this._name.substring(5, 6);
        selectedCol = _root["color"+selectedStrip];
        tricolor.setCol(selectedCol, selectedCol, selectedCol);
    }
};
```

This uses a new function called `fadeText` with our new `fadeAlpha` variable. We still need to define the function, though. After the end of `colTransition`, add the new function `fadeText` as shown.

```
fadeText = function (fadeValue) {
   var fadeValue;
   tricolor.strip0_txt._alpha = fadeValue;
   tricolor.strip1_txt._alpha = fadeValue;
   tricolor.strip2_txt._alpha = fadeValue;
};
```

If you run the FLA now, you'll see that we've now successfully done our sneaky switch-aroundy. You should test the site in a browser to see the full deception (CONTROL+F12), and then run it in normal test mode (CONTROL + ENTER) to see what's going on behind the scenes.

The FLA for this point is included as `stun_section5_part4.fla` and implements the storyboards so far. What we want to do now is create a *new* tricolor full of three new strips.

> *At some point the navigation will have to display pages of content as well as simply linking to new pages, but we'll come to that part in due course. At the moment we're really only concerned with getting the main concept working. We've already largely decided where content needs to go in our navigation (the area on the inside edge of the border area), so we're not belittling the need for there to be content later, it's just that our UI scripts are not yet ready to support it.*

We still have a pretty unfinished site, but we're moving forward at a pace now. We only need to bring in the `colTransition` event script to complete the main site graphic transitions.

The use of diagrams that define how the code works and what it actually needs to do is one of the cool things about Flash. You don't put away the drawing pencils when you start coding. Most of the time you'll need to sharpen them and get ready for half an hour of playing about and experimenting on paper, before trying your ideas out in ActionScript and the Flash environment.

This can be an exciting and rewarding pastime in itself, because, unlike traditional graphic design, with Flash you don't end up with pretty logos and typography – you end up with things that *move*.

I remember the first site I put together. For ages it was a load of ideas on paper and graphic mockups in Photoshop, but over a few days something changed as it got fed into Flash; *it started to come alive*. It moved and reacted.

That's where Flash is totally different, and if you're just looking over the diagrams and sketches in this section, you'll never get the feel of Flash. It's all about *motion* and saying '*look at that move! Cool, this is going somewhere!*'

And the best thing of all is that Flash is still relatively new, so you might be the first person who's done it your way, and the web is out there waiting to see it.

Section 6 - Finishing the forward navigation

In this section, we'll complete the event driven site animations. We'll then start to think about adding some data to allow Flash to create the site structure.

So far we have got the position transition sorted out, but the color transition is not implemented. At the moment, when we click on a strip, the selected strip zooms in correctly, but doesn't split off into three new strips to present further navigation options to take us deeper into the site.

Wiring colTransition in

At the moment the function `colTransition` is neither completed nor linked up to our previous events, `navigate` and `posTransition`.

Let's link `posTransition` up to our `colTransition` first.

At the end of the last section, the end of `posTransition` and the beginning of `colTransition`, we had this in our file `stun_section5_part4.fla`:

```
            this.onEnterFrame = undefined;
            // then place tricolor back at start position...
            tricolor._y = border;
            tricolor._xscale = tricolor._yscale=100;
            selectedStrip = this._name.substring(5, 6);
            selectedCol = _root["color"+selectedStrip];
            tricolor.setCol(selectedCol, selectedCol, selectedCol);
        }
    };
    colTransition = function () {
        // We finally do the color transition that makes the page
        // split back into 3 here
```

We need to 'wire up' the `colTransition` function into our animation sequence so far. To reach the starting point for our initial file in this chapter, `stun_section6_part1.fla`, we have changed the line

```
        this.onEnterFrame = undefined;
```

at the end of `posTransition` to

```
this.onEnterFrame = colTransition;
```

This means that when we've finished the position transition, we'll move on to the final phase of our navigation transition, the color transition that splits the page back into three strips. Now that we've wired `colTransition` into the loop, we can concentrate on this function and get it working. To allow us to do this quickly, we've also got rid of all the previous placeholder code within `colTransition`.

The game plan...

So what do we want to do? You guessed it, storyboard time! Everyone sitting comfortably? Then I'll begin...

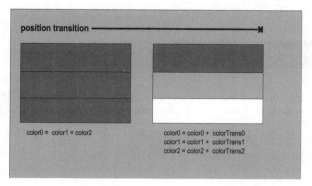

At the start of the color transition, we have all three strip colors the same. We need to fade them to three colors that are different from the original color, and different from each other.

We'll do this by making all three final colors brighter, and we do this by adding something to the current color value. The storyboard above shows us adding three values `colorTrans0` to `colorTrans2`. So our `colTransition` code has to fade from the three mono-colored strips to the three uniquely colored strips on the right.

Okay, that's the direction we'll take. We now need to know how to implement it. There are two things we need to know:

- How do we perform the fade so that it is smooth?
- What will our target colors (`color+colorTrans`) be?

Fading color

If we wanted to fade between black (0x000000) to white (0xFFFFFF), in a gradual transition, how would we do it?

Well, we could simply add 1 to the starting color every frame, until we reach the final target color, white. That doesn't actually work. You don't get a smooth transition from black to white through all the grays; you get a transition from black to white that goes through all the colors of the rainbow!

The way to do it is rather like you mix colors in the Color mixer panel when you create new colors with the RGB model; you treat the red, green, and blue components *separately*. So to move from black to white, while only sticking to the colors that are actually between black and white (i.e. all the grays) rather than different hues (red, blue, green, etc), we have to add 1 to the red component, one to the green component and one to the blue component every time.

That gives you 256 different steps (0 to FF for each color channel R, G and B). That's actually a lot of colors, so instead we'll add a larger number. I'll be changing the green and blue channels only during the transitions, because I want the new strips to be fairly close to each other to give a more subtle color graduation. Leaving one color channel fixed has this effect.

Red also tends to add 'warmth' to an RGB color, and keeping this the same will make for pages that seem to have a consistent 'mood'.

Coding the color transition

1. Anyway, let's get coding. We first need to define our color variables. Add the following in the INITIALIZE section (or have a look at stun_section6_part2.fla):

    ```
    // Define initial screen colors (further colors will
    // use these colors as their seed)

    color0 = 0x993333;
    color1 = 0x119922;
    color2 = 0x005577;
    colTrans = new Array();
    colTrans = [0x000880, 0x001100, 0x002280];
    ```

    This defines our target colors when we want to re-color our strip; color0's target now becomes color0+colTrans[0], color1's target is color1+colTrans[1], and so on. Notice that color0 is the closest to the original color, and color2 is the furthest away (because we're adding a bigger value to it).

    Finally, we need to use these values to form a new set of colors. We will use a variable that contains the level of change we are applying to the color transition, fadeColor. This will be initially zero, and we will initialize it at the end of the posTransition phase.

    ```
        selectedStrip = this._name.substring(5, 6);
        selectedCol = _root["color"+selectedStrip];
        tricolor.setCol(selectedCol, selectedCol, selectedCol);
        fadeColor = 0;
      }
    };
    ```

> Note that function posTransition *was attached to the strip that was pressed, and not* tricolor. colTransition *will be attached again to the same place; the strip that was pressed. Our event scripts are really 'super button scripts' that go on for as many frames as it takes to complete the animation stages*

2.   Add the following code to replace the existing colTransition:

```
colTransition = function () {
  fadeColor += 0x000202;
  if (fadeColor<colTrans[0]) {
    tricolor.colstrip0.setRGB(selectedCol+fadeColor);
  }
  if (fadeColor<colTrans[1]) {
    tricolor.colStrip1.setRGB(selectedCol+fadeColor);
  }
  if (fadeColor<colTrans[2]) {
    tricolor.colStrip2.setRGB(selectedCol+fadeColor);
  } else {
    // we are now at the new page...
    color0 = tricolor.colStrip0.getRGB();
    color1 = tricolor.colStrip1.getRGB();
    color2 = tricolor.colStrip2.getRGB();
    this.onEnterFrame = undefined;
  }
};
```

So what does this do? Well, what we're doing is slowly incrementing fadeColor. This increases from 0x000000, which means it starts off as black and slowly gets brighter. We add this color to the starting colors, color0, 1 and 2, and using the color objects colStrip0-2 we defined earlier via function stripCols, we gradually add fadeColor to the existing strip colors. We stop adding this new color to each strip once it has reached its target color, colTrans.

Because strip 2 is the one with the highest colTrans value, we know all three color transitions are completed when this one is done, so that's when we stop. When we've completed the full color change, we replace the original colors with the new strip colors.

```
color0 = tricolor.colStrip0.getRGB();
color1 = tricolor.colStrip1.getRGB();
color2 = tricolor.colStrip2.getRGB();
```

This means that the colors are unique for each page in the site, and these colors tell you something about where you are in the navigation. In fact, if you look at the finished site (linked to from friends of ED.com,) you may notice that apart from the stun logo and strap line, everything else is tied in to the navigation; the colors, the text, in fact, *everything except the content!* There are no little graphical extras to 'make it look nice', and this is part of its charm; the pared down design has a very modern feel to it (the fact that the core UI comes in at about 12-15k once it is on the web is also cool).

As you navigate through the FLA with the new code in place, you will notice two things:

- We have forgotten to bring the text back once the new page is created.
- If you navigate too far into the site, the colors start to break up, and you lose the graded color scheme.

We will sort out the first problem in a moment. The second problem is something we're seeing because we're going much further into the navigation than would normally be expected. Normally, the 'three-click' rule applies – if the user cannot get where they want to go within three clicks, your site has poor navigation. We will arrange the content later so that all pages can be reached within three clicks, and the color break up will never be seen.

> *The technical reason for the breakup is that we have overflowed on one of the color channels. One of the channels (blue or green, because those are the ones we are changing in the transition) has gone over 0xFF. We lose the subtle tonal changes when this happens because we have suddenly shifted to a different position on the color spectrum*

Finishing the text transition

1. Bringing the text back again is actually remarkably easy because we already have the function to fade text (fadeText). All we have to do is set up the variable we used to fade the text out so that this time, we fade back in (and you can see the changes in stun_section6_part3.fla if you don't want to do the typing):

```
selectedCol = _root["color"+selectedStrip];
   tricolor.setCol(selectedCol, selectedCol, selectedCol);
   fadeColor = 0;
   fadeAlpha = 0;
   }
};
colTransition = function () {
  fadeColor += 0x000202;
  fadeAlpha += 4;
  fadeText(fadeAlpha);
  if (fadeColor<colTrans[0]) {
    tricolor.colstrip0.setRGB(selectedCol+fadeColor);
  }
  if (fadeColor<colTrans[1]) {
    tricolor.colStrip1.setRGB(selectedCol+fadeColor);
```

```
    }
    if (fadeColor<colTrans[2]) {
      tricolor.colStrip2.setRGB(selectedCol+fadeColor);
    } else {
      // we're now at the new page...
      color0 = tricolor.colStrip0.getRGB();
      color1 = tricolor.colStrip1.getRGB();
      color2 = tricolor.colStrip2.getRGB();
      fadeText(100)
      this.onEnterFrame = undefined;
    }
  };
```

At the end of the routine, we've explicitly set the text alpha value to 100. This is to make sure that we end up with fully faded in text even if we make the other transitions quicker (in which case the alpha fade would not be finished in time).

Reviewing the code so far

If you have a look at the FLA in test mode, you'll now be able to see the full color transition of our UI, and how the variables and events change as the animations progress if you test the FLA in debug mode. Have a look at the variables tab of root (level0), and the way the various color and fade variables change two distinct ways as posTransition and colTransition are at work. It's almost like a watching a clockwork mechanism.

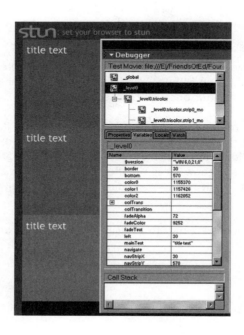

You can also have a look at the true relationship between `tricolor` and the three strips inside it by having a look at the variables tab for their timelines:

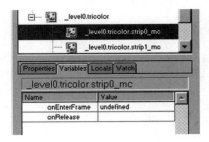

The `tricolor` movie clip is simply a carrier of the three strips and the background functions to drive it all. The individual `strip` movie clips are the things that control the animation (via the `onRelease` events, which are always attached to the strips) and initiate the animation, and control the `onEnterFrame` events which become attached to the `strip` that was pressed once animation takes place.

Notice also that the `onEnterFrame` events that control the animation become undefined as soon as the animation navigation has completed. So what does Flash do when there are no animations going on? *Nothing!*

It just sits there, waiting for a mouse click on one of the three strips. That's actually a *very good thing*. Some Flash designers blame Macromedia for sluggish graphics, but that's usually because their UI code is always running in the background, and this makes the final content sluggish. Our UI takes up none of the Flash player's precious performance budget when it's not doing anything, and that makes our site processor friendly – it will never be the cause of performance bottlenecks that our final content may experience!

Cool Flash UIs that are always animating even when the user is not interacting with it are cool as long as they know when to stop and get on with the important task of providing quick and responsive navigation, and then let the content do its stuff once it's reached.

Talking of content and site structure, our site so far is very colorful. It has the look of a Pantone swatches book (the ones all graphic designers look at and say 'Wow, that looks kind of cool, if only we could actually do something that looks as colorful as that!'). Guess what, that was one of the influences to this site. I've always wanted to somehow design a site that looked like a swatch book or a paint swatch brochure. However, we don't really seem to be *going anywhere*. We always end up at pages marked '*title text*'.

In this final part of this section, we'll turn to actually adding some structure to our navigation.

Thinking about navigation

The whole site so far kind of does something like this:

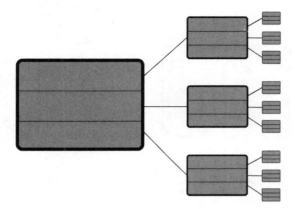

There's a home page, and clicking on any strip zooms us into a new page, which then magically splits again into another three-strip. This goes on forever, taking us down an endless series of three-way crossroads. We need to add some information here to tell Flash how to do this in a structured way that allows us to:

- Add unique titles for each page.
- Form definite paths. This includes the ability to close off certain paths where we don't want all three strips to take us somewhere.
- Allow us to add a new type of page that doesn't turn into more `linkPages` but allows us to display content (`contentPages`).

And while we're at it, we might as well push the boat out and add some other cool stuff that normal tween-based sites can't do; we'll make the content general by adding the following.

- Allowing us to define the content as something that is currently in the library
- Allowing us to define content that needs loading in as a SWF file

Wow! That's a lot of stuff. Now there are two ways we could do this. One is that we could define a set of arrays for each full page, and the other is that we could have all the information for the full site in one place. We're coming on in leaps and bounds, so we will go for the latter, because we're feeling confident about all this.

To do this we need to set up a set of **records**, one per page. Within each record, we will have **fields** that define each page, covering all the above information in a structured way.

> *So, our site is structured on at least two levels; the code itself is written in a structured way using functions, and on another level, the data that drives the actual content is itself also structured!*

So, exactly what bits of information do we need to know? Well, for the pages we have seen so far (pages that link to other pages or `linkPages`) we have:

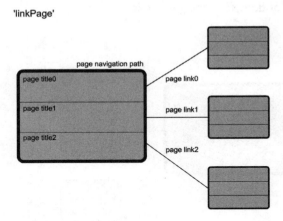

We need to know:

- Three items that define links to other pages.
- Three page title strings plus one page navigation path. We can either get the UI to work this last one out, or just put up a string that we have defined (we will go for the latter).

If the page will actually show some content, we want another game plan that looks something like this:

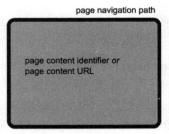

Here, we're more concerned about the content we'll show. We need to know:

- The movie clip linkage identifier if we're going to pull content from the Flash library.

- The URL that the content lives at if it's a SWF.

Now here's the big question. If we wanted to represent all this information as a *general* set of data that Flash could understand, how would we do it?

Well, we know about arrays from Chapter 2, but we couldn't really use them, because an array only stores a *list*. We need something more structured. The answer is that we need to produce an *object*.

As you learned earlier in the book, objects have properties that describe them. Properties are just raw data, and it's up to us to decide what the properties mean. Well, we have some information we want to define for our site, so how about we do that? *Property* is just a fancy programmer way of saying 'thing that describes something'. Well, we have a bunch of things that we want to describe our web pages, so how about we do that with this odd *Object* thing?

We need several properties, but there's a problem. We have two kinds of page! How do we do it? Well, we can have two objects, one for the content pages, and one for the link pages. That is not how programmers think; they like to *generalize*. In this context, generalize means 'what do we have to do for there to be only one kind of page? See if you can guess, without going on to the answer...

The answer is *we make the page type a property as well!*

So we'll have a thing called page with properties as follows (all of which I've taken from the previous diagrams):

- Page type

- Page links

- Page titles

- Page content linkage identifier

- Page content URL

And that's everything we need to define our site pages. In fact, in principle, it's almost enough to define *any* web page!

> *The final product of this little trial is included as* stun_database.fla

So let's create an object in Flash that has these properties. Open a new FLA (you can do this even if you already have something else open in Flash) and type this in frame 1 of the Actions panel.

```
page = new Object();
page.pType = "this is the page type; content or linking";
page.plink = "this defines all the page links";
page.pTitle = "this is the page navigation title";
page.pID = "this is the content linkage identifier";
page.pURL = "this is the content URL";
```

Test the FLA in debug mode again. This time you'll find this in the variable tab of _level0:

Name	Value
$version	"WIN 6,0,21,0"
⊟ page	
pID	"this is the content linkage identifier"
plink	"this defines all the page links"
pTitle	"this is the page navigation title"
pType	"this is the page type; content or linking"
pURL	"this is the content URL"

Okay, so now you're thinking, that's fine, but some of the properties of our pages have properties of their own. For example, the pTitle part will need four titles, one for each strip, and one for the navigation bit at the top right. So we're stumped, right? Well, sort of. There are two ways to fix this problem.

One is to build a constructor function that creates sub-properties. The other, much simpler way is to use the fact that properties can be *any* primitive data type themselves, and that includes strings, numbers, Booleans and **arrays**.

If we go through and define our properties as the actual variable types we need, and make those that contain multiple sub-properties into arrays, we can encapsulate all our descriptive data for a single page into a single object. Let's do that now. Change our code as follows:

```
page = new Object();
page.pType = new String();
page.plink = new Array();
page.pTitle = new Array();
page.pID = new String();
page.pURL = new String();
```

This gives us a structure to our properties, but doesn't put any data in it. We should do that next. Add the following lines to what you have so far:

```
// add the data for a general page...
page.pType = "linkPage or contentPage";
page.pLink = ["strip0 link", "strip1 link", "strip2 link"];
page.pTitle = ["navigation", "strip0 title", "strip1 title",
"strip2 title"];
page.pID = "content library identifier (optional)";
page.pURL = "content URL (optional)";
```

Now run the FLA in debug mode again. This time you'll see a much larger structure of properties. In fact, there are enough branches on our tree to *fully define our two kinds of page*. We have all the titles, where to get the content from, and the list of links (including the back button link) of each page.

Name			Value
	$version		"WIN 6,0,21,0"
⊟	page		
		pID	"content library identifier (optional)"
	⊟	pLink	
		0	"strip0 link"
		1	"strip1 link"
		2	"strip2 link"
	⊟	pTitle	
		0	"navigation"
		1	"strip0 title"
		2	"strip1 title"
		3	"strip2 title"
		pType	"linkPage or contentPage"
		pURL	"content URL (optional)"

In the same way that the folder your doctor has of your medical history is called your medical record, this structure is a page record. Your medical record defines your health history since birth. The stun:design site's page record fully defines the page.

We have one last problem. We only have one record. We have many pages in our site. We need some way of building more of these, and like a filing cabinet of medical records (where the surgery staff need to be able to look up any patients medical history before the patient can be treated) we need to be able to do the same for the current page the UI needs to display, so that Flash knows what to show, where to link to when a strip is pressed, and so on for all the properties of every page.

Well, let's say there are fifty pages. We need fifty of the structures above. How many lines do you think that we'll have to add to our listing so far? Guess!

Okay, it's not many. Handling large quantities of repetitive data (or to use a polite programming term, *structured data*) is something computers are very good at. We only have to add three new lines, (and one of them is a brace, so it's really two!). You also have to change all the references to page to page[i]:

```
page = new Array();
for (i=0; i<50; i++) {
  page[i] = new Object();
  page[i].pType = new String();
  page[i].plink = new Array();
  page[i].pTitle = new Array();
  page[i].pID = new String();
  page[i].pURL = new String();
  // add the data for a general page...
  page[i].pType = "linkPage or contentPage";
  page[i].pLink = ["strip0 link", "strip1 link", "strip2 link"];
  page[i].pTitle = ["navigation", "strip0 title", "strip1 title",➡
  "strip2 title"];
  page[i].pID = "content library identifier (optional)";
  page[i].pURL = "content URL (optional)";
}
```

So what have we done? Well, we have created an array of size 50 called page. We have made each array element, page[i], an object, which allows us to add the properties of page number i.

Cool! So now we have a data structure (it's actually a simple *database of records*) that we can use to make Flash create all our page titles and links! You can see it in the debugger if you debug the FLA one last time. You'll see that there are now 50 sets of records (0 to 49). If you open any of them, you'll find the familiar page definition structure.

Name			Value
⊞ 33			
⊞ 34			
⊞ 35			
⊟ 36			
	pID		"content library identifier (optional)"
	⊟ pLink		
		0	"strip0 link"
		1	"strip1 link"
		2	"strip2 link"
	⊟ pTitle		
		0	"navigation"
		1	"strip0 title"
		2	"strip1 title"
		3	"strip2 title"
	pType		"linkPage or contentPage"
	pURL		"content URL (optional)"
⊞ 37			
⊞ 38			
⊞ 39			
⊞ 40			

Looking at it from the medical record analogy, we have just created a filing cabinet full of records. Our patients are called 00 to 49, and we've filed the records numerically. At the moment, each record is filled with basic default information, but we'll soon make the records specific to each page in our site.

We've come a *very* long way here. We've started with basic variables, and have just built the sort of structure that would have made Flash 5 creak (trying to show 50 records in the Flash 5 debugger would have run the risk of crashing the application, for example!). Flash MX lives for this sort of thing because Macromedia have designed it to allow you to build something called an **application front end** as well as normal web sites. The structure we have created is defined as an array of objects called page, and the data required to fill it will be hardcoded into the site itself in the next section. There is, however, nothing stopping you defining this code externally.

> *Some of you may recognize the tree structure above as something you could define via a separate XML file, that the final SWF will load at runtime.*

We're on the verge of building something in-between – a web site that could (given the addition of the appropriate interfacing functions) easily be converted to an application front end because it's driven internally by a well-defined data structure.

In the next section I do something to this information called **parsing**; Flash will decode the records on the fly to create web pages in our site.

Before we move on...

I've thought long and hard about building a site that was based around a set of records. Many existing Flash 5 designers would see this as advanced.

In the end I knew I had to do it this way if I was going to teach you how to use Flash MX. Anything else and you would be learning 'Flash 5.5' (Flash MX with *some* of the new bells and whistles), but we'd have missed the whole *point* of Flash MX. Flash MX ActionScript is a big step away from the 'motion graphics only' Flash 5. It's there to be used for more complex things that require data to be captured and manipulated as well.

That in itself was a compelling reason for building the stun: design site the way we have, but it is still not the main one...

You're learning Flash MX because you want to make money as a designer. The days of Flash sites that do clever tricks with dots or whatever running around and looking pretty are as dead as the dotcom bubble. To learn Flash well enough to make it big time, you have to know about how ActionScript can also handle *data*, because Flash is set to become the front end of business sites as well as experimental designer sites, and that's where your hot meals and beer money may well come from as a professional Flash designer. If we did not teach you to build a site that had the core scripts to do this sort of thing in it, we would have taken the easier route, but sold you short, and we couldn't do that.

Section 7: Navigation and data

So far we've thought about adding our navigation structure as data, but haven't implemented it. We also have only given Flash a way to move **forward** in the site, and still cannot move **back**. There is actually a very good reason for this; without our data that defines the forward path, we can't go back!

> *The fact that the site currently appears to let you go forward is an illusion as well... it only shows the forward animation; it still doesn't actually go anywhere!*

Something you may have picked up is that in defining our navigation links as data, we've separated it from the actual content. Normally, you write a web page, adding all the links on the individual buttons within the page and the linking data is therefore part of the content.

In this site we're about to add the links on a site that is still free of *any* content. Although this may go against the grain when compared with simple sites you may have designed before, it actually leads to a very flexible design. Our site UI and the navigation links *are separate from the final content*, and so we can define the overall UI separately from the client content.

Obviously, there is the issue of the graphics; the UI look and feel has to match seamlessly with the content. This isn't an issue for the code though, which will stay the same.

What we'll do...

We need to make the final connections that turn our UI from a pretty set of interactive color swatches into something that we can actually use as a website.

- The first thing we'll do is to create our data structure. We've already done that in the last section, so all we really need to do is to transfer it into our site.

- The second thing we need to do is to populate the data structure with our navigation data.

- Finally, we have to get Flash to use the data, so that when you click on a strip, it takes you to the appropriate page.

Creating the data structure

The first of the three things on our 'to do' list is to create the data structure. We've already more or less defined this in the previous section, so the only thing to do is to write a function that creates the structure, and put it somewhere appropriate in our code.

The starting point of this chapter, stun_section7_start.fla has the initial new code included, but if you want to do your own thing, you can use your FLA so far. If you want to carry on from the last chapter, start with stun_section6_part3.fla and add the code as specified below.

We'll create a new function navigationData() that defines our data structure. The place to add this is after the DEFINE MAIN SETUP SCRIPTS block of functions:

```
// DEFINE SITE NAVIGATION DATA

navigationData = function () {
  // define and populate page data structure...
  //
  page = new Array();
  for (i=0; i<50; i++) {
    // define structure...
    page[i] = new Object();
    page[i].pType = new String();
    page[i].pLink = new Array();
    page[i].pTitle = new Array();
    page[i].pID = new String();
    page[i].pURL = new String();
  }
};
```

We haven't finished though, because we also need to call this function from somewhere... the question is where? Well, we're initializing something to do with the UI, so lets place it in the INITIALIZE block (the bit at the end of the listing).

```
// Initialize UI...

stripPage.apply(tricolor);
navigationData()

// Set UI colors...
```

That's the basic data structure in place. If you now run the FLA in debug mode, you will see this data structure appear on _level0:

Name		Value
	color1	1153314
	color2	21879
⊞	colTrans	
	colTransition	
	fadeText	
	i	50
	left	30
	mainText	"title text"
	navigate	
	navigationData	
	navStripX	30
	navStripY	570
⊞	page	
	posTransition	
	right	770

Hitting the little '+' will reveal our fifty page entries.

Okay, we've got our data structure set up, now comes the tricky part – what to put in it!

Defining our data

We have a number of parameters that define our website, and we need to decide what values each should take.

Some of you might be thinking 'hey, this is a bit like the parameters in components'. Well, if you did, congratulations, you are right on the money! Components are dependent on parameters that define their look and feel. These parameters *configure* the components, and the full set of parameters is sometimes called the *configuration data*. What we're doing can be thought of as the next level up; the whole site is just one big component, and right now, we're sorting out the parameter list on a rather large site-wide Property inspector!

Page type pType

This is one of the easier parameters, because we can only have two possible values; contentPage and linkPage. we'll therefore make our page type a string value "contentPage" and "linkPage".

```
pType = "contentPage" or "linkPage"
```

Page links pLink

This is one of the difficult parameters to tie down because there seem to be so many possible configurations. Each strip can either link to another page, or there is the possibility that there is no link. So you can have any number of links from zero to the maximum number of links, three. How do you represent that?

Well, the Romans had the same problem. They could represent any positive number, but they didn't see the logic in representing 'no number' (what we now call zero) as a number. Arabic includes a zero, and that's why we use the Arabic digits 0 to 9 when we count; *because it allows us to fill the spaces where there is no value.* The Romans didn't appreciate the beauty of this concept, and had a strange number system that is useless for representing large numbers, because it requires so many different symbols.

In the same way, as long as we treat 'no link' the same as an actual link, *we thus always have the same number of links, and our link data for each page becomes the same.* How do we represent a non-link? Well, a common programming trick is to give 'non data' a special value. We'll make a non-link point to a page that doesn't exist, page -1 (we can't use zero, because that is a valid page). If a -1 is seen, then the code should be written to recognize that this actually means 'no link'. If any other number is seen, (such as 23 or 2) the link should be taken as valid.

```
pLink[0] = link for strip 0 (number or -1 for no link)
pLink[1] = link for strip 1 (number or -1 for no link)
pLink[2] = link for strip 2 (number or -1 for no link)
```

Okay, that's a rather esoteric set of information. Let's show by example. Suppose page 6 links to:

- Page 4 if we hit strip 0

- Page 3 if we hit strip 1

- Nowhere if we hit strip 2

We could represent this by the following:

```
page[6].pLink = [4, 3, -1];
```

page[6].pLink[0] tells us that when we hit strip 0, we need to jump to page 4, and page[6].pLink[2] tells us that if we click on strip 2, no navigation should occur because the link points to page -1.

page 6

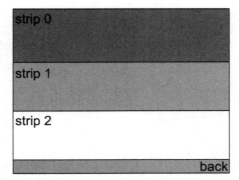

strip 0

strip 1

strip 2

back

Page titles `title`
There are four titles we need in all.

- One for the navigation title (top right)

- One for each strip

That's four in all, and because we need four separate strings, we'll need to use another array.

```
title = [mainTitle,titleStrip1, titleStrip2, titleStrip3]
```

The home page of the final site has titles as shown; it has a main title of 'home' and the three individual strip titles 'stun: design', 'stun: work' and 'stun: people:

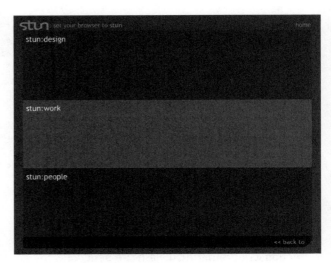

To define the titles for this page (noting that the home page is page 0) we would use;

```
page[0].titles = ["home","stun:design","stun:work","stun:people"];
```

Content Linkage ID and URL

These final two parameters define where to get the content from. They only need to be used if the current page is a contentPage, and they will all be string values. The only minor issue is what to set them to if they're unused. We'll set them to 'non', although we could just as easily leave them undefined.

> *Some of you may notice that we're actually defining more information than we need to; Flash can infer the values of some of the parameters from other parameters. For example, if a page is a* contentPage, *then you know that you will not linking to anywhere via the strips, so* pLinks *0, 1 and 2 will all be –1. Although you could do it that way, I prefer to always define enough data to make it clear to me and not just the computer. Clarity of the code is usually more important than efficiency when you're writing large bits of code. Redundant data can also act as an aid in debugging (in fact, all error detection relies on redundant data).*

Populating the data with default values

We next need to populate our data with default values. Why? Well, it's actually efficient to do so; not only does it make debugging easier (everything has a definite value rather than being undefined), but it shows up the final data structure before any real data is entered.

Add the following code to the function navigationData().

```
    page[i].pURL = new String();
    page[i].pData = new String();
    // populate with default values...
    page[i].pType = "non";
    page[i].pLink = [-1, -1, -1];
    page[i].pTitle = ["warning > unlinked page > site error",➡
                      "please contact the site owner", "", ""];
    page[i].pID = "non";
    page[i].pURL = "non";
}
```

Populating the data values

We're finally ready to start defining the data. It should be noted that, because this is a book on ActionScript rather than Flash site design, I won't go too much into the reasoning behind the pages, page content and the nature of the general site page structure, although it is fairly self-evident.

Although we will introduce the whole data for our site, during actual development only a small subset of the data was used to allow for fine-tuning. For the purposes of continuity, we have included the full site data up front.

> *Another point worth mentioning is the use of the word* **field**. *It is actually identical to the term* **property**, *although it is used when describing databases. The reason for this is that the records that describe each page are obviously actually objects. 'Obviously' comes from the fact that every bit of data (apart from the low level primitive data types* string, number *and* boolean*) is invariably an object whenever you use any modern computer language.*

To begin, let's have a look at how the pages will look and how they'll link. We have three links and four titles for each page page [pageNumber]. Taking this as my template, I decided on a general hierarchy for my pages:

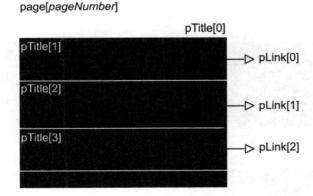

The home page will look like this. (Note – This shows a cleaned up version of the original sketches I used; if you later want to define your own site, you are advised to draw your site out in the same way as shown here before defining your data).

I have decided on three main areas.

- Stun: design tells the user about the *stun* design house.

- Stun: work includes a client list and links to a portfolio of personal work.

- Stun: people includes information about the stun: designers.

The data to define this page is:

```
page[00].pType = "linkPage";
page[00].pLink = [01, 20, 30];
page[00].pTitle = ["home","stun:design", "stun:work",➡
                   "stun:people"];
```

The stun:design link will send us to page 1, and the links from strips 1 and 2 will take us to pages 20 and 30 respectively.

> *Because the linking scheme in our website is actually very flexible, and we can link any page to any other, the page numbering scheme is arbitrary. In fact, the number of pages is also arbitrary, as is the fact that you don't have to use all the pages you define (you can have lots of 'spare' pages that are unlinked). The numbering system I've chosen makes sense to me because of the number and types of page I am creating, although you can choose another system if you decide to use this design for your own site.*

Pages 00, 20, and 30 look like this:

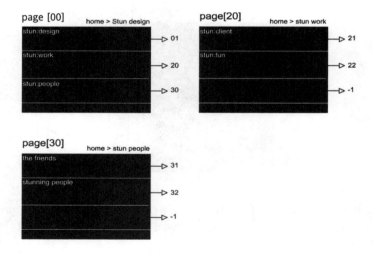

The code to set this up is as follows:

```
// Page 01 - stun: design (linking page)
page[01].pType = "linkPage";
page[01].pLink = [02, 03, 04];
page[01].pTitle = ["home > stun design", "web design", "stun:in print",➡
     "contact"];
```

```
// Page 20 - stun: work (link page)
page[20].pType = "linkPage";
page[20].pLink = [21, 22, -1];
page[20].pTitle = ["home > stun work", "stun:client", "stun:fun", ""];

// Page 30 - stun: people (linking page)
page[30].pType = "linkPage";
page[30].pLink = [31, 32, -1];
page[30].pTitle = ["home > stun people", "the friends",➡
                    "stunning:people", ""];
```

There are a couple of things to notice here:

- Unused strips are given a link of –1

- Unused titles are given a text string of ""

You can see the function with this data added as stun_section7_part1.fla. The navigationData() function within this FLA looks like the code below. Copy the new code into your work in progress if you're following this tutorial by hand:

```
navigationData = function () {
  // define and populate page data structure...

  page = new Array();
  for (i=0; i<50; i++) {
    // define structure...
    page[i] = new Object();
    page[i].pType = new String();
    page[i].pLink = new Array();
    page[i].pTitle = new Array();
    page[i].pID = new String();
    page[i].pURL = new String();
    // populate with default values...
    page[i].pType = "non";
    page[i].pLink = [-1, -1, -1];
    page[i].pTitle = ["warning > unlinked page > site error",➡
                      "please contact the site owner", "", ""];
    page[i].pID = "non";
    page[i].pURL = "non";
  }
  // HOME LEVEL

  // Page 0 - home (linking page)
  page[00].pType = "linkPage";
  page[00].pLink = [01, 20, 30];
  page[00].pTitle = ["home", "stun:design", "stun:work",➡
                      "stun:people"];
```

```
// FIRST STRIP NAVIGATION TREE

// Page 01 - stun: design (linking page)
page[01].pType = "linkPage";
page[01].pLink = [02, 03, 04];
page[01].pTitle = ["home > stun design", "web design", "stun:in ➥
                print", "contact"];

// SECOND STRIP NAVIGATION TREE

// Page 20 - stun: work (link page)
page[20].pType = "linkPage";
page[20].pLink = [21, 22, -1];
page[20].pTitle = ["home > stun work", "stun:client", "stun:fun", ➥
                ""];

// THIRD STRIP NAVIGATION TREE

// Page 30 - stun: people (linking page)
page[30].pType = "linkPage";
page[30].pLink = [31, 32, -1];
page[30].pTitle = ["home > stun people", "the friends",➥
                "stunning:people", ""];
};
```

You can see the data represented in the debugger if you debug the movie. Shown below is the page entry for our new page 20.

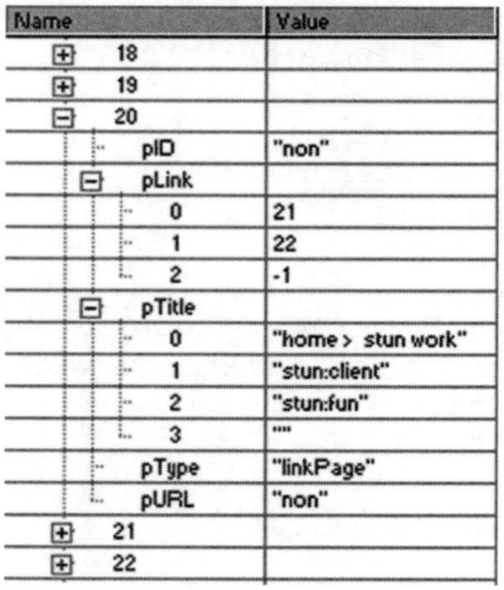

Name			Value
⊞	18		
⊞	19		
⊟	20		
		pID	"non"
	⊟	pLink	
		0	21
		1	22
		2	-1
	⊟	pTitle	
		0	"home > stun work"
		1	"stun:client"
		2	"stun:fun"
		3	""
		pType	"linkPage"
		pURL	"non"
⊞	21		
⊞	22		

I've added the remaining data in `stun_section7_part2.fla`.

Getting Flash to read the data

Okay, a quick recap to make sure we all understand where we are. We have just defined all our navigation data into the page object. This object is a large multi-property data structure. Our last task for this chapter is to get Flash to start reading it. There are a number of bits of information we need to pull from page to successfully create a new display for our UI. Let's have a look at two of the easiest first.

- Populating the titles

- Adding the link data to the current page

Populating the titles

We'll create a new block of functions to do this, called BUILD PAGE AND DYNAMIC UI ELEMENTS. Add this after the existing DEFINE EVENT SCRIPTS block.

```
    tricolor.strip0_txt._alpha = fadeValue;
    tricolor.strip1_txt._alpha = fadeValue;
    tricolor.strip2_txt._alpha = fadeValue;
};

// BUILD PAGE AND DYNAMIC UI ELEMENTS

populateTitles = function (pageIndex) {
  var pageIndex;
  main_txt.text = page[pageIndex].pTitle[0];
  tricolor.strip0_txt.text = page[pageIndex].pTitle[1];
  tricolor.strip1_txt.text = page[pageIndex].pTitle[2];
  tricolor.strip2_txt.text = page[pageIndex].pTitle[3];
};
```

This function takes an argument pageIndex and uses it to retrieve the titles for page page[pageIndex]. It then populates our four text fields with the appropriate text strings, as defined by the data we just defined in the last section.

Okay, apart from the fact that we don't have a pageIndex argument generated anywhere yet, that's the text titling sorted out. Next stop, the linking.

Add the following code below the populateTitles() function we just added:

```
populateEvents = function (pageIndex) {
  var pageIndex;
  if (page[pageIndex].pLink[0] != -1) {
    tricolor.strip0_mc.onRelease = navigate;
    tricolor.strip0_mc.useHandCursor = true;
  }
  if (page[pageIndex].pLink[1] != -1) {
    tricolor.strip1_mc.onRelease = navigate;
```

```
                        tricolor.strip1_mc.useHandCursor = true;
                }
        if (page[pageIndex].pLink[2] != -1) {
                tricolor.strip2_mc.onRelease = navigate;
                tricolor.strip2_mc.useHandCursor = true;
                }
        };
```

All this function does is to look at the current page (page[pageIndex]) and adds an onRelease event that's defined as our old friend navigate(), so that if a link exists for a strip, it's made to act like a button (thus enabling the user to follow the link). It does this *unless* any strip has a −1 link defined for it.

> The useHandCursor *lines are there to fix a feature of Flash MX. We will address this in a moment.*

Okay, now add this function (directly below populateEvents()), which does the reverse, it *removes* all the events:

```
        unpopulateEvents = function () {
                tricolor.strip0_mc.onRelease = undefined;
                tricolor.strip1_mc.onRelease = undefined;
                tricolor.strip2_mc.onRelease = undefined;
                tricolor.strip0_mc.useHandCursor = false;
                tricolor.strip1_mc.useHandCursor = false;
                tricolor.strip2_mc.useHandCursor = false;
        };
```

This function deletes all our button events, so that the UI no longer responds to button clicks on the three strips. This in itself doesn't get rid of the hand cursor though, so to stop that we have to change a property, useHandCursor, to false (and when we give them button events again via populateEvents, we make this property true again for those strips that are links in the new page).

We now need to modify our existing functions to use our new events.

The first thing we don't yet know is the page we're on. Well, actually, we know what page we're on to start off with; we always start at the home page, and that is page 0. When we navigate to another page, we should be able to tell where we are from the link data.

> *Although some of you may see immediately which bit of our data will tell us this, using data in a website in this manner will be new to many, so we'll move slowly and explain it so that we lose no-one.*

If we look at the sketch for page 0 again, we see immediately what bit of data we need; *the link number.* This tells us the page number straight off!

For example, if we click on strip 2, we go to page 30, and that becomes the new page number. When we use the `populateTitles(pageIndex)` and `populateEvents(pageIndex)` functions, we want `pageIndex` to hold the value 30. This will cause page 30 to be built as the next page.

page[0]

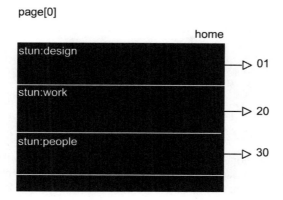

Looking at the more general diagram below, it becomes obvious that the current page is:

- Page 0 when we start.

- As soon as we click on a strip, the new page becomes `pLink[strip]`, where `strip` is the strip number (0, 1, 2).

page[*pageNumber*]

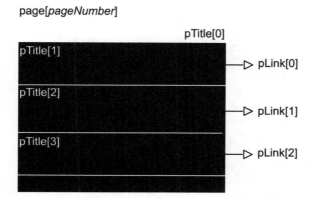

Let's try the page 0 bit for starters. Given that we know we're on page 0 to start with, we'll assign this value to a variable that tells us the current page number, `currentPage`. Add this to the INITIALIZE section (at the end of the listing):

```
        // Initialize UI...

    stripPage.apply(tricolor);
    navigationData();
    currentPage = 0;

        // Set UI colors...

    tricolor.setCol(color0, color1, color2);

        // Build First page...

    populateTitles(currentPage);

        // now sit back and let the event scripts handle everything ;)
    stop();
```

Test your FLA (or use our version, stun_section7_part3.fla). You will see that we now have titles correctly showing on the home page. The only trouble is that when you click on a link, the titles don't change. Well, they wouldn't; we haven't added that part yet...

The next step is to ensure that we *always* see the correct titles. We need to do this by changing currentPage when we see a new page, and populating the page based on the new value. The place to do this is at the end of posTransition; once the position transition has occurred and the current titles have faded out:

```
    posTransition = function () {
        s -= (s-sTarget)/4;
        y -= (y-yTarget)/4;
        fadeAlpha = 300-s;
        tricolor._y = y;
        tricolor._xscale = tricolor._yscale=s;
        fadeText(fadeAlpha);
        if (Math.abs(s-sTarget)<5) {
            // if so, disconnect this function from onEnterframe...
            this.onEnterFrame = colTransition;
            // then place tricolor back at start position...
            tricolor._y = border;
            tricolor._xscale = tricolor._yscale=100;
            selectedStrip = this._name.substring(5, 6);
            selectedCol = _root["color"+selectedStrip];
            tricolor.setCol(selectedCol, selectedCol, selectedCol);
            currentPage = page[currentPage].pLink[selectedStrip];
            populateTitles(currentPage);
            fadeColor = 0;
            fadeAlpha = 0;
        }
    };
```

If you test the FLA you'll see our titles appearing. Unfortunately, you can still navigate to pages you shouldn't be able to (i.e. page −1, or empty links), and to fix that we need to look at integrating `populateEvents()` with the main code.

Populating the events

We now need to sort out the site so that it reads and acts upon `pLink`. The first step is to remove all button events as soon as any of the strips are clicked. This is so that we can add a new set of events via our `populateEvents()` function.

Add the following code to function `navigate()`:

```
navigate = function () {
    // remove existing events...
    unpopulateEvents();
    // set up target for animation transition...
    s=100, x=border, y=border;
    yTarget = -3*this._y+border;
```

This strips our button events from all strips in the tricolor. Once we're at the new page, we want to add the events back in, but only for those strips that are actually valid links.

> We have to do this, because our page always actually remains the same; we never really actually go to a new page, but simply keep re-using tricolor!

All we have to do now is put the new events back onto the strips when the navigation has completed, and that occurs at the end of `colTransition()`. Add the following line at the end of this function;

```
        color0 = tricolor.colStrip0.getRGB();
        color1 = tricolor.colStrip1.getRGB();
        color2 = tricolor.colStrip2.getRGB();
        this.onEnterFrame = undefined;
        populateEvents(currentPage);
        fadeText(100);
    }
};
```

The FLA to this point is saved as `stun_section7_part4.fla`. If you test this, you'll see that we're *almost* there. Although the pages now work for link pages, as soon as we hit a content page, the site messes up, because it still changes to the three strips. On a content page, the UI will simply act as a dumb background until the content is loaded, so we don't want it to do that. We need to make the UI read the `pType` value and act accordingly.

Reading content pages

We only want to use `colTransition()` if the new page happens to be a link page. If it isn't, we don't need to fade the three strips in again. To make this change, add the following code at the end of `posTransition()`;

```
      // if so, disconnect this function from onEnterframe...
      this.onEnterFrame = undefined;
      // then place tricolor back at start position...
      tricolor._y = border;
      tricolor._xscale = tricolor._yscale=100;
      selectedStrip = this._name.substring(5, 6);
      selectedCol = _root["color"+selectedStrip];
      tricolor.setCol(selectedCol, selectedCol, selectedCol);
      currentPage = page[currentPage].pLink[selectedStrip];
      // if this is a link page, create another tricolor...
      if (page[currentPage].pType == "linkPage") {
        populateTitles(currentPage);
        fadeColor = 0;
        fadeAlpha = 0;
        this.onEnterFrame = colTransition;
      } else {
        // otherwise place the content...
        placeContent();
      }
    }
  };
```

If the current page happens to be a link page, we carry on as before. If it isn't, we do something else; we go to a new function `placeContent()`. Don't worry! This is a very short function, and then we'll be done for this section.

Add the following function below `unpopulateEvents()`.

```
placeContent = function () {
  _root.attachMovie("placeholder", "placeholder", 10000);
  _root.placeholder._x = border;
  _root.placeholder._y = border;
};
```

At the moment we'll add the same content placeholder movie clip (this is a movie clip with linkage identifier `placeholder`) in front of the UI. You need to create a suitable clip in the library, which can be simply a movie clip with the text 'placeholder' in it. Alternatively, you might consider creating a standard placeholder (they are actually quite useful) and using that. Anyway, I've used my own version of a placeholder, suitably branded with my home site. You can see it in action in the final FLA for this chapter, `stun_section7_part5.fla`.

We,ve now got a working interface. Everything is actually in place except the back button. We'll fix that, as well as looking at how to load in content properly in the final two sections.

Section 8: Going back

We've now got a website UI that looks almost complete. There is in fact only one remaining thing we have to do before we can finally start thinking about adding our content; we need to implement the back navigation.

In this section we'll add the code to read the back path and will then build the back animation into the existing code. This means that we also need to add the little icons representing the back path (the 'breadcrumb trail').

Adding the back path

If you have a look at the final version of the site, you will see that the back strip has a number of icons that appear at the bottom left. Clicking on one takes you back one or more pages through the current navigation, and clicking on the first icon takes you back to the home page.

We already have the symbols for our icons, built and ready in the library. This symbol is exactly the same as page, except that there is no text.

We need to create the functions to drive the icons, and then we need to integrate them with the existing code so that the functions are called at the appropriate times.

So what do we need? Well, there are a number of stages we need to consider.

We need to create each icon as new pages are added

Initially, at the home page, there are no icons as shown below.

As soon as you click on a strip, the icon to go back to the home page appears.

As you click on further strips that take you deeper into the site, more icons appear, each color coded to look like small versions of the page they represent. Thus, a breadcrumb trail that shows you the path you have taken is created.

We need to delete icons as they are used to navigate back

A given icon can only be used once; as soon as you have used one to go back, it is no longer needed and should disappear, as should the 'back history' from that point onwards. For example, if we click on the second icon in a breadcrumb trail, you'll no longer need the second or third icon to remain.

So clicking on the home icon should result in all icons disappearing, because you have gone back all the way to the start:

We need to show a new animation transition that shows the effects of going backward through the navigation

The final site has a separate animation to represent the user moving backwards. Because this is different from the forward animation (the selected icon grows from the back strip to become the new page), we need to code a new function to handle the back animation.

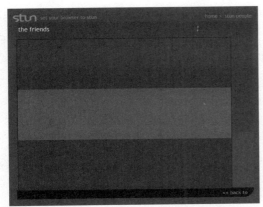

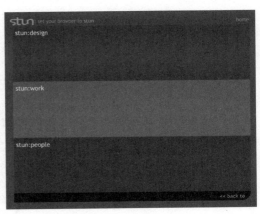

We need to make sure that the UI knows where it needs to return to!

An obvious point, but perhaps the hardest point so far; we need to recreate the page that the icon represents! So what do we need to do this? Three things:

- We need to know the page number of the page each icon represents. This value is held in variable currentPage when the page is being or has been displayed, so we need to somehow store this so that each icon knows what the currentPage value was when the page we're going to was last displayed.

- We need to know the colors of the new page we'll be going back to. Remember that the color of each page (except the home page) is not predefined; it is calculated on the fly. However, the icon already 'knows' the page colors, because it is colored using the same scheme!

- If the current page contains content, we need to delete it from the screen before we go backwards. An interesting question is '*what if the new page we want to go back to also has content on it?*' Well, that one caused me some worry initially, but the answer is actually very simple; *that never happens so you don't have to worry about it.* The navigation is designed so that only the last page in any navigation is a content page; all the others leading up to it are link pages.

> *Although the back strip functionality looks and feels totally simple/intuitive, and is one of the little touches that makes the navigation look so sweet, you will have realized by now that it is actually one of the hardest parts to design! Ergonomic simplicity is usually one of the more difficult things to code up for all but the most basic UIs.*

Okay, so we've defined the problem, let's turn to looking at the coding solution. We'll split the functionality into two parts.

- The part that looks after the building of the icon (and related data and event handlers), buildIcon()

- The part that looks after the animation transition, `iconTransition()`

The starting point for this is `stun_section7_part5.fla` from the last section. The second FLA, `stun_section8.fla` contains all the new code to handle the back navigation.

> *One thing I've done to the icon movie clip since Chapter 8 is to put a black outline around it. This was added during final testing. Because some of the colors are very close to each other, it was found necessary to differentiate between the growing icon and the background tricolor, and this is what the border does.*

We also need to keep a track of the number of icons we have, and so the first thing I've done is to create a new variable, `iconCount` (it's in the INITIALIZE block).

```
// Define navigation strip variables...

iconCount = 0;
navStripX = border;
navStripY = bottom;
```

The next thing we'll look at is where we'll be building the new icon. Well, it's a good idea to build it as soon as a new page is created, and that means at the beginning of `navigate()`:

```
navigate = function () {
   // undefine any existing strip events...
   unpopulateEvents();
   // build icon to get back to current page...
   buildIcon(currentPage);
   // set up target for animation transition...
   s=100, x=border, y=border;
```

The `buildIcon()` function is actually very similar to the code we have created for the tricolor, and we'll be using many of the same functions. Because of this, I'll go through it fairly rapidly, and concentrate on the stuff that is unique to the icons.

Okay. we'll put `buildIcon()` directly after `unpopulateEvents()`. Here it is:

```
unpopulateEvents = function () {
   tricolor.strip0_mc.onRelease = undefined;
   tricolor.strip1_mc.onRelease = undefined;
   tricolor.strip2_mc.onRelease = undefined;
   tricolor.strip0_mc.useHandCursor = false;
   tricolor.strip1_mc.useHandCursor = false;
   tricolor.strip2_mc.useHandCursor = false;
};
buildIcon = function (pageIndex) {
```

```
    var pageIndex, iconName, iconDepth;
    // initialize...
    iconName = "icon"+iconCount;
    iconDepth = 100+iconCount;

    // create Icon and attach functions...
    _root.attachMovie("icon", iconName, iconDepth);
    stripCols.apply(_root[iconName]);

    // set colors, size and position...
    _root[iconName]._xscale = _root[iconName]._yscale=4;
    _root[iconName].setCol(color0, color1, color2);
    _root[iconName]._x = navStripX+(40*iconCount)+10;
    _root[iconName]._y = navStripY+5;

    // update iconCount by one for next icon and store current
    // page details onto the icon stack...

    iconCount++;
    _root[iconName].currentPage = currentPage;
    _root[iconName].color0 = color0;
    _root[iconName].color1 = color1;
    _root[iconName].color2 = color2;
    _root[iconName].iconCount = iconCount;

    // add the animation functions to this icon...
    // define icon button script...

    _root[iconName].onRelease = function() {
      // delete all icons after this one...
      for (i=this.iconCount; i<=iconCount; i++) {
        _root["icon"+i].removeMovieClip();
      }
      // delete any content on the current page...
      _root.createEmptyMovieClip("dummy", 10000);
      // zoom icon into the new current page...
      s=4, x=this._x, y=this._y;
      xTarget = border;
      yTarget = border;
      sTarget = 100;
      this.onRelease = undefined;
      this.onEnterFrame = iconTransition;
    };
};
placeContent = function () {
  _root.attachMovie("placeholder", "placeholder", 10000);
  _root.placeholder._x = border;
  _root.placeholder._y = border;
};
```

Uh... what's all that about then? Let's have a look around...

The first thing is that we have an argument for our `buildIcon()` function, `currentPage`. Looking at the code we added in `navigate()` just now, this is simply our old friend `currentPage`.

When we start, there are no icons on stage, and we'll have to place them on stage with code. There are three ways to do this.

- Drag a version of the icon movie clip, icon, onto the stage manually now, and put it somewhere off screen where the user won't be able to see it. When we come to needing icons to appear, we copy them via the `duplicateMovieClip()` method.

- Copy the icon clips directly from the library using `attachMovie()`.

- Create an empty movie clip and draw an icon inside it using the drawing API.

Well, the first method is what folks used in Flash 5, but we have better ways to do this now. The third method is cool, but there's not really any reason for getting so complicated, so I've plumped for the middle one.

To create movie clips dynamically, you have to have three things in place.

- You have to set up the symbol to be attached properly in the library by giving it a **Linkage ID** and getting Flash to export it correctly. More on this in a moment.

- You have to give the movie clip you want to copy (or 'attach to the stage') an instance name. We'll have to give each icon a unique name because we'll need to selectively remove them as well later.

- Finally, you have to give each icon a unique **depth**. Flash places everything on screen using depth. This defines the order that things are drawn in; the higher the depth, the more 'in front' it is. This is rather like layers.

> *Layers don't actually exist in Flash SWFS they are there as an authoring tool for us designers. Layer order is used (amongst other things) to define the depth order, which is what the Flash player understands. Stuff placed on stage has a negative depth, and this is assigned by Flash itself during the process of converting a FLA into a SWF. When attaching content directly to the stage at runtime, the depth is positive, and this means that the things we attach will always be in front of any content placed manually during author time. Valid and supported depths that we can use are any integer between 0 and approximately 16000.*

We said 'rather like layers' because there's one major difference; there can only be one thing at each depth. If you try to put a movie clip at depth 100 when there is already something occupying that depth, the 'something' will be deleted and replaced by your new movie clip. The upshot of this is that when we assign depths, we have to make sure that we don't overwrite existing and already occupied depths. There is an easy way to do this; *make sure that each depth we use is unique.*

So what does all that mean for us? Well, the linkage ID and export options are set up for you in the files I have provided, but if you are working through your own FLA from scratch, you need to do the following.

1. In the library, locate the icon movie clip (it's in the User interface > active UI stuff library folder), and right-click/Alt-click on it. Select Properties...,then click the Advanced button to bring up the extra options

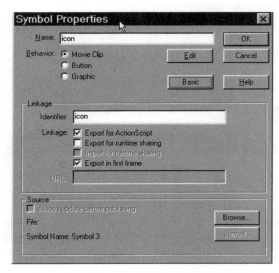

2. You need to have the symbol properties set up as shown. To do this, simply check the Export for ActionScript checkbox and accept the defaults that appear in the now un-grayed Identifier text entry box and Export in first frame checkbox.

    The reason we have to do all this is as follows...

    The identifier is simply the name Flash will use to recognize the movie clip when it is in the library.

    Normally, Flash doesn't include any symbols that are not used in the final SWF. By 'not used in the final SWF', we mean that the symbol doesn't appear on any timeline of the FLA. That's cool, but if we're going to place content dynamically at runtime, *it will not appear on any timeline at the time when Flash creates the SWF.* Left to its own devices, Flash would not include such content in the SWF library. By checking Export for ActionScript, we're overriding Flash, and saying 'well, it's not on any timeline now, but put it in the SWF because we'll need it during runtime'.

    Okay, so we've told Flash that we need a symbol. The next thing Flash needs to know is *when* it will be needed. Flash usually arranges things in the SWF so that the symbols that are needed early on (that appear in the first few frames of the timeline) stream in first. Stuff that is exported for ActionScript will *never* appear on a timeline of the FLA, so Flash has no idea when it is required. Flash therefore has two options; load stuff marked for Export for ActionScript first, or load it in last.

We're best off downloading the symbol on the first frame, because then we at least know that it is there straight away. This is why you should *always* have Export in First Frame selected when you Export for ActionScript. There are a few advanced reasons why you would not do this, but they are very far and few between, so it's a good rule of thumb.

Meanwhile, back at the ranch, the first few lines of buildIcon() do all the icon creation:

```
// initialize...
iconName = "icon"+iconCount;
iconDepth = 100+iconCount;

// create Icon and attach functions...
_root.attachMovie("icon", iconName, iconDepth);
```

Our instance name is "icon" plus the value of our new variable, iconCount. The first icon we create will thus be called "icon0". If we increment iconCount every time we create a new icon, then the second icon will be called "icon1" and so on; in other words, the instance names are *unique*.

The depth is also based on iconCount. I have started the icon depths at 101 (there is a chance that we may need to attach other, more permanent stuff on _root, so I have left free depths 0-100 to do this).

The last line creates our icon movie clip by copying the movie clip with Linkage ID "icon" to _root.

We need to change the strip colors within the icon. Fortunately, we can do that using code we have already defined for tricolor. The icon and page movie clips are very similar, and this is the reason why; so that we can use the same code to control the color changes in both! The next line attaches the stripCols function to the icon we just created.

```
stripCols.apply(_root[iconName]);
```

We next need to position and scale the icon. At the moment, the icon is the same size as the tricolor instance, so we need to make it much smaller. The following line does this by making it 4% of its original size:

```
// set colors, size and position...
_root[iconName]._xscale = _root[iconName]._yscale=4;
```

Next, we need to color it:

```
_root[iconName].setCol(color0, color1, color2);
```

Finally, we need to position it on the backstrip. This took a bit of tweaking, but here are the values I came up with. Note that the position is dependent on the icon number iconCount; as we add more icons, the position changes so that no two occupy the same position:

```
_root[iconName]._x = navStripX+(40*iconCount)+10;
_root[iconName]._y = navStripY+5;
```

Finally, the important part; we need to store the current position so that we can get back to 'here' if the icon is clicked on later. We *could* be clever here, and create an array a bit like page, which lists the back path, but I prefer to keep it simple by being devious; I've stored the values that allow us to build the current page again by storing the variable values *inside the icon itself.* More correctly, I copied the values that describe the current page on the timeline of the current icon. I have also updated iconCount here, so the next icon after the home icon ("icon0") will be called "icon1", and so on.

```
// update iconCount by one for next icon and store current
// page details onto the icon stack...
iconCount++;
_root[iconName].currentPage = currentPage;
_root[iconName].color0 = color0;
_root[iconName].color1 = color1;
_root[iconName].color2 = color2;
_root[iconName].iconCount = iconCount;
```

Our icons are actually buttons, and that means that we have to attach a button script to them. This occurs via the next bit of code. The icon we just created is given an onEnterFrame script.

```
// add the animation functions to this icon...
// define icon button script...
_root[iconName].onRelease = function() {
  // delete all icons after this one...
  for (i=this.iconCount; i<=iconCount; i++) {
    _root["icon"+i].removeMovieClip();
  }
  // delete any content on the current page...
  _root.createEmptyMovieClip("dummy", 10000);
  // zoom icon into the new current page...
  s=4, x=this._x, y=this._y;
  xTarget = border;
  yTarget = border;
  sTarget = 100;
  this.onRelease = undefined;
  this.onEnterFrame = iconTransition;
};
```

What does this script have to do? Well, remembering what the icons do in the final site:

- When we press on an icon, all icons to the right of it have to be deleted because they're no longer needed.

- Any content currently displayed has to be deleted.

- The icon has to grow to become the new page.

The first part is done here:

```
// delete all icons after this one...
for (i=this.iconCount; i<=iconCount; i++) {
    _root["icon"+i].removeMovieClip();
}
```

This deletes all icons between the local value of `iconCount` (i.e. the value that `iconCount` was when this icon was created) and the current value of `iconCount`. This has the effect of deleting all icons that were placed on screen since this icon was created.

We then delete any content that may exist. Rather than check if there's any content to delete, we'll simply delete it whether we need to or not. Deleting nothing does nothing, and is easier to do than checking first.

```
// delete any content on the current page...
_root.createEmptyMovieClip("dummy", 10000);
```

The code to handle content is still code in progress; so don't get too worried about this at the moment. we'll have a look at that in the next (and final) section of our project.

The last part of the `buildIcon()` function is much like the `navigate()` function. We set up for the position transition and delete the current `onRelease` event (so that the animation cannot be stopped once it has started). We set up the target size and position we want the icon to end up as (at position (`border`, `border`) and size 100%, which is what it has to change to before it looks like the tricolor in position and size).

```
// zoom icon into the new current page...
s=4, x=this._x, y=this._y;
xTarget = border;
yTarget = border;
sTarget = 100;
this.onRelease = undefined;
this.onEnterFrame = iconTransition;
```

The last part of `buildIcon()` attaches the `iconTransition()` function as the `onEnterFrame` script for the icon. This new function animates the icon as it grows to cover the current page. It is very similar to the previous function `posTransition()` with one subtle sting in the tail; when the icon totally covers the old page, it *doesn't* become the new page. Instead, the icon is deleted and the current tricolor changes so that it looks like the icon. It might look like the icon grows and becomes the new page, but this is not the case.

Why do we do this? Well, the site UI is written to animate tricolor. Changing this clip for a new icon clip causes no end of problems, so we do the sneaky switch-aroundy to keep life simple.

The last thing this function does is to set `iconCount` to the value of `iconCount` held in the icon (`this.iconCount`). This has the effect of resetting the `iconCount` value so that it now reflects the fact that some icons have been deleted.

```
iconTransition = function () {
  s -= (s-sTarget)/4;
  x -= (x-xTarget)/8;
  y -= (y-yTarget)/4;
  this._x=x, this._y=y;
  this._xscale = this._yscale=s;
  // have we reached the target?
  if (Math.abs(y-yTarget)<3) {
    // change page to new page...
    tricolor.setCol(this.color0, this.color1, this.color2);
    currentPage = this.currentPage;
    populateTitles(currentPage);
    populateEvents(currentPage);
    // update page color variables...
    color0 = this.color0;
    color1 = this.color1;
    color2 = this.color2;
    // update the icon count and remove this icon...
    iconCount = this.iconCount-1;
    this.removeMovieClip();
  }
};
```

You can see the `iconCount` value, and the way the icons store the current state of the navigation by debugging this FLA (or use mine, `stun_ch11back.fla`). When the site starts from home, you'll see that there are no icons.

As you navigate deeper into the site, you'll see the breadcrumb icon trail build up, and you can see the icon movie clips created in the debugger.

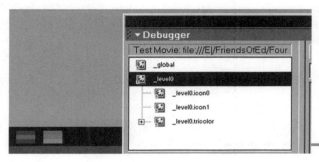

Look inside an icon (select an icon and then look at the Variables tab) and you'll see the local variables that are stored inside each icon instance (color0, color1, color2, currentPage, iconCount). These variables are used to return to the page represented by the icon when it is pressed later.

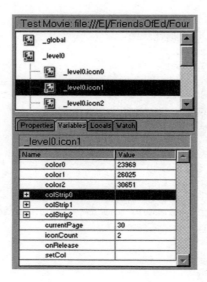

Also worth looking at is the way _root.iconCount changes as you interact with the icons.

We've now created our core UI. This is the site navigation system without any content. In the final installing enthrallment, we'll look at adding the sound controller we built in Chapter 10. We'll also look at adding content to our site.

Almost finished!

Section 9: Content and sound

In this final section we'll add the content to our site. This content includes:

- Stuff to fill the actual pages

- The stun soundtrack

The complied SWF that makes up our site is actually very light in file size (it's just over 12K, something that would load up within 3 seconds on even a 56K modem).

Notice how we have not gone for a graphic rich site in our design. There is no bandwidth-heavy artwork that makes up our UI, and neither is there any real eye candy to hold the attention.

The way we have added interest is in the way the site moves. This is something that is very bandwidth-light because it is defined by the code, and not any bandwidth-heavy graphics, video or other effects!

To maintain the low download sizes that our site UI has when content is added, we also need to think about how the content will stream in.

First we'll add the sound controller. We'll also alter its color scheme via `globalStyleFormat` so that the components that make it up (and any other components we choose to use) change their color and style in keeping with the changing web site colors.

Next, we'll make final alterations to our code so that it can handle the loading of content.

Adding sound

Because of the way the sound controller was written, it's actually very easy to incorporate it into this (or for that matter, any other) site design, as we shall see.

The starting point for this exercise is the file `stun_section8.fla`. The file `stun_section9_sound.fla` has the sound controller already added. You will also need the files `stun_soundControlB.fla` and `soundtrack.swf` which we created in Chapter 10.

Open `stun_section8.fla`, and add a new layer on `_root` called soundControl as shown below. Lock all layers except soundControl (locking a folder locks all layers inside it).

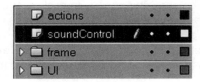

We'll be putting our sound controller on this layer in a moment. First though, we have to find it. Next, open the file `stun_soundControlB.fla`. Select the sound controller and copy it (hit CONTROL+C). Go back to the site (you can go to it by selecting it at the bottom of the Window menu) and paste it into the soundControl layer. Move it so that it is positioned as shown, in the top right hand corner of the site.

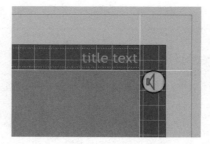

The next part assumes that `soundtrack.swf` is in the same folder as the main site FLA we have just edited (in our case, `stun_section8.fla`). If it isn't, you need to copy it across now.

Test the FLA (or use our FLA, `stun_section9_sound.fla`):

You'll see that our sound controller starts working immediately, with no changes to the code! That's because all the code to drive it is contained within it, and was copied across with it. The sound controller is **modular**; it can be added to any FLA, and will immediately start working with no changes.

The sound controller doesn't quite fit in with the color scheme; those sliders are still the default gray. You will remember that when we created the sound controller, there were some `globalStyleFormat` commands in the FLA to modify the sliders. We'll do the same again here.

First, we need to define a function that changes the `globalStyleFormat` based on the current tricolor colors. Because the sound controller opens up over strip 0, we want its color scheme to be based around `color0`.

I've added the new function after the `placeContent()` function.

```
// COMPONENT COLOR CHANGER
styleChanger = function () {
  globalStyleFormat.face = color0+0x222222;
  globalStyleFormat.scrollTrack = color0+0x330000;
  globalStyleFormat.arrow = 0xFFEEEE;
```

```
        globalStyleFormat.applychanges();
    };
```

We want to call this every time strip 0 changes color. This will occur:

- At the start of the site (when the strips change from their default gray to the home page colors)

- Every time you navigate to a new page via the forward navigation

- Every time you navigate to a new page using the back navigation

We therefore need to make a call to our function for all three of these occurrences. The first call goes in the INITIALIZE block.

```
    // Define initial screen colors (further colors will
    // use these colors as their seed)

    color0 = 0x993333;
    color1 = 0x119922;
    color2 = 0x005599;
    colTrans = new Array();
    colTrans = [0x000880, 0x001100, 0x002280];
    // change component styles to reflect color scheme...
    styleChanger();
```

The next place is near the end of colTransition().

```
    // we're now at the new page...
    color0 = tricolor.colStrip0.getRGB();
    color1 = tricolor.colStrip1.getRGB();
    color2 = tricolor.colStrip2.getRGB();
    // change component styles to reflect new page...
    styleChanger();
    this.onEnterFrame = undefined;
    populateEvents(currentPage);
    fadeText(100);
```

The final location is at the end of iconTransition().

```
    // update page color variables...
    color0 = this.color0;
    color1 = this.color1;
    color2 = this.color2;
    // update component styles to reflect new colors...
    styleChanger();
```

If you run the FLA now, you'll see that the sound controller is always a similar color to the site background. We've succeeded in integrating the components with our site design!

> *One thing to notice is that the site runs slightly slower with sound running (or will do on anything less than a Pentium PIII 500 in our tests). Playing sound has a slight performance hit, particularly if you are using a high frame rate as we are (we have it set to 18fps).*

Only one last thing to do and we're finished...

Adding content and managing downloads.

So far we're only using a placeholder movie clip. The function that loads content, placeContent(), simply attaches our placeholder movie clip instead of real content. That's okay for building our site, but we're beyond that now. We need to replace this with *our* (or more importantly, *your*) content.

From section 7 of this case study, we know that two properties of page refer to content; page.pID and page.pURL. These define where the site will look for the content.

- If the pID property is not "non", then it contains the Linkage identifier of the library movie clip that contains the content.

- If the pURL property is not "non" then it contains the URL that points to the SWF we need to load to bring in our content.

The reasoning for this is as follows:

Some content is small in size and we can simply include it in the site SWF as a library item. This type of content will be loaded in along with the main site, and to retrieve it, we simply need to grab the movie clip from the library and attach it to the stage.

Other content can be very large in size. Loading this type of content will lead to a very long site download time if we load it in at the same time as the main site UI. Rather than do this, it would be better to load it in on demand (i.e. when the user asks to see it). This sort of content is what pURL is all about; content that'll be loaded in after the main site has loaded in.

Okay, that's the theory. Here's the code, as found in stun_section9_content1.fla.

```
placeContent = function () {
    // is the content already in the library?
    if (page[currentPage].pID != "non") {
        // if so, attach it to the stage...
        _root.attachMovie(page[currentPage].pID, "content_mc", 10000);
    } else {
        // ...otherwise it must be at a remote URL, so
        // load it in into a new movie clip...
        _root.createEmptyMovieClip("content_mc", 10000);
        content_mc.loadMovie(page[currentPage].pURL);
```

```
        }
        _root.content_mc._x = border;
        _root.content_mc._y = border;
    };
```

So what does this do? Well, we'll always end up with a movie clip called content_mc. If the current page's pID is not "non", then the code creates content_mc as the library clip containing our content. If it *is* "non", then that must be because pURL is what we really need to look at, and in that case, we need to load our content from the URL, placing it into a new movie clip called content_mc.

If you test the FLA, nothing much changes. This is because all the pages define placeholder as the content. To change any page, you simply create a new movie clip in the library and give it a unique linkage ID. Then, you have to change the pID value so that it is the same as the linkage ID of the new page.

Our FLA has one page that uses this function. Have a look at the entry for page 02 in navigationData(). Instead of the usual "placeholder" for the pID, we have changed it to "webDesign".

```
// Page 02 - web: design (content page)
page[02].pType = "contentPage";
page[02].pLink = [-1, -1, -1];
page[02].pTitle = ["home > stun design > web design", "", "", ""];
page[02].pID = "webDesign";
```

You can see this movie clip in the Library. This has a Linkage ID of "webDesign".

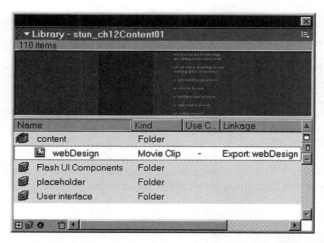

You can see the page by testing the FLA and navigating to stun:design > web design.

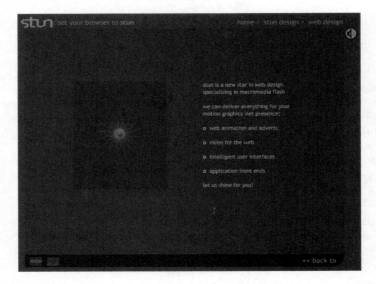

Supposing we wanted to load this page in on demand. Well, the FLA `stun_section9_content2.fla` does this. You need to have the file `webDesign.swf` in the same directory as this FLA when you test it for the next exercise to work.

The entry for our page looks like this:

```
// Page 02 - web: design (content page)
page[02].pType = "contentPage";
page[02].pLink = [-1, -1, -1];
page[02].pTitle = ["home > stun design > web design", "", "", ""];
page[02].pURL = "webDesign.swf";
```

This time, we're setting `pURL`, which means that `pID` will stay at its default value of `"non"`. The `placeContent()` function will thus look for the `webDesign.swf` file, and the URL we've given Flash will cause it to look for this SWF in the same directory as the site SWF.

Running this FLA will result in the same page showing up, but in terms of streaming on the web, this method is very different; the content is only loaded when it's required.

Preloading the main site UI

There's actually very little need to add a preloader for the main site, because it's a pretty small SWF anyway. What we'll do is add a little 'loading...'' message. Have a look at `stun_section9_load.fla`. This is essentially the same site, but there is now a first frame with a little 'loading' message (you can see it in the library as the movie clip loadingMessage).

The final site files

The final site files (for our version of the site) can be found in the downloads for this chapter. The code is essentially the same as the basic site we've just built, except that the page data is fully populated with the pURL and pID values, and the content movie clips and SWFs are included to make up the full site.

Parting Shots...

Now that you have the finished site, the real journey - building your first ActionScript heavy site - has just begun. You can base your site on our site, or you can even have a look at earlier versions of the stun:design site (available from the downloads page for the previous version of this book). The best thing is to take the ideas developed in this site and make them your own.

The look and feel of the stun:design site can be changed by changing the basic tricolor navigation. You can actually use a number of other geometries:

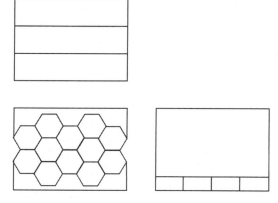

The tricolor is just one of several designs you can use. All the geometries shown above are simply incremental changes away from our basic UI design.

The current site uses scaling rectangles. By using the drawing API to draw the rectangles on the fly, you can add all sorts of weird and wonderful transitions. How about a single page that splits up *organically*? (rather like a piece of silly putty being stretched until it becomes two pieces).

We've just touched the surface here, because we don't want to put too many ideas in your head; we'd rather you came up with them yourself. Just add inspiration...

After all, that's what Flash is all about.

You've come a long way, but the journey doesn't end here. In this book you've been given the fundamental skills and understanding that will allow you to take your ActionScripting onwards and upwards. We hope that the book has also provided you with inspiration, and excitement at the massive amount of creative options opened up by efficient and imaginative coding.

ActionScript's possibilities are limitless – gotoAndPlay!

Index

The index is arranged hierarchically, in alphabetical order, with symbols preceding the letter A. Many second-level entries also occur as first-level entries. This is to ensure that users will find the information they require however they choose to search for it.

Flash MX Studio

The principle behind this book is to advance your skills in Macromedia Flash MX and hone them for a real-world scenario. How does your work stand up in the freshly competitive environment of the Flash MX marketplace? How can you streamline your ideas to give them greater usability? Where can you take your ideas next?

This book examines all the avenues open to professional or aspiring professional Flash MX designers. It gives guidance on building whole new structures for Dynamic Content, video, animation, and other media benefiting from the latest Macromedia Flash version.

DESIGNER TO DESIGNER™

friends of ED writes books for you. Any suggestions, or ideas about how you want information given in your ideal book will be studied by our team.

Your comments are valued by friends of ED.

For technical support please contact support@friendsofed.com.

Freephone in USA:	800.873.9769
Fax:	312.893.8001

UK contact
Tel:	0121.258.8858
Fax:	0121.258.8868

Registration Code: 073X1Y8961795R01

Foundation ActionScript for Macromedia Flash MX – Registration Card

Name ....

Address ....

City ....State/Region ....

Country ....Postcode/Zip ....

E-mail ....

Profession: design student ☐ freelance designer ☐
part of an agency ☐ inhouse designer ☐
other (please specify) ....

Age: Under 20 ☐ 20-25 ☐ 25-30 ☐ 30-40 ☐ over 40 ☐

Do you use: mac ☐ pc ☐ both ☐

How did you hear about this book?...

Book review (name)...

Advertisement (name) ....

Recommendation ....

Catalog ....

Other ....

Where did you buy this book? ....

Bookstore (name) ....City...........................

Computer Store (name)...

Mail Order..

Other...

How did you rate the overall content of this book?
Excellent ☐   Good ☐
Average ☐   Poor ☐

What applications/technologies do you intend to learn in the near future?...
....

What did you find most useful about this book? ....
....

What did you find the least useful about this book? ....
....

Please add any additional comments ....
....

What other subjects will you buy a computer book on soon?
....
....

What is the best computer book you have used this year?
....
....

Note: This information will only be used to keep you updated about new friends of ED titles and will not be used for any other purpose or passed to any other third party.

friendsof

DESIGNER TO DESIGNER™

NB. If you post the bounce back card below in the UK, please send it to:

friends of ED Ltd.,
30 Lincoln Road,
Olton,
Birmingham.
B27 6PA